AFRICAN-AMERICAN PERSPECTIVES AND PHILOSOPHICAL TRADITIONS

R o u t l e d g e
New York and London

AFRICAN-AMERICAN PERSPECTIVES AND PHILOSOPHICAL TRADITIONS

Edited and with an Introduction by

John P. Pittman

Published in 1997 by
Routledge
29 West 35th Street
New York, NY 10001

Published in Great Britain by
Routledge
11 New Fetter Lane
London EC4P 4EE

Printed in the United States of America on acid-free paper.

Library of Congress Cataloging-in-Publication Data

African-American perspectives and philosophical traditions / edited by John Pittman

p. cm.

Published also as v. 24, no. 1–3, of The philosophical forum. bibliographical references and index.

1. Afro-American philosophy. 2. Philosophy, African.

3. Philosophy I. Pittman, John.

B936.A37 1996

19 ' . 089'96073—dc20 96–43485

CIP

CONTENTS

INTRODUCTION TO THE ROUTLEDGE EDITION

John P. Pittman

THE ARTICLES collected in this volume originally appeared in a special triple issue of the *Philosophical Forum*, published in December 1992. That was the second issue of that journal devoted to the work of African-American philosophers; the first was published fifteen years earlier, entitled "Philosophy and the Black Experience." Some of the writers appearing here also had articles in that earlier issue, but most did not: much has changed since 1978.

This introduction has two parts. The first is a revised version of the introduction appearing in the journal issue. In it I try to sketch in broad terms what might be called the "institutional-philosophic" context in which these articles came into being, to situate the issue of African-American philosophers in the academy. These comments represent my own, personal observations. The second part, freshly written, provides an introduction to and perspective on the essays themselves. I review them seriatim and highlight themes and connections that figure in the concerns and prospects of the African-American philosophy appearing in this book.

I

Here in the last quarter of the twentieth century members of historically excluded and marginalized groups—women, people of color, gays and lesbians—have just begun to fight their way into being represented and recognized. These groups have sought recognition in more than a symbolic way, in socially prestigious and culturally influential occupations, including the academic faculty. African-Americans have now begun to enter the academic philosophic institutions and engage the traditions by appeal to which those institutions identify themselves and justify their activity.[1] We are now, given this achievement, confronted with the realities of institutionalized philosophic practices—realities posing distinctive problems for those who would think through the experiences of people of color in this Western world. These realities include a complex of presumptions that tend to regulate the way philosophy is taught in the academy.

One persistent presumption that remains broadly operative in mainstream philosophical culture—despite coming under increasing challenge in the last fifteen years—has it that philosophy is that academic discipline in which the process of fully justifying one's claims and one's standpoint can and should be done with the greatest completeness, rigor, and coherence. This presumption is often expressed in the belief that such justification can be accomplished absolutely if only the proper discursive means have been grasped. Much of the stuff of philosophic debate concerns the nature of these means.[2] Proper employment of these means allows the achievement of what might be called an "absolute standpoint," because these means are taken to be grounded in the necessary structure of knowing and/or being.[3] As such they are taken to be significant not merely in their local applicability in philosophical discourse. They are regarded as having universal and absolute sovereignty, even if the executors of that sovereignty choose to exercise it strictly only in (certain) departments of philosophy.

The presumption concerning philosophy's unique role in the academy is not only expressed in explicit pronouncements advanced and contested in philosophical discussion: there is also a broad implicit practical agreement about what kinds or styles of writing, what venues—journals, conferences, publishers—and what questions, problems, and precursor texts and authors are appropriate to genuinely philosophical productions. This broad agreement is enforced as much by tenure committees as by peer reviewers and editorial boards. It is generally part of the "prereflective" culture of academic philosophy, internalized by graduate students as defining in part the standards of their chosen calling. Something analogous is true of other academic disciplines also, but in philosophy the conventionality of this culture is perhaps particularly invisible to those involved in it because of the weight of the traditional philosophical conceptions used to supply justifications of it.

The philosophical conceptions aligned with this presumption have come under sustained intellectual attack in the last fifteen years, but they could not be said to be in retreat. Rather there has been a fragmentation of the philosophical culture, and, to some extent, a politicization of the relations between various subgroups and academic departments and factions. This situation has arisen against a backdrop of a larger ferment created by the infiltration into the academy of conceptions having a—broadly speaking—antisystemic impetus in the radical sixties, and their confrontation with a still-thriving mainstream.

This attack can be seen as part of a longer-term effort to waken philosophy from its analytic slumbers, and to substitute for the foundationalist dream of a purely rational universal language of truth a sensitivity to and exploration of the actually existing plurality of contingent social practices. In varying degrees, and in their own ways, Dewey and the later Wittgenstein can be taken as champions of such an awakening.[4] To do so, of course, is to read their work from a point of view oriented by a particular take on current issues and problems. Here the demand to justify *that* point of view might be raised, and the specter of an absolute standpoint invoked once more.

To dwell on the absolute standpoint for a minute: here it is a matter of eliminating all that is "purely accidental."[5] The appearance—or hope, or pretense—of having done so is what makes the conventionality, and contrivance, of tradition invisible to some "traditionally-minded" philosophers. This philosophical sleight of hand—this pretense masquerading as an accomplishment—has repercussions that go beyond those of the usual parlor trick. To try to adopt such a standpoint (in order to justify ourselves philosophically) means to forswear any identity that might not be equally well ascribed to any other person—for the purposes of thought. This equality might be seen precisely as one of the advantages of becoming members of the "club" of fully-accredited philosophers—a leveling of the playing field, if only in thought. But this invitation to think behind a "veil of ignorance," as it were, seems to amount to a requirement that *our* thinking, too, should be color-blind—now that *we* have become philosophers.

The reminder implicit in this last phrase pushes us once again from the ideal of an absolute standpoint that has been the dominant philosophical tradition's core conception back into the prereflective culture of philosophers, the earthly grave from which that specter has arisen. The presumption has always been that those engaged in philosophical reflection in the Western academy are white men, and that they are writing about white men for other white men. This presumption is now being challenged, but it has not disappeared; despite all the "post-"s (or perhaps, partly, because of them) the fifties are still with us. One indication of the challenge is the defection, for example, of increasing numbers of philosophical writers, from the traditional practice of using the *male* third-person singular pronoun "he" as the generic designation. But this is no small example: that this practice carries with it an implicit conceptual content only became "visible" to the community of philosophical practitioners as such in the wake of concerted efforts—by women—to show that this was the case.[6]

This last-named presumption, embedded in the traditional culture of academic philosophy, has derived some strength and plausibility in the eyes of philosophical practitioners because of one simple fact: until quite recently, those engaged in philosophical reflection in the Western academy *have been* (almost exclusively) white men. This fact is as much a result of the presumption as it is a determinant of it. We can say of this fact, however contingent, that "it is no accident." Though it could not be "rationalized" by all the philosophy in the world, it is of a piece with the entire history of the United States, and of what is still called "Western civilization." But I don't want to allow room for the temptation some may feel at this point to respond, "Yes, admittedly, philosophers may have been susceptible to the dangers implicit in the practices you have indicated. But this is not distinctive of philosophy; it is rather a general problem of the culture that has been formed by centuries of European and Anglo-American development." My first reaction to such a response is, admittedly, a mere reflex: "Where was your absolute standpoint then, when you needed it most?"

The response, and the temptation it expresses, skirts, and thereby raises, is a question that any black or brown philosopher eventually confronts. How complicit has the dominant (European) philosophical tradition been in the exclusion of peoples of color—and their intellectual and moral traditions—from participation in the centers of power of Western civilization? Here, I think, the centrality of the absolute standpoint to so much of the history of the dominant tradition helps to explain how that tradition abetted or at least tolerated that racist—not to mention sexist—exclusion.[7] For the idea of this standpoint has been the flip side of what I have described as a prereflective culture, and a set of presumptions, that has been exclusionary. If it is true, as I think it must be, that these presumptions carry a conceptual "payload"—as has been shown in the case of the generic "he"—then the damage that is done by that culture must surely be aggravated by a consistent refusal to treat the "accidental"—including, of course, the presumptions themselves—as worthy of attention.[8] For what appears to be "accidental"—including skin color, gender, or sexual orientation—has been ensnared in, and largely constituted by, historical formations of oppression, repression, and exclusion. These historical formations are contingent, but by no means "accidental"—they are the product of entrenched and ideologically positioned structures of action, decision, and response that have too often been labeled "natural," "God-given," and "inevitable."

Indeed, the force and "givenness" of many of these entrenched structures of action is often imperceptible though efficacious—these presumptions only become noticeable through the force of an opposing movement of thought—and practice. Consider the conventions of what might be called "stylistic individualism." When not wholly inaudible, the authorial voice with which philosophy is written is typically first-person singular. The expectation that this is so gives an initially strange feeling to the uses of "we" that have for that reason stood out in my writing here. This stylistic individualism may be enforced by the humanistic professionalization of academic philosophy; its rationale can perhaps be traced back to the absolute standpoint and what is a correlative demand to silence those distinctions of origin and voice that are defined as "accidental."

The presumptions I have been discussing are not easily put aside; they have the force of habit, memory, and institutional identity propping them up. Thus, "philosophy" is usually introduced to college audiences by displaying the writings of some select group of "dead white men," all European or Anglo-American. This is traditional, and it is here that the weight of tradition is heaviest. This tradition is far too often upheld by the professional activity of people of color and women themselves. The presumption is still dominant in the teaching institutions of academic philosophy: there may have always been "Asian philosophy," and now maybe there's "feminist philosophy" and "Africana philosophy," but most of what's done is just "philosophy," indifferent to, and glorying, by contrast, in the implied particularism of these other upstart breeds.

I do not want to suggest that any philosopher of African-American descent is for these reasons compelled to reject the possibility of an absolute standpoint as a basis for their philosophical thinking. Some of the authors in this volume, and many philosophically schooled African-American writers in the past have, I think, accepted something like that conception as informing their work. But insofar as the presumptions I have discussed still lie unspoken at the heart of many institutionalized philosophical practices, the acceptance of such a stand-point will be problematic for us in ways that it could not be for "white" philosophers.[9] There is at least a further cause for initial ambivalence toward the state of professional philosophy, one that can only be exorcised by a clear demonstration that the dominant traditions of philosophical reflection originating in the social movements of European history are not compromised at their conceptual roots by racism. Such a demonstration has yet to be attempted.

That such a task is put on the agenda is symptomatic of the critical need for a stock-taking by the profession, one that aims to replace the studied traditionlessness of abstract philosophizing with a critical examination of the socially constructed canons of the dominant traditions. This examination also needs situating in the social conditions of philosophy's professionalization. The fact that up until Kant none of the canonical philosophical writers were "professionals" often escapes notice—it is one of the "accidents." Yet the canon is clearly determined by a range of problems and issues deemed significantly "philosophical" by that grouping of contemporary professionals who regard themselves as the collective inheritors of the legacy of those "founders." This despite the fact that even in this century many of those considered central to the development of those traditions that are now legitimated in the academy have had tenuous, and ambivalent, relations to that academy—Sartre and Wittgenstein, for example. The professionalization of philosophy in the twentieth century exacerbates a problematic feature of the dominant traditions' canon-formation—an exclusive inward focus on "highly literate," "high-cultural"—if not technical—productions. The journal article is paradigmatic, of course. What gets left out is an entire world of intellectual life, and for traditionally excluded groups, any "representation" at all. An African-American tradition that harked back only to professionally-trained writers concerned exclusively with philosophical issues canonically defined is a naked impossibility...and absurd. But that it is absurd is the mark not simply of a specific difference of the African-American historical experience, but of a programmatic narrowness and exclusivity that constituted and still constitutes much of the dominant Anglo-European philosophical tradition.

That the accomplishment of philosophy might be something more than the generation of a specialist literature is also a hope sustained by many black philosophers' commitment to a historical community and a people. We cannot but be keenly aware of the unfinished agenda captured by the title *From Slavery to Freedom*.[10] Of course such an orientation and motivation were central to the task of philosophy as conceived by many of the foundational figures in the pantheon of the modern Western tradition. Yet in those cases the commitment was not to an embattled racial community but to a political project, and was not grounded in socio-cultural identity but in ideological conviction. That commitment has come to take the form, in our time, of a reliance on "top-down techno-bureaucratic initiatives" to socially engineer the redemption (in the image of capitalism) of peoples kept all the while at arm's length.[11] For us commitment can have no such stand-offishness. Often we are taken as representative in the very terms of our professional employment.

II

The narrowness of the reigning conception of philosophy—and its problematic applicability beyond the context of Western European modernity—is an issue in recent debates among African philosophers. The issue focuses on the status and usefulness of what has been termed "ethnophilosophy"—the attempt at systematic articulation of the philosophical conceptions implicit in the way of life, stories, sayings, and more basic linguistic practices of traditional communities of African peoples.

In an article whose title poses the question for some of the contributors to this volume, Anthony Appiah considers that earlier discussion and its relevance for African-American philosophers. After criticizing some naive presumptions about the object and goals of ethnophilosophy, Appiah sketches a notion of "critical ethnophilosophy" and suggests that it could be part of what African-American philosophy is. But also, noting that "'philosophy' is the highest status label of western humanism," Appiah pairs this with a call to "demystify" the "canonical respect"

(27) we are accustomed to show to the foundational figures of the Western philosophic academy.

Kwasi Wiredu gives an account of what he calls the "Akan tradition of philosophy," a tradition which consists of both a traditional (oral) and a modern (written) component. He devotes the lion's share of his piece to a brief overview of some of the conceptual elements of Akan traditional philosophy: he is practicing ethnophilosophy, or, as he puts it, "the critical and reconstructive treatment of the oral tradition." (35) His account of Akan traditional philosophy, informed by his native speaker's understanding of the Akan language, is at the same time comparative, carefully contrasting Akan views to Western ones in terms of which it has often mistakenly been glossed. In concluding he suggests that "sub-African categorizations of philosophy such as Akan or Yoruba" will increasingly "lose point" (56–7) as the ethnophilosophical reconstructions of the materials found in the oral traditions are completed.

Wiredu's account is of traditional conceptual resources sustained in preliterate culture by the linguistic activity of speakers, most often without reflecting on the speculative potential of their ways of speaking. The oral tradition thus reconstituted issues in many judgments of a "metaphysical" or philosophical kind. Appiah challenges the inference that the elaboration and speculative exploration of those resources yields a philosophy that all speakers of the language would have assented to; nonetheless he takes critical analyses of such conceptual resources as part of what might constitute a philosophical tradition. Indeed, he answers the question with which he titles his essay in suggesting that critical ethnophilosophy is what Du Bois was, in fact, doing in *The Souls of Black Folk*. Both Appiah and Wiredu write of traditions that are only now being uncovered, as it were; that they are discovered now, and that their discovery is revisionary of the mainstream philosophical canon, is only indicative of the partiality and narrowness of that mainstream, on this view.

This picture involves an objectivist account of tradition—that is, Appiah and Wiredu seem to take themselves to be reporting, in a non-partisan manner, a state of affairs independent of their own activity. Lucius Outlaw and Leonard Harris take a more critical approach to philosophical traditions as such. They take themselves to be constructing or inventing a tradition, since that is the most that any writer can do. This approach serves immediately to demystify tradition in a more radical way than the first one does; Harris goes so far as to propose—as the title of his piece suggests—that a rational tradition would be a self-destructive one. While Harris focuses on an account of tradition which he then applies to the traditions of American and African-American philosophy, Outlaw goes global, exploring the idea of a tradition of the philosophical activity of all African-descended peoples. Outlaw gives a bibliographically dense account of the sources and traditions of African philosophy, and a similar overview of the works of African-American philosophical reflection. These are propaedeutic to a discussion of the "gathering" or "umbrella" notion of Africana philosophy as a self-consciously constructed disciplinary formation. Outlaw's approach is exploratory and tentative, matching his own vision of such a "gathering" tradition against Molefi Asante's Afrocentric methodology. Though sympathetic with Asante's project, Outlaw finds questionable the Afrocentrist's insistence on "the deployment of 'African' as though the term has the unifying power of a trans-historical, transgeographic *essence*." (82) Outlaw employs the Foucauldian distinction between "total" and "general" history to argue for the importance of discontinuities and differences in the experiences of African-descended peoples; at the same time he insists on adherence to shared and public rules of discourse in the construction of a philosophical view. Africana philosophy cannot be interior to the subjective experience of African-descended peoples, even though committed to reconstructing "life-defining meaning connections to lands and cultures of the African continent, to its peoples and their histories." (76)

Harris shares with Appiah and Outlaw a concern that "the guardianship and administration of the word 'philosophy' as an honorific term"(75, Outlaw's wording) not become a motivation for inquiry into the question of an African-American philosophical tradition. Harris is much bolder than either of the other two, however, in characterizing his own intentions and just what exactly he is doing. Noting recent accounts of traditions as "invented," Harris produces a picture of tradition as horrific, staged, and oppressive. But then he says of himself that "I consciously participate in the creation of a tradition [of African-American philosophy] that did not exist as such before." (111) This is not a self-standing tradition, on Harris' account, for the writers who constitute it are "western intellectuals"—the paradigmatic figures he mentions are Olaudah Equiano, David Walker, Alexander Crummell, and Alain Locke. Their rightful place, he suggests, is in the tradition of American philosophy from which they have been excluded. They were, and continue to be, denied their rightful place in part because the texts they produced arose out of "personal and intellectual struggle which is not university-bound, nor confined to the central issues in the history of philosophy, nor reflective of the accepted American grain." (110) The African-American philosophical tradition is necessarily an adversarial tradition, made up of intellectuals who spoke to "those disenfranchised, stereotyped, stigmatized as parasites, raciated as inferior, and immiserated," (112) even in the rare case—that of Alain Locke, for instance—that those intellectuals were professional academic philosophers.

Harris also suggests that the created African-American philosophical tradition, as a progressive tradition, "should entail recognition of its formation and continuation as an ongoing invention," that it should be "metaphorically a jazz tradition." (114) Since all traditions are "reformations of previous authorial voices," there is a danger of conservatism and "canonization" inherent in any tradition. Thus, the process of invention should be guided by the functional utility of the African-American tradition as subversive of racism and domination, for Harris. In the case of Locke, Harris argues that only if "Locke's authorial voice, as a subtext, is honestly treated and works well to help reshape the western and American tradition, destroy its hegemonic control over who and what count as important, forces consideration of the racism that infests western philosophy"(113) should it be foregrounded in the invented tradition.

Harris' energetic essay exhibits the jazziness it commends. Such a style is rarely encountered in traditional venues for philosophical productions. Bernard Boxill's contribution is a model of one standard approach to the kind of invention employed in mainstream philosophical research journals. The genre I am referring to is the contrastive juxtaposition of two writers addressing a single issue, tracing their differing positions to distinct constellations of logically connected philosophical views. In this case Boxill contrasts the views of Frederick Douglass and Martin Delany, who are cast as paradigms of assimilationist and separatist political thought, respectively. Boxill sketches Delany's explanation of the enslavement of blacks as resulting from the imbalance between self-interest and sympathy on the part of their more powerful white oppressors, and its implication for black separatism as a strategy for empowering blacks to secure their own interests. By contrast, Douglass' insistence on the "self-evidence of human nature and human rights" supports a strategy of moral suasion, especially when it is shown how the reality of the moral equality of slaves and masters provokes cruelty from those who would obliterate the awareness of that fact, how slaves are naturally bound to resist such brutalization and the denial of rights which it obscures, and how that resistance is a form of moral suasion itself. Interestingly, the philosophical backdrop is drawn from the canonical tradition of British philosophy: Boxill compares Douglass' moral theory to John Locke's, while his account of Delany is framed by references to the views of Thomas Hobbes and David Hume.

If Boxill's reading of the traditions he discusses is Anglophone in the way it stages the confrontation between them, Frank M. Kirkland's piece is formed in the crucible of German critical theory. Kirkland mines the "substantial tradition of African-American reflection...about how the facts of 'race' and the demand for justice may be accommodated to each other" (to use Appiah's words), yielding a rich reading of certain themes in the writing of Frederick Douglass, Alexander Crummell, Booker T. Washington, and W. E. B. Du Bois. Kirkland argues that of these four only Du Bois gives an adequate account of "modernity in black" as distinct from "modernity in the west." The problem of "modernity in black" is "the problem of the color line"—that of the historical fate in the modern world of a people whose conditions of existence are governed by a legacy of enslavement, and the currency of "material poverty, stifled moral gallantry, melodious and resonant expressiveness, and irrepressible religious faith on the other." (150) Kirkland explores this issue in terms of these writers' distinct accounts of the tasks facing African-American intellectuals, both theoretically—in interpreting the legacy of enslavement and its impact on the "future-oriented present" of African-

Americans—and practically—in guiding the mass of black folks in confronting the challenges of that present. His core argument involves a reading of Du Bois' well-known concept of double consciousness in terms of his earlier account of the "Talented Tenth" as those who would lead black folks to claim their rightful place in modernity. Kirkland concludes that the task Du Bois set for the talented tenth in the period of modernity is that of "inculcating in African-Americans that cultural uplift and progress must be historically redemptive" (162).

While the focus of Kirkland's piece is Du Bois' 1903 *Souls of Black Folk*, Tommy L. Lott considers the "Conservation of Races," an address Du Bois gave six years earlier to the American Negro Academy. This early piece has attracted considerable attention recently, having been linked with the controversy over whether there is an irreducible biological referent in the concept of race. Du Bois has been read as arguing for a sociohistorical conception of race, one not founded on biological classifications. This account was subjected to sustained criticism by Anthony Appiah in a much-commented article, "The Uncompleted Argument," published in 1985; Lott is, in part, answering Appiah's criticisms and arguing in support of Du Bois' "revisionist" concept of race. Du Bois pins his account of 'race' on the existence of "common history, traditions and impulses" shared by a "vast family of human beings." Appiah had argued, to simplify somewhat, that history, traditions, and impulses themselves had to be individuated, and that could only be done by specifying *whose* history, etc. That involved specifying some physical or biological characteristics, which is just what Du Bois is generally regarded as having wanted to get away from. Lott urges that Appiah's logical point is misplaced; Du Bois' piece must be read in the context of late nineteenth-century African-American social views, and of Du Bois' overall political project. Because Du Bois' "main concern was with the impact of racism on African-American group identity," (176) he held that African-Americans "must *invent* a conception of themselves that [would] contribute to their social elevation as a group." (168) In that sense, the definition Du Bois advanced was prescriptive or revisionary, not systematic or theoretical; on this reading, there was no argument in need of completion.

Let me pause at this point to draw some threads together. Appiah characterized Du Bois' *Souls of Black Folk* as *critical* ethnophilosophy: that identification formed part of his answer to the question whether there is an African-American philosophical tradition. Kirkland cites the same work as presenting Du Bois' interpretation of the task of black intellectuals in the face of modernity. In part that interpretation demanded that social elevation not come at the expense of sociocultural group identity, but rather that "an ethical/historical identity" (161) be advanced capable of redeeming the history of African peoples in America. Lott's discussion seems to mesh with Kirkland's: his account of the 1897 speech is consistent with Kirkland's take on the book of 1903. Part of what Du Bois argues for in the 1897 essay is the duty of Blacks to "maintain their race identity" (166); if race is primarily a sociohistorical construction, preserving one's race becomes a cultural task of the sort Kirkland describes, rather than one requiring a policy against, say, intermarriage as such. Race then is something we do as much as something we just are. Against this Appiah seems to maintain that race, if it is anything at all, should have its reality independently of how we think of it or what we make of it. Toward this end he distinguishes between criteria for membership in a race and the a posteriori properties of a racial group. His point is a conceptual one, and as such claims a force beyond an insistence that the facts do not support Du Bois' view. We seem to be poised between the force of strategic considerations of the kind discussed by Lott, and the demand for theoretical coherence made by Appiah.

Lott argues that Du Bois' definition of "race" on the strength of the "common history, traditions, and impulses" of all peoples who have historically been designated "Negro" is *both* aimed at advancing the unity-in-action of black folk in America *and* more adequate to the actualities of the deployment of the race concept in racialized political contexts. In doing so he is following up on what he calls Du Bois' "sociohistorical essentialism," the view "that there is something universal, or essential, in the cultures of all the various black ethnic groups, viz., a common history of oppression." (178) Indeed, the attempt to adequately characterize the experience of being black in a white society has been a persistent and substantial concern of African-American philosophers. This has often taken the form of a search for invariant features of the lives of people of color and a general account of those features as products of the dynamic of a racist society. Boxill's account of the views of Delany and Douglass is a good indication of how important—and philosophically fertile—such efforts have been to the tradition of African-American social thought. A similar concern can be seen in the efforts of some thinkers—discussed by both Outlaw and Appiah in this volume—to trace the source of an African-American—or, more generally, a black—philosophical tradition, to common features of the experience of African-American and/or African-descended peoples both in Africa and the African diaspora. As Outlaw indicates in his article, such efforts have often been understood as directed toward, and formulated in support of, specific practical approaches to the emancipation and "elevation" of the "race."

That understanding again suggests that the question of our identity cannot be for us simply a problem about ontological sameness and individuation, nor a romantic attempt at creative individual self-redefinition, but involves the pursuit of a hard-fought collective relation to a social designation devised and enforced by a hostile culture. That seems to involve a notion of philosophic activity—as constitutively concerned with the prospects and fate of a specific historical community—which is not the mainstream view, even, I think, among African-American professional philosophers. Nonetheless, the commitment to advancing the freedom agenda—conceived differently by different writers—with the weapons of philosophical argument is widely shared by black philosophers.

These concerns—to identify and analyze the universals of the historical experience of African-descended peoples, and to bend that analysis toward the project of emancipation—emerge as closely linked in the essays composing the last third of this book. Adrian Piper explores some of the cognitive errors that can underlie racism as a form of xenophobia, and argues that those errors can be accounted for by a version of Kantian rationalism, which suggests the possibility of a xenophilia as well. Laurence Thomas argues for the "downward social constitution" of the characters of members of minority groups through seemingly routine interactions with members of other social groups, necessitating the practice of moral deference on the part of members of downwardly constituting groups. Michele Moody-Adams discusses self-respect as a social construct, claiming that the development of robust self-respect can be thwarted in members of a society who are systematically denied access to institutions and practices that promote it or are the vehicles for its expression. Anita L. Allen examines the the "role model" argument for affirmative-action hiring of faculty who are members of minority groups and argues that its use serves to perpetuate racist attitudes and institutional bad faith. Howard McGary discusses the impact of racism and its relation to alienation, and emphasizes the role of the community in keeping the one from becoming the other.

Racism, if anything, has been a "universal" in the experiences of people of color in the Western diaspora. A concern to account for the ubiquity of racism has motivated much recent philosophical reflection. Adrian M.S. Piper takes up the issue in a novel way: she provides an account of the general category of xenophobia in terms of a reading of Kant's theory of the a priori constitution of the self through rational categories. Piper argues for the claim that xenophobia represents a "defect in rationality" (189). She shows how four cognitive errors add up to give the xenophobe, who categorizes others in terms of honorific and derogatory stereotypes, "a conception of the other as an inscrutable and malevolent anomaly that threatens that theory of the world which unifies one's experience and structures one's expectations about oneself and others." (221) But Piper finds Kantian grounds for rejecting the view that "xenophobia is a hard-wired cognitive disposition that is impervious to empirical modification." (222) Rather, she points to a crucial ambiguity in Kant that she reads in a way to support the possibility of xenophilia, or "a positive valuation of human difference as intrinsically interesting and therefore worthy of regard." (225)

Piper's argument implies that Kantian rationalism has the resources for contributing to our understanding of, and resistance to, racism and other forms of xenophobia. Other authors also try to employ standard mainstream philosophical theories in accounting for the experiences of oppression, with mixed results. Laurence Thomas concludes that Humean moral theory "must be adjusted to take into account the reality that the emotional makeup of persons can be configured along dimensions other than cultivation." (241) Thomas focuses on what he calls the differential "emotional category configurations" of persons from "diminished social categories"; much of his essay is given to analyses and examples of how members of diminished social categories are victims of a process of "downward social constitution" effected through the attitudes, expectations and actions of others. The notion of moral deference plays both a theoretical and practical role for Thomas: it serves "to stand in opposition to the idea that there is a vantage point from which any and every person can rationally grasp whatever morally significant experiences a person might have." (233) Yet Thomas advances the notion of moral deference "as a bridge between individuals with different social category configurations owing to the injustices of society." (234)

The concern to explain important differences of character and fortune in terms of social injustice also occupies Michele Moody-Adams' article on self-respect. Drawing on the social-scientific research of Kenneth Clark, Robert Merton, Gordon Allport, and William Julius Wilson, she articulates a conception of self-respect as socially-constructed, and argues that "in America, the social construction of self-respect continues to bear the complex and often unacknowledged stamp of racial discrimination." (259) Moody-Adams uses examples to highlight the ravages such social construction can effect when "a scheme of discrimination is rooted in a complex network of degrading and dehumanizing fictions about its victims." (255) Distinguishing between self-respect and self-esteem, she claims that while "the influence of class position is usually registered most directly on the phenomenon of self-esteem," "the influence of racial designations is typically registered most directly on self-respect." (257) She discusses the devastating effects of these factors on young people in Black communities in poor urban areas.

The phenomena described by Thomas and Moody-Adams affect the experience of virtually all people of color in the west, and as such they constitute the social conditions which affirmative-action policies have been aimed to address. One argument for such programs that has particular relevance to these social conditions is the "role model" argument. Anita L. Allen analyzes the "role model" argument for the hiring of African-American faculty in the academy and especially law schools. The "role model" argument starts from the need of students of color for same-kind role models or mentors among faculty ; as such it is a forward-looking argument connected to the increasing numbers of such students in postgraduate educational institutions. Allen makes a case for same-kind role models based on anecdotal insight into the experiences of black women. Yet, paradoxically, she shows how some of the most common uses of the "role model" argument can serve to perpetuate racist and unequal expectations of minority faculty, and she argues ultimately for the abandonment of the "role model" argument in discussions of affirmative action.

If, as Allen maintains, "minority students have special role modeling needs that minority faculty are uniquely placed to service," this is because of "a fundamental sense of abandonment" such students feel (279–80). That sense, and the kinds of experiences discussed by Thomas and Moody-Adams, have suggested a "new account of alienation" to some theorists, according to Howard McGary. On that account, "alienation exists when the self is deeply divided because the hostility of the dominant groups in the society forces the self to see itself as loathsome, defective, or insignificant, and lacking the possibility of...ever becoming a self that is not defined in the hostile terms of the dominant group." (283) McGary weighs this account of alienation against the liberal and Marxist conceptions. He concludes that some liberal authors can't fully capture the phenomena the new account addresses "because their emphasis on the external constraints causes them to underestimate the internal ways that people can be prevented from experiencing freedom," while the Marxist view fails because it is "too quick in dismissing the significance of race-consciousness." (287, 291) McGary concludes that while the liberal tradition has the conceptual tools necessary to account for "the particular estrangement that blacks experience," it does not have "the theoretical wherewithal to resolve the problem." (290)

McGary suggests that resolving the problem requires the presence of "supportive communities" which have existed throughout the history of black people in America, and have contributed to our ability to "maintain healthy self-concepts through acts of resistance and communal nourishment." (292) A similar idea plays a role in Moody-Adams' account of how, despite oppressive circumstances, many African-Americans have developed a robust sense of self-respect. Something like "communal nourishment," of a one-on-one variety, is what the need for same-kind role modeling is, I take it. If these resonances ring true, might we not also turn back and, looking beyond our local communities, seek "communal nourishment" in the notion of "a vast family of human beings...of common history, traditions and impulses"? Such a thematic drawing together of the essays in front of us is tempting. It should be clear by now as well how powerful that impulse has been and still is for African-American philosophers. There is, however, a countervailing consideration, also in evidence here: that the experiences of people of color, and the social and institutional hostilities which we face, are not completely unique to us, but are shared by other groups who have felt the brunt of oppression. This sense comes out most strongly in Piper's and Thomas' essays, but is also evident in Moody-Adams', and Harris', and Lott's, and others' as well.

There is another conclusion, suggested also by this last train of thought, to which I am finally tempted. Each of the writers engaged in the conceptual analysis of aspects of "the black experience" is also doing something else—contributing to other lines of discussion, addressing other audiences as well. Adrian Piper attempts to account for xenophobia from within the context of the Anglo-American tradition of Kant scholarship and interpretation, on which she comments critically at the same time. Laurence Thomas is mainly concerned to make a case for the category of "moral deference," yet his reflections begin with an allusion to the work of the mainstream ethical theorist, Thomas Nagel, and his discussion coils around repeated returnings to the views of David Hume. Michele

Moody-Adams articulates a conception of self-respect as socially-constructed; in doing so she both draws on and distinguishes her views from the work of John Rawls on self-respect. Howard McGary questions whether the "African-American experience" necessarily results in a condition of "alienation"; his answer is formulated in terms of, and in response to, the mainstream liberal tradition of political-philosophical theory. In varying degrees—and this could be said of those writing about tradition(s) as well—the philosophers writing in this volume can be seen grappling with a sense of dual commitments, a sense attributable in part, at least, to a professionalized version of the "double consciousness" remarked by Du Bois more than ninety years ago.

NOTES

1 David Hoekema counts 37 "Black philosophers" among APA members, which adds up to 1.7% of the total. See the *APA Proceedings* for June, 1992 (Vol. 62, No. 7), p. 42. Leonard Harris updates and discusses the numbers in his "'Believe it or Not' or the Ku Klux Klan and American Philosophy Exposed," in the *APA Proceedings* of May, 1995 (Vol. 68, No. 5), pp. 133–137.

2 "The aim of epistemology is the formulation of a method for the justification of cognitions (Erkenntnisse)"—that is the first sentence of Rudolf Carnap's *Pseudoproblems in Philosophy*, translated by Rolf A. George, and published in one volume with *The Logical Structure of the World* (Berkeley: University of California Press, 1969), p. 305.

3 The phrase I am using should be distinguished from Bernard Williams' "absolute conception," but not too much. See Williams' *Descartes: The Project of Pure Enquiry* (Harmondsworth: Penguin, 1978), pp. 65ff.

4 Such an interpretation has been the brunt of the work of Richard Rorty since his 1979 book *Philosophy and the Mirror of Nature* (Princeton University Press).

5 "Philosophical reflection has no other object than to get rid of what is accidental." G.W.F. Hegel, in *Die Vernunft in der Geschichte* , as cited by Odo Marquard in *In Defense of the Accidental*, translated by Robert M. Wallace (Oxford University Press, 1991), p. 109.

6 This process eventually led to the APA's publication—without "formal endorsement"—of *Guidelines for NonSexist Use of Language* (Newark, DE: APA, nd) explicitly modeled after similar documents released earlier by the American Psychological Association and the National Council of Teachers of English.

7 For a good example of an "abettor," consider some of the research documenting and discussing the racist views of David Hume. See the articles by Richard H. Popkin, "Hume's Racism," *The Philosophical Forum*, Vol. 9, No. 2–3, Winter-Spring 1977–1978, pp. 211–226; and "Hume's Racism Reconsidered," *The Journal of the Society for the Study of Black Philosophy*, Vol. 1, No. 1, Winter–Spring 1984, pp. 61–71. In the latter article Popkin credits the unpublished dissertation of Henry Louis Gates, Jr. for providing documentation to show that Hume "knew his [racist] views were being taken as authoritative by the color racists

and the defenders of slavery" and that this "shows he was no innocent," but a "biased" and "dishonest researcher." More recently, Emmanuel Chukwudi Eze has examined the racist claims Immanuel Kant made in articulating his conception of anthropology; see his "The Color of Reason: The Idea of 'Race' in Kant's Anthropology," in *Anthropology and the German Enlightenment*, ed. Katherine Faull (London: Bucknell & Associates University Press, 1994), pp. 200–241.

8 Indeed, it is to be expected that some will say to this: "it is only an accident that the ideal absolute standpoint has been allied in this way with what you call the presumption underpinning the history of Western philosophic practice." An attempt to address such a remark has been made by Cornel West in "A Genealogy of Racism: On the Underside of Modern Discourse," *The Journal* of the SSBP, Vol. 1, No. 1, pp. 42–60.

9 This situation takes its characteristic form in the current period in the phenomenon of affirmative action: the race and ethnic background of candidates, say, only becomes visible if they are non-white; white candidates are taken to be evaluated solely on their merits. This expresses the fact that the presumption I am discussing is no chimera but a deep operative feature of the whole institutional context: to be "white" is to be colorless, unburdened by distinguishing idiosyncratic secondary qualities.

10 John Hope Franklin, *From Slavery to Freedom: A History of American Negroes* (New York: Alfred A. Knopf, 1947); Sixth Edition, co-authored with Alfred A. Moss, Jr., 1987. As if in response, and characterizing our historical setting, Howard McGary and Bill E. Lawson entitled their conceptual study of slavery *Between Slavery and Freedom: Philosophy and American Slavery* (Bloomington: Indiana University Press, 1992).

11 Richard Rorty, "Love and Money," in *Common Knowledge*, Vol. 1, No. 1 (Spring 1992), p.15.

AFRICAN-AMERICAN PERSPECTIVES AND PHILOSOPHICAL TRADITIONS

INTRODUCTION

JOHN P. PITTMAN

The Winter–Spring 1977–78 issue of the *Philosophical Forum* was a double issue devoted to "Philosophy and the Black Experience." It included papers given at a conference of the same name at Tuskegee Institute in 1973, as well as several other articles written especially for the issue. The "general question of whether there is a distinctive Black Consciousness, and moreover, a Black philosophy," was a central concern of the issue. A footnote was added to the "Editors' Note," when the issue was already in proofs, referring to the Supreme Court's Bakke decision, which had just been handed down. How much has happened in the fifteen years since then: that was before Reagan, before Gorbachev, before Clarence Thomas.

There is a sameness, nonetheless, about the issues confronting us—as African-Americans, as academics, as philosophers—then and now. Previously excluded groups have, in the last quarter of the twentieth century, just begun to fight their way into being represented and recognized, in a more than token/symbolic way, in socially prestigious and culturally influential occupations, including academia. African-Americans in greater numbers have become a part of the academy and its traditions.[1] Yet this achievement—taken together with the partial implementation and seemingly imminent dismantling of affirmative action programs—is now a new mark of our distinctness. We must either fit in or stand out. If we are to be recognized *for who we are,* our membership in excluded groups looms large—it is the relevant difference that our just having arrived in the hallowed halls signifies. We are expected to do African philosophy, and not just the analytic philosophy of language. And, with this distinctness, comes marginalization: we have not *really* arrived, but are being kept in an anteroom. Otherwise, the price of admission to the "inner circle" is a disavowal of our past—a participation in the pretense that nothing really has changed, that who we are and what we feel has no significance for what we think.

This caught-between-two-demands scenario is surely not new, and it is certainly not peculiar to African-Americans. The form it takes for us, in philosophy as an academic discipline, and at this particular time, is perhaps novel enough to warrant a few words. One persistent presumption has it that philosophy is that academic discipline in which the process of fully justifying one's claims and one's standpoint can and should be done with the greatest completeness, rigor, and finality. This presumption is often expressed in the belief that such justification can be accomplished absolutely if only the proper discursive means have been grasped; much of the stuff of philosophic debate concerns the nature of these means.[2] Proper employment of these means allows the achievement of what might be called an "absolute standpoint," since these means are taken to be grounded in the necessary structure of knowing and/or being. As such they are taken to be significant not merely in their local applicability in philosophical discourse; they are regarded as having universal and absolute sovereignty, even if the executors of that sovereignty choose to exercise it strictly only in (certain) departments of philosophy.

The presumption—concerning philosophy's unique role in the academy—is not merely expressed in explicit pronouncements advanced and contested in philosophical discussion. There is also a broad implicit practical agreement about what kinds or styles of writing, what venues—journals, conferences, publishers—and what questions, problems, and precursor texts and authors are appropriate to genuinely philosophical productions. This broad agreement is enforced as much by tenure committees as by peer reviewers and editorial boards. It is generally part of the "prereflective" culture of academic philosophy, internalized by graduate students as defining in part the standards of their chosen calling. Something analogous is true of other academic disciplines as well. But in philosophy the conventionality of this culture is perhaps particularly invisible because of the weight of the traditional philosophical conceptions that have been used to supply justifications of it.

These philosophical conceptions have come under sustained intellectual attack in the last fifteen years. Two philosophical authors prominently identifiable with that attack are Richard Rorty and Alasdair MacIntyre. Their efforts have been part of a larger ferment created by the infiltration into the academy of ideas from the radical sixties with a broadly antisystemic impetus. The specifically philosophical aspect of this ferment has focused attention on *tradition* as constitutive of current philosophical practice in a way that is conventional and not merely rational.

Or merely natural. The attack mentioned above can be seen as part of a longer-term effort to waken philosophy from its analytic slumbers, and to substitute for the foundationalist dream of a purely rational universal language of truth a sensitivity to and exploration of the actually existing plurality of contingent social practices. In varying degrees, and in their own ways, Dewey, the late Wittgenstein, and Quine can all be taken as championing such an awakening. To do so, of course, is to read their work from a definite point of view, oriented by a particular take on current issues and problems. Here the demand to justify *that* point of view might be raised, and the specter of an absolute standpoint invoked once more. But even the paths to that beguiling, elusive standpoint, always just beyond reach, lead past the landmarks of an imaginary philosophical lineage.

To dwell on the absolute standpoint for a minute: here it is a matter of eliminating all that is "purely accidental."[3] The appearance or hope, or pretense, of having done so is what makes the conventionality of tradition invisible to some "traditionally-minded" philosophers. This philosophical sleight of hand—this pretense masquerading as an accomplishment—has repercussions that go beyond those of the usual parlor trick. To try to adopt such a standpoint, in order to justify ourselves philosophically, means to forswear any identity that might not be equally well ascribed to any other person—for the purposes of thought. This equality might be seen precisely as one of the advantages of becoming members of the "club" of fully-accredited philosophers—a levelling of the playing field, if only in thought. But this invitation to think behind a "veil of ignorance," as it were, seems to amount to a requirement that *our* thinking, too, should be color-blind (and gender-neutral)—now that *we* have become philosophers.

The reminder implicit in this last phrase pushes us back from the absolute standpoint that has been the dominant philosophical tradition's ideal to the prereflective culture of philosophers, the earthly grave from which that specter has arisen. The presumption has always been that those engaged in philosophical reflection in the western academy are white men, and that they are writing about white men for other white men. This presumption is only now being challenged, in part, by the defection, for example, of increasing numbers of philosophical writers, from the traditional practice of using the *male* third-personal singular pronoun "he" as the generic designation for persons. That this practice carries with it an implicit conceptual content only became "visible" to the community of philosophical practitioners as such in the wake of concerted efforts—by women—to show that this was the case.[4]

This last-named presumption, embedded in the traditional culture of academic philosophy, has derived some strength and, I suppose, plausibility, in the eyes of philosophical practitioners because of one simple fact: until quite recently, those engaged in philosophical reflection in the western academy *have been* white men. This fact is as much a result of the presumption as it is a determinant of it. We can say of this fact, however contingent, that "it is no accident." Though it could not be "rationalized" by all the philosophy in the world, it is of a piece with the entire history of the United States, and of what is still called "western civilization." But I don't want to allow room for the temptation some may feel at this point to respond: "Yes, admittedly, philosophers may have been susceptible to the sort of dangers implicit in the practices you have indicated. But this is not distinctive of philosophy; it is rather a general problem of the culture that has been formed by centuries of European and Anglo-American development.'' My first reaction to such a response is, admittedly, a mere reflex: ''Where was your absolute standpoint then, when you needed it most?''

The response, and the temptation it expresses, skirts, and thereby raises, a question it is unwise to put off. How complicit is/was the dominant (European) philosophical tradition in the exclusion of peoples of color—and their intellectual and moral traditions—from participation in the centers of power of western civilization? Here, I think, the centrality of the absolute standpoint to so much of the history of the dominant tradition helps to explain how that tradition abetted or at least tolerated that racist—not to mention sexist—exclusion.[5] For the idea of this standpoint has been the flip side of what I have suggested is a prereflective culture, a set of presumptions that has been both racist and sexist. And if it is true, as I think it must be, that these presumptions carry a conceptual ''payload''—as has been shown in the case of the generic ''he''—then the damage that is done by that culture must surely be aggravated by a consistent refusal to treat the ''accidental''—including, of course, the presumptions themselves—as worthy of attention.[6] For in this case what appears to be ''accidental''—including the color of a person's skin, their gender, or their sexual orientation—has been ensnared in, and largely defined by, historical formations of oppression, repression, and exclusion. These historical formations are contingent, but by no means ''accidental''—they are the product of entrenched and ideologically positioned structures of action, decision, and response that have too often been labelled ''natural,'' ''God-given,'' and ''inevitable.''

I do not want to suggest that any philosopher of African-American descent is for that reason going to reject outright the concept of an absolute standpoint as a basis for their philosophical thinking. Some of the authors in this volume, and many philosophically schooled African-American writers in the past have, I think, accepted something like that concept as informing their work. But insofar as we are the objects of the racist presumption that still lies unspoken at the heart of many institutionalized philosophical practices, the acceptance of such a standpoint will be problematic for us in (additional) ways that it could not be for ''white'' philosophers.[7] There is at least a further cause for initial ambivalence, one that can only be exorcised by a clear demonstration that the dominant traditions of philosophical reflection originating in the social movements of European history are not compromised at their conceptual roots by racism. This is part of the reason why the theme of ''traditions'' in philosophy is a central focus of the inquiries contained in this issue. Anthony Appiah, Bernard Boxill, Frank Kirkland, and Lucius Outlaw all discuss, in different ways, the constitution of African and/or African-American philosophical traditions. Leonard Harris, in arguing that traditions in philosophy are inherently conservative, urges the construction of an African-American tradition that is radically antitraditional.

It would be wrong to assume a unanimity of opinion about the existence, nature, and prospects of an "African-American philosophical tradition" on the part of the authors collected here. We do not need to *do anything* at all to have our efforts—whatever form or direction they may take—categorized, pigeonholed, and marginalized. This is not merely a personal and psychological, but also a disciplinary and professional process of isolation. The presumption is still dominant in the halls of academic philosophy: there may have always been "Asian philosophy," and now maybe there is "feminist philosophy" and "Africana philosophy," but most of what is done is just "philosophy," indifferent to, and set above in the implied particularism of, these other upstart breeds. Pluralism, circa 1992!

"Philosophy" is usually introduced by studying the writings of some select group of "dead white men," all European or Anglo-American. The fact that up until Kant none of these writers were "professionals" escapes notice—it is one of the "accidents." Yet the canon is clearly determined by a range of problems and issues deemed significantly "philosophical" by that grouping of contemporary professionals who regard themselves as the collective inheritors of the legacy of those "founders." This despite the fact that even in this century many of those considered central to the development of those traditions that are now legitimated in the academy have had tenuous, and ambivalent, relations to that academy—Sartre and Wittgenstein, for example. The professionalization of philosophy that has occurred in the twentieth century exacerbates a problematic feature of the dominant traditions' canon-formation—an exclusive inward focus on "highly literate," "high-cultural"—if not technical—productions. The journal article is paradigmatic, of course. What gets left out is an entire world of intellectual life, and for traditionally excluded groups, any "representation" at all. An African-American tradition that harked back only to professionally-trained writers concerned exclusively with philosophical issues canonically defined is a naked impossibility . . . and absurd. But that it is absurd is the mark not simply of a specific difference of the African-American historical experience, but of a programmatic narrowness and exclusivity that constituted and still constitutes much of the dominant Anglo-European philosophical tradition.

The narrowness of the reigning conception of philosophy—and its problematic applicability to the experience of peoples other than those whose experience is central to West European modernity—is an issue in recent debates among African philosophers. The issue focuses on the status and usefulness of what has been termed "ethnophilosophy"—the attempt at systematic articulation of the philosophical conceptions implicit in the way of life, stories, sayings, and more basic linguistic practices of traditional communities of African peoples. Kwasi

Wiredu's article presents something like an ethnophilosophical discussion of the Akan people. Anthony Appiah, though critical of the excesses and abuses that ethnophilosophy is susceptible to, argues that a provisional, critical ethnophilosophy can be part of what African philosophy, and African-American philosophy, are about. Lucius Outlaw discusses the relation of African to African-American philosophical discussions, and examines Molefi Asante's fashionable proposal for an "Afrocentric" theoretical perspective.

That the accomplishment of philosophy might be something more than the generation of a specialist literature is also a hope sustained by a commitment to a historical community and a people. We cannot but be keenly aware of the unfinished agenda captured by the title "From Slavery to Freedom."[8] Of course such an orientation and motivation were central to the task of philosophy as it was conceived by many of the foundational figures in the pantheon of the modern western philosophical tradition. Yet in those cases the commitment was not to an embattled racial community but to a political project, and was not grounded in sociocultural identity but in ideological conviction. That commitment has come to take the form, in our time, of a reliance on "top-down techno-bureaucratic initiatives" to socially engineer the redemption of peoples kept all the while at arm's length.[9] For us commitment can have no such standoffishness. Often we are taken as representative, and as committed to those whom we represent, in the very terms of our professional employment.

This again points up why *identity* is not for us simply a philosophical problem about ontological sameness and individuation but a question of our hard-fought collective relation to a social designation devised and enforced by a hostile culture. That designation, involving the idea of race as a morally significant pseudo-biological essence, has been the focus of a racialized ideology justifying and perpetuating African-American social and political inferiority. Some of the articles in the collection address issues related to the nature and consequences of that ideology. Adrian Piper explores some of the cognitive errors that can underlie racism as a form of xenophobia, and argues that those errors can be accounted for by a version of Kantian rationalism, which suggests the possibility of a xenophilia as well. Laurence Thomas argues for the "downward social constitution" of the characters of members of minority groups through seemingly routine interactions with members of other social groups, necessitating the practice of moral deference on the part of members of downwardly constituting groups. Michele Moody-Adams discusses self-respect as a social construct, claiming that the development of robust self-respect can be thwarted in members of a society who are systematically denied access to institutions and practices that promote it or are the vehicles for its expression. Anita Allen examines the "role model" argument for affirmative-action hiring of faculty who are members of minority groups and argues that its use serves to perpetuate racist attitudes and institutional bad faith. Howard McGary discusses the impact of racism and its relation to alienation, and emphasizes the role of the community in keeping the one from becoming the other.

Of course, race and our identity as a people has been a basic issue in the philosophical writing of African-American intellectuals since 1619, and a number of articles explore that heritage in detail. Bernard Boxill presents Frederick Douglass and Martin Delany as representatives of distinct traditions of political philosophy, and traces their differences about strategy to different moral psychologies and conceptions of the significance of race. Tommy Lott argues that W. E. B. DuBois formulated a social conception of race and argues for such a conception, showing that racial and ethnic identifications and categories have always been socially constructed as well as politically employed. Frank Kirkland revisits DuBois's dictum that the problem of the twentieth century is the problem of the color line: he argues that DuBois was expressing the problem of the African-American intellectuals' confrontation with modernity, a confrontation that he traces in the writings of Alexander Crummell, Booker T. Washington, and DuBois himself.

The philosophy collected and expressed in this special issue is many-faced and divergent, though not nearly as much as it might have been but for the inevitable limitations of space. This is in keeping both with the character of the *Philosophical Forum*, and with the diversity of "African-American perspectives." We have gotten beyond the insistence on a single "Black experience"; we are hopeful for a dialogue and more, a polyglot of traditions. Our purpose is still the fulfillment of freedom: freedom from the demand for a uniformity into which we cannot fit; freedom to participate, with all others, in a community of many voices.

John Jay College of Criminal Justice, City University of New York

NOTES

1 David Hoekema counts 37 "Black philosophers" among American Philosophical Association members, which adds up to 1.7% of the total. See the *A.P.A. Proceedings* for June 1992 (Vol., 62, No. 7), p. 42.

2 "The aim of epistemology is the formulation of a method for the justification of cognitions (*Erkenntnisse*)"—that is the first sentence of Rudolf Carnap's *Pseudoproblems in Philosophy,* tr. Rolf A. George, in Carnap, *The Logical Structure of the World* (Berkeley: University of California Press, 1969), p. 305.

3 "Philosophical reflection has no other object than to get rid of what is accidental." G. W. F. Hegel, in *Die Vernunft in der Geschichte,* as cited by Odo Marquard in *In Defense of the Accidental,* tr. Robert M. Wallace (Oxford: Oxford University Press, 1991), p. 109.

4 This process eventually led to the A.P.A.'s publication—without "formal endorsement"—of

Guidelines for Non-Sexist Use of Language (Newark, Del.: American Philosophical Association, n.d.), explicitly modeled after similar documents released earlier by the American Psychological Association and the National Council of Teachers of English.

5 For a good example of an "abettor," consider some of the research documenting and discussing the racist views of David Hume. See the articles by Richard H. Popkin, "Hume's Racism," *Philosophical Forum,* Vol. 9, Nos. 2–3, Winter-Spring 177–78, pp. 211–26; and "Hume's Racism Reconsidered," *Journal of the Society for the Study of Black Philosophy,* Vol. 1, No. 1, Winter-Spring 1984, pp. 61–71. In the latter article Popkin credits the unpublished dissertation of Henry Louis Gates, Jr., for providing documentation to show that Hume "knew his [racist] views were being taken as authoritative by the color racists and the defenders of slavery" and that this "shows he was no innocent," but a "biased" and "dishonest researcher."

6 Indeed, it is to be expected that some will say to this: "it is only an accident that the ideal absolute standpoint has been allied in this way with what you call the presumption underpinning the history of western philosophic practice." An attempt to address such a remark has been made by Cornel West in "A Genealogy of Racism: On the Underside of Modern Discourse," *Journal of the Society for the Study of Black Philosophy,* Vol. 1, No. 1, pp. 42–60.

7 This situation takes its characteristic form in the present period in the phenomenon of affirmative action: the race and ethnic background of candidates, say, only becomes visible if they are nonwhite; white candidates are taken to be evaluated solely on their merits. This expressed the fact that the presumption I am discussing is no chimera but a deep feature of the whole institutional context: to be "white" is to be colorless, unburdened by distinguishing idiosyncratic secondary qualities.

8 John Hope Franklin, *From Slavery to Freedom: A History of American Negroes* (New York: Alfred A. Knopf, 1947); the sixth edition in 1987 was coauthored with Alfred A. Moss, Jr.

9 Richard Rorty, "Love and Money," *Common Knowledge,* Vol. 1, No. 1 (Spring 1992), p. 15.

AFRICAN-AMERICAN PHILOSOPHY?[1]

K. ANTHONY APPIAH

Briefly, and in conclusion, African philosophy exists, but it is not what it is believed to be.[2]

Paulin Hountondji, *African Philosophy: Myth and Reality*

The condition of native is a nervous condition.[3]

Epigraph to Tsitsi Dangarembga's *Nervous Conditions*

Yes, I was black as they were, but they had a common bond I could but marvel at.[4]

Charles Johnson, *Middle Passage*

WHAT WOULD IT MEAN TO PURSUE AN AFRICAN-AMERICAN PHILOSOPHY?

At least since Herder—you can tell I am not an historian, such grandly vague formulations being anathema to Ranke's heirs—questions of this sort, seeking after the connection between a people and the majestic projects of philosophy, literature, and the arts, have been central, in a familiar way, to *nationalist* argument. Herder taught us to think that the minimum condition for being the sort of collectivity—a nation—that required and deserved a state for its historical realization was the possession of a shared *Sprachgeist;* and at the heart of the culture of the Volk, the folk-culture embodied in the language, were certain principles, a certain *Weltanschauung,* that we should naturally call a philosophy.

For Herder, the history of nations is above all the history of cultures, of civilizations. In the *Reflections on the Philosophy of the History of Mankind,*

Herder's history of Greece is the history of "the Grecian language . . . the most refined of any in the world; the Grecian mythology, the richest and most beautiful upon Earth; the Grecian poetry, perhaps the most perfect of its kind, when considered with respect to time and place," as well as the history of their arts, religion, "moral and political wisdom," and "scientific acquirements."[5] Each person inherited the conceptual materials and the philosophical principles that defined the spirit of her nation. This idea, which was so original in Herder, became part of the common sense of Euro-American high culture in the nineteenth century; a common sense that W. E. B. Du Bois expressed, in 1897, in the observation that like "[t]he English nation . . . the German nation . . . [and] the Romance nations . . . the other race groups are striving, each in its own way, to develop for civilization its particular message, its particular ideal."[6] What is attractive, always, in Du Bois's rendering of the issue (as here in the "Conservation of Races") is that the message of his race is always seen (in a way that is, I think, more fully realized than in Herder's talk of *humanität*)[7] in the perspective of humanity: for Du Bois it is as one voice in the chorus of races that the Negro sings.[8]

Du Bois's attachment to this Herderian principle is evident, too, in his definition of a "race" as "a vast family of human beings, generally of common blood and language . . . who are both voluntarily and involuntarily striving together for the accomplishment of certain more or less vividly conceived ideals of life."[9] But we shall find the same claim in Edward Blyden—who wrote in 1883: "Among the conclusions to which study and research are conducting philosophers, none is clearer than this—that each of the races of mankind has a specific character and specific work."[10] This claim is also found in Alexander Crummell and in Martin Robinson Delany[11]—in short in most, perhaps all, of those black intellectuals in the anglophone New World who articulated the beginnings of the Pan-Africanist vision.

These African-American intellectuals mobilized a rhetoric of race, rather than one of nation, and thus, in an age when race was increasingly understood through the sciences of biology and physical anthropology, the connection was made, at least implicitly, not to a *Sprachgeist,* expressed and transmitted through the institutions of language, but to the more material substrate of physical inheritance.

This way of speaking would not have pleased Herder, who remarks in the *Reflections on the Philosophy of the History of Mankind* that "[r]ace refers to a difference of origin, which in this case does not exist . . . Complexions run into each other."[12] But the primary consequence of Du Bois's view was the same as of Herder's: from such a perspective, African-Americans and Africans represent philosophical principles in the world and nothing could be more natural, *from such a viewpoint,* than talk of an—indeed talk of *the*—Negro philosophy. We might think that there would be a difference of opinion between Herder and Du Bois as to the relations between African and African-American philosophy. For Du Bois, after all, African-Americans are representatives of the African race in America, and so this African-American philosophy will be an expression of the very principles that are embodied in African philosophy. But Herder wrote that "[i]n India . . . the Arab and the Chinese, the Turk and the Persian, the Christian and the Jew, the Negro and the Malay, the Japanese and the Gentoo are clearly distinguishable: thus everyone bears the characters of his country and way of life to the most distant shores."[13] For Herder, too, then blacks in America might well have belonged together with their African cousins. Within this tradition of reflection, therefore, the questions "Is there an African-American philosophy?" and "Is there an African philosophy?" are, in effect, the same question.[14]

By itself this would be a pretty feeble excuse for turning (as I shall in a moment and for a while) from the quest for an African-American philosophy to the question of an African philosophy, since, unlike Du Bois or Blyden or Crummell, we have good reason not to speak of races as the expression of philosophical principles (indeed, as I have often argued, we have good reason nowadays not to speak of races, as Du Bois and Blyden and Crummell understood them, at all).[15]

But I do not follow this path merely because it is well-trodden. First of all, it is an issue of contemporary relevance: these days when proponents of Afrocentricity assert the significance of something called "African philosophy" for the projects of today's African-American education and culture, I take it that it is this familiar nationalist argument that they have in mind. Jahnheinz Jahn's *Muntu: African Cultures and the Western World*—a work that specifically seeks to give a unified account of African and African-American cultures rooted in an African philosophy—has recently been re-released with a new introduction by Calvin Hernton, who tells us "I got my first understanding of what it means to be an African when I read Jahnheinz Jahn's remarkable book."[16]

Among the ideas that made Africa so happily available is the concept of NTU—this is the stem of the Kinyaruanda-Bantu words "Muntu" (person), "Kintu" (thing), "Hantu" (place and time), and "Kuntu" (modality), and it is a morpheme that does not occur unprefixed in Kinyaruanda—"NTU," Jahn writes with the gravitas of revelation, "is the universal force as such."[17]

Reading this I found myself irresistibly drawn toward fantasizing an African scholar, returning to her home in Lagos or Nairobi with the important news that she has uncovered the key to Western culture. Soon to be published, *THING: Western Culture and the African World,* a work that exposes the philosophy of ING, written so clearly on the face of the English language. For ING, in the

Euro-American view, is the inner dynamic essence of the world. In the very structure of the terms do*ing* and mak*ing* and mean*ing*, the English (and thus, by extension all westerners) express their deep commitment to this conception: but the secret heart of the matter is captured in their primary ontological category of th*ing:* every th-*ing* (or be*ing* as their sages express the matter in the more specialized vocabulary of one of their secret societies) is not stable but ceaselessly changing. Here we see the fundamental explanation for the extraordinary neophilia of Western culture, its sense that reality is change.

Muntu is often cited as an Afrocentric source book in the media. It is important that Jahn explicitly and firmly repudiates (as a German scholar working in the 1950s emphatically would) any notion that (as he puts it) "culture is tied to the chromosomes."[18] And in so doing he seeks to escape the racialization of culture that Du Bois, Crummell, and their contemporaries inherited in the general intellectual climate of nineteenth-century theorizing about difference. Still the appeal of an account of African philosophy of this sort for many African-Americans surely lies in exactly the sort of nationalist search for identity that is common to the discourse of race and of nation.

Jahn's own argument for the relevance of an African philosophy to the black cultures of the New World is based on historical claims (of the sort made familiar in America by Herskovitz) as to the survival of mainly Dahomeyan, Yoruba, and Kongo cosmology, ritual, and aesthetic notions in Haiti and Cuba. I shall say more about this aspect of his account a little later.

But I also have a reason of my own, a reason that survives the rejection of the romantic racialism of the early Pan-Africanists, for exploring the debate on an African philosophy, a debate pursued with a great deal of vigor and in a climate formed, in part, by the culture to which Du Bois and his peers were so central. That reason is that it seems to me that anyone interested in the question of an African-American philosophy can learn a great deal more from the trajectory of that well-established debate than we could from a more abstract reflection on the relationship between peoples, on the one hand, and philosophies, on the other, in Europe (or, indeed, in the great philosophical traditions of South and East Asia). Since the debate *is* so well established, we can pick and choose, with Minerva's owl, among its more illuminating moments: I promise to spare you a detailed narration of the last 30 years of postcolonial African academic philosophy.

Let me proceed, then, with a quotation from Paulin Hountondji, a Beninois philosopher, perhaps the leading francophone philosopher in Africa today; a quotation that anyone even slightly familiar with recent African debates will identify as the opening sentence of his *African Philosophy: Myth and Reality* (1976).

> By "African philosophy" I mean a set of texts, specifically the set of texts written by Africans themselves and described as philosophical by their authors themselves.[19]

This is a definition that knowingly sidesteps what has been one of the cruces of philosophical debate in postcolonial black Africa. As we have puzzled over whether philosophers who happen to share a continent should for that reason be classified together, we have wondered, too, what sorts of intellectual activity should be called "philosophy." And, despite Hountondji, we know that not any answer to that question will do. If Sir Isaac Newton had lived in Africa, *Principia* would be, by this criterion, a work of African philosophy: for Newton called this, the first great text of modern theoretical physics, a work of natural philosophy. And thousands of books published each year in the United States on astrology or bogus Hindu mysticism would count by an analogous criterion as American philosophy.

Yet there is something to be said for Hountondji's strategy. While philosophers in Africa are seeking a role for themselves—or wondering, perhaps, whether they have any role at all—it may be as well not to rely too much on restrictive definitions. The worst that can be said, after all, against someone who calls a cookbook a contribution to the philosophy of cooking is, perhaps, that "philosophy" is, in this context, a rather flashy word.

We do well to be especially careful in applying definitions borrowed from the European philosophical traditions in which contemporary African university philosophers have been trained, because even within these traditions there is a notoriously wide range of opinion about the tasks and the topics of philosophy. And the disagreements within the western academy about the character of philosophy pale into insignificance when we seek to give a unitary explanation of what makes both Confucius and Plato philosophers or of what makes certain Indian and Chinese and Latin writings all *philosophical* texts.

So that, though we *could* try to approach the question of African philosophy by the method of definitions, asking what the word "philosophy" means and what it means to be African, settling the issue by definitional fiat is unlikely to be productive. A cookbook might better not be called the philosophy of cooking," but it might be a good cookbook nevertheless. I suggest we start instead by examining the range of things that have come to be called "African philosophy" and asking which of these activities is worthwhile or interesting—and in what ways; once we have surveyed this territory we can turn to asking whether these projects have plausible African-American counterparts.

I should first observe parenthetically, however, that a more direct application of Hountondji's strategy would, interestingly, yield surprisingly little in this country in the case of African-American philosophy: for few of the major texts of African-American intellectual life—the work of Alain Locke being the most notable counterexample—were, in Hountondji's formula, "described as philosophical by their authors themselves." There have, of course, been African-Americans with philosophical trainings, but their most influential works were not described as philosophical. Du Bois studied philosophy here at Harvard in the days of James and Santayana and Royce; but his Ph.D., as we know, was the *Suppression of the African Slave Trade,* a work of history, even if it was guided by an ethical vision. Du Bois's concern with the practical business of racial uplift (a commitment that has sometimes been connected with Jamesian pragmatism) makes his lack of interest in technical philosophy easy to understand. Alain Locke, whose work as midwife to some of the talents of the Harlem Renaissance is best known through his editing of *The New Negro* and whose championing of African and African-American art and poetry played a major role in the development of an audience for African-American writing in the mid-century, was also a Harvard philosopher; and he pursued the subject at the doctoral level. But his "professional" philosophical work—in axiology—was largely unpublished in his lifetime and had little impact either on his reputation as an African-American intellectual or on the development of the field.

If I were to begin an explanation of why this is, I would start with the fact that in the professionalization of philosophy in America for the last fifty or sixty years—no doubt, in part, because American philosophy in the period is the work of British and German and Austrian and French-born scholars as much as of native-born ones—the American-ness of philosophy in America has not been a dominant preoccupation. As a result, the few African-Americans with philosophical trainings have thought of their being African-American as important to their philosophical work, not in determining that they should explore the conceptions of the African-American community, but rather that they should concern themselves with those critical issues in ethics and political theory raised especially acutely by the American practice of racism. Because, as Bruce Kuklick and, following him, Cornel West have argued, the development of the subject as an academic discipline in this period has taken it increasingly away from the articulation of an American public philosophy (in the manner of Emerson or James), philosophy has, I suspect, seemed until recently a poor point of departure for the effective intellectual articulation of anti-racist arguments. And, as West has also argued, there is no doubt that public discourse on these issues both within and out of the black community has been dominated not by philosophers, like Alain Locke, but by clerics and theologians, like King.

It is only in recent years, in part because of a general sensitivity in the academy to questions of ethnocentrism, in part, I think, through the revival of what is taken (by its proponents) to be a distinctively American tradition of pragmatism, that allegations of the cultural—the national and, perhaps, the ethnic—specificity of philosophical practices in this country have become the object of serious attention. Which makes it, I think, an especially apt moment to pursue the question with which I began.

What projects, then, *should* philosophers concerned with finding a role in Africa pursue? The philosopher Richard Wright (no relation) has provided an accurate survey of the answers to this question that are currently on offer:

> (1) the thought of the African people[20] is intrinsically valuable and should be studied for that reason, if for no other; (2) it is important to the history of ideas that we discover and understand the relation between (or influence of) African thought and the thought of the Western world. For, if Western civilization had its origin on the African continent . . . the correct pattern of intellectual development . . . will become clear only as we begin to understand the basis and direction of that development . . . (3) it is important in understanding practical affairs that we clearly delineate their underlying philosophical motivation.[21]

It will be clear at once that the understanding of philosophy that underlies these various conceptions is curiously ethnographic. Reflect what would be the result of offering these reasons for studying, say, German philosophy: "true," one would respond to the first point, the thought of Germans is valuable and worthy of study, "but that study is not going to be philosophy. If the thoughts in question belong to the literate high culture, then intellectual history is the field to aim at; if they are the practical ideas operative in everyday life, then, perhaps, sociology is the answer." To the second point—and supposing an analogous, if more modest, claim to have been made about the role of German culture in shaping, say, modern European civilization—we should reply, once more, that philosophy seems at best a modest part of what is in question. (Ethnography, it is fashionable to say, is the study of Others; and Wright's second strikingly Euro-American rationale for studying the ideas of Africa, a rationale whose appeal to Africans might seem less obvious, is ethnographic in that sense also).

As to the third point: well, it is certainly important to practical affairs to understand motivation, but that the underpinnings of most practical affairs are importantly philosophical would have to be argued, since, if "philosophical" connects in any way with the formal discipline of philosophy, it cannot be said to be, on the face of it, especially plausible. Try as I might, I cannot see an exposition of Quine's *Word and Object* as germane to an understanding of the Kennedy administration, which followed its publication (or of the Eisenhower administration that preceded it).

It is no surprise, therefore, that a significant proportion of what is served up under the title of African philosophy, in Africa as in the American academy, consists of what Hountondji has called "ethnophilosophy," the attempt to explore and systematize the conceptual world of Africa's traditional cultures. It amounts, in effect, to adopting the approach of a folklorist or ethnographer:

doing the natural history of "traditional" folk-thought about the central issues of human life.[22]

Herder was surely right in maintaining that there is in every culture a folk-philosophy of this sort to explore; right, too, I think, in insisting that this folk-philosophy bears an intimate relationship to the language of the *Volk*. We can add to Herder's claims, at least for our purposes, a recognition that implicit in the folk-philosophy of every human culture are concepts that look close to those central concepts—of good and evil, for example, of spirit, or mind—around which academic philosophers in the west have built their work. We should subtract from Herder's vision the cozy organic unity of the *Volk:* within national and ethnic traditions there are collisions and contradictions of perspective, there is dissension as well as consonance. Not only are there differences between individuals and groups in their understanding of the moral and metaphysical order (some of them centering in obvious ways on gender or age or status), there are in every position contradictions that no one has raised or knows how to resolve.

Clearly, there have not been in every society people who pursued a systematic critical conceptual inquiry; but at least in every culture there is work for an ethnophilosopher, should one come along, to do. In Africa many have come along: and the result, as I say, has been a substantial body of ethnophilosophy.

I shall leave, for the moment, to one side the question whether the analysis of such material is something for which a philosopher's training, in the Euro-American style that has been inherited by Africa's postcolonial universities, especially prepares one. Much ethnophilosophy has, in fact, been practiced by scholars in anthropology and religious studies; philosophers, ill-prepared to carry out the kind of "field work" that will yield a coherent picture, are likely to explore, at most, the traditions of their own mother tongues; and, in so doing, they practice the armchair skills of the native speaker that are presupposed by the philosophical practice of conceptual analysis.

It is easiest to see both the promise and the pitfalls of ethnophilosophy in the context of a specific case. So let us consider these issues in the context of the interesting discussion of Fanti philosophy of mind in the work of the Ghanaian philosopher Ben Oguah. For reasons that will become clear, I shall begin by saying a little about the philosophical psychology of the Asante people, of my home in central Southern Ghana, whose culture and language belong to the same Twi-speaking Akan culture area as the Fanti people, who live towards the west of the hills and plains that lie behind the Ghanaian coast.

According to most "traditional" Asante people, a person consists of a body (*nipadua*) made from the blood of the mother (the *mogya*); an individual spirit, the *sunsum,* which is the main bearer of one's personality; and a third entity, the *okra*. The *sunsum* derives, it is said, from the father at conception. The *okra,* a sort of life force, departs the body only at the person's last breath; is sometimes, as with the Greeks and the Hebrews, identified with breath; and is often said to be sent to a person at birth, as the bearer of one's *nkrabea,* or destiny, from God. The *sunsum,* unlike the *okra,* may leave the body during life and does so, for example, in sleep, dreams being thought to be the perceptions of a person's *sunsum* on its nightly peregrinations; yet, in the day, one's shadow (which never leaves one) is also referred to sometimes as a *sunsum*. Since the *sunsum* is a real entity, dreaming that you have committed an offence is evidence that you have committed it, and, for example, a man who dreamed that he had sexual intercourse with another man's wife was liable for the adultery fees that were paid for walking offenses.[23]

In speaking thus I have already broken one of the precepts that I suggested we add to Herder's conception of folk-philosophy. We should recall, I said, that there are collisions and contradictions of perspective. The ideas I have described are certainly part of the baggage of ideas you acquire (or, at least, used to acquire) as you learned the words *sunsum, okra* and *nipadua* in Asante; but assent to these doctrines was never constitutive of a grasp of the relevant concepts, and we should not assume that it was taken equally seriously by everybody as a *theory*. Rather the concepts were mobilized largely in everyday life in discussions, for example, of personality and its inheritance, good and bad fortune, or ill-health.

So, for example, it used to be widely believed that some foods are tabu to one's *okra;* and, if one ate those foods and became ill, a priest or healer, who was able, with the use of medicines, to "see" one's *okra,* might tell one to pacify it by offering it food and drink. Or, in a more ordinary case, a person with bad fortune may be described as one whose *okra* has failed to guide him. Or a wicked person might be said to have a bad *sunsum;* and a powerful person a strong one. It is not clear that these usages, the ones that *are* part and parcel of being able to talk about a person and her personality, characteristics, and fortune, commit one to any very specific ontology. No more am I committed to any entity other than the person when I observe that Ama has a good soul, or is in fine spirits, or has changed her mind.

Still, if you ask about *sunsum, okra,* and *nipadua* and don't get into a very deep discussion, this is what you will be told: and only once you have got into deeper discourse will you discover that not everyone shares the official theory of their relations. In what follows, these reservations should be borne in mind.

Now Asante-Twi and Fanti-Twi are largely mutually intelligible, and it is natural, I think, to consider Oguah's account in the light of these Asante conceptions.[24] Oguah asserts that the Fanti conceptual scheme is dualist—in fact, Cartesian. But at least three caveats need to be entered about this claim.

First, since Fanti is an Akan language and the word *okra* which Oguah translates as "soul" is, you will recall, the same as the word for what, in Asante, I identified not with the mind but with the life-force, we might wonder why there is no mention, in Oguah, of the *sunsum*. Naturally, there is no reason that the Fanti should have precisely the tripartite system that we find among the Asante (and other Akan peoples in, for example, Akuapem); and there is some tendency among modern Asante speakers as well to use the words *okra* and *sunsum* almost interchangeably, even while insisting, when asked, on the distinctness of their senses. But Oguah's access, as a contemporary native speaker of Fanti-Twi, is to these terms as mediated by the many Christian influences that have settled in the coastal regions of Ghana, after four centuries of trade and missions from Europe, and over a century of an extensive British cultural presence in the Gold Coast Colony. Even if, therefore, there is, for the Fanti, no *sunsum,* we are not free to infer that this is a fact about unadulterated Fanti traditions: it might be the result of Christianization.

I emphatically do not wish to imply that Christian beliefs are *in se* un-African. But the Fanti live on the coast of modern Ghana and this case allows us to focus on the question whether, in cultures that have exchanged goods, people, and ideas with each other and with Europe (or, in East Africa, with the Middle and Far East) for many centuries, it makes sense to insist on the possibility of identifying some precolonial system of ideas as *the* Fanti tradition. For a Fanti-speaker today the beliefs of her ancestors are surely not intrinsically more valuable than the beliefs of her contemporaries and it is perfectly reasonable for Oguah to treat the concepts as he finds them—now—in his own culture. But the fact that there is reason to suppose that these beliefs are the product of a history of cultural exchanges, the fact that they are not, as the elders sometimes claim, the unadulterated legacy of immemorial tradition, *does* bring into sharp relief the question why these particular beliefs should be granted a special status. If our ancestors believed differently, why should not our descendants? Such reflection is bound to make especially compelling the demand for African intellectuals to give a critical—which does *not* mean an unsympathetic—reading of the modes of thought of their less Western-influenced sisters and brothers.

Second, however—and putting aside the question whether this reportage is, by itself, what is needed—the evidence that the Fanti are now dualists, and Cartesian dualists at that, is surely not very compelling. For a Cartesian dualist, mind and body are separate substances: and this doctrine—which I admit to finding, even after years of training, less than easy to understand—is not one I would expect to find among the Fanti. The Fanti, for example, according to Oguah's own account, hold that "what happens to the *okra* takes effect in the *honam*"[25]—i.e., the body. And Oguah offers no evidence that they find this idea at all problematic. But if that is so their dualism must be at least in some respects different from Descartes', since, for a Cartesian, the relation of mind and body *is* felt as problematic.

More than this, there is, as Kwame Gyekye—another distinguished Twi-speaking philosopher—has pointed out, a good deal of evidence that the Akan regard the psychic component of the person as having many rather physical-sounding properties. So that even if there were not these problems with the general notion of the Fanti as Cartesian interactionists, Oguah's insistence that the "*okra,* like the Cartesian soul, is not spatially identifiable"[26] looks to me like a projection of the ideas of Western philosophy. For if, as I suspect, my Fanti step-grandmother would have agreed that the *okra* leaves the body at death,[27] then there is no doubt that at least sometimes—namely as it leaves the body—it is thought of as having a spatial location. Most of the time, it would be thought strange to ask where it was since the answer, for a living person, is obvious—in the body; and for a dead person is likely to be regarded as speculative at best.

I do not myself believe that any of Ghana's Akan peoples are dualist. But I do not think that it makes sense to say that they are monists either: like most Westerners—all Westerners, in fact, without a philosophical training—most simply do not have a view about the issue at all.[28] For the examination and systematization of concepts may require us to face questions that, prior to reflection, simply have not been addressed. To organize these concepts and their relations into a coherent system is the task of what Peter Strawson—one of Oguah's teachers—has called "descriptive metaphysics."[29] But, as many philosophers have observed in discussing Strawson's work, though this sort of careful conceptual analysis is indeed a helpful preliminary to the philosophical project, it is surely *only* a preliminary to the "revisionary metaphysics" that seeks to assess our most general concepts and beliefs, to look for system in them, to evaluate them critically, and, where necessary, to propose and develop new ways of thinking about the world.

More than this, the systematization of what exists prior to the sort of organized, written collaborative discourse that academic philosophy represents inevitably changes the character of our ideas. The image of philosophy presented by British conceptual analysis in the 1950s and 1960s as an activity that takes as its material the raw stuff of everyday conceptual life, merely organizing and articulating it, is false to the experience of doing philosophy. We may agree with J. L. Austin that the structure of the concepts with which people ordinarily operate is highly complex and subtly nuanced without supposing that the process of making the implicit explicit leaves the prereflective texture of our thought unchanged.

A simple example will make the point for me. If we were reporting, as ethnographers, the views of rural French men and women, we should have to accept that many of them believe that something of them—their spirit, as we might say—survives the death of their bodies. But to systematize this sort of view, we should have to decide whether this entity had a location in the ordinary world of space and time. Many of these people, if asked, would be likely, if they took any view of the matter at all, to answer that it did not. We can imagine that, for them, the idea of disembodied existence is essentially subjectively conceived as the having of experiences without the possession of a body. But philosophical reflection stretching back through Wittgenstein to Descartes has led many of us to conclude that this notion is just incoherent. And since anyone with a western philosophical training knows that there are grounds for thinking it incoherent, there is something less than sane in the intellectual project of recovering this notion without at least considering whether, in the end, it makes sense.

The fact is that philosophers in Africa are bound, by their position as intellectuals educated in the shadow of the West, to adopt an essentially comparative perspective. Even if it is their "own" traditions they are analyzing, they are bound to see them in the context of European (and often Islamic) as well as other African cultures. No one can be happy celebrating her own tradition in the knowledge that it makes claims inconsistent with other systems without beginning to wonder which system is right about which issues. A cozy celebration of one's own conceptual and theoretical resources is a simple impossibility. For one has to live one's life through concepts; and, despite the fact that people everywhere constantly inhabit inconsistent presuppositions, in one life at one time there can sometimes be space for only one system. That system does not have to be either "western" or "traditional": it can take elements of each and create new ones of its own. But the life of reason requires the integration of elements: for intellectuals elements in different systems or within the same system that are recognized as incompatible pose a problem that cannot be ignored like the unremarked practical inconsistencies of everyday.

What the Fanti have is a concept—*okra*—ripe for philosophical work; and what is needed is someone who does for this concept the sort of work that Descartes did for the concept of the mind: and, in doing this, like Descartes, this Fanti philosopher will be covering new territory.

I deferred somewhat earlier the question whether a philosopher's training is apt for this kind of work; and my answer, which is not one that will surprise you now that we have seen some, is: "Yes: insofar as the concepts under exploration are the sorts of terms with which philosophers are familiar, and insofar as what is at stake is not only the analysis and articulation of these concepts but their organization, assessment, critique, and development." Indeed, because the issues of the truth and the intelligibility of traditional ideas are bound to be at the heart of any intellectual project conceived of by someone with a Western conception of a reflective life, the purely descriptive ethnophilosopher faces, as a result, the following dilemma.

If, on the one hand, his view is that European and, say, Fanti concepts are the same but their beliefs are different, a crucial question is who is right. (This can be an entirely practical matter: should I go to the shrine to pacify my *okra* or to the psychiatrist to deal with my neurosis?) And if, on the other, the concepts are different, the interesting question is whether the Fanti concepts are more appropriate to the world than European ones, or, if not, at least more appropriate to the problems and form of life of the Fanti. In either case, to refuse to go beyond mere description of the conceptual situation seems at best eccentric, at worst simply irresponsible.

These problems will often turn out to involve matters addressed by the natural and biological sciences or by psychology or by anthropology: but a philosopher, with a philosopher's training, who speaks the language, is at least trained in the articulation of concepts. And, at all events, in the present African situation this preliminary work must be done by somebody, if the inescapable task of deciding who is right—and therefore if (and if so which) "traditional" Fanti modes of thought should be modified or abandoned—is to be rationally accomplished. Philosophers of physics learn physics; philosophers of biology learn about molecular genetics; philosophers of history (good ones, anyway) study history and historical narrative; there is nothing to stop African philosophers seeking what they need to follow the questions that their situation has posed for them. Not to address the adequacy of the ideas we have inherited from the process of encounter with our colonizers is to leave the outcome in the hands not of reason but of chance; or, perhaps, to leave the intellectual future of the Fanti-speaking peoples, and that of other Africans, to be decided exclusively by the fact of the economic and technological superiority of the already hegemonic cultures of the metropolitan world.

Ethnophilosophy, then, strikes me as, at its best, a useful beginning; a point from which to strike out in the direction of negotiating the conceptual lives—which is, in a sense, to say the lives *simpliciter*—of contemporary Africans. But, as I have argued, without an impetus toward such interventions (or, worse, as a substitute for them), it is merely a distraction.

I indicated at the start that it was not my view that African philosophy as a racial inheritance had nay relevance for African-American life. But what I believe is best in Jahn's book—the accounts of *voodoo* and of *santeria* at the start—shows how an intelligent reading of the cultural meaning of African "survivals" requires a knowledge of the ethnophilosophy of the slaves' cultures of origin. That, at least, is a modest contribution that African ethnophilosophy can make to African-American studies; and we can hope that it will be carried out with more care in the future as our scholarly understanding deepens and without Jahn's insistence on a continental unanimity.[30]

Given the continuing role of *Muntu, Nommo,* and the like even in recent discussions of Afrocentricity, it may be useful to insist on the implausibility of that assumption of what Hountondji has called ''unanimism'': the factual assumption that there is some key body of ideas that is shared by black Africans quite generally. Consider a representative passage from *Muntu,* which has the advantage over other more recent texts that follow in its train, of being by an author who is no more among us.

> Adebayo Adesanya, a Yoruba writer, has found a pretty formulation to characterize briefly the harmony of African conceptions.
>
> ''. . . Philosophy, theology, politics, social theory, land law, medicine, psychology, birth and burial, all find themselves logically concatenated in a system so tight that to subtract one item from the whole is to paralyse the structure of the whole.''
>
> The unity of which Adesanya is speaking here holds not only for Yoruba thought, but presumably also for the whole of traditional thinking in Africa, for African philosophy as such.[31]

What a heavy burden is borne by that ''presumably.'' Why should the Zulu, the Azande, the Hausa, and the Asante have the same concepts or the same beliefs about those matters that the concepts are used to think about and discuss? Indeed, it seems they do not. If similarities are expected, it should be on the basis of the similarities between the economies and social structures of traditional societies or as the result of cultural exchanges: but the cultural exchange across the continent at the level of ideas has been limited by the absence of writing, and the socioeconomic similarities are often exaggerated.[32] Many African societies have as much in common with traditional societies that are not African as they do with each other. It is not reassuring that Jahn asserts at one point that ''[s]ince African culture appears as a unity, it makes no difference from which African language a term is derived''[33] or that his only observation in defense of his procedure is that ''the question of whether or not a plurality is understood as a unity is to a great extent one of interpretation.'' For the issue is not whether Africa is to be understood as a unity but whether it is to be seen as united in these highly specific philosophical doctrines. Skepticism on this point is hardly met by Jahn's observation that, since Egon Friedell has stated that ''[a]ll history is saga and myth'' the ''neo-African intelligence'' whose work Jahn is reporting is ''entitled to declare authentic'' whatever in its past it believes to be so.[34]

For the unity at the core of the African world that Jahn alleges involves attachment to principles drawn from Alexis Kagamé's work in Rwanda on the Bantu culture zone, from the Dogon sage Ogottemêli of Mali, and from various writers on Yoruba culture. Thus we are told that it is part of African philosophy that ''[f]orce and matter are not being united'' in the conception of NTU; ''on the contrary, they have never been apart.''[35]

But it seems to me that ascribing philosophical doctrines of this level of abstraction and generality to the speakers of a language on the basis of anything other than the widespread enunciation of that doctrine (which is nowhere in evidence in this case) is intrinsically not very plausible. It is not that there are *no* philosophical doctrines that one can educe from the way people ordinarily operate with their words and thoughts. It might make sense, I think, to suppose that all of us are committed, in some sense, by the way we argue about right and wrong to the ethical doctrine, for example, that "ought" implies "can": most people will agree that "I can't" is, at least, a good first response to "You ought to." But it is hard to see what grounds would lead one to suppose that we must all think anything in particular that can be stated in such distinctively philosophical terms as that "force and matter are one."

It is, therefore, even more astonishing to find it being claimed in *Muntu* that highly abstract philosophical notions, originally identified in the structure of some Bantu languages, are the folk-philosophy also of people who speak languages in West Africa as remote from Kinyaruanda as German is from Hindi. (I am aware that such comparisons lack clear sense but you will gather my general drift.) Alexis Kagamé himself, from whom these claims are borrowed, like his teacher the Belgian priest, Placide Tempels, made claims only about the ideas implicit in Bantu *languages*. And though it is indeed odd to suppose, with some unanimists, that a people should share the same beliefs on all the major issues in their lives, it is not at all odd to suppose that people who speak the same language should share concepts, and thus at least those a priori beliefs whose possession is constitutive (on one plausible view) of a grasp of concepts. If there is a case to be made for the relevance of African ethnophilosophy to African-American life, the tradition (transmitted by Jahn) of Father Tempels' *La Philosophie Bantoue* is, on these grounds alone, a poor place to start.[36]

One further debate in African philosophy of relevance to our case deserves briefer mention. In the recent discourse of Afrocentricity it has often been argued that "classical Egyptian philosophy" provides a solid foundation for an Afrocentric education. A similar debate has gone on in Africa, where the importance of ancient Egyptian philosophy for contemporary African intellectual life has been argued with most vigor in the writings of the Senegalese man of letters, Cheikh Anta Diop. Diop's work makes clear, I think, the primary motivations of the school. In *The African Origins of Civilization,* Diop summarized his claims: "Ancient Egypt was a Negro civilization. . . . The moral fruit of their civilization is to be counted among the assets of the Black world." Because "[a]nthropologically and culturally speaking, the Semitic world was born during protohistoric times from the mixture of white-skinned and dark-skinned people in Western Asia . . . [and] all races descended from the Black race"[37] it follows that the first great human civilization—one from which the Greeks, amongst others, borrowed much—was a black civilization. Since he had also argued in

L'Unité culturelle de l'Afrique Noire for the existence of "features common to Negro African civilization,"[38] Diop exhibits, in our own day, the essential elements of the romantic racialism of Crummell, Blyden, and Du Bois: and he makes quite explicit the connections between claims about Egyptian philosophy and the projects of Pan-African nationalism. For it is the historical depth of the alleged tradition, along with its putative négritude, that makes Egyptian thought a suitable vehicle for contemporary racial pride. Since philosophers have succeeded in persuading many in the west that philosophical ideas are central to any culture—a trick that depends on an equivocation between "philosophy," the formal discipline, and "folk-philosophy"—and since these are Western-trained intellectuals, it is natural that they should see in Egyptian philosophy the continent's proudest achievement.

Yet it seems to me that Diop—whose work is clearly the best in this tradition—offers little evidence that Egyptian philosophy is more than a systematized but fairly uncritical folk-philosophy, makes no argument that the Egyptian problematic is that of the contemporary African, and allows for a hovering, if inexplicit, suggestion that the Egyptians are important because the originators of the earliest dynasty were black.

I have never seen any particular point in *requiring* European and American philosophers—*qua* philosophers—to study the pre-Socratics: their work is a mixture of early "science," poetry, and myth, and if it is important for modern philosophy at all it is important partly because it creates the world of texts in which Plato began—or, should we say, took the first faltering steps toward?—the business of systematically reflecting on and arguing about the concepts of folk-philosophy; and partly because it has been the subject of sustained attention from philosophers in the western tradition. No analogous argument exists for the study of ancient Egyptian thought in contemporary Africa: there are no founding texts, there is no direct or continuous tradition.[39]

If Diop and his followers—a group we might call the "Egyptianists"—are right, then ancient Egypt deserves a greater place than it currently has in the study of ancient thought: and if they are right then it should be studied intensely in Africa and Europe and America and Australasia, wherever there is an interest in the ancient world.[40] If European or American or Australasian intellectuals are too blinkered or too deeply chauvinistic to accept this, then maybe these matters will only be studied in Africa. But that would be a matter for regret.

In the appeal to Egypt there are echoes of Oguah's appeal to a Fanti tradition; and I think there is something important to be diagnosed in the urge to find an authentically Negro or an authentically Fanti point of departure. I myself detect here the magical power of a "reverse discourse." We have been led to think that this philosophy, this history that flows from Plato to Frege, is theirs, that it belongs to Europe and to her New World diaspora. The wrong reaction is to accept this claim and run off after a philosophy of our own. The right reaction is surely Du Bois's: to master and claim what is useful in that tradition, to chide it for its errors, to offer it the insights of the other traditions one has inherited.

Still, I don't want wish to minimize the importance or deny the intelligibility of one important motivation for the work both of the ethnophilosophers and of the Egyptianists: namely, the desire to recover for Africa a history in philosophy, to deny the claim that "Logic or Philosophy" are absent from the continent's traditional thought. Surely nothing much is achieved by insisting that *something* had better be called African philosophy. After all, as Marcien Towa once observed tartly:

> The concept of philosophy thus enlarged is coextensive with the concept of culture. . . . It . . . remains indistinguishable from any other cultural form at all: myth, religion, poetry, art, science, etc.[42]

If ethnophilosophy is not much like what is practiced in the American academy; if there is nothing that stands to African intellectual life as Greece allegedly stands to the high culture of Heidegger; why can we not simply accept that there is no more reason to suppose that every intellectual activity in the west should have had an African twin than there is to suppose that there must have been African harpsichords or African sonnets?

The answer, of course is that "philosophy" is the highest-status label of western humanism. Few black philosophers are undisturbed when they discover the moments when Africa is banished from Hegel's universal history and when Hume declares, in the essay on "National Characters" that blacks are incapable of eminence in action or speculation (likening in the same place Francis Williams, the Jamaican poet, to a "parrot who speaks few words plainly.") The urge to find something in Africa that "lives up to" the label is, in part, a question of wanting to find something in Africa that *deserves* the dignity; that warrants the respect that we have been taught (in our western or westernized schools and colleges) is due to Plato and Aristotle, Kant, and Hegel. And part of a proper response to this impulse is to demystify that canonical respect; something that requires only, surely, that we remark the preposterous foundations upon which it is established.

Our textbook histories of western culture may insist that Plato and Aristotle are at the root of its pivotal insights; but if we ask ourselves what is most valuable in Euro-American culture, we shall surely want to mention, for example, democracy, to which Plato and Aristotle—and, for that matter, Kant and Hegel—were opposed; applied science and technology, to which Plato contributed nothing and Aristotle provided a long false start whose overthrow in the Renaissance finally made possible the scientific revolution; and a literary culture that refers back to Plato and Aristotle almost exclusively in moments of Christian religiosity (which they would have repudiated) or snobbism or hocus-pocus. The point is not that these are authors we should not read—reading them has provided me, as it has provided many others, with some of the greatest pleasures of my reading life—but rather that we should not read them as repositories of forgotten truth or sources of timeless value. Plato and Aristotle are often interesting because they are wicked and wrong; because they provide us with access to worlds of thought that are alien, stretching our conception of the range of human thought; because we can trace, in tracing the history of reflection on their work, a single fascinating strand in the history of the mental life of our species.

What are the lessons for the prospects of an African-American philosophy from the African debate about ethnophilosophy? I think there are five major points that bear discussion.

First, ethnophilosophy at its best has been rooted in an exploration of the distinctive conceptual worlds of various ethnic groups and has often done so by exploring key *terms* in their languages. And there are terms in the multifarious dialects of American Black English—*signifyin'* for example, will hardly have escaped your attention—that deserve a good deal of the exploration and analysis they are beginning to receive. Like many of the terms that are analyzed in African ethnophilosophy, they gain their full sense in the context only of certain social practices; and describing these practices and the role of concepts in them is, as the ethnophilosophers have discovered, an activity that may require the interpretative and descriptive skills of the ethnographer as well as those of the philosopher, even when the culture is, in some sense, your own.

Second, the best ethnophilosophy has not assumed that even within cultures there will be unanimity on all questions; that there is, in the end *an* Akan or *a* Yoruba philosophy. Even if "whether or not a plurality is understood as a unity is to a great extent one of interpretation," there are important differences in the normative ideals and the metaphysical commitments of African-Americans that are obscured by talk of *the* view of "*the* black community."

Third, it has recognized that in drawing a system from the practical mobilization of these concepts in everyday life there are decisions to be made that inevitably take one beyond what is already implicit in that everyday practice. In building a vision of the world rooted in some aspect of, say, African-American experience, one is creating as well as describing.

Fourth, it has led on to a critical engagement with the conceptual traditions it discusses; in part because, fifth and finally, it has always been comparative. Indeed, in the United States, it seems quite inconceivable that this project should be carried out in isolation from other work of the same sort in American Studies, in departments of religion, in philosophical and literary-theoretical debates about modernity. An African isolationism, a delinkage, of the sort that has been suggested by Samir Amin in Senegal, at the intellectual rather than at the economic level, is an imaginable, though, in my view, undesirable and unlikely outcome. But for us here this is surely not even a possibility.

If we dub a project that meets these five desiderata a *critical* ethnophilosophy we can ask whether there is a body of African-American reflection that satisfies most (and sometimes all) of these conditions; and it is, I think, clear that the answer is: Yes. You will find just such work as long ago as in *The Souls of Black Folk*.

Are people with academic trainings in philosophy uniquely equipped for the project of a critical ethnophilosophy of African-American cultures? Certainly not: for some of the best such work is being done in African-American Studies by theologians, legal scholars, political scientists, literary theorists, and sociologists. But, while feeling free to borrow from other disciplinary traditions—in ethnography and literary studies and sociology—I think that the philosophers' taste for system and argumentative style can make useful contributions in this area.

So there are theories and tendencies—as Cornel West, Cedric Robinson, and others have argued in the domain of political and social thought; as Skip Gates, Claudia Mitchell-Kernan, and others have argued for verbal behavior—that are interestingly embedded in particular African-American communities. But the intellectual leadership of the African-American community has been overwhelmingly provided by intellectuals trained in the same traditions as other American intellectuals and in conversation with them and with Europeans, and African-Americans have been schooled in American schools for several generations, so that there is little likelihood that an African-American ethnophilosophy would turn up ideas that differ radically from those of most other American communities in fundamental philosophical psychology or ontology. And this is an important difference from the situation that still obtains in Africa's cultures today.

The lessons of the first years of philosophy in the postcolonial African university for the prospects of an African-American philosophy are modest but not wholly negative: in particular I believe there are real, if limited, possibilities in what I have called a critical ethnophilosophy, pursued by people with philosophical trainings alongside others. But the more important lesson to be drawn, I think, is from one significant reaction of African philosophers to their recognition of the limitations of ethnophilosophy: which has been to turn to what Odera Oruka, the Kenyan philosopher, has dubbed "national-ideological philosophy": toward, in other words, the reflective articulation of the great ethical and political questions raised by the struggle through colonialism and toward postcolonial social and economic development. For African-Americans the great ethnical and political questions are raised by the history of racism; and they involve more than political philosophy narrowly conceived, since there are cultural issues centrally raised by the African-American identity. And while racism has played so significant a negative part in shaping that identity, we need to remember also the positive experiences of racial community, what Blyden called "the poetry of politics" that is "the feeling of race," the feeling of "people with whom we are connected."[43]

Thinking about how the facts of "race" and the demand for justice may be accommodated to each other and to the realities of our various identifications and identities: nothing could be a more recognizably philosophical project. And what Du Bois called the "social heritage of slavery; the discrimination and insult" as well as the contemporary meaning of "racial difference" need always to be borne in mind if these discussions are to hew to reality. Here, so it seems to me, we have a substantial tradition of African-American reflection that includes—along with Du Bois and Crummell and Delany—intellectuals like Frederick Douglass and Henry Highland Garnett, who were (to use a term that risks, like much shorthand, obscuring as much as it clarifies) more assimilationist than Du Bois, which continues to our own day. If anyone wants to know of a substantial tradition of philosophical work by African-Americans and relevant to their circumstances, surely that is it.[44]

It is true, as I said at the start, that not much of this work was carried on in philosophy departments, not much was labeled "philosophical" by its authors. But the work of their successors now can be, should be, and, is beginning to be carried on in philosophy departments; and the profit will flow (as it has already begun to flow) in both directions.

These issues, which are crucial for questions of race in public life quite generally, intersect with a more narrowly academic range of questions in what I suppose we could call not so much the philosophy of education as the philosophy of the academy, questions about how racial identities and racist histories have shaped our disciplinary heritages. Philosophers (like others) have not always been good at seeing clearly the historical formation of their own discipline; so that we have often offered "essentialist" accounts of the subject, stories that seek to explain the connection between Plato and Frege by postulating a common transhistorical relation to shared methods or questions. But as philosophers of science, in conjunction with historians and sociologists of science, began to recognize the ways in which the natural and social sciences develop, both as pedagogical and as research traditions, and as that wonderfully plastic notion of the paradigm filtered back into the general discourse of philosophy (as it filtered into general discourse, *tout court*), it has occurred to many of us that the disciplines of the humanities too usually have histories more interesting than we realized.

Feminist philosophers have argued that the structure of philosophical discourse reflects the longstanding exclusion of most women and women's concerns, first from the life of intellectuals, then, as it developed, from the university; and their lesson is not simply that here, as elsewhere, sexism has damaged women and men but that it has clouded our understanding. There has not been an equally extensive exploration of the question how racism has misguided our more abstract reflections; of how the absence of black voices has shaped our philosophical discourse. Some of the most surprising results of feminist philosophical scholarship have come from reflecting on how discussions that do not explicitly mention gender at all reflect (in the preoccupation of political philosophy, for example, with a certain conception of the public sphere) the exclusion of women. After these lessons, it seems simply astonishing how little of the political philosophy of the philosophers explicitly acknowledges the distinctive and different significances of race and other kinds of collective identity as well as of gender to the questions that arise at the intersection of the state with morality.

It is as well to remind ourselves that there is less at stake, in the broader scheme of things, in the "contest of faculties" than in the management of "race" in our public life, even though the latter does not proceed entirely independently of the former. Even if we get it right, or, at least, righter, here in our studies and seminars, there is no guarantee that we shall get it right in our legislatures or on our streets. But within these hallowed halls, the contest of faculties raises crucial issues about the future of American education; and this is one discussion to which a philosopher's perspective can, I believe, make a humble—in the spirit of pragmatism, let us say a useful—contribution.

NOTES

1 Some of (but not all of and not only) these ideas appear also in "Ancestral Voices," which is to appear in *Salmagundi*. A fuller discussion of African ethnophilosophy appears in *In My Father's House* (New York: Oxford University Press, 1992).

2 Paulin Hountondji, *African Philosophy: Myth and Reality,* (Bloomington: Indiana University Press, 1983), p. 69.

3 Cited from an introduction to Franz Fanon's *The Wretched of the Earth*. Tsitsi Dangarembga, *Nervous Conditions* (New York: The Seal Press, 1989).

4 Charles Johnson, *Middle Passage: A Novel* (New York: Atheneum, 1990), p. 132.

5 Johann Gottfried von Herder, *Reflections on the Philosophy of the History of Mankind* (Chicago: University of Chicago Press, 1968), pp. 172, 186, 195.

6 W. E. B. Du Bois, ed. *Writings* Nathan Huggins (New York: Library of America, 1986) p. 819.

7 What I have in mind here is the discussion of "Humanity as the end of human nature" in Book XV of Herder, *Philosophy of History*.

8 There are equally benign echoes of this same idea in the shibboleths of multiculturalism: we'll provide the rhythm, you'll bring the discipline, they'll contribute the curry powder.

9 Du Bois, "The Conservation of Races," American Negro Academy Occasional Papers, No. 2, 1897; reprinted in *W. E. B. Du Bois Speaks: Speeches and Addresses 1890-1919*, ed. Philip S. Foner (New York: Pathfinders Press, 1970), pp. 75–76.

10 E. W. Blyden, *Christianity, Islam and the Negro Race* (1887), reprinted (Edinburgh: Edinburgh University Press, 1967), p. 94; from an address to the American Colonization Society given in 1883.

11 In Howard Brotz, *Negro Social and Political Thought 1850–1920* (New York: Basic Books, 1966), pp. 104, 110. "Africa to become regenerated must have a national character. . . . Our policy must be—and I hazard nothing in promulgating it; nay, without this design, there would be a great deficiency of self-respect, pride of race, and love of country, and we might never expect to challenge the respect of nations—*Africa for the Africans and black men to rule them*. By black men I mean, men of African descent who claim identity with the race." See also the paragraph at pp. 84–85.

12 Herder, *Philosophy of History*, p. 7.

13 Herder, *Philosophy of History*, p. 10.

14 These contrasts between Herder and Du Bois are meant to suggest contrasts between 18th and 19th century thought about difference, in particular to reflect the rather larger part a biologized notion of race plays in the latter; but obviously it would take a great deal more discussion to get clear what one can infer from Herder's discussion about his views on what we mean by "race." For Du Bois, see my "The Uncompleted Argument: Du Bois and the Illusion of Race," in "*Race*," *Writing and Difference*, ed., Henry Louis Gates, Jr. (Chicago: University of Chicago Press, 1986), 21–37.

15 See K. A. Appiah, "The Conservation of 'Race,' " *Black American Literature Forum* 23 (Spring 1989): pp. 37–60; "Race" in *Key Words in Contemporary Literary Studies*, eds. Frank Lentricchia and Tom McLaughlin (Chicago: Chicago University Press, 1990); pp. 274–287; "Racisms" in *Anatomy of Racism*, ed. David Goldberg (Minneapolis: Minnesota University Press, 1988), pp. 3–17.

16 Jahnheinz Jahn, *Muntu: African Culture and the Western World* (trans. Marjorie Grene, intro by Calvin Hernton) (New York: Grove Weidenfeld, 1989), p. xix.

17 Jahn, *Muntu*, p. 101.

18 Jahn, *Muntu*, p. 233.

19 Hountondji, *African Philosophy: Myth and Reality*, p.33.

20 The implications of this reference to *the* African people here will, I hope, strike those who have followed me this far as worrying.

21 Richard Wright (ed.), *African Philosophy: An Introduction* (Washington, D.C.: University Press of America, 1979), pp. 26–27.

22 Many of the references in the thorough bibliography of Richard Wright's collection are to anthropological reports of the concepts and beliefs of the folk-philosophies of various groups in Africa, reflecting the editor's view that ethnophilosophy is indeed a major philosophical preoccupation.

23 These notions are to be found in the writings of Rattray, who was the first ethnographer to give a written account of Asante ideology, and they can be confirmed by discussion with elders in Asante today; see R. S. Rattray, *Ashanti* (London: Oxford University Press, 1955), p. 46. They are discussed also by Wiredu in Wright's *African Philosophy*, p. 141, and Kwame Gyekye in "Akan Language and the Materialism Thesis," *Studies in Language* I, no. 1 (1977), and more recently in his *African Philosophical Thought* (Cambridge: Cambridge University Press, 1987).

24 Indeed the literature on Akan ideas does not often distinguish among the various Twi-speaking

Akan cultures; that it is potentially different schemes that are being compared is thus an issue that has not usually been raised.

25 Oguah, ''African and Western Philosophy: A Comparative Study'' in Wright, *African Philosophy,* p. 170.

26 Oguah, ''African and Western Philosophy: A Comparative Study,'' p. 177; compare Gyekye, ''Akan Language and the Materialism Thesis,'' *Studies in Language* I, no. 1 (1977).

27 But my step-grandmother was a very active Methodist and would probably have taken me to be asking only about the Christian soul: about which she would, however, probably have believed the same.

28 I say ''most'' because Kwasi Wiredu is a monist and Kwame Gyekye a dualist: each of them is the product, of course, of an extensive Western training.

29 See P. F. Strawson, *Individuals: An Essay in Descriptive Metaphysics* (London: Methuen, 1959).

30 I think, however, we should be careful to proceed with a realistic sense of the relationship between the ideas and practices of religion in the cultures from which the slaves came and their syncretisms with Christianity in the New World. In bringing together in Haiti or Cuba or Brazil ideas from a variety of African cultures and mobilizing them together in the languages developed in the New World and in working them into new practices, it is obvious that those ideas change their meaning. We understand the practices better as we see them grow out of these older practices in response to new circumstances: but it is as well to remember (to take an analogy that is to hand) that when I explain the rituals of the Black Sabbath by beginning with an explanation of the Eucharist, I do not thereby show that the Black Sabbath is ''really'' Christian. Nor, to pursue the point a step further, does the Christian origin of the symbolism settle in the affirmative for a Christian the question whether she should adopt it.

31 Jahn, *Muntu,* pp. 96–97.

32 The other obvious possibility for generating African commonalities is that there are universals of human thought, but this won't give us a distinctively African philosophy.

33 Jahn, *Muntu,* p. 27.

34 Jahn, *Muntu,* p. 17.

35 Jahn, *Muntu,* p. 101.

36 In constructing this discussion of ethnophilosophy I have drawn a good deal from the critique of ethnophilosophy that recent African philosophy has constructed. See Chapter 5 of *In My Father's House*.

37 Cheikh Anta Diop, *The African Origin of Civilization: Myth or Reality* (New York, Lawrence Hill and Company, 1974), p. xiv–xv.

38 Diop, *The African Origin of Civilization,* p. xvi.

39 Even what we might call the historicist view that understanding a concept involves understanding its history does not justify the study of either Greek or Egyptian ''philosophy'': for the transformations that the conceptual world of Africa and Europe have undergone since, respectively, the fifth century BC and the eighteenth dynasty are so great, and our forms of life so different, that the level of understanding to be gleaned by historical research is surely very limited. The understanding of the prehistory of a concept is only helpful in present conceptual enquiries if the prehistory is genuinely and deeply understood: and the distance and the paucity of data from ancient Greece or Egypt are enough to preclude any deep historical understanding, certainly if the study of that history is regarded merely as a propaedeutic. Besides which, the historicist claim is only plausible where there are important social and intellectual continuities between the various stages of society in which a concept is studied. And I deny that this condition is satisfied in the relationship between ancient Egypt and modern Africa, or ancient Greece and modern Europe. Even if I am wrong I find nothing in Diop to persuade me otherwise. (There is, incidentally, something paradoxical about the insistence that we must work with the great *written* texts of

philosophy in Africa. For if we are trying to get away from European stereotypes, then surely the view that all interesting conceptual work is written and the property of an individual and that all interesting analysis has to be of written texts is one that we should discard faster than many others?)

40 The work of Diop challenges the claim to Greek originality: unlike their other claims, this one seems to me plausible and worth examining; and the best case for it, so far as I know, is in Martin Bernal's recent *Black Athena: The Fabrication of Ancient Greece 1785–1985,* vol. 1 (New Brunswick, N.J.: Rutgers University Press, 1987). I think one of the most important lessons of Bernal's work is that it makes a strong case for the centrality of racism—directed against both "Negroes" and "Semites" in the rewriting of the official history of the Greek miracle that occurred in the European Enlightenment; a rewriting that rejected the ancient commonplace that the Greeks learned much from Egypt. Bernal does not count as an Egyptianist, for me, because he does not make his argument the basis for a view about what contemporary black intellectuals should care about. He is simply concerned to set the record straight.

41 Robin Horton, "African Traditional Religion and Western Science," *Africa* 37, nos. 1 & 2 (1967), p. 159.

42 Marcien Towa, *Essai sur la problématique philosophique dans l'Afrique actuelle* (Yaoundé: CLE, 1971), p. 26.: Le concept de philosophie ainsi élargi est coextensif à celui de culture. . . . Il . . . demeure indiscernible de n'importe quelle forme culturelle: mythe, religion, poésie, art, science, etc . . .[11]

43 Brotz, *Negro Social and Political Thought,* p. 197.

44 There are issues here about the way in which intellectuals don't count as the *real* African and the *real* African-American. "[S]trangely enough," V. Y. Mudimbe has written with characteristic irony, "Africanists—and among them anthropologists—have decided to separate the 'real' African from the westernized African and to rely strictly upon the first." (V. Y. Mudimbe, *The Invention of Africa* (Chicago: University of Chicago Press, 1988), p. x.) For "African" read "African-American"; for "westernized" read "educated" and you will find yourself with a parallel.

AFRICAN PHILOSOPHICAL TRADITION: A CASE STUDY OF THE AKAN[1]

KWASI WIREDU

INTRODUCTION

Philosophical thinking is a significant feature of African life. This fact is likely to be hidden from anybody who identifies philosophy with the discipline of academic philosophy, for the latter is predominantly an ensemble of written meditations, whereas writing, as a widespread cultural habit, is comparatively recent in most parts of Africa. This is not to say, of course, that writing, as such, or even written philosophy, was historically unknown to Africa. Philosophical conceptions were put into writing in Egypt long before the practice was heard of in the western world or its antecedents. Moreover, some African peoples south of the Sahara, the Yorubas, for example, are known to have invented scripts of their own. Nevertheless, with few exceptions, such as in the case of Ethiopia,[2] traditional philosophy in Africa south of the Sahara (which, for historical reasons, will henceforward be the referent of "Africa" and its cognates) is an oral rather than a written tradition.

To be sure there is a rapidly developing tradition of written philosophy in Africa today. It is probably recognized by all concerned that an important task of that emerging tradition is the recording and interpreting (in script) of the oral philosophy mentioned above. But, beyond this, what the exact relation between the two types of effort in philosophical thinking should be is, currently, a most contentious issue.[3] In my opinion the agenda for contemporary African philosophy must include the critical and reconstructive treatment of the oral tradition and the exploitation of the literary and scientific resources of the modern world in pursuit of a synthesis. One rationale for this is that the character of contemporary African culture has been determined by the interplay between African traditional modes of life and thought and Christian and Islamic customs and ideas along with the impact of modern science, technology, and industrialization. If in this process of synthesis contemporary African philosophers take critical cognizance of all these strands of the African experience, the resulting tradition of modern African philosophy should be rich in its variety and vital in its relevance to contemporary existence.

This does not mean that every single African philosopher is duty bound to grapple with all the many sides of contemporary African life. Division of labor is as good a policy in intellectual as in economic production. Thus a contemporary African who specializes in the philosophy of mathematics or natural science and devotes a lifetime to this field might be making potentially valuable contributions to modern African philosophy even if she does not take up in her work issues arising from the traditional strand of our culture.[4] There is only one proviso, and it is that for her work to become a part of the African tradition it should eventually have a linkage, in some kind of organic manner, with a significant body of African efforts in philosophy which, *mutatis mutandis,* is the only way in which a thought product could become an integral part of an intellectual tradition.[5] Nevertheless, for a long time to come a study of the oral tradition is going to have a prominent place in the preoccupations of African philosophers, as a class, because of the relative neglect that befell it in the period of western colonization.

SOURCES OF AFRICAN TRADITIONAL PHILOSOPHY

An oral tradition of philosophy has both strengths and weaknesses. A major weakness is that it tends not to develop sustained and readily accessible expositions of speculative thought, such as you have in Kant's *Critique of Pure Reason,* or elaborate and architectural systematizations of thought *forms,* such as you get in Russell and Whitehead's *Principia Mathematica*. Nor, consequently, do you encounter an easily observed dialectic of diverging schools of thought with the excitement of an inevitable variegation of insight and illusion. The readiest sources of an oral philosophical tradition are communal proverbs, maxims, tales, myths, lyrics, poetry, art motifs, and the like. These are often single statements or sets (which may be numerous) of relatively brief pieces of discourse as opposed to the lengthy exercises in assertion, explanation, and justification that are so characteristic of developed traditions of written philosophy.

The point is not that an oral tradition is condemned to philosophical superficiality or logical obtuseness. On the contrary, some of the folk sayings of African societies express profound conceptions about reality and human experience. And as to logical acuity, there are conceptual absurdities in the *Critique of Pure Reason* that would be promptly laughed out of court among any group of abstractly inclined Akan elders, for instance. Nevertheless, the lack of writing is a definite handicap in the preservation and enhancement of a philosophical tradition.

The situation just mentioned has been aggravated by the manner in which traditional African philosophy has tended to be researched and studied. Attention has seemed to be principally focused on the sort of sources mentioned above. But, although these are the readiest sources, they are not the only ones possible. At least two other sources can be mentioned. The first of these should be obvious on only a little reflection. Proverbs and other folk sayings do not materialize out of the void; they originate in the brains of specific individuals, and although in most instances ascription of authorship is impossible, there still are in Africa today indigenous philosophic thinkers not significantly influenced by foreign philosophies who are capable of expatiating at length on these thought-materials or advancing fresh ones through their own reasoning.

This should inspire another thought about the communal philosophies of traditional societies. It should be apparent that these are, to a large extent, the amalgamation in the communal imagination of truncated residues of the thought of the speculative thinkers and wise conversationalists of the group. The word "truncated" is used here advisedly. It cannot be expected that the details of the reasonings of various remarkable thinkers would be retained in the memory of the common people over the course of many generations. It is striking enough that some of their more memorable remarks have been preserved more or less intact in spite of the deleterious possibilities of this form of thought-transmission. The fact of this preservation is suggested by the near uniformity of doctrinal report that one frequently encounters in widely separated parts of a traditional society. There is, of course, never a total unanimity; but so high a degree of uniformity with regard to basic conceptions can only be thanks to the extraordinary powers of memory that people are apparently apt to develop in the absence of a reliance on writing.[6]

It develops, accordingly, that in the African traditional setting there are two types of exponents of traditional philosophy. There are the traditionalist reporters of the communal philosophy, and there are the indigenous thinkers of philosophic originality. The former are, as a rule, content with, or even insistent on, the transmission of the heritage through quotation, paraphrase or, at best, exegetical flourish, and do not take too kindly to the idea of criticism and reconstruction. The latter—a rare species in any society—are usually appreciative of the tradition and cognizant of its rationale, but are not hidebound to it. They can reject or amend aspects of received conceptions and innovate with their own contributions. As it happens the former are the ones who have tended to be tapped into service as "informants" by researchers into African philosophy. Of course, *if the results are formulated with due conceptual circumspection*, some insights into one level, namely, the folk level, of African traditional philosophy, should accrue. Without at this stage pursuing the question whether this proviso has usually been met, it is worth emphasizing that it is a mistake to proceed as if folk philosophy exhausts the whole range of traditional philosophy, for there is the thought of the indigenous individual thinkers of traditional society. An even more egregious error, replete with atavistic forebodings, is that of equating African philosophy with African traditional philosophy.

But, to return to the individual philosophic thinkers of African traditional society, it is only comparatively recently that their existence or importance has received substantial notice; it may well be that the Kenyan philosopher H. Odera Oruka's *Sage Philosophy: Indigenous Thinkers and Modern Debate on African Philosophy,*[7] published in 1990, is the first publication giving extended exposure to the views of named members of that class. M. Griaule's celebrated *Conversations with Ogotemmeli*[8] was somewhat in this direction, though that author's main interest in Ogotemmeli seems to have been as a depository of the communal (but not common) knowledge of his society. (Be that as it may, the complexity of the combination of empirical cosmology and speculative cosmogony that emerges from the talk of that African sage cannot but raise mind-tickling speculations as to what tomes of scientific and philosophic research his society might have produced had it been wedded to the art of writing.)

The reader will get some idea of the intellectual venturesomeness of the indigenous traditional thinkers of Kenya studied by Professor Oruka from the following brief quotations taken from some of the articulations of their conceptions of God. Oruka Rang'inya (1900–1979) asserts, "It is . . . quite wrong to personalize him. He is an idea, the *idea* which represents goodness itself. God is thus a useful concept from a practical point of view."[9] This thinker had no formal education. His conception of God, by the way, is one that would have warmed the heart of John Dewey, who in *A Common Faith,*[10] criticized the personalization and generally the "hypostatization" of the concept of God and proposed using the word "God" to denote "the unity of all ideal ends arousing us to desire and actions."

In striking contrast to the position of Oruka Rang'inya is that of Okemba Simiyu Chaungo (1914–87), another of the philosophic sages, as Professor Oruka calls them. He says, "I think that God, in fact, is the sun. . . . Well, the doings of the sun are big. It heats the land all day and its absence cools the land all night. It dries things: plants use it to grow. Surely, it must be the God we talk about."[11] Similar to this in some ways but also intriguingly dissimilar in others are the views of Stephen M'Mukindia Kithanje (born 1922). This sage explains, "When I try to have an idea of God he appears to me as a *mixture of heat and cold*. When these two merge (fuse) there comes up life. . . . The act of fusion, which brings forth life, is what we call *God*. And that is what we mean when we say that God created the universe."[12] The sum total of his western education was six months in elementary school.

Even when one of these sages seemed to have embraced Christianity, his perspective on God displayed a personal twist. Paul Mbuya Akoko (1891–1981) had western elementary school education and professed both Christianity and his indigenous religion (the religion of the Luo of Kenya) in which he was regarded as a spiritual leader. His reasoning in regard to God was as follows: "God in my language is *Nyasaye*. But God is one for all communities. The Luos thought differently. They thought their god was not god over other ethnicities. They were wrong. God is one Supreme Being for all peoples. This I can show by reference to the fact of the uniformity of nature. If there were many gods with similar powers, nature would be in chaos, since there would be conflicts and wars among the gods. But nature is uniform, not chaotic: a dog, for example, brings forth a dog not a cat. And a cat produces a cat not a dog or a hen. All this is proof of One Supreme Mind ruling nature. But what exactly is God? This nobody knows and can know."[13] In this quotation African and western influences are fused and transmuted by means of a personal dialectic in a manner that deserves, in its appropriate place, a cultural as well as philosophical analysis.

I will conclude these exhibits from Prof. Oruka's *Sage Philosophy* with the thoughts of a Kenyan indigenous skeptic. Njeru wa Kinyenje (1880–1976), who had no western education at all, regarded organized religion, by which he meant Christianity, as the white man's witchcraft. "This witchcraft," he notes, "has triumphed over the traditional African witchcraft. Today I recognize its *victory* but not its *truth*. . . . I do not pray to God nor do I consult witch doctors. Both religion and witchcraft . . . have no truth in them. My greatest wish is that I should be spared interference from religion and witchcraft."[14]

In 1986 The Nigerian philosopher J. O. Sodipo and his American colleague Barry Hallen published a book on *Knowledge, Belief and Witchcraft: Analytic Experiments in African Philosophy*[15] in which they also relied on the quoted views of some *onisegun,* masters of Yoruba indigenous medicine—regarded as philosophical colleagues rather than "informants"—in making some interesting crosscultural comparisons of the Yoruba conceptual framework with the English-speaking one. It turns out, on their showing, that, for example, there is a more uncompromising insistence in Yoruba than in English discourse on first-hand sensible experience in the validation of knowledge claims. Another recent work in which some attention is called to the opinions of individual indigenous thinkers of an African society—with names attached in this case—is Gyekye's *Essay on African Philosophical Thought,*[16] though the main focus of the book is on the communal philosophy of the Akans of Ghana. This is an elaborate study commanding the greatest interest.

Both of the last-mentioned books evince also a notable sensitivity to the philosophical intimations of the languages of the African peoples studied; which brings me to the second type of additional source for African traditional philosophy. I have in mind here the fact that certain features of the vocabulary and syntax of a language may have conceptual consequences of the highest philosophical interest. In the matter of the influence of language on philosophy, it is well to understand from the outset that language inclines but does not necessitate. Nevertheless, that influence can be tremendous and, moreover, can be to the good or ill.

Considerations of language have a double urgency in connection with African philosophy; for in addition to their basic philosophical relevance, there is a need to unravel, by their means, the conceptual distortions that have accumulated in accounts of African traditional thought through the legacy of years of a self-assumed western spokesmanship. The early European adventurers, missionaries, and anthropologists, who offered to explain to the western world how Africans think (or fail to think), naturally formulated their narratives in terms of the conceptual schemes of their own upbringing. The fit between those frameworks and the African thought materials was most imperfect; but, unfortunately, these antecedents in the literature established paradigms of conceptualization which, in basic essentials, remain operative to this day in the work of foreign as well as of indigenous scholars. In many parts of Africa the power of western formal education and Christian indoctrination over the African mind has been so great that, as one knows from one's experience, it is only by dint of a deliberate mental effort that an educated African can begin to think, in theoretical matters, in terms of the categories of thought embedded in his own language. That effort does not seem to be a widespread phenomenon among contemporary African sophisticates—not even among those who are most prolific in nationalistic protestations. Yet, conceptual sanity, like charity, ought to begin at home.

The assumption is not that truth necessarily resides in the speculative promptings of the African vernacular, but only that an indispensable preparation for crosscultural evaluations of thought is conceptual clarity at both cultural ends. Because the hoped-for conceptual perspicacity presupposes not a little linguistic competence, I propose in what follows to draw on my native understanding of the Akan language to attempt a brief account of elements of Akan traditional philosophy. Such culturally specific studies seem to me to be a necessary propaedeutic to any future generalizations about African traditional philosophy that shall have substance, depth, and legitimacy.

Let me, as a preliminary, give a list of some of the concepts and conceptual contrasts that have frequently been misapplied in expositions of Akan thought:

> Concepts: God, Nature, Person, Mind, Truth, Fact, Free Will, Responsibility.
>
> Conceptual Contrasts: the Material and the Spiritual, the Secular and the Religious, the Natural and the Supernatural, the Mystical and the Nonmystical.

In a number of articles and public lectures, I have tried in some detail to separate Akan ideas with regard to these topics from foreign-oriented entanglements and to elucidate the former with due attention to their natural linguistic environment.[17] Here I can only give a selective summary, which, by reason of its brevity, is likely to give an unintended impression of dogmatism.

THE CONCEPT OF GOD AS A COSMIC ARCHITECT

The religious sphere is that in which there is the greatest misrepresentation of Akan (and in general African) thought. The Akan, as indeed the African, cosmos is regularly said to be a preeminently religious universe—a universe full of spiritual entities at the apex of which God, the *ex-nihilo creator* of heaven and earth, reigns supreme. It is true that most—but, note, not all[18]—traditional Akans do believe in the existence of a supreme being. In fact, one of the commonest sayings in Akanland is that no one teaches the supreme being to a child (*Obi nkyere akwadaa Nyame*). But this being is supreme, or if you like, omnipotent only in the qualified sense that he can accomplish any well-defined task.[19] By comparison with some well-known western conceptions of the omnipotence of God, this concept of supremacy might be thought to be vitiated by too impious a rider, especially considering the sorts of things that are not regarded by the Akans as well-defined. For example, is it possible for the supreme being to reverse that law-likeness of phenomena that defines the cosmic order as we know it? The Akan answer is "No!" Thus the state drummer, a veritable public metaphysician, in the course of rendering condolences, on his "talking drums," to an Akan ruler on the occasion of a bereavement would "say," among other things, "The creator created death and death killed him."

The late K. A. Busia, sociologist and once Prime Minister of Ghana, an Akan scholar deeply steeped in Akan culture by both royal birth and sustained research, commenting on this quote, remarks,

> "Akan drum language is full of riddles that conceal reflective thought and philosophy . . . The drummer is emphasizing the inevitability of death. Man must die. The drummer is saying to the ruler: Condolences; do not mourn; remember the creator made man to die; and when the destined time comes, it is not only beyond the skill of the physician to save the sick, but also *beyond the creator himself* to exercise his power to save this man, for the creator has decreed that every man must die, and so he is unable to stop death from exacting the payment due to him"[20] (my italics).

It should be stressed that the idea is not that God just decides not to forestall this or any other death but rather that, by the very nature of the laws by which he fashioned the cosmic order, *he cannot do so*. So strong is the Akan sense of the universality of law and its indefeasibility that the process of creation itself is viewed not as the outcome of motivated decision making on the part of the supreme being but as the necessary result of his nature. This is the point of another famous metaphysical drum text:

> Who gave word,
> Who gave word,
> Who gave word,
> Who gave word to Hearing,
> For Hearing to have told the Spider,
> For the Spider to have told the Creator,
> For the Creator to have created things?

In venturing an interpretation of this text we are following a time-honored practice of the speculative elders of Akan society. A very well-known saying in this society is that to a wise person you speak in proverbs not in literal language. This is the reason why, as Busia notes, Akan drum language, as indeed other forms of wise discourse, is full of riddles and paradoxes. Inevitably, someone has to provide solutions, since, especially in the more abstract cases, not too many curious people can immediately penetrate such enigmas. Accordingly, one of the accepted credentials of wisdom is the ability to offer the needed explanations. But since, even in much less subtle matters, another Akan consensus has it that "two heads are better than one," no one's explanation is taken as final. Thus the art of interpretation is a continuing dialectic.

One contemporary Ghanaian philosopher of Akan extraction who has devoted considerable effort to the interpretation of the cosmological text under discussion is G. P. Hagan of the Institute of African Studies at the University of Ghana, Legon. He suggests that the lesson of the riddle is that "We must not look for the will to act and the reasons for acting in God's reliance on other entities. Beyond Odomankoma [the Creator] there is no other being to which the Akans assign any role in creation."[21] This is correct as far as it goes. But there is an even more radical lesson to be drawn: not only must we not look for reasons beyond God for creation, but also we must not look for God's reasons for creation, for there can be no such reasons. Why? Because once we start talking of reasons for creation, we would be *en route* to a wild goose chase, for what is to prevent us from pressing for the reasons behind those reasons and so on *ad infinitum?* This, clearly, is the logic behind the iteration and the rhythmic relay of the thought movement before us. We are, accordingly, left with the notion that the creator created the world by the very law of his own being.

But what sort of creation are we talking about? There are doctrinal as well as linguistic reasons for thinking that the Akan conception is one of a demiurgic fashioning out of order from a preexisting indeterminate stuff rather than creation out of nothing. Again, the doctrine is "concealed" in a riddle: The supreme being is likened to a bagworm, and the question is raised as to how the bagworm got into its case. Did it weave it before getting into it or did it get into it before weaving it? One might easily suppose that this precipitates no real antinomy; for, surely, the bagworm couldn't have gotten into a nonexistent case. But suppose now that it wove it before getting into it. Very well, then we had no bagworm to begin with, for without the "bag" you have no bagworm; and how could a nonexistent bagworm have woven its case or anything else? The corresponding cosmogonic paradox is this: either the creator was somewhere before creating everywhere or he was nowhere while creating everywhere. In either case there is a contradiction. Moral: creation can only have been a process of transformation. By means of somewhat different reasoning about this same bagworm paradox Hagan derives a by-and-large equivalent conclusion: ". . . The Akan view is that both he and his creator are part of this world. With such a philosophic assumption the quest for the explanation of the universe reduces itself to the quest for the explication of the *internal structure* of the universe."[22]

Hagan's formulation can hardly be improved. But the thought can be reinforced with the following linguistic consideration. In Akan the concept of existence has an explicitly locative connotation. To exist is to "wo ho," i.e. to be *there,* at some place.[23] Ultimately, the same is true, I believe, of the concept of existence in the English language. But in English there is an appearance to the contrary. Through the so-called existential sense of "is" or "to be" the impression is fostered that "to be there" might be interpreted as "to exist in that place"; from which it then appears that existence in itself (as expressed by the verb "to be") has nothing to do with location. Thus, apparently, something might exist, *be,* without *being* in some place. In Akan there is no such pretense, for there is no analogue of the supposedly pure existential "is" or "to be." To say "Some thing is there" in Akan we say, "Biribi wo ho." If called upon to translate "Some thing *is*" we must insist on the same locution: "Biribi wo ho," for if you eliminate the localizer "ho," the remainder is simply meaningless.[24]

Lest it be thought that an exclusively locative conception of existence must rob the Akan of the wherewithal to call attention to the existence of abstract entities, such as numbers, possibilities, reasons, hopes, fears, etc., it should be observed that a simple option is available. It is open to us to argue that an abstract entity is only figuratively an entity (though not for that reason unimportant); and to a figurative entity corresponds only a figurative location. This, in fact, is the construal of abstract entities that is consonant with the bent of the Akan language, but I must forebear to expatiate on it here.

In the present connection what we need to note is the following cosmological implication of the locative conception of existence. If a creator exists, he exists in space somewhere, and his creative activities can only have taken *place* in space. Thus he exists exactly in the same sense, though, of course, not with the same powers and properties, as the things he created. Compare: Jack exists in the same sense in which the house that Jack built exists. Logically, the comparison is not outlandish, for the creator, on the Akan view, must also have operated on some preexisting raw stuff. True, prior to creation there were no mundane entities x, y, or z, but the existence of the creator entails some cosmological environment, however indeterminate. That he could not have existed in the midst (!) of absolute nothingness is also implied in the Akan word for "create," which is "bo". To "bo" something is to fashion out a product: and, actually, it is closer to the Akan *intension* to describe the supreme being as a cosmic architect than as a creator, given the transcendental conceits of the latter English term in contexts like this.

In Akan the idea of to "bo" something out of nothing carries its contradictoriness on its face. In English the semantical incongruity of creation out of nothing is well enough concealed to allow it to be an orthodoxy among great numbers of people. Yet, if to create is to *cause* something to come into existence, then absolute nothingness must be a logically immovable impediment. Consider a creator working in such a splendid metaphysical isolation. Suppose he exerts himself and then something appears. The question is: what, in principle, is to make the difference between *post hoc* and *propter hoc* in such circumstances or, more strictly, lack of circumstances? Given the hypothesis, the answer is "nothing," and with it disappears any simulacrum of causation. Personally, I do not believe in either the Akan or the Christian creator, but it seems to me that the conceptual problems besetting the former pale into insignificance in the face of those afflicting the latter. I might point out parenthetically that I have not, here or elsewhere, taken the mere linguistic portrayal of an Akan conceptual scheme, in contrast to, say, a western conceptual set-up, as proof of its truth or validity. Such considerations are germane only to the purposes of conceptual description and comparison, which, when there are significant differences, is a substantial enough objective in itself. But where, as in the present paragraph, I have offered an evaluation, I have endeavored to adduce, or at least hint at, *independent* considerations, whose intelligibility and (therefore) merits or demerits do not depend essentially on the peculiarities of the conceptual framework of a given culture. As surface facts, such peculiarities undeniably exist and can impede intercultural understanding. But at the deeper reaches of human conceptualization, they are not crossculturally irreducible[25]; and that is why independent arguments are possible. In this paragraph my argument for the incoherence of the concept of creation out of nothing is not based on the fact that it does not make sense in Akan but rather on the fact that there are logicoconceptual considerations against it which are crossculturally intelligible or at least intelligible in both English and Akan discourse.

It might be of some interest, however, to expatiate a little on the reasons for the incoherence of the notion of creation out of nothing within the Akan conceptual framework. It is incoherent therein not only on account of the meanings of "wo ho" (to exist) and "bo" (to "create") but also because of the comparable empirical orientation of the Akan concept of nothingness. Significantly, there is no abstract noun in Akan for this concept. The only available translations are in terms of a gerund in some such formulation as "the circumstances of there not being something *there*" (*se biribiara nni ho* or *se hwee nni ho*). In general, the Akan language, as apparently many an African language, is very economical in abstract nouns, preferring gerundive and other periphrastic devices. From this it has sometimes been inferred—absurdly—that Africans tend not to think in abstract terms. In fact, periphrases can be as abstract as single-word abstract nouns. Besides, against the verbal economy achievable through abstract nouns is to be weighed the tendency of the availability of such words to inspire—I do not say compel—the spinning of webs of ontological fantasy. Consider the thesis that number is a species of object. Now, number is rendered in Akan as the how-many (*dodow*) of things. Accordingly, when the thesis is faithfully translated from Akan back into English it becomes something like "The how many of things is a species of object." Anyone is likely to have problems thinking this to herself let alone selling it to others. Again, considerations of this sort are not decisive as to truth or validity. My own antipathy towards the postulation of abstract entities (in semantic analysis and anywhere else) is based not only on my Akan linguistic sensibilities but also on independent argumentation intelligible in English. The burden of my critique (expounded elsewhere)[26] is that this practice, whose frank name is hypostasis, thrives on a conflation of the categories of signifier, referent, and object, especially the last two.

But let us return to *nothing*. It is clear that in the Akan way of thinking it presupposes *something;* it has an intrinsic spatial context. In consequence, any notions of a total and absolute nothingness devoid of all context can have no accreditation in Akan philosophy. If one now reviews the bagworm riddle, its antitranscendental message with regard to creation should be even more evident. That message and its framework of concepts have further momentous metaphysical implications. For example, if the spiritual is conceived, in the manner of Descartes, as that which is absolutely nonspatial, no such category of being can have a home in Akan thought; which implies that the question of the spiritual/material antithesis does not arise therein.

The natural/supernatural distinction fares no better.[27] If everything is according to law, even including the creative activities of the supreme being, as pointed out earlier on in connection with the dialectic of Death and the Creator, then there is no separating one order of being, as nature, from another, above it, as supernature; which means that the ontology entertained is a homogenous one in which the concept of nature itself is otiose. True, there is a conception of a hierarchy of existences, starting with inanimate things at the bottom and climbing through the realms of plants and the lower animals to that of human beings, the ancestors and a variety of extrahuman beings and forces up to the supreme being at the apex. (Having touched upon inanimate things, let me take the opportunity to debunk the routine attributions of animism to all Africans. The Akans, at least, regard some things as lifeless. For them dead wood is quintessentially *dead,* and what is so tragic about a corpse is that it is lifeless—the life-principle has left it!) Different realms of being, then, are postulated, but the important thing is that all of them are viewed, as Hagan well remarks, as *parts* of one comprehensive universe.

Thus, suppose an event or situation in the human realm seems to resist all the commoner modes of explanation. For example, an illness may be defying all the best herbal and psychiatric treatments. Very well, then the explanation, for a traditional Akan, may be that the patient is being punished by an ancestor for some sins of commission or omission. In having recourse to a hypothesis of this sort, there is no feeling of going out of the "natural" order, for no such concept is germane to the thought system under discussion. As can be understood from our earlier remarks, the Akan starts with the axiom that everything has its sufficient reason. (No shades of Leibniz! That there is a sufficient reason, an appropriate explanation, for everything, *biribiara wo ne nkyerease,* is a commonplace of the Akan oral tradition.) Given this axiom, what is more *natural* than to seek the explanation for a given phenomenon apparently inexplicable in terms of the factors of one part of the world from another *regular* part? Pardon the pleonasm. By the Akan definition of the universe, everything is a regular part of the system of reality.

Even more inappropriate than calling the kind of Akan explanation we have just cited supernaturalistic is the application of the term "mystical" to it. This last term is often used loosely to mean the same as supernatural. In that case it is subject to the disclaimer already entered. But if it is used with a more serious semantical intent, then we have a bigger mistake on our hands.[28] Mysticism in the stricter sense refers to a special experience in which the subject is supposed to attain unity with the highest reality, directly apprehending everything as identical with everything else and yet as distinct, with an associated sense of purest bliss. Nothing is farther from traditional Akan modes of thought and experience than mysticism in this sense. Apart from anything else, the contradictory language, apparently beloved of mystics, is likely to get on Akan nerves and elicit the traditional admonition that there are no crossroads in the ears (*asumu nni nkwanta*), an aphoristic advocacy of the principle of noncontradiction. Here, again, let it be conceded, in principle, that mysticism may, after all, be an avenue to higher truths; only many Akans, including the present writer, will take a lot of convincing.[29]

That the concept of the mystical is so inapplicable to the world view of the Akans is due to the extensively empirical character of their conceptual framework. This is not the same, by the way, as saying that their beliefs necessarily have empirical warrant. The proposition that our departed ancestors are alive and kicking in the world of the dead and can punish the errors of the living may not be empirically justifiable, and I, for one, have the gravest doubts. Yet, the conception itself of the ancestors and their habitat is empirical in orientation.

It has not escaped any moderately attentive student of Akan thought—and of African thought in general—that the ancestors and their world are conceived very much on the model of the living and their world.[30] For example, access to the *post mortem* world is believed to be by land travel during which there is a river-crossing involving the payment of a toll; which was the reason in olden times for the stuffing of coffins with money and other travelling needs. In fact, the Akan world of the ancestors is so like this world that our political order is supposed to be continued there (in perpetuity) in terms not only of structure but also of personnel. Take away the temporal imagery of the conception and nothing is left. The reader who recalls the empirical character of the Akan conception of existence is unlikely to be surprised by this.

But though the ancestors are conceptualized in terms of a this-worldly imagery, they are not supposed, in their interaction with the living, to be constrained by all the laws that govern human motion and physical interaction. Thus they are normally not perceivable, though the initiated are supposed to be capable of entering into communication with them. Again, although they are conceived in the image of persons, they are not vulnerable to the physical perils of this fleeting world. I have elsewhere[31] called entities conceived in this way quasimaterial. Entities of this sort—material in image but not in dynamics—are obviously very important in the Akan world view. Actually, they are also important in various brands of western thought. The Christian belief in the resurrection of the body clearly involves quasimaterial conceptions. So too do parapsychological narratives about poltergeists and other apparitions, spiritualist claims of human communication with the dead and occult theories of astral bodies. The interesting and important difference between Akan thought and all these varieties of western thinking is this regard is that in the west quasimaterial ideas coexist with Cartesian notions of spiritual substance while, as previously indicated, conceptions of spiritual entities in the Cartesian sense simply have no place in the Akan ontology.

THE CONCEPT OF A PERSON AS BOTH DESCRIPTIVE AND NORMATIVE

What has just been said has a substantial implication with respect to the Akan concept of a person. One can straightaway rule out any prospect of a Cartesian dualism of body and mind. In the Akan language the word for mind (*adwene*) does not signify any kind of entity, except in some figurative uses when it denotes the brain (as when we comment on the *adwene* in someone's head). The regular word for the brain is *amene,* and there is little temptation to identify the mind, the *adwene,* with the brain, the *amene*. But there is not even the possibility, short of a linguistic revolution, of identifying the *adwene* with a Cartesian spiritual substance. In our (Akan) conceptual scheme mind is primarily the capacity to think thoughts, feel emotions, construct arguments, imagine things, perceive objects and situations, dream dreams of both night and day and so on.[32] A difference of considerable interest between the Akan concept of mind and many western conceptions of mind is that sensations viewed in isolation from conceptualization or, if you like, from intentionality, do not count as mental, i.e., as having to do with *adwene,* whereas some very famous discussions of mind in western philosophy are full of earnest meditations on sensations.[33] The Akan way of viewing this matter prompts the hypothesis that, perhaps, there is no one uniform theory that will illumine the nature of both thought and sensation, though they all, as the Akans are very much aware, depend on the brain. Incidentally, except in regard to the reference to the brain, this is a suggestion to which Aristotle would probably have resonated more readily than many of his spiritual descendants in contemporary philosophy of mind.

It would be an agreeable exercise to enlarge upon the advantages of the Akan view of mind but that belongs to another place. Here it might be of greater immediate interest to see what in addition to mind the Akans conceive to be involved in the constitution of persons. There is, most visibly, the assemblage of flesh and bones that form the body (*nipadua,* literally, person tree). But, reason the Akans, something must make the difference between a dead, inert body and a living one. This they attribute to an entity called the *okra,* which they consider an actual particle of the supreme being. Since in respect of this divine constituent all persons are exactly alike, they all are deserving, in equal measure, of a certain dignity and respect—a notion that motivates a strong ideology of human rights. However, in all other respects, every individual is different from every other; they differ not only in terms of spatiotemporal specifics but also in terms of moral, psychological, and social circumstances, which, in combination with humanly imponderable contingencies, produce achievements and failures, fortunes and misfortunes, and shape individual lives in myriad ways. We might, in light of this thought, sum up one aspect of Akan thinking on human personhood by saying that destiny is the principle of individuation of the *akra* (plural of *okra*), the divine specks that constitute the principle of life in the human frame.

A principle of individuation for the *akra* in terms of mundane circumstances is needed because otherwise they would, from a human point of view, be indistinguishable, being all specks of the divine substance. Prior to incarnation, a given *okra* is, by definition, the *okra* of a person envisaged in a determinate life-story, which the creator knows in its full completeness *ab initio* but we, humans, can only learn by empirical installments as the individual concerned plays out his or her destiny on this earth day by day. There is here some analogy with Leibniz' individual concept of a person, which, in the mind of God, "includes once for all everything which can ever happen to him."[34] Both conceptions are faced with the problem of human responsibility. Of this problem the Akans are very acutely aware. Yet, interestingly, the very notion that each individual has her own antecedently defined destiny is often appropriated in Akan discourse as a basis for the right of individuals to make their own decisions unhindered by others. Since the Akans—and Africans generally—are strongly communalistic in outlook, this stress on what might be called the metaphysical right of decision is significant as indicating a certain balance between the sense of communal dependency and the belief in individual rights. Such metaphysical proclamations of individuality take the form of pointing out that when one was receiving one's destiny from the supreme being no one else was there.

It is important to understand that the doctrine of preappointed destinies is, logically, integral to the Akan belief in the universal reign of law encompassing even the process of divine creation. The class of facts and events constituting the destiny of an individual is only an instantiation in miniature of the cosmic order. The idea that individuals have each their own unique destinies is expressed in Akan communal thought in the following dramatic form.[35] In the making of a human individual, God (the Akan cosmic architect, not the Christian *ex-nihilo* creator) apportions a part of himself in the form of an *okra* for dispatch to the earth to be born of man and woman. Before the departure there is a ceremony at which the *okra,* alone before God, takes leave of his or her maker. (In fact, the Akan word for destiny, which is *nkrabea,* means, literally, manner of taking leave). The high point of the proceeding is the announcement of destiny. God reveals to the *okra* what career awaits her on earth and how it shall be brought to a conclusion. Thereupon, the *okra* descends to be incarnated into human society to fulfill the blueprint. (When a person descends from on high, says an Akan maxim, she lands in a town.)

The incarnation is, of course, in large part a biological process which starts with the intimacy of man and woman. Accordingly, the physiologic make-up of a person is attributed to both partners. To the mother the Akans ascribe the origin of a person's *mogya* (literally, blood). Socially, this is the most important constituent of a person, for it is taken as the basis of lineage or, more extensively, clan identity. Since the Akans are a matrilineal people, it is this kinship status that situates a person in the most visceral relationships and brings him into the most existential of the networks of obligations, rights, and privileges that characterize Akan communalism. To the father is attributed the origin of an aspect of human personality which is, conceptually, somewhat elusive. The father's semen is held to give rise to something in a person which accounts for the degree of impact which that individual makes upon others by his sheer presence. Both the inner cause and the outer effect are called *sunsum* in Akan. This is a human characteristic to which the Akans are especially sensitive.

Descriptively, then, the highlights of the Akan conception of a person are the life principle (*okra*), the "blood" (*mogya*) and the distinctive personality ingredient called *sunsum*. Ontologically, there is a greater affinity between the *okra* and the *sunsum,* for they are both quasimaterial. But the *okra* survives death to become an ancestor whereas the *sunsum* perishes with the demise of its possessor. Indeed, an individual may die because his *sunsum* has been attacked and destroyed or even devoured by some extra-human agent such as a witch. Only a constitutionally weak *sunsum,* though, is supposed to be susceptible to this kind of attack; a strong *sunsum* will withstand it. Of a person with a strong *sunsum* the Akans say: *Ne sunsum ye duru,* literally, "His *sunsum* is heavy"; and a weak sunsum is said to be light (*hare*). The locution is metaphorical, but the quasimateriality of the conception of the *sunsum* is evident. Indeed, for the Akans, the *sunsum* is, as Abraham puts it in his classic exposition of Akan philosophy, "that second man who is a *dramatis persona* in dreams,"[36] a temporary duplication of a person who *actually* sallies forth from a sleeping person to indulge in all the goings-on of the dream state.

The difference in ontological character, then, between the *okra* and the *sunsum,* on the one hand, and the *mogya* and the bodily frame as a whole, on the other, is only one of degree of materiality, the body being fully material and the other constituents only partially material in the sense already explained. Carefully to be distinguished from this conception is the Cartesian notion of a material body and an immaterial soul. On this latter conception, any talk of the incarnation of the soul is simply self-contradictory; on the former, there is at least a preliminary coherence. If one is going to talk of an embodiment, it is, surely, a conceptual requirement that the thing to be embodied should be spatial, which is what a Cartesian soul diametrically is not. Both the *okra* and the *sunsum,* being spatial in conception, satisfy this condition, though whether there actually are such entities is severely open to question. (This skepticism, by the way, is without prejudice to the utility of a nonhypostatic construal of these two concepts in the analysis of human personhood.) One thing, in any case, should be absolutely clear: neither the *okra* nor the *sunsum* can be identified with the immaterial soul familiar in some influential western philosophical and religious thinking (with all its attendant paradoxes). This western concept of the soul is routinely used interchangeably with the concept of mind while the concepts of *okra* and *sunsum* are categorically different from the Akan concept of mind (*adwene*), as our previous explanations should have rendered apparent. Thus Descartes (in English translation) can speak indifferently of the soul *or* the mind and appear to make sense. In Akan to identify either the *okra* or the *sunsum* with *adwene* would be the sheerest gibberish.

Our remarks about the Akan concept of a person so far have been occupied, broadly speaking, with its descriptive aspect, even though some very significant normative consequences have been shown to flow from it, as, for example, the idea that every human being has an intrinsic worth because of the divine element in her being. But it is of the utmost importance to note that in addition to such normative implications there is a normative layer of meaning in the concept itself. In Akan thinking, as indeed in the thinking of many other African peoples, a person in the true sense is not just any human being, but one who has attained the status of a responsible member of society.[37] The characterization of this status will also be the characterization of the Akan system of values. Only the baldest statement is possible here. A responsible member of society, from the Akan point of view, is the individual whose conduct, by reason of a sense of human sympathy, shows a sensitivity to the need for the harmonious adaptation of his own interests to the interests of others in society and who, through judicious thinking and hard work, is able to achieve a reasonable livelihood for himself and family while making nontrivial contributions to the well-being of appropriate members of his extended kinship circles and his wider community. The first component of this conjunction of necessary conditions provides, in fact, the essentials of a definition of morals in the strictest sense, while the second gives intimations of the communalist ethos of Akan society.[38] That ethos also holds the key to Akan political philosophy which we must leave unexplored on account of space limitations.[39] On the question of ethics in the strict sense, let me point out in the briefest possible manner that Akan ethics is a humanistic ethics in the precise sense that it is founded exclusively on considerations having to do with human well-being and, contrary to widespread reports, has nothing to do, except very extrinsically, with religion.[40]

On the above showing, personhood is susceptible to degrees. Moreover, it is not an attribute that one is born with but rather an ideal that one strives to achieve in life. In the path of improvement there are, theoretically, endless vistas of higher personhood. But the downward path has a certain critical line of demarcation. In reflecting on this matter we will be brought back to the problem of destiny and human responsibility in Akan thought, to which the makings of an Akan-inspired solution will be proposed.

FREE WILL AS RESPONSIBILITY

Within Akan canons for the appraisal of behavior an individual may fail to be a person (*onipa*) through irresponsible habits, for instance. Such an individual is sure to be the recipient of advice and inspirational prodding from kith and kin and from friends and peers; which, incidentally, should allay any fears that the denial of personhood to a human being might be a prelude to some form of maltreatment. Every human being, as previously noted, has an intrinsic value, since he is seen as possessing in himself a part of God. But suppose the individual in question proves utterly impervious to counsel and slides steadily into the depths of social futility. The typical Akan approach at this stage is to substitute a (solicitous) search for treatment and rehabilitation for moral critique and verbal persuasion. Reason? Irresponsibility has passed into nonresponsibility. The individual is no longer himself. The critical line of human self-identity has been passed. (*Enye onoa,* literally, "It is not himself," or *Enye nania,* literally, "it is not his eyes.") There is no exact equivalent of the English-speaking notion of free will or, in this specific case, lack of free will, within the Akan framework of concepts, but this may be taken as its Akan counterpart.

But notice five things about the Akan understanding of what in English is called free will. First, neither free will nor the lack of it is a universal feature of the human condition; some people have free will, others do not.[41] Second, one and the same individual may have free will with respect to one sphere of conduct but not some other. Third, since there are degrees of personal and social maladjustment, we can speak of degrees of free will. Fourth, the concept of free will has normative as well as descriptive components. Fifth, and, perhaps most interestingly, both free will and responsibility refer to the same aspect of human consciousness and conduct, namely, the ability of an individual to retain his human self-identity in conduct. As is clear from the context, the self-identity in question is not logical self-identity, which even the most confirmed idler must necessarily retain, but a normative species-identity. We are talking, in other words, of whether the individual has the ability to act as a *normal* human being should. (Behold the normative significance of free will writ even larger.)

When, then, is an individual responsible? We can derive the following answer, which I believe to be the correct one, from the brief sketch given above of the Akan approach to the appraisal of human conduct. An individual is responsible (or free) if and only if she is amenable in both thought and action to rational persuasion and moral correction.[42]

Two philosophical consequences of the conception of free will (or responsibility) just advanced should be rapidly noted. First, determinism does not have the slightest tendency to compromise human responsibility in the present conception. Indeed, rational persuasion is a form of determination: it is the form of determination appropriate to normal human behavior. Second, it follows from the conception in question that there can be only one problem of free will *or* responsibility, not two problems, one of free will and the other of responsibility.[43] This is probably the most interesting difference between the Akan-inspired view of free will and soft determinism or compatibilism in western philosophy. The soft determinist also does not think that determinism imperils free will, but he speaks of the problem of free will *and* responsibility as if there are two problems here; which accounts, I think, for the persistence of a certain residual sense of mystery when all the admirable compatibilist arguments have been rehearsed. In spite of the abandonment in many western philosophical circles of the facultative concept of *the will* that may be supposed to be free or unfree, it remains a veritable postulate in much western discussion of the problem in hand that freedom is a descriptive attribute that is either present in the human condition or absent from it independently of normative considerations. It becomes then a truly intractable problem how to establish its existence or nonexistence. This matter requires infinitely more argumentation, but it seems to me to be a distinct advantage of the conceptual economy of the Akan view of "freedom" that it is exempt from this problem.

What of the problem of free will and predestination? The difficulty is that any preappointing of destiny might seem to smack of a freedom-negating manipulation, and it is not at all difficult to imagine a kind of subtle manipulation that might look in principle like divine preappointing. (Think, for example, of a Brave-New-World type of preconditioning updated with all the technical resources for manipulation that have been developed since the classic alluded to was written.) It is appropriate, in answer to this problem, to recall that in the Akan cosmology the predetermination of human destiny (as of everything else) is an integral part of the intrinsically law-governed demiurgic process from which the world order results. The very possibility of such a thing as indoctrination or manipulation presupposes that order, and it is therefore a categorical error to compare any freedom-eroding technique of manipulation that might be devised by humans with the divine preappointing of destiny in the above manner, in spite of the possibly oversuggestive drama of the Akan traditional articulation of the doctrine of destiny. The reason why manipulative conditioning is prejudicial to free will is that it is disruptive of the human way of development on which the Akan conception of free will or responsibility is predicated. That way of development is through nursing, nurture, and the kind of training of the mind that is aimed at producing individuals capable of acting on the basis of judicious reflection—all which, of course, also presupposes the same world order discussed. In my opinion, the validity of this defense of free will within the context of a worldview based on the universal reign of law remains intact even when shorn of the belief in a supreme being.

There is still, however, the problem of fatalism. It might be wondered whether the Akan doctrine of destiny does not entail a fatalistic policy of life. There is, actually, a fatalist strain in Akan thought, due, I suspect, to the tempting conflation of "what will happen will happen" with "what is ordained by God will happen." But the two suppositions are logically independent; the first is a logical truth, the second obviously is not. The first is a premise in the constitutive argument of fatalism, the second is a premise in the doctrine of divine predestination. Fatalism argues: "What will happen will happen, therefore whatever happens happens of necessity," while predestination argues: "What is ordained by God will happen; God had ordained everything, therefore whatever happens is ordained by God." The latter is what is germane to the Akan doctrine of destiny; but the Akan mind, like many minds everywhere, has not been immune the deceptive allurements of the former.

It should be observed, in any case, that, logically, fatalism does not imply a fatalistic policy of life. That policy is premised on pessimism, which is no part of the philosophical thesis of fatalism. From fatalism all that one can deduce is that if success will come, it will come of necessity; and if failure will come it will come of necessity. The person who supposes, for whatever reason, that success will come in his life is unlikely to adopt a policy of resignation. Only those who somehow come to acquire the feeling that what is in store for them is failure are at all likely to develop that attitude. The underlying reasoning then is: "Failure will come; whatever will come will come of necessity, therefore, failure will come of necessity. So why bother?" It is obvious, by the same considerations, that the doctrine of destiny does not imply a fatalistic attitude to life. One has to add to that doctrine the logically independent information that one is destined to fail before any pretense of an argument for fatalistic inactivity can be made.

It should come, then, as no surprise that although the traditional Akans are, as a rule, believers in the predetermination of destiny and are, to boot, frequently fatalists, they are not generally fatalistic. Some Akans are known to sink into passivity, citing bad fate; others assume a bright destiny and live and work with high motivation even in the face of adversity.[44] Statistically, the optimists would seem to be more typical.

This last reflection brings us to a characteristic of an oral tradition of philosophy, which, I believe, is an advantage. In such a context philosophy tends to have a very direct and palpable effect on practical life. When philosophy becomes a written discipline there is always the danger that some might, though certainly they need not, be tempted to pursue technical virtuosity as somewhat of an end in itself. Such diversions are remote to the concerns of an oral tradition. The Akan doctrine of destiny and how it is played out in daily life provide a particularly conspicuous illustration of this remark.

This same circumstance probably accounts for the possibility of speaking of the communal philosophy of a whole people. The doctrines involved are not necessarily accepted or even dreamt of by all and sundry, but the close interplay of life and doctrine in an oral tradition of philosophy ensures that in the normal course of socialization one's intellectual sensibilities are attuned to certain winds of doctrine. In some this attunement amounts to nothing much more than an inchoate predisposition; but in others it takes the form of highly articulate conceptualizations. The foregoing has been a brief report, interpretation, and critical reconstruction of some of the high points of this intellectual phenomenon as far as the Akan communal tradition is concerned. The potentially more exciting exploration of the individual philosophies of the indigenous thinkers of Akan traditional society remains a thing of the future. But the time is obviously ripe for extensive particularistic studies of both types across the continent of Africa.

CONTEMPORARY AKAN PHILOSOPHY

Meanwhile, there is a growing Akan tradition of written philosophy which is very conscious of its heritage of oral philosophy. By a happy historical circumstance, some of the most industrious scholars among the nineteenth-and early twentieth-century missionaries and anthropologists who studied our culture (from a mixture of motives, facilitation of colonial governance not excluded) were much taken with its philosophical dimensions. Thus the works of Christaller,[45] Rattray,[46] and Westermann[47] on Akan culture give various degrees of exposure to the philosophical conceptions of the Akans. These foreigners were meticulous scholars who lived among our people, learnt their language and their ways and tried to empathize with their psyche. Their insights have been appreciated, though their limitations have not gone unnoticed by indigenous Akan scholars[48] (many of them trained philosophers), who, since the beginning of this century, have taken in their own hands the task of expounding their culture and its philosophy. The most celebrated of these was J. B. Danquah (1895–1965),[49] lawyer, politician, philosopher, poet, playwright, whose *Akan Doctrine of God* is a classic of Akan philosophy. An earlier lawyer, politician and scholar, who, though not as technical a philosopher as Danquah, wrote books relevant to Akan philosophy was J. E. Casely Hayford (1865–1930). His books, especially *Ethiopia Unbound,*[50] are among those that sowed the seeds of twentieth-century Pan-African nationalism. Internationally, of course, the most important Ghanaian political leader was Kwame Nkrumah (1901–72), first President of Ghana. Also an Akan, Nkrumah studied philosophy, among other things, in the U.S.A. and Britain. In Britain his thesis supervisor (at the University of London) was A. J. Ayer, under whom he wrote a doctoral dissertation on *Knowledge and Logical Positivism*[51] in the mid-1940s. His supervisor notwithstanding, Nkrumah was heavily Marxist-Leninist, and in 1947 published a manifesto of African radicalism called *Towards Colonial Freedom,* in which he adapted Marxist-Leninist philosophy to the purposes of African liberation. Later on, in *Consciencism: Philosophy and Ideology for Decolonization with Particular Reference to the African Revolution* (1964),[52] he argued that Marxism agreed in many points with the indigenous philosophy of his own society. Another Akan scholar-statesman, the sociologist K. A. Busia, Prime Minister of Ghana after Nkrumah's regime, who also had some philosophical background, wrote a number of expositions of Akan culture and philosophy among which the most important, at least from the point of view of Akan traditional political philosophy, was his *Position of the Chief in the Modern Political System of Ashanti* (1951).[53]

Current Akan workers in philosophy are generally professional philosophers.[54] Of these W. E. Abraham, an all-round philosopher, as much at home in mathematical logic as in the history of philosophy, is something of a pioneer in the exposition of Akan philosophy. His *Mind of Africa* (1962),[55] integrates a survey of Akan traditional philosophy with a discussion of the political and economic problems of Africa. Gyekye's *Essay on African Philosophical Thought* (1987)[56] is the latest full-length work on Akan traditional philosophy. It is both expository and reconstructive. Contemporary Akan philosophers, as indeed many contemporary philosophers of other parts of Africa, in spite of their attachment to their tradition of oral philosophy, are not parochial in their philosophical interests, and the corpus of their work displays a variety which reflects a sensitivity to both their own tradition and the intellectual environment of the modern world.[57] There is also another kind of variety in their work. There are differences in the way they interpret and build upon their oral tradition, as is to be expected in any enterprise of philosophy undertaken by different minds.[58]

It is apparent from all the above that the Akan tradition of philosophy includes a traditional and an emerging modern component. The reference of "traditional" here is different from that of the same word as it occurs in a phrase such as "British traditional philosophy." In the latter context it refers to the writings of the historical philosophers of Britain. In the former, that is, in relation to a preliterate society of the past, "traditional" refers to the body of thought orally transmitted from generations long past. This asymmetry of reference arises from an asymmetry of importance. As remarked earlier on, in Africa, owing to the intervention of colonialism, the resources of the oral tradition remain either untapped or only insufficiently tapped. That tradition therefore has a contemporary importance not matched in various other places. This is why there is a need for the kind of particularistic investigations to which attention has been drawn more than once in this discussion. But, certainly, as this situation is more and more attended to and contemporary African philosophers exploit their background of traditional philosophy to construct philosophies suited to modern existence, sub-African categorizations of philosophy such as Akan or Yoruba or

Luo philosophy will increasingly lose point in the arena of contemporary concerns. I leave the question of the possibility of an analogous melting down of racial categorizations in the global theater of philosophy to the rational imagination of the reader.

University of South Florida

NOTES

1 As to the identity of the Akans, let me quote a previous description of mine. "The word *Akan* refers both to a group of intimately related languages found in West Africa and to the people who speak them. This ethnic group lives predominantly in Ghana and in parts of adjoining Ivory Coast. In Ghana they inhabit most of the southern and middle belts and account for about half the national population of fourteen million. Best known among the Akan subgroups are the Ashanti. Closely cognate are the Denkyiras, Akims, Akwapims, Fantes, Kwahus, Wassas, Brongs, and Nzimas, among others." ("An Akan Perspective on Human Rights," in Abdullahi Ahmed An-Na'im & Francis M. Deng (eds.), *Human Rights in Africa: Cross-Cultural Perspectives* (Washington, D.C.: Brookings Institution, 1990), p. 243.) The Akans have been the subject of some famous anthropological, linguistic, and philosophical studies. On this see notes 45–50.

2 Professor Claude Sumner of Addis Ababa University, Ethiopia, has brought out five volumes of historic writings in Ethiopian philosophy in a continuing program of publication under the general title *Ethiopian Philosophy,* Vols. 1–5 (Addis Ababa: Central Printing Press, 1974–82). See also Sumner's "Assessment of Philosophical Research in Africa: Major Themes and Undercurrents of Thought," in *Teaching and Research in Philosophy: Africa* (Paris: UNESCO, 1984), esp. pp. 159–67 and his "An Ethical Study of Ethiopian Philosophy," in H. Odera Oruka & D. A. Masolo, *Philosophy and Culture* (Nairobi, Kenya: Bookwise Ltd., 1983). Of interest also is the appendix on "Ethiopian Sources of Knowledge" in V. Y. Mudimbe's *The Invention of Africa* (Bloomington: Indiana University Press, 1988).

3 Practically the entirety of a recent anthology on African philosophy is devoted to this controversy. I refer to Tsenay Serequeberham (ed.), *African Philosophy: The Essential Readings* (New York: Paragon House, 1991). An earlier anthology edited by Richard A. Wright (*African Philosophy: An Introduction* (New York: University Press of America, 1977)) contained quite a number of articles dealing with the controversy. A powerful catalyst was Paulin J. Hountondji's *African Philosophy: Myth and Reality* (Bloomington: Indiana University Press, 1983), first published (in French) in 1976. My own *Philosophy and an African Culture* (New York: Cambridge University Press, 1980), among other things, gave considerable attention to the issues involved, and Kwame Gyekye's *An Essay on African Philosophical Thought* (New York: Cambridge University Press, 1987) contains a good balance of discussions of this methodological question and of substantive issues. Two recent books by H. Odera Oruka are also very relevant here. Much of his *Trends in Contemporary African Philosophy* (Nairobi, Kenya: Shirikon Publishers, 1990) is occupied with the debate in question. The same is true of his *Sage Philosophy: Indigenous Thinkers and Modern Debate on African Philosophy* (Nairobi, Kenya: African Center for Technology Studies Press, 1991). This is the local version of the work of the same title published in 1990 by E. J. Brill. The book's section on the "indigenous thinkers" has an importance which will be commented on below. A great part of the earlier phase of the controversy was taken up with the critique of the

conceptions of African philosophy represented by Placide Tempel's *Bantu Philosophy* (Paris: Presence Africaine, 1959), first published in French translation from the original Dutch in 1945, and John S. Mbiti's *African Religions and Philosophy* (London: Heinemann, 1969).

4 The potential importance to the modern African tradition of philosophy of work that exploits the literary and scientific resources of the modern world but that is not rooted in African culture beyond the fact that Africa also exists in the modern world is sometimes questioned by foreign (as well, *mirabile dictu,* as African) scholars. Thus, commenting on my "Classes and Sets" (*Logique et Analyse,* Jan. 1974), an article in which I discussed some issues in the conceptual foundations of set theory, Professor Ruch, a European teacher of philosophy in Africa, declares that, "when such an eminent African philosopher as, for example, J. E. Wiredu ["J.E." being my former initials] writes a scholarly article on the logic of classes and sets his philosophical article contains nothing specifically African." Such work, therefore, according to him, could never become part of African philosophy. See E. A. Ruch & A. K. Anyanwu, *African Philosophy: An Introduction to the Main Philosophical Trends in Contemporary Africa* (Rome: Catholic Book Agency, 1981), p. 16 (in a chapter written by Ruch). I appreciate Professor Ruch's gracious address, but I cannot embrace the abridged prospects he holds up for African philosophy in the modern world. When an African expresses sentiments akin to Ruch's that can only be attributed to a backward-looking tendency, which though understandable in view of what Africa has historically suffered at the hands of Western imperialism, etc., will not help Africa in her existence in the modern world. True, there is absolutely no question but that contemporary African philosophers, as a breed, ought to investigate the philosophical thought in their culture and build upon its insights, of which I believe there are plenty, as will be apparent from this paper. But not to appropriate for their own tradition any resource necessary for the philosophical understanding of the modern world on the grounds that it is not rooted in their culture would be nothing but pointless self-abnegation.

5 On this see further Kwasi Wiredu, "On Defining African Philosophy," in Serequeberham, *African Philosophy,* esp. p. 92ff.

6 To have some conception of the wonders of memorization that some human beings in an oral tradition are capable of, consider how many *Odu* (groups of versified recitations with addenda) a would-be master of the Ifa divination system of the Yorubas must memorize. According to Professor E. Bolaji Idowu, "We cannot tell exactly how many of the recitals there are within the corpus. However, we know that they are well grouped under headings to which are given the generic name of *Odu.* There are two hundred and fifty-six of these *Odu;* and to each of them . . . are attached one thousand six hundred and eighty stories or myths called pathways, roads or courses." *Olodumare: God in Yoruba Belief* (London: Longman Group Ltd., 1962), pp. 7–8.

7 Leiden, Netherlands: E. J. Brill, 1990.

8 Oxford: Oxford University Press, 1965; original French version, 1948.

9 Oruka, *Sage Philosophy,* p. 119. This quotation and the others to follow are translations into English by Professor Oruka of taped remarks made to him or his colleagues in the vernacular by the Kenyan sages.

10 New Haven, Conn.: Yale University Press, 1934.

11 Oruka, *Sage Philosophy,* pp. 115–16.

12 Oruka, *Sage Philosophy,* p. 134.

13 Oruka, *Sage Philosophy,* p. 37; see also p. 137.

14 Oruka, *Sage Philosophy,* p. 38.

15 London: Ethnographica Ltd., 1986.

16 New York: Cambridge University Press, 1987.

17 See the citations below.

18 The late Okot p'Bitek, Ugandan poet, man of letters and conceptual analyst of no mean standing,

argued with vigor and sophistication that his ethnic group, the Central Luo, do not even have a place in their conceptual scheme for any concept of creation or of a supreme being. This he did in two books, namely, *Religion of the Central Luo* (Nairobi, Kenya: East African Literature Bureau, 1971) and *African Religions in Western Scholarship* (Nairobi: East African Literature Bureau, 1970). In the case of the Akans, although skeptics are not unknown, there is a widespread belief in the existence of some kind of a supreme being.

19 J. B. Danquah, in his *The Akan Doctrine of God: A Fragment of Gold Coast Ethics and Religion,* the most famous book on Akan philosophy, suggests an even more drastic Akan qualification on omnipotence. "The Akan idea is of an ancestral creator and head of the very real and near community. . . . The omnipotence of the high-father cannot be greater than the reality of this community" (p. 24); see also pp. 55–56 & 87–89. The book was first published in 1944 and reissued in 1968 with a new introduction by Prof. Kwesi Dickson (London: Frank Cass and Co., Ltd.).

20 *The Challenge of Africa* (New York: Frederick A. Praeger, 1962), pp. 11–13. The first three chapters of this book are especially relevant to Akan philosophy. The first two chapters of his *Africa in Search of Democracy* (New York: Frederick A. Praeger, 1967) are similarly relevant. Busia also contributed a celebrated chapter on "The Ashanti" to the volume on *African Worlds: Studies in the Cosmological Ideas and the Social Values of African Peoples,* ed. Daryll Forde (Oxford: Oxford University Press, 1954). There is a briefer piece on "The African World-view" in Jacob Drachler, ed., *African Heritage* (New York: Macmillan, 1963). Both articles are extremely useful for the investigation of Akan philosophy. Worthy of mention, finally, is *The Position of the Chief in the Modern Political System of Ashanti* (London: Frank Cass and Co. Ltd., 1968), which, though not a philosophical text, contains valuable sources for the study of Akan political philosophy.

21 "Black Civilization and Philosophy: Akan Tradition of Philosophy," presented at the festival of African culture (FESTAC) held in Lagos, 1976.

22 Hagan, "Black Civilization and Philosophy."

23 I discussed this locative conception of existence and its implications for the concept of nature in "An African Conception of Nature," presented at the Boston Colloquium in the Philosophy of Science, Boston University, Massachusetts, February 1986. Gyekye also insists on the locative character of the Akan conception of existence; see his *Essay,* p. 179.

24 This seems to be a widespread characteristic of African languages. Thus Alexis Kagame, the late well-known Bantu metaphysician and linguist says, "Throughout the Bantu belt, the verb 'to be' can never express the idea of existence, nor, therefore, can the word 'being' express the notion of existing. The celebrated axiom 'I think, therefore, I am' is unintelligible, as the verb 'to be' is always followed by an attribute or by an adjunct of place: I am good, big, etc., I am in such and such a place, etc. Thus the utterance '. . . therefore I am' would prompt the question: 'You are . . . what? . . . where?' " ("Empirical Apperception of Time and the Concept of History in Bantu Thought" in *Cultures and Time,* ed. Paul Ricoeur (Paris: UNESCO, 1976), p. 95.

25 See Kwasi Wiredu, "Are There Cultural Universals?", presented at a Symposium of the 18th World Congress of Philosophy, Brighton, U.K., August 1988, and published in *Quest: Philosophical Discussions,* Vol. IV, No. 2, December 1990 (University of Zambia, Lusaka).

26 See my four-part series on "Logic and Ontology" in *Second Order: An African Journal of Philosophy* (Ile-Ife, Nigeria: University of Ife Press (now Obafemi Awolowo University Press), 1973–75, especially the last two. See also my "A Philosophical Perspective on the Concept of Human Communication," *International Social Science Journal,* Vol. XXXII, No. 2, 1980.

27 For more discussion of the notions of the spiritual and the supernatural, see my "Universalism and Particularism in Religion from an African Perspective," *Journal of Humanism and Ethical Religion,* Vol. 3, No. 1, Fall 1990.

28 Such premeditated attributions of mysticism to Africans may be observed in, for example, E. G. Parrinder's "Mysticism in African Religion," in J. S. Pobee, ed., *Religion in a Pluralistic Society* (Leiden, Netherlands: E. J. Brill, 1976).

29 See chapter 7: "Philosophy, Mysticism and Rationality," in my *Philosophy and an African Culture*.

30 I have discussed this and related issues in "Death and the Afterlife in African Culture," originally presented at a colloquium at the Woodrow Wilson International Center for Scholars, Washington, D.C., 1988, and published in *Perspectives on Death and Dying: Cross-Cultural and Multi-Disciplinary Views,* ed. Arthur Berger et al. (Philadelphia: Charles Press, 1989).

31 See, for example, the article cited in note 27.

32 For details see my "The Concept of Mind with Particular Reference to the Language and Thought of the Akans," in G. Floistad (eds.), *Contemporary Philosophy,* Volume 5: African Philosophy (Boston: Kluwer, 1987).

33 For example, J. J. C. Smart, "Sensations and Brain Processes," *Philosophical Review,* 1959; reprinted in Paul Edwards & Arthur Pap (eds.), *A Modern Introduction to Philosophy* (New York: Collier Macmillan, 1973), and in several other anthologies.

34 *Leibniz: Basic Writings,* tr. George R. Montgomery (La Salle, Ill.: Open Court Publishing Co., 1962), p. 19.

35 The Yorubas have an even more picturesquely dramatic and elaborate formulation of essentially the same doctrine; see, for example, Idowu's *Olodumare,* p. 174.

36 *The Mind of Africa* (Chicago: University of Chicago Press, 1962), p. 60. With an epigrammatic economy of words and a dense richness of information and reflection Abraham manages to cover all the main aspects of Akan philosophy in chapter 2 of the book (pp. 44–115).

37 This point and various others in regard to the Akan concept of a person are discussed in my article, "The African Concept of Personhood," presented at the conference on "African-American Perspectives on Biomedical Ethics: Philosophical Issues" held at Georgetown University, November 1990 (forthcoming in the proceedings of the conference). On the normative aspects of African conceptions of human personality, see also Ifeanyi A. Menkiti, "Person and Community in African Traditional Thought," in Richard A. Wright (ed.), *African Philosophy: An Introduction* (New York: University Press of America, 1984), and Meyers Fortes' "On the Concept of the Person Among the Tallensi," in *Religion, Morality and the Person: Essays on Tallensi Religion* (New York: Cambridge University Press, 1987).

38 See Kwame Gyekye's *Essay,* chs. 8–10. Also Kwasi Wiredu, "The Moral Foundations of African Culture" (presented at the conference mentioned in the immediately preceding note).

39 Busia's *The Position of the Chief,* cited in note 23, is the most accessible source of the raw materials of the Akan philosophy of politics. Abraham's discussion of Akan philosophy includes accounts of the Akan theory of government and of its legal system (see *The Mind of Africa,* pp. 75–88). G. P. Hagan has an extremely interesting paper entitled "Is There an Akan Political Philosophy?" (paper presented at seminar on Ghana Culture at the University of Ghana, Legon, April 1975). B. E. Oguah in his "African and Western Philosophy: A Comparative Study," a generally thought-provoking essay, has some useful comments on Akan political philosophy. The paper is included in Richard A. Wright's anthology, *African Philosophy*. I have some brief comments on the Akan political system in "An Akan Perspective on Human Rights," in An-Na'im & Deng, *Human Rights in Africa*.

40 See J. B. Danquah, "Obligation in Akan Society," *West African Affairs,* No. 8 (London: Bureau of Current Affairs (for the Department of Extra-Mural Studies, University College of the Gold Coast, 1952); J. N. Kudadjie, "Does Religion Determine Morality in African Societies?—A Viewpoint," in J. S. Pobee (ed.), *Religion in a Pluralistic Society* (Leiden, Netherlands: E. J. Brill, 1976); Kwasi Wiredu, "Morality and Religion in Akan Thought," in H. Odera Oruka

& S. A. Masolo (eds.), *Philosophy and Culture* (Nairobi, Kenya: Bookwise, Ltd., 1983); Gyekye, *Essay,* chap. 8; Wiredu, "The Moral Foundations of African Culture" (paper mentioned in note 37).

41 See my *Philosophy and An African Culture,* p. 19.

42 John Hospers, a soft determinist at bottom, but a hard determinist in rhetoric, suggests a basically similar criterion as far as (the English-speaking concept of) responsibility is concerned in "What Means This Freedom?" in Sidney Hook (ed.), *Determinism and Freedom in the Age of Modern Science* (New York: Collier Books, 1958), p. 131. His "Free Will and Psychoanalysis" (*Philosophy and Phenomenological Research,* 1950, reprinted in Edwards & Pap, *Modern Introduction*) also, on the whole, makes a lot of sense from an Akan standpoint.

43 Moritz Schlick, in chapter 7 of his *Problems of Ethics* (reprinted in Edwards & Pap, *Modern Introduction,* chapter 6: "When is a Man Responsible?"), almost arrives at this result.

44 See my *Philosophy and An African Culture,* p. 17.

45 Christaller was responsible for the first full-length dictionary of the Akan language: J. G. Christaller, *A Dictionary of the Asante and Fante Language Called Tshi* (*Twi*) (Basel, Switzerland: Evangelical Missionary Society, 1881, 2nd ed. 1933). He also wrote a grammar of Akan: *A Grammar of the Asante and Fante Language called Tshi* (Basel, Switzerland: Evangelical Missionary Society 1875). The verbal formation "Tshi" is an outcome of European struggles to pronounce "Twi," which is the name of the version of Akan spoken by the Ashanti, the Akims, the Kwahus and the Akwapims, these being subgroups of the Akan people. The Fante are another subgroup, speaking another, thinly varied version of Akan. An extremely interesting discussion of Akan philosophy through its Fante wing is B. E. Oguah's "African and Western Philosophy: A Comparative Study," in Wright, *African Philosophy.*

46 R. S. Rattray wrote a great deal about the Akans. Of particular interest are the following books: (1) *Ashanti Proverbs* (Oxford: Oxford University Press, 1916); this is a translation and exegetical annotation of a selection from J. C. Christaller's *a Collection of 3600 Tshi Proverbs* (Basel, Switzerland: Evangelical Missionary Society, 1879), which was published in the vernacular; (2) *Ashanti* (Oxford: Oxford University Press, 1923); (3) *Religion and Art in Ashanti* (Oxford: Oxford University Press, 1927); and (4) *Ashanti Law and Constitution* (Oxford: Oxford University Press, 1929).

47 Diedrich Westermann, *Africa and Christianity* (Oxford: Oxford University Press, 1937).

48 See, for example, J. B. Danquah's critique of Rattray and Westermann in chapter 2 of his *Akan Doctrine of God* (London: Frank Cass, [1944] 1968). K. A. Busia enters a gentle demurer with respect to Rattray on page xi of his *Position of the Chief.*

49 Of interest here in addition to his *Akan Doctrine of God,* is his *Akan Laws and Customs* (London, 1920) and his article on "Obligation in Akan Society," in *West African Affairs,* No. 8 (London: Bureau of Current Affairs; 1952).

50 London, 1911. One might mention also his *Gold Coast Native Institutions* (London, 1903).

51 Nkrumah was just about getting ready for the oral defense of his thesis when the cell went to him from his country to return home to participate in the leadership of the independence struggle. He left at once.

52 The first edition (1964) of Kwame Nkrumah's *Consciencism* was published by Heinemann Educational Books Ltd., London. The second edition was brought out by Panaf Books Ltd., London, in 1970. The second edition of *Towards Colonial Freedom* came out in 1962 from Heinemann.

53 London: Frank Cass, 1968 (see also note 20).

54 However, Akan workers in other fields, especially religion, have produced works relevant to Akan philosophy. We may note the following: Peter Sarpong, *Ghana in Retrospect* (Accra-Tema, Ghana: Ghana Publishing Corp., 1974); Kofi Asare Opoku, *West African Traditional Religion*

(London: FEP International Private Ltd., 1978); John S. Pobee, *Towards an African Theology* (Nashville, Tenn.: Abingdon, 1979); Kwesi A. Dickson, *Aspects of Religion and Life in Africa* (Accra, Ghana: Ghana Academy of Arts and Sciences, 1977) and *Theology in Africa* (New York: Orbis Books, 1984). A remarkable book by one of Ghana's most famous artists, the late Kofi Antubam, on *Ghana's Heritage of Culture* (Leipzig: Koehler & Amelang, 1963), had considerable materials of a philosophical significance in the study of the Akans. As in the beginning, some of the recent philosophical studies of the Akans have been done by foreign scholars. A perceptive treatment of Akan philosophy in its Akwapim version is contained in "Causal Theory in Akwapim Akan Philosophy," by Helaine Minkus, in Wright, *African Philosophy*. This material is a spin-off from the author's doctoral dissertation (Northwestern University, 1975) on *The Philosophy of the Akwapim Akan of Southern Ghana*. Earlier ventures into Akan philosophy by another foreigner were much more controversial and, in part, somewhat obscure. We are referring to the following writings of Eva L. R. Meyerowitz: (1) *The Sacred State of the Akans* (London: Faber and Faber, 1951); (2) "Concepts of the Soul among the Akans of the Gold Coast," *Africa*, Vol. XXI, No. 1, Jan. 1951; and (3) *The Akan of Ghana: Their Ancient Beliefs* (London: Faber and Faber, 1958).

55 Chicago: University of Chicago Press, 1962. In 1964 Abraham wrote an article on "The Life and Times of Wilhelm Anton Amo," in *The Transactions of the Historical Society of Ghana*. This was about a Ghanaian who taught philosophy in Germany in the eighteenth century. An interesting question that arises is: He was an African and a philosopher, but did his work constitute an African philosophy? The answer is that his work was in the German tradition of his time and place, but if a significant number of Africans should take up his work and build on it, it would become an integral part of African philosophy and thus come to belong to the two traditions, which is not at all a rare species of philosophical interconnection. The first part of this answer occurs to Ruch (see note 4), but not the second.

56 New York: Cambridge University Press, 1987.

57 See my "On Defining African Philosophy" in Serequeberham, *African Philosophy*, pp. 104–5, for a list of a small sample of the varied publications of contemporary African philosophers.

58 For example, the reader of Gyekye's *Essay* will note that there are some very substantial differences in the way he and I interpret and use the tradition which we share.

AFRICAN, AFRICAN AMERICAN, AFRICANA PHILOSOPHY

LUCIUS OUTLAW

INTRODUCTION

Nearly fifty years ago, arguments that certain modes of thought of African peoples should be regarded as "philosophy" were advanced—in important instances by persons of European descent—and became a matter of serious debate.[1] Both the context and the debates were structured by the domination and exploitation of Africans by peoples from Europe, and rationalized with strategies drawing on rank-ordering distinctions and infected with racism. That Africans could philosophize was for many a bold declaration or proposal, at the very least, in light of the rationalizing, redefining, and attempted remaking of African peoples as subordinates to "civilized" peoples of Europe.

Today, of course, there are a significant number of formally trained African philosophers throughout the world. And, to a great extent the *explicit* development of discursive formations within the discipline of philosophy that invoke "Africa" has been unfolding through efforts to identify, reconstruct, and create traditions and repositories of thought by African and African-descended persons and peoples, in both oral and written literatures, as forms of philosophy. In the context of such endeavors, persons past and present, who were and are without formal training or degrees in philosophy, are being worked into developing canons as providing instances of reflections, on various matters, that are appropriately characterized as philosophical.[2]

Similar (and related) circumstances and developments condition efforts to give shape and meaning to African American philosophy as a disciplinary enterprise. When we look through the tables of contents of collections of writings organized under the heading of "American Philosophy," we find, in virtually every case, *no* writings by persons of African descent. Histories of American philosophy tend to be equally silent about thinkings and writings of Africans-becoming-"Americans" as instances of philosophy. There are, of course, long, rich traditions of critical, more or less systematic thought by women and men of African descent articulated in speeches and writings of various kinds that are now being appropriated as instances and traditions of philosophizing.[3] And during the last two decades in particular, with the significant increase in the number of persons of African descent with formal training in philosophy (nonetheless, still a very small number—fewer than one percent of professional philosophers in the United

States), many of whom underwent this training during the highly charged historical periods of the civil rights, black power, and African independence movements, efforts to construct a disciplinary formation and to identify and refine traditions of intellectual praxis as distinctively African American philosophy were a major concern of a few engaged and determined persons.[4]

"Africana philosophy" is the phrase I use as a "gathering" notion under which to situate the articulations (writings, speeches, etc.), and traditions of Africans and peoples of African descent collectively, as well as the subdiscipline- or field-forming, tradition-defining or tradition-organizing reconstructive efforts, which are (to be) regarded as philosophy. However, "Africana philosophy" is to include, as well, the work of those persons who are neither African nor of African descent but who recognize the legitimacy and importance of the issues and endeavors that constitute the disciplinary activities of African or African American philosophy and contribute to the efforts—persons whose work justifies their being called "Africanists." Use of the qualifier "Africana" is consistent with the practice of naming intellectual traditions and practices in terms of the national, geographic, cultural, racial, and/or ethnic descriptor or identity of the persons who initiated and were/are the primary practitioners—and/or are the subjects and objects—of the practices and traditions in question (e.g., "American," "British," "French," "German," or "continental" philosophy).

Yet, what is it that is characteristic of the philosophical practices of African and African-descended thinkers that distinguishes—or should distinguish?—the efforts *by virtue of their being those of persons African and/or African-descended*? Is there, or can there be, a properly determined field of philosophy that is constituted by the efforts of persons of a particular racial or ethnic group? Given the global dispersal of African peoples and the subsequent development of regional (e.g., Caribbean), more or less complex local-national (e.g., African American), and nation-state groupings ("Nigerian," "Kenyan"), can we speak of "Africana philosophy" in a cogent way?

These are some of the questions I wish to explore in what follows. In the process, I hope to clarify, for myself especially, the extent to which it makes sense to continue speaking of "Africana philosophy" as an "umbrella" notion under which can be gathered a potentially large collection of traditions of practices, agendas, and resulting literatures of African and African-descended peoples. I propose to review, briefly, developments in what is now referred to as African philosophy and particular instances of African American thought. However, I wish to also explore whether it makes sense to speak of "Africana philosophy" in even stronger terms: as a venture which should be bound by *particular* norms appropriate to discursive practices by and/or in the interests of African peoples (that is to say, which have their origins, justification, and legitimacy in the life-worlds of African peoples) in contrast to norms of the life-worlds of other peoples. In this regard, I intend to test the adequacy of what, in some quarters, is at present the most prominent—and contested—effort to define an agenda and strategies for inquiry about and in the interests of African peoples, namely, Molefi Kete Asante's notion and project of "Afrocentricity."

AFRICAN PHILOSOPHY[5]

On the continent of Africa, the publication in 1945 of Placide Tempels' *La Philosophie Bantoue,* one of the earliest and most influential explicit acknowledgments of African intellectual efforts and achievements as philosophy, marks the initiation of contemporary discussions of African philosophy.[6] Emerging during the apex of European colonization in Africa, the discussion, both in form and content, was shaped by this context, and no less so by subsequent anticolonial struggles. The focus of the discussion was whether African peoples could *have* or *do* philosophy. But this was only the surface issue. The deeper and more pressing question was whether Africans were fully human as defined by the reigning Greek-cum-European philosophical-anthropological paradigm centered around the notion of "rationality."

There were strong reactions to Tempels since the major thesis of the book—that Bantu Africans had a "philosophy"—challenged the rationalizations of the colonization, enslavement, and exploitation of Africans and the resources of Africa. In addition, a significant number of African intellectuals felt that the humanity of Africans as beings of "reason" was defended and vindicated, all the more so by a European. Even further, certain Europeans who were in some ways more knowledgeable of, sympathetic to, and respectful of Africans than was Tempels were likewise happy to see their views confirmed in Tempels' report of African achievements in philosophy.[7]

Tempels challenged the claim that Africans were inherently or developmentally incapable of the level of thought required for "true" philosophy, the standards for which were those operative in the traditions and practices of mainstream European philosophy. Franz Crahay, in his criticism of *Bantu Philosophy,* argued against what he regarded as the mistaken acceptance of the book as an instance of Bantu *philosophy,* rather than as what he termed an "impetus" for philosophy.[8] A "frank appraisal," he argued, required the conclusion that philosophy did *not* exist at present (circa 1965) among the Bantu "within the admissible sense" of "philosophy": that is, as "explicit, abstract analytical reflection, sharply critical and autocritical, which is systematic, at least in principle, and yet open, dealing with experience, its human condition, and the meanings and values that it reveals."[9] Crahay went on to specify what he took to be the necessary "dissociations" constitutive of the appropriate conceptual conditions under which a Bantu philosophy might be founded, conditions, in his judgment, not then fulfilled by Bantu thinkers:

- dissociation of subject and object through reflection; dissociation of I and others;
- dissociation of the natural from the supernatural, of technical action and acts of faith; dissociation of the concrete and the abstract leading to dissociation of the named object and the term;
- dissociation of time and space;
- development from a limited concept of corporeal freedom to a *mature* concept of freedom involving a synthesis of corporeal freedom, the faculty of decision, and the "assumption of responsibility for one's actions and their rationally recognized consequences"; and
- a desirable attitude, i.e., the avoidance of temptations of "shortcuts" or the "cult of difference."[10]

This was the context within which debates regarding the humanity of Africans were forced by Tempels' *Bantu Philosophy* and its reception. Other scholars during the same period (1930s–40s and subsequently) who were investigating the thought-systems of various African peoples made substantial contributions to the debate. It was in this same historical context that the voices of Africans concerned with the liberation of African peoples from colonial domination and with the reclamation of the indigenous cultures of African peoples were raised (for example, during the Négritude movement) to challenge the caricatures of black peoples perpetrated by peoples of European descent. Efforts to identify and elaborate "African philosophy" have to a large extent been endeavors of this kind. And it is this historical, contextual framing that, in part, gives identity to the efforts as comprising a distinct field of discourse, one that is conditioned by European legacies (e.g., in being called "philosophy") while, in many instances, challenging the claims to truth, exclusivity, and predominance that for centuries were driving forces, theoretically and practically, in the imperialist encounters of European peoples with native peoples in Africa and elsewhere.[11]

That debate has now given way to a broader range of concerns. On the African continent this has resulted in the emergence of different trends or "schools" of thought, the growth of diverse bodies of philosophical literature, the formation of national and international professional philosophical associations, and the development of programs offering advanced degrees in philosophy in African institutions with strong emphasis, in a number of instances, on African philosophy. Critical self-consciousness regarding developments in African philosophy has led to the articulation of various taxonomic overviews or "mappings" of the field. There is H. Odera Oruka's discussion of the four "trends" of African philosophy (i.e., "ethno-philosophy," "philosophic sagacity," "nationalist-ideological" philosophy, and "professional" philosophy).[12] Alphonse J. Smet[13] and O. Nkombe[14] offer a more insightful and nuanced mapping of trends.[15] *Ideological* is their name for a trend that, for them, includes such developments as "African personality,"[16] Pan-Africanism,[17] Négritude,[18] African humanism,[19] African socialism,[20] scientific socialism,[21] Consciencism,[22] and "authenticity."[23] The rule for inclusion in this trend is that all of the works and discussions are geared primarily to redressing the political and cultural situation of African peoples under the conditions of European imperialism, enslavement, and colonization. Their second trend includes works which recognize the existence of philosophy in traditional Africa, examine its philosophical elements as found in its various manifestations, and systematically explore complexes of traditional thought as repositories of wisdom and esoteric knowledge.[24] The principal criterion for placement in this trend is the shared motivation on the part of the thinkers surveyed to contest the pernicious myth that Africans are peoples of a decidedly "primitive mentality."

Smet and Nkombe's third trend, the *critical* school, is shaped by reactions to the first two trends. It is from the critical trend that we get the label "ethnophilosophy" applied to the thinkers in the traditional and ideological groupings as a way of questioning the relevance and validity of their work as instances of philosophy proper.[25] On the other hand, there are those in the critical group who also criticize western conceptions of science and philosophy, particularly in the context of the deployment of those enterprises as part of the European expansion into Africa. Finally, the Nkombe/Smet taxonomy includes a fourth grouping, one they term the *synthetic* trend. Here are to be found the works and practices of persons who use philosophical hermeneutics to explore issues and new problems which emerge in the African context.[26]

The Nkombe/Smet survey of African philosophy has been given even greater detail by Mudimbe who identifies a first group (the principle of placement which Mudimbe uses being the idea that the participants make use of a "wide sense" of the term "philosophy"[27]) that is made up of two subgroups: the *ethnophilosophical,*[28] which includes "works arising from the need to express and to render faithfully the unity and the coherence of traditional philosophies" and the *ideologico-philosophical,* which includes works "qualified by an explicit intention to separate and to analyze present constraints of African society, marking the present and future situation, while remaining true to African ideals. . . ."[29]

Mudimbe's second group is made up of persons whose works are structured by the notion of philosophy "in the strict sense" (i.e., in something like the sense articulated by Crahay). Sub-groupings include persons who are involved in reflections on the conditions of possibility of African philosophy (e.g, Fabien Eboussi-Boulaga, Marcien Towa, and Paulin Hountondji) and persons who reflect on the significance of western sciences, the anthropological/ethnological social sciences in particular, in terms of both their developments and their applications as forms of knowledge in African contexts (Stanislas Adotevi, Ngoma-Binda, Mudimbe himself). Writings in a third group (those of Atanganga, Njoh-Mouelle, and other writings of Eboussi-Boulaga), which involve reflections on philosophy "as a critical auxiliary to the process of development," Mudimbe regards as high points in the field. Finally, the works of Nkombe, Ntumba Tshiamalenga, I. P. Leleye, John Kinyongo, and others Mudimbe includes in the subgroup of writings which share a concern for philosophical hermeneutics.[30]

AFRICAN AMERICAN PHILOSOPHY

The crucible for New World Africans has been (and continues to be) the complex of factors involving various forms of racial oppression and class exploitation, further complicated by matters having to do with sex and gender. In a dialectic of racist imposition and creative response in the process of survival and reproduction, New World African descendants-become-Americans have had to form and perpetuate new ways for getting on with their lives. A recurrent feature of life in the racialized crucible has been the struggle to resolve major tensions infecting identity-formation and all that follows in their wake, the tensions involving the ambiguities and ambivalences of being, in some senses, both "African" and "American." Historically, how these tensions were mediated by particular persons in the forging of an identity was crucial to forming or sharing in agendas and exercising strategies devoted to securing *freedom,* for the person and the "race." For this and other important reasons, differences have always existed among thinkers of African descent in the United States which have resulted from and led to distinct foci, strategies, and objectives of discursive traditions and practices. A brief rehearsal of several complexes of socially engaged thinking will provide examples of what today is being claimed as instances of African American philosophy that, in the words of Leonard Harris, was, indeed, "philosophy born of struggle."[31]

From the earliest presence of Africans as slaves in the portion of the New World that was later to become the United States of America, militant antislavery agitation was a prominent endeavor among "free" persons of color in the North and East (less so from the early 1850s to the Civil War). Frederick Douglass was one of the most well-known participants in the movement to abolish slavery. (The movement had its foundations in the efforts of black folk, though white abolitionists came to play dominant, controlling roles.) Two decades of post-Reconstruction separatist and emigrationist activity (mid-1860s–1880s) followed the Civil War but were soon eclipsed by a period (1880–1915) during which the accommodationist strategy of Booker T. Washington was predominant, though not without "radical" challenges from W. E. B. DuBois and others who initiated the Niagara movement to counter the effects of Washington's agenda and to press for full citizenship rights for African Americans. The National Association for the Advancement of Colored People (N.A.A.C.P.), which grew out of the Niagara movement, and the National Urban League were organized toward the end of this period (in 1909 and 1910, respectively) and would play major roles in promoting the melioration of racial apartheid by utilizing legal attacks and organized protests to attack invidious racial discrimination in schools, workplaces, and public accommodations.

Booker T. Washington's death in 1915 resulted in the declining significance of his accommodationist strategy. Major transformations in the American and world economies including industrialization in the North and Northeast; world war; the pull of jobs; the hope for less restricted social life; and the push of agricultural transformations in the South all led to significantly increased migration of African Americans to the American industrial heartland and the development of conditions which were nurturing soil in which various forms of nationalism flowered (again) among people of African descent (during the period 1916–1930). The organizational activities and achievements of Marcus Garvey and the Harlem Renaissance were two of the most significant nationalist developments. Further, recovery from the Depression and its attendant dislocations, spurred by a second world war and, later, the Korean war, conditioned several decades of economic expansion which led to rising prosperity for urban, industrial workers in particular. Among these were a significant minority of black persons who ushered in the rise of the modern black middle class and who were to champion, after the decline of nationalist groups and projects as significant forces, "civil rights" and "integration" as objectives of black struggle (1940s–mid-1960s). This period was followed, and momentarily eclipsed, by yet another resurgence of black nationalism, the black power movement of the mid-1960s to the early 1970s.[32]

Assimilation is the name for projects which would have one racial and/or ethnic group absorbed, physically and/or culturally, by another, the former taking on the defining characteristics of the latter and relinquishing its own racial and/or ethnic distinctiveness. For African American assimilationists, the "official" cultural, social, political, and economic ideals of the American republic have been sufficient and appropriate goals for African American life, and people of African descent should pursue these ends "without regard to race, creed, or color." Frederick Douglass is one of the most well-known of African American assimilationists.

Accommodation was the prevailing agenda and strategy during the period when the influence of Booker T. Washington, its most successful purveyor, was dominant. For Washington, the economic and political hegemony of white folks was not to be challenged directly but was to be finessed by subtle strategies of seeming accommodation while black folks prepared themselves for economic self-reliance and eventual full political citizenship "earned" by forming and exercising good character and responsibility through education for and the practice of honest work.

Washington's strategy was fervently opposed by the likes of W. E. B. DuBois.[33] One of the foremost intellectuals in American history, DuBois was a proponent of what I term *pluralist integration*: that is, the commitment to achieving a society that is integrated socially, politically, and economically though made up of a plurality of racial and ethnic groups which maintain and perpetuate their racial and ethnic distinctivenesses to the extent that doing so does not threaten the integration of the social whole.[34] DuBois was thus something of a *nationalist* in being committed to the proposition that black folk should articulate and appropriate a racial identity based, in part, on biologically-based shared characteristics, but including, as well, shared history and culture. In this respect he might best be classed as a cultural nationalist. Other forms of nationalism include economic (capitalist or socialist) and political nationalism (democratic, socialist, or dictatorial) either form of which might—but need not—promote varying degrees of racial and/or ethnic integration or separatism.[35]

In contrast to those who have been called "Left nationalists" (i.e., nationalists committed, as well, to socialist or communist agendas and strategies, such as C. L. R. James and Grace and James Boggs[36]), there are those African American thinkers who have been committed socialists or communists for whom "race" is at best an epiphenomenon secondary to the primary contradictions of class-conflicted capitalist societies. For such persons racial (or ethnic) distinctions will disappear with the transformation of capitalist social formations into self-managing socialist or communist societies in which neither race nor ethnicity will be of any social significance.

Such thought/praxis complexes are among some of the most ready candidates for being regarded as instances of African American philosophy. Of course, organizing, examining, and representing the articulations of these persons and movements as "philosophy" involves positioning them in ways and contexts not intended by the "authors" themselves. W. E. B. DuBois was one of the very few to study philosophy formally, and even considered pursuing it professionally. Alain Leroy Locke was one of the first persons of African descent in America to earn a doctoral degree in philosophy (Harvard University, 1918). Over the last half-century, a small number of African Americans joined the ranks of professional philosophers. And the need and desire to identify and/or forge distinctive philosophical traditions, literatures, and practices were given major impetus by the modern black power movement. Early in the 1970s, a number of attempts were made to articulate a "Black," or "Afro-American," and later "African American" philosophy.[37] Over the years a number of American Philosophical Association (A.P.A.) sessions have been devoted to these discussions, organized by the A.P.A.'s Committee on Blacks in Philosophy. (A.P.A. recognition of these efforts as having opened a legitimate discursive field was accorded in 1987 with the decision to list "Africana Philosophy" as a specialty in the discipline.)

Leonard Harris's edited *Philosophy Born of Struggle: Anthology of Afro-American Philosophy from 1917* remains the only widely available, somewhat historically organized collection of writings by African American philosophers. An important earlier collection is Percy E. Johnston's *Afro-American Philosophers*.[38] However, for the most part writings devoted to the formation of African American philosophy as a discursive context so named remain largely unpublished. A significant number of these writings were presented during the special A.P.A. sessions and during conferences held, for the most part, at historically black colleges and universities (e.g., Tuskegee and Morgan State Universities) during the 1970s and early 1980s. Of particular note are the following essays: "Value and Religion in Africana Philosophy: The African-American Case" by Robert C. Williams (deceased); George Garrison's "Afro-American Philosophical Thought: The Early Beginnings and the Afro-Centric Substratum"; and Cornel West's insightful critical survey "Black Philosophers and Textual Practice" in which he examines what he terms the "ideological character" of the textual practices ("academic dovetailing," "professional criticism," and "counterhegemonic praxis") of black philosophers in the twentieth century.[39] Other texts in the genre include a continuously expanding corpus of writings by Cornel West; Charles A. Frey's *From Egypt to Don Juan: The Anatomy of Black Studies* and *Level Three: A Black Philosophy Reader*[40]; and endeavors by others that are now bearing fruit and must be noted, among them the presentations and discussions of the writings of such persons as Alain Locke by Johnny Washington[41] and Leonard Harris[42]; and writings in ethics and social and political philosophy by Laurence Thomas, Adrian Piper, Michele Moody-Adams, William Lawson, Howard McGary, Jr., Bernard Boxill, Robert Birt, and others.

Nonetheless, there is a striking aspect to the recent work of African American philosophers: namely, for the most part this work is conducted with little or no knowledge of, or attention to, the history of philosophical activity on the African continent or elsewhere in the African diaspora. At the very least, this lack of awareness and attention may well contribute to deficiencies in our historically informed self-understandings and, to that extent, will have important implications for the work we do whether or not we take our work to be distinguished, or at least conditioned in significant ways, by our being persons of African descent. African philosophers have generally been much more successful in advancing the enterprise of philosophy, theoretically and practically, as a venture conditioned by explicit commitments and linkages to the histories and historical situations and to the interests of African peoples. It is my judgment that the development of traditions of thought by African American philosophers has been seriously curtailed by the absence of more refined, explicit, and shared agendas, conditioned by a sense of shared identities and shared histories. Further, a comparison of instances and traditions of philosophizing of African philosophers in various African countries to the work of particular African American thinkers or traditions highlights sharp differences in the degrees of institutionalization of philosophical praxes and legacies distinctively conditioned by what was called the "black consciousness movement." African and African-descended philosophers in America are perhaps long overdue for coming together for a sustained, systematic, critical reconstruction of our intellectual histories. However, the historical connections and more or less similar experiences of persons of African descent in the United States, in the African diaspora generally, and on continental Africa, do not warrant uncritical appropriations and celebrations of our racial connectedness, nor of the glories of philosophical insight from the African "Motherland" to which we should all turn to be shown the way to the primordial "ancient wisdom" that simply waits to be reclaimed.

AFRICANA PHILOSOPHY

Have the all too brief and incomplete surveys of some of the trends and traditions of thought and praxis in African and African American philosophy provided even a glimpse of what would be required in the way of commonalities to support grouping them all under the same heading and, further, support efforts to articulate distinctive agendas, practices, ends, and norms characteristic of the philosophizing of African and African-descended thinkers? In the first instance, the range of universality of the term "Africana," its boundaries and "contents," coincide with the experiences and situated practices of a dispersed *geographic race*[43]: that is, not a genetically homogeneous group but persons and peoples who, through shared lines of descent and ancestry, share a relatively permanent geographical site of origin and development from which decedents were dispersed, and, thereby, who share a relatively distinctive gene pool that determines the relative frequencies of various physical characteristics, even in the diaspora; and persons who share—more or less—evolved social and cultural elements of life-worlds that are, in part, traceable to those of the "ancestors." In turn, geographical, cultural, social, and natural-selection factors influence the shared gene pool and cultural practices to condition *raciation:* that is, the formation and evolution of the biological and cultural factors collectively characterizing the "race."

But, this first instance provides only an initial circumscription of the primary distinguishing feature of some practitioners, and the "objects" or subjects, of the discursive practices of Africana philosophy: i.e., ''African'' and ''African-descended'' peoples. The strategy of circumscription is so far at best a point of departure. To avoid undue simplicity—or, worse still, biological or racial essentialism—more is required: namely, to identify the features that make certain intellectual practices and legacies of persons who are situated in geographically and historically-socially diverse societies ''philosophy,'' features characteristic of—though not necessarily *unique* to—these persons *as members of a dispersed race*.

While I have offered a sketch of several forms of thought as possible candidates for inclusion under the heading of Africana philosophy, a key commitment influencing my discussion is the belief that there is no timeless essence shared by any and all forms of thought called ''philosophy'' that is a function of, say, logical or epistemological characteristics. A serious study of the writings of persons included in canons of western philosophy will disclose thinkings that are the same only in the most general sense of being reflections on . . . thinking, ethics, politics, etc. However, the agendas (motivations), strategies, and achievements involved are extremely diverse. Philosophizing is inherently grounded in socially shared practices, not in transcendental rules. When we view philosophical practices historically, sociologically, and comparatively, we are led inescapably to conclude that ''philosophical practice is inherently pluralistic,'' and ''[a]ll philosophical ideals are local'' to communities of thinkers.[44] We mislead ourselves if we require that there be something more than ''family resemblances'' common to all the instances we recognize as instances of ''philosophy,'' where the common feature is more or less systematic *reflection* on various aspects, in various areas, of experience to the end of facilitating ordered, meaningful existence. There are no transcendental rules *a priori* that are the essential, thus defining, feature of ''philosophy.''

Likewise for ''Africana philosophy.'' To the extent that this phrase identifies a discursive venture or ''field'' with determinate contours and subregions, it does so, in large part, by constructing the field *ex post facto:* that is to say, through discursive strategies—mine, in the present case—which seek to organize ''data'' (i.e., instances of reflection and/or accounts of the same) in particular ways including, in important cases, practices and traditions of discourse which were not themselves conditioned by an explicit sense on the part of those involved that they were engaged in something called ''philosophy'' or ''Africana philosophy.''

Further, since African peoples are ethnically—hence culturally—diverse and geographically dispersed, very important aspects of these ethnic and geographical diversities were fueled, in significant part, by the incursions of Europeans and others into Africa. Even before the incursions and subsequent related dispersals, however, there were diversities among the peoples of Africa which were manifest even as the herding of slaves began. Thus, the practices, traditions, and literatures comprising "Africana philosophy," because they are tied, in the first instance, to the life-worlds of numerous African peoples, have diverse histories, sites, and conditions of emergence. Africana philosophy is constituted by diversity.

How, then, to speak of "commonalities" or "unity" in Africana philosophy? The unifying commonality sought for to provide both boundaries and coherence is provided initially through third-order organizing, classificatory strategies: to the discursive practices that are the focus of discussion, practices which are themselves second-order reflections on the first-order lived experiences of various African and African-descended persons and peoples. Further, the presentation of commonalities sufficient to support gathering the practices of dispersed persons under a single heading proceeds by disregarding other factors of difference. The presentation of commonality is a function of my discursive agenda. But not mine alone. It is an agenda for others, as well—indicated, for example, in the efforts of others to develop African American philosophy or African philosophy as disciplinary fields. In the case of African philosophy, Kwame Gyekye's posture is worthy of review:

> I believe that in many areas of thought we can discern features of the traditional life and thought of African peoples sufficiently common to constitute a legitimate and reasonable basis for the construction (or reconstruction) of a philosophical system that may properly be called African—African not in the sense that every African adheres to it, but in the sense that philosophical system arises from, and hence is essentially related to, African life and thought. Such a basis would justify a discourse in terms of "African philosophy". . . .[45]

This search for "unity" is also a political project of long standing, as in that complex tradition of endeavors known as Pan-Africanism. However, is the search for "unity" in African, African American, or Africana philosophy but an instance of a romanticism that distorts the enterprise of philosophy? That remains to be seen. Each case of an appeal to, or purported demonstration of, unity or commonality in the discursive practices of philosophy of African and African-descended persons requires an appraisal on its own merits. What allows initially for the grouping of diverse intellectual endeavors of diverse persons under a single heading is, as indicated, the identity (in part) of the persons that are the subjects-objects of the endeavors as either African or African-descended, thus sharing socially and culturally conditioned biological characteristics, cultural traditions, and historical experiences more or less distinctive of the race. Yet, these characteristics are sufficient only for providing an *initial* distinguishing that groups persons by race. Doing so, however, provides no immediate and/or necessary insight into the forms, agendas, strategies, or ends of their discursive traditions and practices. It is to these traditions and practices, along with the agendas and strategies structuring their formation and deployment, situated in the context of the cultural life-worlds of those who practice and mediate them, that we must turn to answer questions regarding commonalities and differences. Only there are to be found life-world conditions and practices with shared "unities" sufficient to support a notion of a comprehending, encompassing disciplinary "field." We must take care to avoid conflating calls for unity among African peoples as a function of political mobilization with unity among the subjects-objects—and thereby the discursive norms and practices—of disciplines.

For Kwame Gyekye, the commonalities identified in comparative studies of "traditional" African thought are to be found in the customs, beliefs, traditions, values, sociopolitical institutions, and historical experiences of African societies.[46] The rupture of "traditional" experiences came when millions of heretofore relatively distinct groups of African peoples were thrown together in the crucible of the system of colonization, enslavement, and dispersion fashioned by that unstable racial and ethnic cultural complexity referred to as "European civilization." These mediators were themselves generally unified in the oppression of African peoples and in the shared sense that "they," contrary to African "others," constituted (or were the harbingers of) "civilization." Hence, the emergence of "philosophy" in Africa and the diaspora as a posttraditional discursive enterprise bearing that name is conditioned by the historical circumstances of domination of Africans and people of African descent by "Europeans" and European descendants.

While what is referred to as "Africana philosophy" is initially constituted through a third-order surveying and arranging of discursive practices and literatures according to an agenda exercised through the arranging and naming, the practices named do not require this arranging and naming as security for their meaningfulness or integrity, nor for their validity. Their meaning, integrity, and validity are local to the contexts within which they emerged and are (or were) exercised, not to my naming. This naming is conditioning only of those practices—mine and others'—that are deployed under this name self-consciously. It is not decisive that many (if not all) of the discursive traditions and practices that might be included under "Africana philosophy" were not so named by those involved in them, or in important cases were not even called "philosophy." That we call the overall "family" of such practices and traditions "philosophy" is a matter of historical, cultural, social, and political circumstance. I wish those of us involved in this enterprise to be free of the pernicious ordering and privileging that has been involved too often in the guardianship and administration of the word "philosophy" as an honorific term reserved for certain practices of certain persons of certain racial/ethnic groups.

Still, what, beyond the race and ethnicity of the thinker, if anything, is common to the endeavors I have included under the "Africana philosophy" heading?

In general, for posttraditional thinkers it is the effort to forge and articulate new identities and life-agendas to survive, and then to flourish—in the face of the limit-situations of racialized oppression and New World relocations; it is, as well, the effort to recover or reconstruct life-defining meaning-connections to lands and cultures of the African continent, to its peoples and their histories.

These efforts have given rise to reconstructions of the history of western philosophy and its relations to peoples on the African continent, to endeavors to recover and rehabilitate African-descended thinkers from earlier periods as precursor and pioneer black philosophers, and to significant moves to deconstruct and revise narratives of the histories of philosophical enterprises in the west and particular aspects of their agendas. The recent vintage of these efforts notwithstanding, they have been of major significance for the self-understandings and identities of African, African-descendant, and, even, non-African thinkers. When considered against the context of the history of western philosophy as narrated and practiced by some of the dominant figures, and against the explicit derogations of African peoples by a number of these figures, the advent of discussions about African and African American philosophy is *necessarily* "deconstructive." Thus, for example, each instance of an attempt to identify and/or articulate a philosophizing effort as distinctively African or African American is, at the outset at least, an important challenge that decenters the very idea, as well as the discursive practices, of "philosophy" into the history of their construction and maintenance, into the historicity of the philosophical anthropology that informs them via the valorized and racialized notion of "rational man." Furthermore, efforts to articulate the norms and boundaries of a distinctly "African" or "African American" philosophy expose the agendas of the persons who constructed and articulated that philosophical anthropology, and the practices through which it was institutionalized, in service to interests and objectives that were more than simply "philosophical" in some restricted, academic sense, but were intimately connected to sociopolitical projects, whether real, anticipated, or desired. Here the reconstructive efforts of a number of persons, and the issues raised in and by their work, demand serious attention: George G. M. James,[47] Henry Olela,[48] Lancinay Keita,[49] and the work of a number of persons in the Association for the Study of Classical African Civilizations, especially Maulana Karenga's and Jacob H. Carruthers' collection, *Kemet and the African Worldview: Research, Rescue and Restoration,*[50] and Carruthers' own *Essays in Ancient Egyptian Studies*[51]; and more recently Martin Bernal's multivolume *Black Athena: The Afroasiatic Roots of Classical Civilization.*[52] Along with the earlier work of William Leo Hansberry[53] and Frank M. Snowden, Jr.,[54] all of these efforts deserve serious attention.

Still, the discussion so far has focused on the objects of Africana philosophy, that is, on the articulated reflections of various African and African-descended peoples. But what about Africana philosophy *as a disciplinary venture*? There are major challenges to be met in the further articulation of its discursive norms and practices, as well as its agenda. One of the striking developments over the past few decades, in the United States in particular, is the extent to which these challenges—with all too few exceptions, to my knowledge—have *not* been taken up by professional philosophers of African descent, but have been by scholars and theoreticians in other fields (literary theory, sociology, history, art, music), especially those contributing to efforts in Black and/or African Studies. The proposals of Molefi Asante, the leading proponent of an ''Afrocentric'' approach to an ''Africalogical'' disciplinary agenda and practices (his attempted recasting of Black or African American Studies), is one of the most prominent and contested current attempts to take up these challenges.[55]

Asante's proposal centers on the concept of ''Afrocentricity,'' which, along with its dialectical corollary ''Eurocentricity,'' has come to have a pervasive life of its own in discussions regarding intellectual ventures that focus on black folks. ''Afrocentricity'' is the name for the principle that instructs us, when pursuing or articulating knowledge of (or about) African peoples, to always ''center'' our perspectives on norms drawn from the ''African Cultural System'' in which, Asante has claimed, *all* African people participate ''although it [this cultural system] is modified according to specific histories and nations.''[56] The core of Afrocentricity, he has said, is *Njia:* ''. . . the collective expression of the Afrocentric worldview based in the historical experience of African people. . . . Incorporating Njia into our lives, we become essentially ruled by our own values and principles. Dispensing with alien views at our center, Njia puts us in and on our own center.''[57] With Njia, we become ''Africa-centered'' in our objective and normative commitments and, thereby, in practices structured and guided by them. Thus, ''Afrocentric'' or ''Afrocentricity.''

When oriented and guided by Afrocentricity, Asante argues, a new criticism emerges. ''It introduces relevant values, denounces non-Afrocentric behavior, and promotes analysis . . . the Afrocentric critical methods start with the primary measure! Does it place Africans in the center?''[58] For the present, the primary task of this new criticism is the ''recapturing of our own collective consciousness . . . . It is reclaiming Egypt, deciphering the ancient writing of Nubia, circulating the histories and geographies of Ibn Khaldun and Ibn Battuta, and examining records of Africans in Mexico and other places in the new world.''[59] On the way to this collective consciousness there are five levels of awareness:

1. *skin recognition*—''when a person recognizes that his or her skin is black and or her heritage is black but cannot grasp any further reality'';
2. *environmental recognition*—seeing the environment ''as indicating his or her blackness through discrimination and abuse'';

3. *personality awareness*—"It occurs when a persons [sic] says 'I like music, or dance or chitterlings'. . . ." Even if the person speaks truthfully, this is not Afrocentricity;
4. *interest-concern*—"demonstrates interest and concern in the problems of blacks and tries to deal intelligently with the issues of the African people." This level is also not Afrocentricity since "it does not consume the life and spirit of the person";
5. *Afrocentricity*—is achieved "when the person becomes totally changed to a conscious level of involvement in the struggle for his or her own mind liberation."[60]

Once achieved, Afrocentricity allows one to predict the actions of whites and non-Afrocentric persons "with certainty." Further, one does not refuse to "condemn mediocrity and reactionary attitudes among Africans for the sake of false unity."

What does this mean for disciplinary practices devoted to studies "centered" on Africans and peoples of African descent? For Asante it means that such studies ("Afrology" in an earlier formulation, "Africalogy" in *Kemet, Afrocentricity and Knowledge*) must be guided by norms that are "rooted in the social, political and economic values of our people." Asante offers two "theoretical propositions" which will "set the tone" for an analysis of the emerging discipline of Afrology with its Afrocentric core:

> Afrology is primarily pan-Africanist in its treatment of the creative, political and geographic dimensions of our collective will to liberty. . . . A second proposition is that the Afrologist, by virtue of his perspective, participates in the coming to be of new concepts and directions. His perceptions of reality, political and social allow him to initiate novel approaches to problems and issues. Not being encapsulated by the Western point of view he is a person who is mentally as free as possible. . . . In fact, the Afrologist . . . is a person who is capable of participating in both the African and the Western point of view; however, as a practicing Afrologist he must act Afrocentrically. What he has learned is the value of every viewpoint.[61]

The future of Afrology?

> Since Afrology is based upon an Afrocentric interpretation and a particular conception of society, the results of our work will alter previous perceptions and set standards for future studies of African peoples. It is here that Afrology comes into its own as an organizing methodology, and a reflective philosophy, able to open the door to a more assertive, and therefore proper, consciousness of cultural and historical data. Such a proper consciousness is founded upon the genuine acceptance of our African past, without which there is no Afrological discourse or basis for peculiar analysis.[62]

In *The Afrocentric Idea* Asante continued his articulation of Afrocentricity.[63] In this text Afrocentricity is further defined and deployed as "a critique that propounds a cultural theory of society by the very act of criticism'' and proposes ''a cultural reconstruction that incorporates the African perspective as a part of an entire human transformation.'' The object of critique: ''Eurocentricism,'' that is, ''the preponderant . . . myths of universalism, objectivity, and classical traditions [that retain] a provincial European cast.'' Afrocentric analysis will ''reestablish . . . the centrality of the ancient Kemetic (Egyptian) civilization and the Nile Valley cultural complex as points of reference for an African perspective in much the same way as Greece and Rome serve as reference points for the European world.'' Afrocentricity, as the foundation of the discipline of Afrology, will ''expand . . . the repertoire of human perspectives on knowledge.''[64] The goal: ''a post-Eurocentric idea where true transcultural analyses become possible''[65]:

> Sustained by new information and innovative methodologies, Afrology will transform community and social sciences, as well as arts and humanities, and assist in constructing a new, perhaps more engaging, way to analyze and synthesize reality. Perhaps what is needed is a post-Western or meta-Western metatheory to disentangle us from the consuming monopoly of a limited intellectual framework . . . .[66]

In his more recent *Kemet, Afrocentricity and Knowledge,* Asante has more to say about the adoption of an ''Afrocentric'' perspective and its importance:

> . . . one steps outside one's history with great difficulty. In fact, the act itself is highly improbable from true historical consciousness. There is no antiplace, since we are all consumers of space and time . . . . Our place is the constantly presenting and re-presenting context, the evolving presentation context, the perspective—that is, history to us.
>
> The Afrocentrist sees knowledge of this ''place'' perspective as a fundamental rule of intellectual inquiry because its content is a self-conscious obliteration of the subject/object duality and the enthronement of an African wholism. A rigorous discipline is necessary to advance the intellectual movement toward a meaningful concept of place. In saying this I am challenging the Afrocentrist to maintain inquiry rooted in a strict interpretation of place in order to betray all naive racial theories and establish Afrocentricity as a legitimate response to the human conditions. All knowledge results from an occasion of encounter in place. But the place remains a rightly shaped perspective that allows the Afrocentrist to put African ideals and values at the center of inquiry. If this does not happen then Afrocentricity does not exist . . . . The Afrocentrist seeks to uncover and use codes, paradigms, symbols, motifs, myths, and circles of discussion that reinforce the centrality of African ideals and values as a valid frame of reference for acquiring and examining data. Such a method appears to go beyond western [sic] history in order to re-valorize the African place in the interpretation of Africans, continental and diasporan.[67]

Asante's project is of a kind with established efforts in the sociology of knowledge and ideology critique. Further, I take seriously Asante's concern to contribute to the opening of democratically informed intellectual spaces to accommodate the creative and constructive play of a plurality of knowledge formations in which norms and agendas from the cultural life-worlds of European peoples—or of any particular people—are no longer hegemonic. To this extent Asante is on to something very important; and he has taken up and furthered an agenda with a long history among African and African-descended (and other) thinkers.

Asante's efforts have their source in a complex of endeavors that comprise modern Black Studies, which has been radically and consistently historicist. A major portion of his programmatic efforts have involved the critique of, and struggle against, institutionalizations of the histories of peoples of Europe and Euro-America as the supposed evolutionary flow of reason embodied, simultaneously, in the discursive practices of persons of European descent and those socialized by them into disciplinary enterprises. Black Studies emerged in the space opened by this historicist, relativizing critique, and in its cultural-nationalist orientations remains firmly wedded to this position. Asante's program continues this line of development.

From a critical antifoundationalist perspective, a close reading of Asante's agenda reveals that it involves a critique of, and opposition to, claims by some that "Eurocentric" styles of rationality[68] are, in fact, the telos of all of humankind. However, Asante then moves to substitute an equally originary "African" foundation by way of reclaiming, rehabilitating narratives offering reassurance of our "Afrocentricity" through identification with forms of Africanness or Africanity seemingly preserved in their essence across all spaces and times. The discontinuities resulting from the spatial and temporal disruptions of historical, geographical, cultural, and sociological dispersions do not seem to be taken seriously.

Likewise the "ready-made syntheses" such as *the* "spirit" or "value system" of all African peoples (e.g., Njia), or "African history" involve attempts to satisfy our need to secure and reclaim originary "truths" established "at the beginning" (during the times of ancient Kemetic and Nubian civilizations, the original "African" civilizations for Asante) which escape historical determination and discontinuities. As noted by Foucault, the consequences of such efforts for historiography are not insignificant:

> . . . history, in its traditional form, undertook to "memorize" the *monuments* of the past, transform them into *documents,* and lend speech to those traces which, in themselves, are often not verbal, or which say in silence something other than what they actually say; in our time, history is that which transforms *documents* into *monuments*. In that area where, in the past, history deciphered the traces left by men, it now deploys a mass of elements that have to be grouped, made relevant, placed in relation to one another to form totalities. There was a time when archaeology, as a discipline devoted to silent monuments, inert traces, objects without context, and things left by the past, aspired to the condition of history, and attained meaning only

> through the restitution of a historical discourse; it might be said, to play on words a little, that in our time history aspires to the condition of archaeology, to the intrinsic description of the monument.[69]

From the context of the critique of historiography as the raising of monuments the theme and possibility of a "total" history begin to disappear and those of a "general" history emerge. The difference between the two is that a total history seeks to provide a *complete* description that "draws all phenomena around a single centre—a principle, a meaning, a spirit, a world-view, an overall shape. . . ." The aim is to "reconstitute the overall form" of a civilization or society in the identification of its material or spiritual principle, and, thereby, to fix "the significance common to all the phenomena of a period, the law that accounts for their cohesion. . . ." A general history, on the other hand, would "deploy the space of a dispersion. . . ." that is, would be sensitive to the possible *discontinuities* constitutive of a field of discourse.[70]

At issue in the distinction between these two approaches to history is the question whether the lived history of the civilization, society, or people under study can be properly thought to cohere around a material or spiritual principle, or set of norms, that fixes the significance common to all phenomena of the period. In the context of a consideration of Africology or Africalogy, the force of this question opens us to a serious concern for *discontinuity* without the overextended presumptions of unity involved in seeking the total history of all African peoples, across all times and spaces, as is invoked, perhaps, in claims regarding the "cultural unity" of all African peoples, both on the continent and throughout the diaspora. We may be required, then, to reconsider our understandable commitment to historiography as a form of archaeology, in something of the old sense noted by Foucault: as an effort to raise *monuments* that glorify African pasts in correction to the disparaging lies and distortions of racist European and Euro-American historiography.

Certainly we must question the veracity of attempted reclamations and rehabilitations as "total history" given that they are executed from the platform of, and in service to, agendas constructed in the present. Further, such efforts are conditioned by anticipated, desired, or hoped-for futures the likes of which our ancestors did not live. Nor, for that matter, are the presents and anticipated futures the same in all their important particulars for *all* African peoples. The *similarities* of experiences of African peoples as a function of the global political economy of racialized capitalism notwithstanding, at the level of lived experience and its perpetuation as tradition there are significant *differences* among us.

We can speak of such "cultural unity" among African peoples only by disregarding very important dissimilarities. But is the cost of that disregard at times too high for serious, self-critical scholarship that aspires to reasonableness and ''truthfulness'' with regard to the totalities that are involved? The unifying power of ''African'' (''Black'' or ''*African* American'' ''civilization'') will have to be reconsidered: ''unity'' can no longer be presumed to be pregiven and automatically recovered with the deployment of ''African,'' as though the term has the unifying power of a trans-historical, transgeographical *essence*.

In light of these considerations, we are left to consider Africana philosophy as a discursive venture. What we speak about, *who* speaks *how,* using what *concepts,* for what *purposes*—all of these are determined by the *rules of discourse* at work in the constitution of the venture. And if Foucault is right, these rules do not define ''the dumb existence of a reality, nor the canonical use of a vocabulary . . .'' but, instead, involve ''the ordering of objects.''[71] The greater the historical distance from the ''objects'' we order, the more it is distinctively *our* rules of ordering that are in force.

We need only remember just how recent is our (re-) embracing of ''Black'' and ''African'' as definitively constitutive of our identity for evidence of our need to take seriously the historicity of our rules of discourse. First, in regard to *what* we speak about: the terms ''Africa,'' ''African,'' ''African peoples,'' etc., are, in part, backward-looking, second-order constructions that have emerged from historical encounters with Europe and America; in part forward-looking notions in the context of projects seeking the achievement of shared identities and shared historical endeavors. Second, the rules governing *who* speaks are made by those of us involved in the reclaiming, rehabilitative efforts *we* take to be necessitated by the disruptive encounters with Europe. We have authorized ourselves to speak, and seek to justify our doing so persuasively: that is to say, by giving arguments that seek to link our praxis and its justification with the needs and interests of those in behalf of whom we speak. Third, with respect to *how* we speak: in part as persons who have come to identify ourselves as ''Africans'' or persons of ''African descent''; in part as ''persuasive ideologues''not initially authorized by those in whose interest we claim to speak; often from organizational or institutional contexts not of our own making (e.g., historically and predominantly ''white'' institutions). Fourth, via *concepts* shot through with the experience of discontinuity brought on by violent disruptions (forced relocation and enslavement in the ''New World''), concepts forged in a language often not the same as the language of those of whom we speak—whom we reconstruct *as* we speak—concepts (e.g., ''Afrocentricity,'' ''Africana philosophy'') created in service to contemporary needs and projects. For what *purpose?* Precisely to overcome *discontinuity* and the absence of unity; to promote *reconstructions* that we hope will lead to psychic wholeness and health, and to social and political empowerment, through which will come historical integrity.

But these are items on an agenda of the *present* that is conditioned by the lived experiences of disruption and marginalization. The rules of our discourse have thus been formed in the crucible of struggle: contemporary concerns leading to the development of Afrocentricity and Africana philosophy emerged in part from the historical contexts of the modern civil rights and black power movements. The connection between the historicity and dimensions of those struggles and our African "origins" is anything but simple continuity.

To the degree that Africalogy is intended as a *discipline*, for which the most constitutive medium and form of praxis is discourse, it cannot be the case that its governing norms will *inherently* be available only to persons of African descent, even though the discipline emerges out of the life-worlds of African peoples. Discourse is possible, and proceeds successfully, only if participants abide by shared governing rules. And, given the committed *social* imperatives conditioning Africalogy, the rules must be available to those to whom we wish to speak, in whose behalf we speak: in short, the rules of discourse must be *public*.

This is true, as well, for our discursive efforts addressed to others who, by virtue of race and/or ethnicity (or, even, class position), are not members of "our group" but to whom we feel compelled to speak. Our critiques of "Eurocentricism," for example, must be expressed in terms to which these "others" of European descent, among others, will have access *if* we would have them understand the limitations of their perspectives and practices, and come to regard and treat us in ways that are more respectful of our integrity. Thus, "we" and "they" must share a norm-structured discursive context that transcends the bounds of our own racial/ethnic life-worlds. At a deeper level, the basis for this sharing is provided by historical circumstances. When we have proper regard for the discontinuities, as well as the continuities, conditioning the existences of African peoples, we are compelled to realize that the "Africanity" of those of us of African descent in the "New World" is in no way purely "African": we are African *and* American (Caribbean, Cuban, Brazilian, etc.). To that extent, we share, in some instances, to some degrees, important aspects of our being with peoples of European descent. Consequently, a stringently relativist cultural nationalism as a platform for Africalogy would be inconsistent even with our most quotidian praxis: ordinary speech expressed in "American" English and addressed to *both* black and non-black audiences.

More fundamentally, such a cultural nationalism would certainly be inconsistent with intellectual praxis conducted in institutional settings and by way of the disciplinary practices of the modern academy with its "European" legacies. For these legacies provide much of the context within which, and the rules by which, modern Black or African American Studies emerged and was shaped into a "discipline"—the importance and truth of the claims that it was to be a radically *different* discipline notwithstanding. Subsequently, if Africalogy is to involve practices of *systematic* knowledge development, acquisition, refinement, and distribution, and, as part of these efforts, is to contribute to the articulation and institutionalization of appropriate norms for peoples of African descent, its structuring norms must satisfy rules which, among other things, promote such activities as critical and *self*-critical endeavors. Furthermore, since a discipline is an inherently *social* enterprise in which some degree of consensus—at the very least—is necessary, that in itself requires shared rules. Without them there can be no agreement, even among ourselves. The rules—the norms—for obtaining such agreement are not provided by melanin.

These rules are not *necessarily* and *irrevocably* restricted to the particular cultural, historical life-worlds of particular racial/ethnic—or gender—groups. It is possible to have norms that transcend particular groups such that they cover the "intellectual" and "social" life-praxes of different groups in ways, even, that make it *possible* to resolve what otherwise might be "fundamental" disagreements. Norms governing "ways of life" in general, systematic intellectual praxis in particular, are *strategies* serving *choices,* ultimately choices about life "in general," in service to which research enterprises have their ground and being. But these are choices not only about *our* intellectual praxis, but about the world we would co-make and share with others *even as we do so with uncompromising commitment to insuring, as best we can, "our" survival and "our" flourishing, now and in the foreseeable future*.

Thus, a crucial and complex question is: how shall we shape the intellectual praxes of Africana philosophy to serve the best interests of African peoples, first and foremost, and thereby provide practitioners with normative guidance while, at the same time, we preserve norms that secure "truthfulness" and appropriate "objectivity" in larger sociohistorical contexts within which our praxes are situated?

The answer to this question cannot be provided by "us" alone. Even if we would have that sharing based on consensus regarding the rules—a consensus arrived at through *open, free,* and *democratic* discussion—it is also a question whether "others" will abide by these same rules. Still, as an enterprise of the modern academy that seeks to speak authoritatively to black folk and to others for and about black folk, the rules of discourse for Africana philosophy will have to satisfy institutionalized rules governing scholarly practices, even as we continue to refine institutionalized rules. We have helped to change the rules of discourse in the contemporary academy. However, as long as we consent to share in such institutional settings and to participate in national and international publics—whether academic or nonacademic—our discourse cannot proceed by private rules.

But the same questions have to be faced when we are talking just about "us." Some black cultural nationalists continue to argue that the values and norms that should ground and structure the study of black folks exist in the "way of life," the "collective worldview and belief system," the "African cultural system" of *all* African peoples worldwide and throughout history. The rhetorical force of these notions has a great deal to do, I think, with the emotional, even psychological, rehabilitation and satisfaction they provide in the cultivation of an identity that is still crucial to our struggles against racialized domination and hegemony. And deliberately so. But at what price to serious critical thought? Some critics have reaped large harvests challenging the abstract naiveté and romanticism often involved in such declarations, which tend to disregard factors such as class stratifications, gender (black women's experiences, for example), and the subsequent serious disparities in values and practices among groups of African peoples. Such declarations also disregard the fact that no "African" of ancient Egypt or Nubia shares our historical world, nor we theirs.

Further, there are important ways in which the very notion "African" is problematic when we move to apply it to concrete persons, as is always the case with general terms. Asante, for example, in *Kemet, Afrocentricity and Knowledge,* takes the following approach: "By 'African' I mean clearly a 'composite African' not a specific discrete African orientation which would rather mean ethnic identification, i.e, Yoruba, Zulu, Nuba, etc."[72] What is a "composite African"? The unity such a concept harbors is gained at the price of abstracting from many vital aspects and details of historical and daily existence of living African peoples, an abstraction accomplished by we intellectuals who do so, supposedly, in the interest of others who have little or no recall on our efforts. In fact, we appropriate to ourselves the power, the right, the responsibility for doing so. Can real, living persons and peoples called "African," from all over the globe, find themselves in our concepts, in our prescriptions for their futures? Are reconstructions of "Africans" and prescriptions for their future justified simply by claiming solidarity with "the people"? Have we, in rightfully criticizing the racism and ethnocentrism that have historically conditioned many of the norms and justificatory strategies of Europeans and Americans, gone too far, at times, in discarding such strategies completely, in doing so without having fashioned new ones to replace them?

A critical stance toward our own disciplinary endeavors requires that we review the presuppositions and requirements too often invested in totalizing deployments of the notions of "African" and/or "black" as names for identity-formations which, it seems, as in the case of Asante's notion of Afrocentricity, often presume a single, shared subjective position for all persons African and African-descended. Such a presumption follows, I think, from a too easy conflation—or explicit identification—of knowledge production and articulation with psychic rehabilitation and political mobilization: for example, taking cultural *commonalities* shared by diverse African and African-descended peoples as *prima facie* evidence of an immediate *cultural* unity that can be a foundation for *political* unity. "All knowledge is political," we critics of modernity have often said. And I take this to be a fundamental truth in terms of the situatedness of the production and distribution of what passes for "knowledge" in the complexities of historically specific social formations. Still, the truism says nothing about the variety of forms and ends of politics, or about the variety of ways in which the production and distribution of knowledge stands toward and is related to the complex social formations in which these processes take place. Modern Black and African Studies, the Afrocentric approach in particular, emerged in service to particular political agendas and have sought to fashion identity-formations thought to be appropriate to the politics.

However, Stuart Hall is correct in stating that we must recognize

> . . . the extraordinary diversity of subjective positions, social experiences and cultural identities which compose the category "black": that is, the recognition that "black" is essentially a politically and culturally *constructed* category, which cannot be grounded in a set of fixed trans-cultural or transcendental racial categories and which therefore has no guarantees in Nature. . . . This inevitably entails a weakening or fading of the notion that "race" or some composite notion of race around the term black will either guarantee the effectivity of any cultural practice or determine in any final sense its aesthetic value.[73]

Neither politics more generally, nor scholarship, can be properly conducted, as Hall notes, by the simple reversal of replacing "the bad old essential white subject" with "the new essentially good black subject."

Of course, personal and social culturally-informed identities are vital to the well-being of individuals and peoples. How such identities are formed, revised, maintained, or overthrown is always a matter of importance, especially in historical situations conditioned by racialized domination and hegemony. Afrocentrists continue centuries-old traditions of African and African-descended "race-men" and "race-women"—taking up the critical tasks of marshalling meanings into articulate configurations meant to provide rehabilitative and mobilizing identity-formations in and through which black folks would fashion social worlds that provide for flourishing, liberated existences. Stuart Hall is especially insightful and helpful in thinking about how we might approach the business of cultural identity-formation: on the one hand, as a function of a shared ancestry, history, and culture that provide continuous and unchanging frames of reference and meaning out of which is formed a collective "one true self" shared by all; or, on the other, as a matter of recurrent, historicized "becoming": "Far from being grounded in a mere 'recovery' of the past, which is waiting to be found, and which, when found, will secure our sense of ourselves into eternity, identities are the names we give to the different ways we are positioned by, and position ourselves within, the narratives of the past."[74] I would add, identities are the names we give to the different ways we are positioned by/position ourselves, *recurrently,* within narrations of the past, the present, and anticipated or desired futures—since no identity-formation is permanent, individually or socially. Hence the need for critical intellectuals, Asante included, to review the legacies and practices shaping any people's reproduction of themselves, and to mediate the results of the reviews as "knowledge" meant to assist reproduction. And Asante, along with the "race-men" and "race-women" who were his predecessors, as well as those who are his contemporaries, is right to focus on the matter of the self-identifications of the thinkers and scholars involved in, and the normative, informing relation of their identities to, knowledge production and distribution as part of cultural reproduction and the formation of cultural identities more generally.

In light of the "untruth" racking the embodiment of the mainstream narratives of the history of philosophy, the advent of Africana philosophy is of very real importance to this reproductive and formative work. We are required to give greater respect to racial, ethnic, and gender "differences" as conditioners of philosophical praxis in various ways without necessarily invalidating reconstructed notions of "reasoning." This prospect cuts to the very core of mainstream western philosophy—one of the central endeavors of which continues to be to provide the definitive characterizations of what it is to be human. And, in general, the terms in which the characterizations have been articulated are void of explicit references to race, ethnicity, or gender. Certainly the modern enlightenment was a triumph of precisely this mode of characterizing humans. And it was a triumph that made possible substantive progressive achievements without which we would have a world not much to the liking of many of us.

But the victory has meant that attention to the unique, dissimilar, individual, and particular human groups has often been lacking in the exclusive focus on "the universal" that, in truth, has all too often been but the norms of particular Europeans in disguise. Further, the aspirations of universalist philosophy notwithstanding, where race, ethnicity, gender, etc., were supposedly irrelevant to the formulations of key notions, critical reviews are disclosing ethnocentricism and racism, sexism, and class biases at the very heart of the classical western philosophical enterprise.

Does this signal the complete inadequacy of the achievements of ancient and modern "European" Enlightenments? Not necessarily. But the recognition and acknowledgment of inadequacies in basic notions, and of histories of invidious appropriations and applications of them, open us to challenging possibilities for further revising our philosophical practices. Africana philosophy as an enterprise can contribute to a critical review of the "universalist" liberal agenda that has dominated so much of philosophical praxis in the west since the modern Enlightenment.

We are in the midst of a historical conjuncture that is relatively new, one highly charged by efforts to achieve democracy in multi-"ethnic," multi-

''racial'' societies in which ''group thinking'' is a decisive feature of social and political life. I join others in calling for a serious revision of our philosophical agenda and praxes. It is my sincere hope that the expansion of the recognized arenas of discourse in philosophy to include Africana philosophy is indicative of a movement in this direction, and that, as a result, philosophy will come to be practiced without pernicious racism and ethnocentrism.

It is also a sincere hope that Africana philosophy, conditioned by concerns some of which are taken up in Asante's Afrocentric Africalogy, will not only take root and grow, but will be nurtured in this revised context to which it will continue to make substantial contributions. All who have and might contribute to the formation and work of the enterprise need not be African or of African descent. The similarities and commonalities in the experiences of the dispersed race of African peoples in their varied ethnicities are one thing (their differences another); the coherence of an intellectual enterprise yet another. We must not confuse the former with the latter. Racial identity and common experiences, cultural commonalities and shared site of origin, *do not,* automatically and necessarily, provide the essential unifying coherence of a disciplinary enterprise, its norms, agenda, and strategies. ''Africana philosophy'' is indeed a ''gathering notion,'' not a proxy for an immutable essence shared by all African peoples. Gathering together various traditions and practices, various literatures, identified as ''philosophy,'' is just an initial, though important, step. Then real labor begins: interrogating works, learning from them, comparing and contrasting them (with endeavors by African and other peoples) as part of a larger, ongoing effort to catalog and study the many creations of African peoples, the contributions of African peoples to the treasure houses of human civilization.

Haverford College

NOTES

1 Important examples are Placide Tempels, *Bantu Philosophy,* tr. Colin King (Paris: Présence Africaine, 1959) and Marcel Griaule's *Conversations with Ogotemmêli* (New York: Oxford University Press, 1965).

2 An important contribution to these efforts is H. Odera Oruka's *Sage Philosophy: Indigenous Thinkers and Modern Debate on African Philosophy* (Leiden, Netherlands: E. J. Brill, 1990).

3 A very rich collection of texts is available (though not presented as ''philosophy'') in Howard Brotz (ed.), *African-American Social and Political Thought, 1850–1920,* 2nd ed. (New Brunswick, N.J.: Transaction Publishers, 1992).

4 For examples of these recent endeavors, see Leonard Harris (ed.), *Philosophy Born of Struggle: Anthology of Afro-American Philosophy from 1917* (Dubuque, Iowa: Kendall/Hunt, 1983).

5 The following discussion is based on my ''African 'Philosophy': Deconstructive and Recon-

structive Challenges,'' in *Contemporary Philosophy: A New Survey,* Vol. 5: *African Philosophy,* ed. Guttorm Fløistad (Boston: Martinus Nijhoff, 1987), pp. 19–26.

6 Tempels, *Bantu Philosophy.* One finds in the literature of this discussion references to the following works of earlier dates, though they are not concerned exclusively with Africa, if at all: V. Brelsford, *Primitive Philosophy* (1935) and *The Philosophy of the Savage* (1938); R. Allier, *The Mind of the Savage* (no date); and P. Radin, *Primitive Man as Philosopher* (1927).

7 See Marcel Griaule's ''Introduction'' to his *Conversations with Ogotemmêli.*

8 Franz Crahay, ''Conceptual Take-off Conditions for a Bantu Philosophy,'' *Diogenes,* No. 52 (Winter 1965), pp. 55–78.

9 Crahay, ''Bantu Philosophy,'' pp. 55–58.

10 Crahay, ''Bantu Philosophy,'' pp. 69–71.

11 Certainly one of the most poignant critiques of European encounters leading to the ''invention'' of Africa and one of the most informed discussions of African philosophy is V. Y. Mudimbe's *The Invention of Africa: Gnosis, Philosophy, and the Order of Knowledge* (Bloomington: Indiana University Press, 1988). I am deeply indebted to Mudimbe's great learning, and to his active participation in the formation of contemporary African philosophy as a discursive formation.

12 H. Odera Oruka, ''Four Trends in Current African Philosophy,'' in Oruka, *Trends In Contemporary African Philosophy* (Nairobi, Kenya: Shirikon Publishers, 1990), pp. 13–22.

13 A. J. Smet, *Histoire de la Philosophie Africaine Contemporaine: Courants et Problèmes* (Kinshasa-Limete, Zaire: Departement de Philosophie et Religions Africaines, Faculté de Theologie Catholique, 1980).

14 O. Nkombe and A. J. Smet, ''Panorama de la Philosophie Africaine contemporaine,'' *Recherches Philosophiques Africaines,* Vol. 3: *Mélanges de Philosophie Africaine* (Kinshasa, Zaïre: Faculté de Théologie Catholique, 1978), pp. 263–82.

15 This discussion of the classifications of Smet and Nkombe is aided significantly by the insightful discussion of Valentine Mudimbe in his ''African Philosophy as an Ideological Practice: The Case of French-Speaking Africa,'' in *African Studies Review,* Vol. 26, Nos. 3/4 (September/December 1983), pp. 133–54.

16 The phrase is taken from a complex of arguments the principal source of which are the speeches and writings of Edward Wilmot Blyden, who attempted to articulate the difference between Africans and Europeans in terms of the former's ''personality.'' Blyden's works include: *Africa and Africans* (1903); *Selected Letters of Edward Wilmot Blyden,* ed. Hollis R. Lynch (New York: KTO Press, 1978); *Liberia's Offering* (1862); *Liberia: Past, Present, and Future* (1869); *The Negro in Ancient History* (1869); *Christianity, Islam and the Negro Race* (London, 1888; new edition: Edinburgh: Edinburgh University Press, 1967). For additional readings see Kwame Nkrumah, ''The African Personality,'' and Alex Quaison-Sakey, ''The African Personality,'' in *Readings in African Political Thought,* eds. Gideon-Cyrus M. Mutiso and S. W. Rohio (London: Heinemann, 1975).

17 Pan-Africanism was an organized ideological and political tradition and movement that emerged in the late 1800s, at the instigation of Henry Sylvester Williams, a Trinidadian lawyer, and, later, W. E. B. DuBois, African-American activist scholar and champion *par excellence* of the interests of Africans and people of African descent. The principal manifestations of the tradition were a series of conferences (London, 1900) and congresses (Paris, 1919; London-Brussels, 1921; London-Lisbon, 1923; New York, 1927; Manchester, 1945; and Dar es Salaam, Tanzania, 1974—the first Pan-African congress to be held on the continent of Africa), which called upon Africans and peoples of African descent world wide (hence *pan*-African) to join together in an organized struggle to liberate the continent of Africa from European colonialism, and to free

African peoples everywhere from domination and the invidious discrimination of racism. See Immanuel Geiss, *The Pan-African Movement* (New York: Africana Publishing Co., 1974).

18 The "Négritude Movement," as it has come to be called, takes its name from the central concept which, like Blyden's "African personality," attempts to distinguish Africans from Europeans by defining the African in terms of the complex of character traits, dispositions, capabilities, natural endowments, etc., in their relative predominance and overall organizational arrangements, which form the negro *essence,* i.e., our *Négritude*. Originating in literary circles, at the instigation of Aimé Césaire, Léon Damas, and Léopold Sédar Senghor, the Négritude Movement quickly exploded the boundaries of these circles as the powerful political forces contained in its arguments played themselves out and took root in the fertile soil of the discontent of colonized Africa. See "What is Négritude?" (pp. 83–84) by Léopold Sédar Senghor and "Remarks on African Personality and Négritude" (pp. 67–70) by Alioune Diop, in Mutiso & Rohio, *African Political Thought*.

19 "African humanism" is another recurrent theme in discussions of the past quarter century that have attempted to identify values and life-practices indigenous to African peoples which distinguish them, in non-trivial ways, from peoples of European descent. In the words of M. Gatsha Buthelezi: "Long before Europeans settled in South Africa little more than three centuries ago, indigenous African peoples had well-developed philosophical views about the worth of human beings and about desirable community relationships. A spirit of humanism—called *ubuntu* (humanness) in the Zulu language and *botho* in the Sotho language—shaped the thoughts and daily lives of our peoples. Humanism and communal traditions together encouraged harmonious social relations." "The Legacy of African Humanism," in *Natural History,* 12 (1984), p. 2.

20 In some cases, discussions of African socialism are quite similar to arguments regarding African "humanism" to the extent that the claim is made that "traditional" Africa (i.e., Africa before its colonization by Europeans) was indigenously "socialist," prior to the discussions of Marx and other Europeans, in view of Africa's "communal traditions" (as Buthelezi puts it in the passage quoted above). In other discussions, the objective is to fashion a particularly *African* form of socialism, one more in keeping with the historical and cultural realities of black Africa. See, for example, Léopold Sédar Senghor, *Nationhood and the African Road to Socialism,* tr. Mercer Cook (Paris; Présence Africaine, 1962).

21 An expressly political/ideological venture that, in service to its conception of the goal of African liberation, involves the importation of the Engels-Lenin scientization of "Marxism" and its consolidation and institutionalization in highly centralized, authoritarian, revolutionary political parties and movements.

22 The title of a book by Kwame Nkrumah, first president of the postcolonial independent state of Ghana. In this work Nkrumah offers what he terms "philosophy and ideology for decolonization": "consciencism is the map in intellectual terms of the disposition of forces which will enable African society to digest the Western and the Islamic and the Euro-Christian elements in Africa, and develop them in such a way that they fit into the African personality. The African personality is itself defined by the cluster of humanist principles which underlie the traditional African society. Philosophical consciencism is that philosophical standpoint which, taking its start from the present content of the African conscience, indicates the way in which progress is forged out of the conflict in that conscience." Kwame Nkrumah, *Consciencism* (New York: Monthly Review Press, 1970), p. 79.

23 This the name for yet another cultural nationalist program which emerged during the period of anticolonial struggles in Africa. Here again the objective is to argue in behalf of a complex of indigenous and/or reconstructed values, practices, and social arrangements which, supposedly, will best serve contemporary Africa. The chief proponent of this program has been President Mobutu of Zaire.

24 Important examples of works in this group are Alexis Kagame's *La Philosophie Bantu-Rwandaise de l'Etre* (Brussels: Académie Royale des Sciences Coloniales, 1956); Kwame Gyekye's *An Essay on African Philosophical Thought: The Akan Conceptual Scheme* (New York: Cambridge University Press, 1988); and Segun Gbadegesin's *African Philosophy: Traditional Yoruba Philosophy and Contemporary African Realities* (New York: Peter Lang, 1991).

25 Mudimbe, "African Philosophy as Ideological Practice," p. 138.

26 See, for example, Theophilus Okere, *African Philosophy: A Historico-Hermeneutical Investigation of the Conditions of its Possibility* (Lanham, Md.: University Press of America, 1983).

27 Paulin Hountondji offers one such characterization: "In its popular meaning the word 'philosophy' designates not only the theoretical discipline that goes by the same name, but, more generally, all visions of the world, all systems of virtually stable representation that lie deep beneath the behavior of an individual or a group of people. . . . 'Philosophy', in that sense, appears as something which is held on to, a minimum system of creeds more deep-rooted in the self than any other systems . . . 'philosophy', in that sense, is more a matter of assumption than of observation. . . . It matters little whether the individual or society concerned are conscious or not of their own 'philosophy'; in strict terms, spontaneous 'philosophy' is necessarily unconscious . . . all told, it constitutes a testimony to the intellectual identity of the person or the group." Paulin Hountondji, "The Myth of Spontaneous Philosophy," *Consequence,* 1 (January–June 1974), pp. 11–12.

28 Mudimbe takes care to note that, contrary to other African scholars (notably Paulin Hountondji and Marcin Towa), he does *not* employ "ethno-philosophy" as a pejorative characterization: "I am using the term in its etymological value: ethnos-philosophia or weltanschauung of a community." "African Philosophy," p. 149, note 7.

29 Mudimbe, "African Philosophy," p. 142.

30 Mudimbe, "African Philosophy," p. 142. Mudimbe has provided a more elaborate, subtle, nuanced discussion and critique of the nature and production of knowledge about Africa generally, African philosophy in particular, in his *The Invention of Africa*. A recently published work, *Parables & Fables: Exegesis, Textuality, and Politics in Central Africa* (Madison: University of Wisconsin Press, 1991), is described as a confrontation with "the philosophical problems of otherness and identity through readings of the parables and fables" of the Luba, a colonized people of Zaire. Discussion of this most recent text must await a completed reading.

31 This review will be based on my "African-American Philosophy: Social and Political Case Studies," published in *Social Science Information* (London: Sage) 26, 1 (1987): 75–97.

32 For discussions of these historical periods and their guiding ideas/ideals, see, for example, Robert H. Brisbane, *Black Activism* (Valley Forge, Penn., Judson Press, 1974); and August Meier, *Negro Thought in America,* 1880–1915 (Ann Arbor: University of Michigan Press, 1966).

33 See W. E. B. DuBois, "Of Mr. Booker T. Washington and Others," in *The Souls of Black Folk* (1903); reprinted in Brotz, *African American Social and Political Thought,* pp. 509–18.

34 See, in particular, DuBois' "The Conservation of Races," in Brotz, *African American Social and Political Thought,* pp. 483–92.

35 For discussions of black nationalism see, among others, John Bracey, August Meier, & Eliott Rudwick (eds.), *Black Nationalism in America* (New York: Bobbs-Merrill, 1970), and A. Pinkney, *Red, Black, and Green: Black Nationalism in The United States* (New York: Cambridge University Press, 1976).

36 C. L. R. James, *The Independence of Black Struggle* (Washington, D.C.: All African Peoples Revolutionary Party, 1975); James Boggs & Grace Lee Boggs, *Revolution and Evolution in the Twentieth Century* (New York: Monthly Review Press, 1974).

37 For a survey of African American philosophy, see Leonard Harris, "Philosophy Born of Struggle: Afro-American Philosophy from 1917," in Gerald McWorter (ed.), *Philosophical Perspec-*

tives in Black Studies (Urbana: Afro-American Studies and Research Program, University of Illinois, 1982). For representative essays from the period, see the special issue of the *Philosophical Forum* devoted to "Philosophy and the Black Experience," Vol. IX (Winter-Spring 1977–78), especially William Jones, "The Legitimacy and Necessity of Black Philosophy: Some Preliminary Considerations."

38 Montclair, N.J.: Montclair State College Press, 1970.

39 These three essays were presented during the Africana Philosophy International Research Conference held at Haverford College during the summer of 1982.

40 Lanham, Md.: University Press of America, 1988; and Lanham, Md.: University Press of America, 1980, respectively.

41 *Alain Locke and Philosophy: A Quest For Cultural Pluralism* (Westport, Conn.: Greenwood Press, 1986).

42 Leonard Harris (ed.), *The Philosophy of Alain Locke: Harlem Renaissance and Beyond* (Philadelphia: Temple University Press, 1989).

43 The notion of a "geographic race" makes use, in the first instance, of geographic categories to group peoples who share distinctive biologically-based characteristics but who are not thereby regarded as constituting a "pure" biological type. Hence, I speak of African and African-descended peoples as a geographical, biological, and cultural "race." See Michael Banton & Jonathan Harwood, *The Race Concept* (New York: Praeger, 1975), p. 62.

44 A. J. Mandt, "The Inevitability of Pluralism: Philosophical Practice and Philosophical Excellence," in Avner Cohen & Marcelo Dascal (eds.), *The Institution of Philosophy: A Discipline in Crisis* (La Salle, Ill.: Open Court, 1989), p. 100.

45 Kwame Gyekye, "On the Idea of African Philosophy," in *An Essay on African Philosophical Thought,* p. 191. For arguments in behalf of the "cultural unity" of Africa, see especially, Cheikh Anta Diop, *The Cultural Unity of Black Africa* (Chicago: Third World Press, 1978); and Jacques Maquet, *Africanity: The Cultural Unity of Black Africa,* tr. Joan R. Rayfield (New York: Oxford University Press, 1972).

46 Gyekye, *African Philosophical Thought,* p. 191. For presentations and discussions of African thought and life along these lines, one might note, for example: Griaule, *Conversations with Ogotemmêli;* M. Fortes & G. Dieterlen (eds.), *African Systems of Thought* (New York: Oxford University Press, 1965); Ivan Karp & Charles S. Bird (eds), *Explorations in African Systems of Thought* (Bloomington: Indiana University Press, 1980); Daryll Forde (ed.), *African Worlds: Studies in the Cosmological Ideas and Social Values of African Peoples* (New York: Oxford University Press, 1954).

47 *Stolen Legacy* (New York: Philosophical Library, 1954).

48 "The African Foundations of Greek Philosophy," in Richard A. Wright (ed.), *African Philosophy: An Introduction,* third ed. (Lanham, Md.: University Press of America, 1984), pp. 77–92, and *From Ancient Africa to Ancient Greece* (Atlanta, Geor.: Select Publishing Co., 1981).

49 "The African Philosophical Tradition," in Wright, *African Philosophy,* pp. 57–76.

50 Los Angeles: University of Sankore Press, 1986. Essays in this text were selected from presentations during two Association for the Study of Classical African Civilizations conferences held in February 1984 (Los Angeles) and March 1985 (Chicago).

51 Los Angeles: University of Sankore Press, 1984.

52 *Black Athena: The Afroasiatic Roots of Classical Civilization,* Vol. 1: *The Fabrication of Ancient Greece 1785–1985* (New Brunswick, N.J.: Rutgers University Press, 1987).

53 *Africa and Africans as Seen by Classical Writers: African History Notebook,* Vol. 2 (Washington, D.C.: Howard University Press, 1981).

54 *Blacks in Antiquity* (Cambridge, Mass.: Belknap Press, 1970).

55 See Molefi Kete Asante, *Kemet, Afrocentricity and Knowledge* (Trenton, N.J.: Africa World

Press, 1990), especially "Part I. Interiors," in which he sets out a revised version of his theory and method for an Afrocentric approach to proper knowledge about African peoples which, together (i.e., the approach and the knowledge obtained through it), constitute the field of "Africalogy."

56 Molefi Kete Asante, *Afrocentricity: The Theory of Social Change* (Buffalo: Amulefi Publishing Co., 1980), p. 5.

57 Asante, *Afrocentricity,* p. 26.

58 Asante, *Afrocentricity,* p. 52.

59 Asante, *Afrocentricity,* p. 55.

60 Asante, *Afrocentricity,* pp. 55–56.

61 Asante, *Afrocentricity,* pp. 68–71.

62 Asante, *Afrocentricity,* p. 73.

63 Philadelphia: Temple University Press, 1987.

64 Asante, *The Afrocentric Idea,* pp. 6, 8–9, 16.

65 Asante, *The Afrocentric Idea,* p. 8. ". . . most of the so-called universal concepts fail transculturally, and without transcultural validity there is not universality." *The Afrocentric Idea,* p. 56.

66 Asante, *The Afrocentric Idea,* p. 34.

67 Asante, *Kemet, Afrocentricity and Knowledge,* pp. 5–6.

68 For a discussion of "cognitive style" see Alfred Schutz & Thomas Luckmann, *Structures of the Life-World* (Evanston, Ill.: Northwestern University Press, 1973).

69 Michel Foucault, *The Archaeology of Knowledge and the Discourse on Language,* tr. A. M. Sheridan Smith (New York: Harper and Row, 1972), p. 7.

70 Foucault, *Archaeology of Knowledge,* pp. 9–10.

71 Foucault, *Archaeology of Knowledge,* p. 48.

72 Asante, *Kemet, Afrocentricity and Knowledge,* p. 9.

73 Stuart Hall, "New Ethnicities," *ICA Documents: Black Film British Cinema* (ICA Conference, February 1988), p. 28 (emphasis in original).

74 Stuart Hall, "Cultural Identity and Diaspora," pp. 223, 225.

THE HORROR OF TRADITION OR HOW TO BURN BABYLON AND BUILD BENIN WHILE READING *A PREFACE TO A TWENTY-VOLUME SUICIDE NOTE*

LEONARD HARRIS

What if traditions in philosophy are analogous to traditions in the theatrics of horror? What if traditions in American philosophy since the influence of modern science are analogous to traditions in the theatrics of horror since the advent of movies? If the texts of philosophy perform, and theatrics can be read as text, we can draw an analogy between the traditions in each arena. I first explore what is meant by a "tradition." I then consider the import of the analogy between the traditions of philosophy and the theatrics of horror.

APHORISM I

In a narrow sense, tradition means institutional interactions which are or result in fairly well-defined, repeated communicative events.[1] "Tradition" will be capitalized when I mean it in a narrow sense. Traditions consist of attention-getting activities, as distinct from pedestrian acts or normalized communicative events. Traditions include intrinsically ambiguous categories, extreme salience of meaning, and standardized protocols. Traditional "objects or practices are liberated for full symbolic and ritual use when no longer fettered by practical use."[2] Well-defined Traditions, such as that of the shape of sailor hats, perform no practical function. Sailor hats certainly make reference to their own symbolic meaning, but unlike baseball helmets, they perform no nature-transforming or protective function. This feature of Traditions has long been recognized by investigators of the phenomenon.

Who has an authorial voice to speak the truth is different from what they speak and claim as true. It's been argued, for example, that "what makes certain types of discourse 'traditional' [akin to my narrow sense of Tradition] can be described as a *specific organisation of the claims to truth*."[3] Traditions of philosophy and science determine "who has the right to speak."[4] The presence of Traditions in science and philosophy does not mean that professionals in these fields all share a world view. Traditions help form institutionalized sources for claims to truth in the sense that they provide rites of passage, language, and situations which define authorial voices that can claim to be asserting a truth, especially a truth that is the unspoken existing, or legitimately possible future, consensus.

One important mark of a Tradition, which also helps distinguish it from other forms of historically repeated behavior, is that a Tradition is marked by well-defined revered symbols and archetypal figures. A horror movie that does not begin with eerie music would seem out of character. A horror movie without a manifestly impossible but frightening monster or event is hard-pressed to qualify as a horror movie. Traditions of horror movies will have archetypal figures, particularly monsters, associated with them. Similarly, a Tradition in philosophy will have archetypal figures, texts, and communicative events that are to be repeated as a part of enacting the protocol of the Tradition. The honored seating of philosophers at annual King's College don gatherings or annual Presidential lectures at the American Philosophical Association Eastern Division meeting are Traditions in the narrow sense.

Although I have described Traditions by means of traits commonly found in anthropological studies, the intent has been to describe traits that are central to, but not exhaustive of, well-defined Traditions. There is also a broad sense of "tradition," integrally connected to but distinct from both the narrow sense of Tradition and from a totalized sense.

A web of consensus, shared values, vocabularies, rhetorical devices, institutional recognitions, rules and rituals of protocol, methods, questions, and criteria of evaluation refined generation after generation help define traditions in a broad sense. George Allan captures the broad sense in which "tradition" has been used by him as well as such authors as Foucault and Auerbach:

> . . . tradition is to be understood as a vast Bible, a system of written and therefore objective assertions, a structure of truth serving as the guide and governor for all human activity. This one book of cultural articulation, to which all individual "books" contribute, is precisely what I have meant by the totality of linked importances. It is an objective order of things, functioning to separate meaning from meaninglessness, rationality from madness, truth from error. Under the tutelage of this enduring value system, I learn how to think and act and feel in a civilized way, which is to say in a way that makes me confident that what I do is worthwhile and satisfying."[5]

In this broad sense, intellectuals discuss what they mean by "the Western tradition," the "German tradition of sociology," "the discursive tradition," the "Aristotelian tradition," etc.[6] On Allan's account, the western tradition is exemplified by "Universality arising from particularity as its child and redeemer. A strange idea, although an ever-present seam running through the fabric of those enduring importances that characterize the Western peoples, its light fading now in these times of cultural forgetfulness and breakdown."[7] The concerns of Derrida in *Writing and Difference*, for example, include the existence and efficacy of centered structures and the search for an *arche* between essence and appearance, content and form, representation and the thing itself.[8] These have formed a misguided array of concerns important to western intellectual traditions on Derrida's account. For Richard Rorty, the search for epistemological foundations, particularly rational forms that could dictate what the content of our beliefs should be, has been an important, but misguided, thread in the western tradition of philosophy.[9] These authors rely on a broad sense of tradition for such depictions, although they may use other senses as well.

A broad sense of tradition is also used to depict the activities of fairly well circumscribed social groups, such as professional philosophers. David Hollinger's "communities of discourse," for example, consist of professionals who share a community by virtue of shared values, questions, importances, affinities, vocabulary, methodologies, ideals, and rhetorical devices.[10] They may share common procedures for credentializing new professionals and types of evidence for establishing rank. This application of "tradition" has become common in studies of professionalism.

When tradition is used broadly, its content is especially empty, save what an author supplies, and the already entailed reverence for Tradition. It is the substantive meaning of Tradition that significantly defines the import, and thereby an important boundary, of tradition. The import of tradition is, I believe, always parasitic on that of Tradition. If, for example, an author believes that an Aristotelian tradition of virtue ethics should be redeemed, the author normally does not mean that all of the beliefs and arcane practices of Aristotle or Periclean Athens should be everyone's guide. Rather, the author means that some set of principles, concerns, or attitudes associated with the history of Aristotelian virtue ethics should be redeemed and given broader acceptance. What may be entailed, if not stated, is that the author would like for this tradition (as a set of beliefs or principles embodied in a discourse) to become normalized, i.e., repeated, reiterated, and for it to become a standard through which persons must pass as a condition of their having a claim to other independent or derived truths. This entailment is a distinguishing mark of Traditions.

Traditions and traditions are conservative repositories of claims and possible claims which are enrolled in the project of perpetuating or creating a given consensus; one that is or should become normalized. Traditions and traditions certainly change; the point is that they provide the stage on which legitimate claims can be made, including claims about how or why the Tradition or tradition should change.

They also exclude; exclusion is a necessary function of tradition. The

"West," for example, can only conceive of itself by constructing others as at least external, alien, and separate if not primitive and exotic.[11] "Western" is sometimes identified with "European," but "Europe" doesn't come into existence as an imagined community until the late eighteenth century.[12] It is a nonnatural array of associated states that has come to be considered a culture, continent, and people. To the extent that "Europe" is a social entity, it is not unreasonable to consider what entitlements or rights persons have that maintain their identity as European. Such entitlement or rights would be goods held by Europeans, exclusive of persons that are not members of its cultural/continental community. Who has a *prima facie* stake in speaking, and the status for speaking, about what entitlements or rights are warranted is conditioned on who counts as European. Traditions and traditions identified as European, consequently, have an implied warrant for existence if considered endemic to the social entity of Europe. European history is replete with civil strife over what traditions count as alien, demeaning, not genuine, and bastardizations of an imagined pristine past.

Another sense of tradition is the totalized sense, not always clearly distinct from the broad sense. The totalized sense (hereafter trad) has two always-present ideas—that *all* ideas, practices, and symbols involve or include repetition, and that all persons are normally contextualized or situated in a society engined by prejudgments, a world view, life world, or form of life. The broad sense of "tradition" considers the past as a vast bible; the totalized sense considers every facet of life interwoven into a contextualized, repeated, interlinked well of cognition. The broad sense can be applied to a limited range of practices, for example, language-use or the practices and ideas of anthropologists; the totalized sense necessarily includes all practices.[13] The totalized sense considers all forms of social life as implicated in privileged communicative or cognitive inheritances. For example, agents can be completely unfamiliar with the Bible and thereby excluded from persons said to practice religion in ways associated with its traditions in a broad sense; in the totalized sense, these agents fit in a world inhabited by the Bible and its associated traditions, familiar to them or not. A totalized conception purports to tell us about the world as a whole.

Impartiality of judgment is, on accounts that rely on a totalized sense, as impossible as having a starting point of analysis that is not distorted by uncritical attitudes, beliefs, habits, customs, prejudgments, and prejudices. A metaphysics, ontology, epistemology, or aesthetics is necessarily distorted by communicative practices which invariably include inherited and privileged structures, forms, assumptions, and codes that remained unstated. The subject, on such accounts, may be considered problematic because the subject may inappropriately present its ideas as ones that surmount the limitations of what it is to be a subject—contextually bounded. A method of reasoning, or at least considering various methods of reasoning, for such authors as Gadamer and Rorty is important as a way of approaching the facticity of trad and the need for critical reflection; neither "facticity" nor "critical reflection" escapes contextuality into a pure realm of the impartial but both can have more or less defensible characteristics.

From the broad sense of tradition we can infer claims about the nature of life. The totalized sense, however, can be used to directly depict a conception of life. Tempels' *Bantu Philosophy,* for example, depicts an alleged world view that totally defines the practices and ideas of the Bantu, actually a dubious language grouping, such that any unanticipated event or new idea is necessarily locked into, interpreted by, and explained in terms of preconstituted ideas.[14] Tempels holds that the "being" of the Bantu is defined by its world view and its traditions/Traditions immediately determined by that world view. Humanity is for Tempels the collection of different beings, equal in their entrenchment in inescapable but mutually valuable world views. The deduction from Bantu world views to Bantu practices is reductive, i.e., the practices provide insight into the world view and the world view provides insight into the practices. In effect, the idea that people can build airplanes corresponds to, fits, is inferentially reasonable or deducible from world views just as the idea that people should have reverence for the forest can be read from social practices.

Trads are the manifestation of the totality of "the truth"; at least "the truth" of persons engaged in the trads. Comte Joseph de Maistre and Felicite Robert de Lamennais considered trads the manifestation of common, racial reason lodged in a group's practices. Failure to submit to trad (the Roman Catholic tradition in their case) meant, just as it meant for Tempels, that a "raciated" agent was violating their true being and risking the evil of destroying "the truth"; for Tempels, the truth of the relativity of logic, for de Maistre and de Lamennais, the truth of the Holy Roman Church.

APHORISM II

I resonate with the politicized side of the invention approach to the history of traditions; it holds, in general, that traditions are historical constructions[15]:

> "Invented traditions" is taken to mean a set of practices, normally governed by overtly or tacitly accepted rules of a ritual or symbolic nature, which seek to inculcate certain values and norms of behavior by repetition, which automatically implies continuity with the past. In fact, where possible, they normally attempt to establish continuity with a suitable historic past.[16]

Inventions are not necessarily fabrications, falsehoods, or outright lies. Inventions are imagined, created, discovered; they are contrivances, gadgets, and doohickeys; they are the Alchemy of Finance, the Alchemy of Race, as well as the Alchemy of Community.[17] King Arthur was neither a king nor an important warrior (an intentional lie told by British historians, and repeated year after year); the Pilgrims did not land on Plymouth Rock, Paul Revere was a nobody during his lifetime, and Americans did not lavish sentiment, toys, or education on their children until the mid-nineteenth century.[18] ''Invention'' is intended to include lies and fabrications, but the facets of central importance are imagined ways in which links are conceived. As Benedict Anderson described the way the past is marshalled to establish an imagined link and legitimacy:

> . . . even the most determinedly radical revolutionaries always, to some degree, inherit the state from the fallen regime. Some of these legacies are symbolic, but not the less important for that. Despite Trotsky's unease, the capital of the USSR was moved back to the old Czarist capital of Moscow . . . the PRC [People's Republic of China]'s capital is that of the Manchus (while Chiang Kai-shek had moved it to Nanking), and the CCP leaders congregate in the Forbidden City of the Sons of Heaven.[19]

Similarly, Washington, D.C. was a slave-trading capital and bastion of displaced mercantile aristocrats—no haven for democratic anything. The ''ancien regimes'' of Europe did not see themselves as forming a body of ''aristocrats'' until aristocracy as such was nearly extinct: we see them as a body.

Conceiving traditions as inventions entails accepting the view that the content and form of traditions are historical developments, i.e., there is nothing natural about any particular tradition; they are normative formations, constructed in a myriad of ways. There may be biologically compelling reasons for the existence of mating, for example, but there are no such reasons for mating traditions that favor either patrilateral parallel cousin marriage or exogamy.[20] Similarly, conceiving communities as imagined requires that the content and form of the bonds that define links to persons outside one's immediacy are imagined bonds that make communication, trade, peace, and war possible. There may be geographically and biologically compelling reasons necessitating community cohesion and bonds of trust, care, and compassion among kin and commune; there are no such reasons necessitating the character of existing nation states.

What is occasionally termed discourse analysis—the works of Nietzsche, Foucault, and Said are examples—is closely associated with the invention approach to traditions.[21] They hold in common that discourse does not represent social reality but rather constructs that social reality through an array of linguistic techniques. ''Discourse analysis'' as I use it is intended to emphasize the scholarship on the way discourse is implied in the construction and deformity of what we count as normal and abnormal reality. My argument does not require that the numerous authors associated with the generalization ''discourse analysis'' hold identical philosophies, e.g., they may be more or less Marxist or more or less Husserlian phenomenologists. Discourse is hardly a neutral picturing of reality, on the discourse analysis account, but a social and political mode of presenting and re-presenting the subject and deforming the other. Discourse analysis "cannot safely be founded on redefined "traditions."[22] The reason is that discourse analysis has used the tools of detailed history, ethnography, genealogy, sociology, and linguistics to evaluate discourses that purport to represent a tradition and found that they rely on salient notions that surreptitiously repeat favored dichotomies, stereotypes, and assumptions about authenticity. Traditions are understood as dichotomizing, totalizing, and violent ventures that too often falsely pretend to be expressive of universal, objective, and rational principles rather than actually entrapped provincialisms. Discourse analysts who consider totalities and surreptitious dichotomies unappealing seek to avoid granting traditions significant appeal. However, depending on the author, some form of tradition may be considered important for social cohesion and political struggle. Discourse analysis, I believe, has provided additional weight to the invention approach to traditions.

Philosophers often use the "Western tradition of philosophy" to mean a line of conversation extending from Athens through primarily western Europe (and not including Egypt, the Ottoman and Byzantine Empires, Huns, Moors, and Islam; the United States and Canada may be thrown in as addenda to the "Western tradition," depending on the author). Economists, by contrast, often mean by "Western" industrialized nations such as Japan, Brazil, Europe, United States, Canada, and Mexico. Sociologists may mean by "Western" North and South American. The use of "the Western tradition of philosophy" can refer to a broad range of beliefs, acts, dominant themes, etc.; it is, however, at once inventing itself and simultaneously relying on content that is arguably present, given appropriate erasures and silent voices.

APHORISM III

It is false that people who watch horror movies normally go away and perform acts of terror; just as it is false that people who read philosophy normally go away and perform the acts philosophers take delight in applauding. It is equally false that people replicate, in mirror fashion, the ideas replete in philosophy or the ideas replete in horror movies.

Assume that history is not driven toward an end-state such that the reality of human history is rationally structured and sequenced to achieve that end-state teleologically. Further assume that neither practical reason, reasonableness, nor rationality saturates or is even dominant in the actual cognitive practices of normal persons. Rather, suppose that the sorts of incongruent, heuristic, and fallacious cognitive practices described by numerous naturalizers of epistemology are characteristic of human cognition.[23] Given these assumptions, it is arguable that traditions (broad sense) in philosophy are as contingent on the nature of human imagination as traditions of horror, if such traditions are contingent on how people actually think. The reason this is so is that traditions require us to imagine that the consensus which they embody is, or should be, identified with normality, such that normality is coterminous with a general or particular nature of being. That "nature of being" can be conceived as an ontological essence or intended as a benign nativism depicting our species character. In either case, we can be confident—in watching a horror movie or living our lives—that we are securely moored in normality.

One reason philosophies are not like horror movies, although both can be understood as performances enlivened by texts, is that philosophies have been coconspirators in, or help make possible, genuine terrors. Roughly, terror is distinguished from horror by the extent to which the acts depicted are or can be considered real; acts that are considered unreal or at best a singular aberration of normal possibility can be considered horror. A horror, such as the instant death and maiming of millions, once considered an impossible feat except by divine intervention, can become an actual terror (Nagasaki and Hiroshima), but not the other way around.

Horror movies have yet to be substantively implicated as a cause of or deep contributor to reigns of terror; no horror movie has ever been used as the definitive text to legitimate domination into perpetuity; nor have any horror movies helped form the theoretical basis for revolutions to overthrow exploitation, exclusion, and tyranny. Horror movies have played roles in each of the above situations, but as bit actors within a play; the play, stage, plot, meaning, and characters were deeply entwined with philosophies. This is so not because philosophies are mirrored in practice, but because the type of imaginative scenarios they offer are intended to be, and have been "traditional" sources for, helping people select right thinking to guide practice (e.g., rational, reasonable, dialectic, postmodern, African, or scientific). Imagination plays a role in shaping what fascinates us about philosophies just as imaginative possibilities play a role in shaping what fascinates us about horror movies although horror movies bear no mirroring in shaping what we do in practice.

The thought theory of emotional responses to fiction "maintains that audiences know horrific beings are not in their presence, and indeed, that they do not exist, and therefore, their description or depiction in horror fictions may be a cause for interest rather than either flight or any other prophylactic enterprise."[24] On this account, the categorically impossible beings that inhabit horror movies command curiosity and fascination. The interest and enjoyment we gain from horror movies outweighs the distress. The distress, in fact, may be an integral feature of the enjoyment; the distress is enwebbed in what forms the fascination if not a particular person's enjoyment. Horror movies remain entertaining in spite of and because of the distress.

The "beings" that often inhabit works of philosophy, for example, the virtuous pagan Athenian, the workers that have as their interests universal human interest, the citizen engaged in communicative inquiry, or the sage in the African village who carries the wisdom of ancient Egyptians, are presented as real beings for our emulation. If the practices and reasoning of such beings are believed manifestations of their traditions, their traditions stand for the collective being of those with right dispositions, right thinking, and practices that make possible right choices. Not even Frankenstein was so bold.

There is a difference between "acting as if" such that our acts make the "as if" real, and "acting as though" such that our acts do *not* make the "as though" real. Acting *as if* there really is a community of philosophers makes, *mutatis mutandis,* the community of philosophers; acting *as if* the virtues of Aristotle were the sort we should follow makes, *mutatis mutandis,* the agents followers of the virtues of Aristotle, if they are earnest believers. Imitating a model, for example, provides us in a sense with an initiation into what it is to live like the model. We improvise, imagine, and add our own unique variations until our lives feel comfortable with the model or models woven together to help form our character. However, acting *as though* the virtues of Aristotle were the sort we should follow makes the action the type well-designed for theater. One who acts this way is not necessarily insincere nor a disbeliever, but is an actor, not just an agent. However, if the actor makes the fatal mistake of treating the virtues of every character played as definitive of their being, then the actor is making their characters' virtues real at least in the sense that the actor is living their experience under the aegis of those virtues. The actor ceases acting and ceases having a distinguishable character apart from the various parts played and the process of performing those parts. Acting *as though* a monster in a horror movie is real at best makes us scared—otherwise we would not be in the theater very long.[25] Consequently, imagination in acting *as if* entails a form of reality that differs from acting *as though*. The first is concretized, i.e., I am the concrete agent, I need a passport to get into the imagined community of France. The second makes a community of genuinely lived experience impossible.

In the next three sections I consider several built-in tendencies of conservatism in philosophy that render support for the belief that traditions (all three forms) are intrinsically conservative inventions, inventions that mitigate against lived experiences. I also consider a defensible approach, given the inescapability of traditions, using American and African American philosophy as examples.

APHORISM IV

One reason competitiveness and critique are not as radical a feature of the western tradition in philosophy as might be believed is because traditions, western or otherwise, are highly regarded as sites of hidden truth. The same authors, repeatedly noted as important, are often noted not because they are authors with right answers in western philosophy, but because they are authors whose works pose the right questions, make interesting distinctions, use appropriate prose forms, and provide controversial answers within an accepted range of conceivable answers. By immersion in their works, as one didactically, argumentatively, critically, and competitively cajoles an ancestral spirit, one will be empowered with the potential to speak the truth. Having acquired the potential, the easiest way to maintain the newly acquired power is to speak through the agents who are the conduits of one's authority. That is, to interpret or reinterpret the canonical figures; to critique and revalue the canonical figures; to speak one's own truth as a clearer version of the truth only intimated, implied, or suggested by the canonical figures, is to proclaim that one's truth is the hidden truth long submerged inside the intricacies of the authorities already canonized as being closest to the truth.

No one is born Kantian, Marxist, or pragmatist; and who counts as a legitimate one of these is a continual subject of debate (for example: Is Derrida really appealing to Kant? Was Trotsky or Stalin the genuine Marxist? Is Rorty really promoting the spirit of Dewey's pragmatism or was Emerson really a pragmatist?). Moreover, what the features of a tradition are, are very often, if not contrived, constructed in one of many possible ways. Meanings always differ from person to person; no matter how slightly, weight placed on different knowledge claims shifts, sometimes ever so slightly. The actors invent, over time, the same play that is of necessity a different version. However, in order to maintain authority within a tradition its authorial voices must be interpreted or shown to provide witting or unwitting support. In this fashion, the critical theorist remains Marxist, having advanced or surmounted Marxism; the neopragmatist remains pragmatist, having focused on experience and rejected either-or dichotomies; MacIntyre remains true to Aristotle although he holds hardly any views of Aristotle; Mudimbe remains an Africanist although he deconstructs "Africa"; Wiredu remains an African philosopher although his views on rationality are Kantian in inspiration.[26]

The Egyptian mystery system is not paradigmatic of Pharaonic Egypt without a myopic focus on death, life after death, eternal servants for royalty, and the possibility of obliteration for persons improperly buried. Traditional African philosophy is not paradigmatically African without the moral community defined in kinship and kind terms. Periclean Athens, without practices of infanticide, animalism, human sacrifice, polytheism, and predestination is not Athenian. Thomas Aquinas, without any form of Christianity, conception of the natural subordination of women to men, or God-dependency as the ultimate source of right action is not the same Thomas Aquinas that he aspired to being. Tradition construction invariably involves, to some degree, erasures. A selection of principles, structures, styles, attitudes, or questions which were important to an author are excised, promoted, or erased. The contexts of claims are ignored or emphasized according to whether they are in some way enlightening in relation to the general ideas the construction wishes to promote. The tremendous range of possible routes makes the notion of a rational tradition, understood as an unvaried, unbroken, communicated line of behavior and beliefs worse than superstition. An argument to reinstate Franz Fanon's sense of moral indignation without the regenerative role of violence; an argument to reinstate an Aristotelian sense of virtue without wealthy citizens standing as exemplars of the most virtuous; or an argument to reinstate a Thomistic traditional sense of morals without noblemen as important characters is analogous to arguing for the mass production of Model-T Fords in a Toyota plant. The appearance as form can be exactly duplicated but the content and character of its producers would, in almost no respect, match the original Model-T Ford.

The search for necessary and sufficient conditions of truth, for example, has one of the longest histories in philosophy; or rather, the way "philosophy" has come to be delineated, the history of the search for necessary and sufficient conditions of truth has been constructed as central. The impact of science, in particular, significantly influenced the importance of this issue in the history of American philosophy. It's not that authors addressing this issue were conversant with one another. Cases in which they were are given special importance. In retrospect, the defenses, responses, and lines of reasoning that authors offered are constantly reconstructed as if they were in conversation with one another. The reconstructions, compiled year after year, layer upon layer, makes it easy to imagine that there is a continuous history within this narrow range of literature. As conversations between persons regarding necessary and sufficient conditions of truth increase, imagination comes to instantiate itself and makes itself concrete with more and more real examples of communication. The feat of imagination, even after a multiplicity of real communicative events, is an important feature of tradition as a perpetual construction—each successive wave of commentators looks back to revise and re-envision a debate; each abandons what it considers irrelevant, tacky, indefensible, embarrassing, or simply unimportant to their projects; each appeals to the past for support and legitimation—as if Pharaonic Egyptians, Ogottemeli, Fanon, Periclean Athenians, Aristotle, or Thomas Aquinas would in some form concur with their reformation.

As an aside, Dr. Frankenstein was not at all pleased when his monster did not obey orders.

APHORISM V

I sometimes believe, contrary to popular interpretations, that Frankenstein movies, and quite a few other classics as well, are not horror movies. If an agent, say Dr. Frankenstein, steps beyond the pale of extant knowledge, applies that knowledge, and creates a being that according to extant knowledge is impossible, then the movie appears less classically horrific. If a person is clinically dead, their revival is possible only by accident, divine intervention, or knowledge that exists beyond the pale of extant knowledge. Ruling out accident, Dr. Frankenstein has similar effectual powers as a divine interventionist. Sometimes, upon reflection, however, I believe Frankenstein movies are classical horror movies. Frankenstein rejoins the ranks of classical horror genre if a dead person (unrevivable) is not revivable because "death" outside of accident or divine intervention, is exclusive of life and potential sentient life. As long as death and life are absolute contraries, Frankenstein is a classical horror movie. Frankenstein is a third, categorically impossible, being. If I treat Frankenstein's "categorical impossibility" as an actual, potential, or even a possible option, however, Frankenstein ceases to be horror. The cessation of Frankenstein as horror is paradoxically parasitic on Frankenstein as horror. Like all forms of parasitism, the relationship between the possible and the impossible is unstable and elastic.[27] Whether Frankenstein is horror or not depends on how I treat extant knowledge of reality.

Traditions (narrow sense) and lived experiences are mutually exclusive in the sense that lived experiences occur through inherited symbols of the normal in which we, like chaotic floating signifiers, continually constitute unique meanings necessarily different from what has been inherited. Traditions are dead (unrevivable) bodies that we inhabit and live through. They are horrors incarnate—the categorically impossible past that shapes the actual present.

Fanon, in "On National Culture," had it right when he argued that the colonized often usurp the demeaning stereotypes of the colonizer and reshape them into the stereotypes that define their self-images.[28] The new images, particularly the ones in the service of the bourgeoisie, are used to make traditions that have little to do with the real redistribution of power. The native is vitalistic, sensual, emotive and the colonizer logocentric, scientific, calculating—all praise to vitalism while the population starves and the colonizer produces and owns the products of modernity! The categorically impossible past can give cause for self-esteem; simultaneously it can be used to shroud the lived experience of misery borne by the populace in the name of the nation—but in the material benefit of the ruling elite that in practice care nothing for such trifles. However, without a link to the past—without reclaiming the Forbidden City of the Sons of Heaven, the Islands of the Kings, or the Benin Empire as seats and sources of legitimation—it's not clear that social transformational ideals can sufficiently regenerate a people's sense of having a coherent social nexus and responsibility.

The impossibility of absolute impartiality—because we all have a starting point, a background of inherited, developed, family-influenced unreflective habits, beliefs, customs—is the other side of the impossibility of absolute contextuality, particularly in the modern world. Traditions, in a broad sense, symbolize a peoples' immediacy and ascendancy. Fanon is noted for having failed to appreciate the influence of the past—as a remembering, reliving, source of meaning and guide for future practice. Muslim women, for example, returned to the veil, Islam did not fade, and autocratic forms of association did not disappear as a result of the FLN's participatory form of organization and struggle against the French—any more than the critical Marxism of Serbian intellectuals replaced or prevented deep-seated parochial ethnocentricity. Moreover, Fanon tended to neglect the importance of inherited beliefs about commitment to family, friends, siblings, and future generations; these often form an array of intuitions that motivate people to place their living existence at tremendous risk in order to remain faithful to beliefs that define their person. How social entities are constructed, inclusive of what traditions are taken to be central grounds for bonding, is crucial to the kind of consensus that shapes social entities. Living agents are involved in shaping that consensus, not dead bodies nor a mysterious historical consciousness of remembrances. That's why it is better for a people to write and rewrite their own dictionaries—several university editions of the *Webster Dictionary,* for example, include "Aryan" but not "Akan"; and if one relies on the *Encyclopedia Britannica,* African people hardly exist. The *Encyclopedia of Philosophy* should be renamed the *Encyclopedia of Eurocentric Nationalism*.

Living persons in a multiplicity of associations and networks participate in shaping and reshaping their being, individual and social; that being provides social agency. Persons share a common nature as transvaluing social agents bonding through fluid forms of social identity. The livingness of identity is why E.W. Blyden's *Christianity, Islam and the Negro Race* has an appeal that V.Y. Mudimbe's *The Invention of Africa* does not; Blyden provides a sense of the past and a telos for a collective entity that gives cause to a willingness to sacrifice for future generations and defend African people against the actual murderous and exploiting Europeans.[29] The coherent social nexus Blyden provides is primordial and providential; the nexus Mudimbe provides is accidental, contrived, alien, and the consequence of adaptations to force. Mudimbe has no way of providing a reason to be concerned with future generations because the collective entity of Africa for Mudimbe is invented in the sense that its historicity is not tied to a telos. Its collectivity forms a being through which people can see themselves as instantiations, but not instantiations tied to their nature, character, or even their own imaginative creation. Invention approaches do not provide providential, historical, material, or anthropological natures and inherent personality traits as causes and reasons for behavior. At best, politicized invention approaches are associated with transformational ideals. Experiences are nonetheless mediated through some categorically impossible features of the past; some causally associated or naturally connected links of coherency legitimating current risks.

If what has been termed the Sartre/Roquentin picture of the self is appropriate—a picture that contends persons are disjointed agents without coherent lives as narratives—it is certainly the case that lived experiences are mutually exclusive of traditions.[30] This is so because imagining the past entails constructing causal links between events that are not causally connected. Also, lived experiences can usurp traditions in the service of either progressive transformation or empty platitudes about revising ancient norms to salvage modern insecurities. Moreover, if MacIntyre's picture of the self as a coherent agent is true, i.e., a coherent agent with narrative stories which may include falsifications (in part, because it's not clear what a narrative would be without falsifications, because agents are also authors of their own stories, and coherent life plans tend to have a telos), it is still the case that traditions and lived experiences are mutually exclusive.[31] This is so because lived experiences include, but are not reducible to, causal connections. Having pain is not reducible to an imagined narrative; needing to defecate is not identical to participating in a tradition that dictates the protocol for so doing; killing a colonizer who has spent her life raising sons to rape and exploit the colonized is not identical to saluting a rebel flag—somebody kills and somebody dies.

Personal necessities, choices, accidents and moments of individuated feelings exist. The having and making of such experiences are not *prima facie* necessarily instantiated in what existing or imagined repeated performance define. Even if what is meant by tradition is trad (the totality of human existence), the actual having of feelings and dispositions by an individual cannot be substituted for the actual having of feelings and dispositions by another individual. The repeated practices of others are not identical to my repeated practices. They can be conjoined, mutually influential, similar, and common, but the having is always individuated. Such individuation does not deny the presence of historical, contextual, or situational influences, only that they are not substitutes for individual experience. This view of lived experiences does not deny the existence of viable communities, imagined as they are; but it does deny that existing communities are substitutes for past communities. Given the importance that the past plays in defining identities, existing identities are always themselves being shaped and reshaped by active agents—living through a categorically impossible past.

Traditions are not horrors in the sense that we can step beyond the limitations of extant knowledge through imagination. We can revise, rewrite, and define the past differently. We can include the historically excluded, consider the strengths of persons that were perceived as self-deprecators, and offer new ways for persons to have a sense of belonging and self–respect. Conversations between traditions, conflicts of traditions, new formations, and the death of previous points of reference contribute to imaginative possibilities. The categorically impossible is not expressed by the noun contraries of death and life, but by the instability of their disjunction. Imagination and symbolic meanings are among the goods we use to help define the world of possibility; they are unstable and elastic, thereby allowing inventions, creations, and new forms of authenticity.

If presentation of the structure of the universe in symbol form occurred, generation after generation, it might be considered a custom. Such a custom could be repeated with reverence and generate attention when discussed. In addition, it could be reasonable to revere the knowledge of inherited, repeated symbol systems which present the structure of the universe. That is, repetition and reverence for this symbolic language could become a well-defined Tradition if and only if the symbolic language were useless. If persons who mastered or contributed to the symbol system that presented the structure of the universe were considered claimants to other truths, the symbol system would have additional grounds as a Tradition. The more useless the symbols presenting the structure of the universe, i.e., logical positivism's *philosophia perenia*'s truth, the more they shade toward Tradition; the more useful, the more they face the degradation of immediacy without the shroud of reverence. The more useless cowboys became to the cattle industry, the more cowboys could become symbolic of America's spirit of independence—real cowboys and real people familiar with the experiences knew better.

The symbolic language presenting the structure of the universe could be useful as a recursive, self-referential, language. That is, symbolic language that concerned symbol systems, how well they presented the universe or how we might continually improve the minimal ways their presentation was inaccurate, could be useful. Traditions, however, require an inability to be other directed, e.g., no practiced ethical systems could be actually justified because of a symbolic language.

It is impossible for a tradition to be rational and supply other-directed knowledge if rational means, minimally, the lack of some set of fallacies and the presence of some rules of inference subject to presentation in symbol form. If rational means reasonable, e.g., considering alternatives, evaluating particular instances in relation to general principles and offering justification for beliefs, traditions cannot be reasonable.

A tradition cannot move as if moving from one premise to the next because change within a tradition occurs cognitively in the realm of symbolic or imaginative behavior. Traditions change as if chaotic floating signifiers determine inferences, not track inferences associating particulars to general principles or codify comparative evaluations. That is, no historical array of discourses can match an array of argument designs nor proceed from one set of practices to another as if each practice represented a premise in a reasonable argument. Traditions are at their best when they do not match a strictly preformed model of inferencing within the boundaries of what the tradition symbolizes and do not substantively inform other-directed practices and beliefs.

One tradition can be based on more reasonable principles and sustain more reasonable practices than another; the boundaries of one tradition can afford a more useful array of imaginative options or restrictions than another. However, to treat "traditions" as entities such that they change in ways that parallel reasonable inferencing is to treat traditions as Hegelian modes of consciousness. There is certainly a distinction between conversation that can occur between two reasonable traditions and picturing a conversation between two reasonable traditions as the flow of an argument. The latter erroneously treats "traditions" *as if* they were real entities whereas the former treats "traditions" *as though* they were real entities. Inventions, treated as real, like nations supposing they are really the embodiment of absolute spirit and like performances in which the actor allows the part played to define how the actor shall live after the play is over, are imaginative scenarios that do not require treatment as substances, even if they have properties.[32] This is so because the content of traditions are extremely variable, i.e., what an array of symbols means or warrants can shift radically. American judges, for example, wear robes but are not servants of the queen; kente cloth symbolizes royalty but more often the regality of African people than the royalty of the Asanteheny. The properties of traditions, consequently, are always inadequate to form boundaries the way the boundaries of France can be neatly drawn and concretely maintained without change. (Imagine, saluting the U.S. flag as a sacred symbol of the country in 1776 and saluting the U.S. flag in 1992—the "country" includes children as citizens with rights, women as rights holders identical to men, Blacks as full moral persons—scandalous ideals that were not shared by writers of the Constitution.) The more a discourse is actually involved in shaping lived experience, the more it shades away from being a tradition and may be more properly described as custom, popular practice, contested guidelines, or possibly societal rules of conversation. So doing, of course, involves a loss of the description's surreptitious legitimation or defamation by parasitism on Tradition.

When a collection of philosophies is constituted as a national tradition, it is very difficult for such a tradition to incorporate authors and ideas that mitigate against the very foundation of repetitions intended to be the embodiment of the community or the community that's coming. "American Philosophy," for example, is confronted with just such a challenge in relation to that grain of African American philosophic activity which most involves a sense of struggle. That history and heritage challenges who counts, what issues are important, what life experiences are exemplary, what "America" and "philosophy" means, and what ideas and practices should be repeated. The character of the invention or staging is, in effect, challenged; not what play is to be performed. As indicated in what follows, African American philosophers such as Equiano, Crummell, Walker, and Locke were all staunch believers in fairly popular theologies or philosophies.[33] They challenged traditional views about who had the right to claims of truth, what styles actors should present, and the weight to be placed on different lines in the play—and about what the play means.

APHORISM VI

The Society for the Advancement of American Philosophy's (SAAP) *Newsletter* is adorned with the pictures of eleven archetypal American philosophers: Emerson, Thoreau, Peirce, James, Dewey, Royce, Whitehead, Santayana, Suckiel, and Dooley. Olaudah Equiano (Gustavus Vasa, the African), author of a slave–narrative form of ethical and social critique; David Walker, author of the impassioned call to arms by the enslaved; Alexander Crummell, Cambridge-educated Platonist and a moral suasionist; Alain Locke, critical relativist and radical pragmatist; do not adorn its cover. The latter group is absent, I believe, not because of a malicious intent on the part of SAAP but because the texts of Equiano, Walker, Crummell, and Locke are rarely considered to be philosophy. They arise out of a history of personal and intellectual struggle which is not university-bound, nor confined to the central issues in the history of philosophy, nor reflective of an accepted American grain. The American grain of doing philosophy, as John McDermott aptly describes, does not include righteous indignation to the point of killing or self-sacrifice.[34] To be nostalgic about the lives of Equiano, Walker, Crummell, or Locke is to be nostalgic about a struggle to create a different reality or a reality that includes those despised by both the gentry and radicals of the dominant culture; a struggle that applauds extremes in its name.

Equiano, Walker, Crummell, and Locke are western intellectuals. That is, the way they did philosophy was creatively their own, but through prisms of prose and ideas fairly common in western culture. They were, after all, Christians, Platonists, or pragmatists. The history and heritage of Christianity and of the Greco-Roman-Egyptian world involved their invented ancestors in a way similar to that in which it involved the invented ancestors of white Europeans and Americans. The *subjects* of their world, however, included the enslaved and the segregated as real agents—not phantoms whose rights would eventually be insured by the fiat of evolution, the rational application of the scientific method, social experiments guided by the dialogue of a community from which they were excluded, or the spiritually inspired principles of the progeny and kin of prevailing authorities.

David Walker's *Appeal to the Coloured Citizens of the World* (1848) advocated the violent overthrow of slavery by killing slave masters, running away from plantations, and disregarding claims of property rights when made by slave owners or their accomplices. Walker advocated maroonage, death blows, the rupture of stability, normalcy, and dispassionate rational dialogue. Walker favored the principles of Christianity, democracy, capitalism, and the popular virtues of thrift, frugality, and chastity; he wanted them actualized without regard to race. The future that Walker envisioned did not differ in structural character from popular visions except for the existence of racial slavery—which required a radical break with the rules of civility. Walker offered, in a sense, a negative dialectic.

Walker distanced himself from being "American" so long as "American" meant the legitimation, as it did, of slavery. An "American" was either a slaveowner or one empowered to potentially become a slaveowner. Walker belonged to a group that at best could only be peripheral slave owners, e.g., black owners of slaves could conceivably become slaves; but the worst possible fate white owners faced was indentured servitude. Analogous to the difference between indentured servitude and slavery is the difference between a slave and serf—the realms of personal freedom from harm and potential realizable life plans substantively differ.[35] Walker is an example of what I mean by righteous indignation—right thinking, right making, and right choices for radical change are explicit and intended as derivations from general principles.

If American philosophers are pictured as a motley crew of curious intellectuals, what do we do with those Americans whose very life and intellectual project suggests the sheltered, segregated, and insulated conundrum of the motley crew? What do we do with the ideas of American philosophers regarding race relations when those ideas were not always savory? We can, as has been the case, construct a tradition that remains blind to diversity—particularly to that sector of the American philosophic scene that compels re-valuation of the scene itself—while simultaneously applauding pluralism, difference, and community. The tradition I have decided to promote cannot afford this deceit.

I consciously participate in the tradition of American philosophy. The tip of the iceberg, however, is that I consciously participate in the creation of a tradition that did not exist as such before. It would be bad faith to contend that the tradition of African American philosophy existed prior to its formation and discussion as such, not because discourse defines existence or is fairly analogous to it, but because the texts that form its canon were not texts that "debated" one another. Some authors were in direct conversation, such as W. E. B. Du Bois and Booker T. Washington; but the Du Bois/Washington debate hardly forms a "tradition" in philosophy.[36] It can be constructed as one feature of a tradition, but only after a "tradition" is conceptualized. Neither Du Bois nor Washington saw themselves as philosophers, or offered an array of arguments around the kinds of issues definitive of professional philosophy. Alain Locke, I believe, is the sentinel historical figure in the history of African American professional philosophers because he conjoins an interest in the historically important issues of social well-being crucial to the African American intellectual agenda with central issues in the modern history of philosophy.

I participate in the creation of the tradition of African American philosophy because the definition of philosophy has been so restrictive that it excludes the possibility of insights from intellectuals that spoke to those disenfranchised, stereotyped, stigmatized as parasites, raciated as inferior, and immiserated. There are, I believe, a fair number of nascent and potentially compelling issues addressed by intellectuals that were themselves excluded from the moral and intellectual community of formal philosophy. I remain convinced that the imaginative scenarios encoded in the created tradition of African American philosophy offer the possibility of ideas of moment for human liberation—not because I expect these philosophies as a collective entity or the ideas of anyone in particular to be neatly mirrored in reality—but because their presence helps form imaginative scenarios of emancipation, i.e., their scenarios are, and are about, struggle for liberation. (Moreover, and independent of these concerns, I needed an intellectual community and the community of American philosophy was peculiarly alien.)

It is, however, as inappropriate to look for an Emerson within Black history as it is to look for a Walker within Native American history. It is also inappropriate to assume that every phase of philosophy is replicated, in some mirror-type fashion, among each racial or ethnic group. The idea that the presence of philosophy is evidence of humanity, proof of intellectual potential, or justification for a sense of pride is misguided.

Philosophy Born of Struggle constructed a tradition in the sense that the tradition it portrayed involved unconnected individuals, working through diverse institutions; but individuals with experiences of similar ilk and addressing similar issues.[37] The tradition is formed, not by repletion of a body of codified ideas which individuals intentionally or unintentionally repeated with unique variations, but by showing the sense in which they participated in addressing situations similar to those of their predecessors of the same discipline. It is a construction. It is an adversarial construction, i.e., it is intended to give voice to concerns that have been, within the western tradition of philosophy, considered illegitimate sources of truth because they referenced individuals and situations that call into question the legitimacy, universality, and meaning of the western tradition.

The Philosophy of Alain Locke is an anthology intended to give voice to Alain Locke's philosophy of critical relativism, a form of radical pragmatism.[38] It is first rooted in debates about race in a racist society, and secondly, debates about the merits of science, the importance of individuality, or the value of experience as a reference point for a coherentist view of truth. Race gives voice to an area of concern that helps shape the special features of Locke's radical pragmatism just as the importance of provincialism and nationalism help shape the special features of Dewey's ethical arguments. An appeal to authors that form the African American tradition is an appeal to authors that in many respects confront and reshape the meaning of western, and in particular, American philosophy.

If the picture of the archetypal American philosophers on the front of SAAP's *Newsletter* included Equiano, Crummell, Walker, or Locke, it would no longer be a picture of fairly gentle, contemplative, raucous, cantankerous intellectuals and public activists. It would include the embattled, excluded, protesting, and the image of those still too often considered less than human. There would be something peculiar about a picture of the archetypes enjoying themselves on a beach. It's not only that if they were all alive at the same time some of them would not be caught dead on a beach with others because of sexism and genuine philosophic or personal differences, but because the blacks would not have been allowed on the beach with white women and men. It is this terribly wrenching facet of the national history of America that makes the collective identity of "America" lose some of its luster, some of its myth-making and symbolic power. Alienation from, and redefinition of, America is captured by works that address the continual redefinition of the moral community.[39] A rapprochement or a new moment of the tradition would require a different way of perceiving America.

The African American tradition, however, does not escape a tendency toward conservatism, valorization, and canonization. The character of racism confronted by Equiano and Locke, for example, differs from the character of racism confronted by Broadus Butler and Angela Davis. Locke's arguments, decontextualized, can be well designed. There are certainly strong reasons for believing that Locke has the most warrantable claims. If he does not then his works lose appeal, regardless of how well they might function as foils. If Locke's authorial voice, as a subtext, is honestly treated and works well to help reshape the western and American tradition, destroy its hegemonic control over who and what count as important, forces consideration of the racism that infests western philosophy, it is an authorial voice that should be a text and a subtext. If, in the future, the hegemonies of American philosophy are defeated, and it turns out that Locke's ideas have received regard, the functional utility of Locke should cease; the consensus should be lived as new musicians mount the stage in their own names.

Newly invented traditions are, like all traditions, reformations of previous authorial voices. Traditions whose loyalties are with the least well-off are intended as praise songs for the widow—rituals of moment for adversarial struggles to overcome immiseration and domination. This view of adversarial traditions does not require essentializing the least well-off, as if they were invested with some purity of vision or as if persons who see themselves as promoting the interest of the least well-off were invested with some special truths. Rather, it requires believing that traditions emanating from adversary voices are likely to perceive community as a becoming which includes the least well-off as subjects. If the imagined community that is the home of one's loyalty is the community of the downtrodden, wretched, degraded, raped, victims of cruelty, the object of viciousness, they are subjects integral to the conceptualized community that is to become. Present traditions may be considered corruptions of a previously existing pristine state of affairs or demeaning practices of a chronically racist society; in either case, if the least well-off are considered agents in the moral community the future is a becoming in a way that counts the immiserated—any future consensus takes their voices as meaningful in defining what counts as consensus.

A progressive tradition should include conditions for self-reformation, given the impossibility of self-destruction. Traditions are intrinsically conservative; as a tradition becomes a Tradition, it loses its substance. A progressive tradition, I suggest, should entail recognition of its own formation and continuation as an ongoing invention; an ongoing process of remaking theatrics which should abandon its representatives and valorized forms of consensus in the service of vitalization. Metaphorically, the living actors should clearly stand apart from the characters they portray and take a bow as agents. Failure to do so perpetuates the facade that the living are only embodiments of the past; that the current consensus is given in the nature of being.

A progressive tradition should be metaphorically a jazz tradition. Traditions in jazz are moments to relive the past; moments to pass through, instantiate, overcome, and moments of creation. The being expressed by the agent and the truth that is hidden is a truth that must, as a condition of crucial importance to the definition of jazz, be a truth either uniquely expressed by the agent or itself a function of unique expressions. The uniqueness or newness of an expression is not an intransitive good. Rather, it is a good within the arrangement of goods that make for a jazz tradition. That arrangement includes appreciation of the past, but not its valorization; the being of the jazz agent is not constricted by a particular medium (e.g., Miles Davis is not an inauthentic jazzman on Tutu nor inauthentic for integrating Jimi Hendrix's sound). Jazz evolves, transforms, transfigures, transvalues, and decenters; it constructs, builds, molds, and creates new anew. Designs and content should be continually reformed, i.e., jazzed; neither fantastic nor sheerly relative.[40]

Burn Babylon, otherwise known as Athens. The burning is the building of Benin.

APHORISM VII

Can the discursive formations of nihilists form a tradition? Nihilism, as I mean it here, is a philosophy that mitigates against the idea that there are unchanging or revisable universal principles and supports the idea of sheer relativized principles and a perception of the past as completely invented.

The object of a philosophy is usually to become repeated, orated, performed, acknowledged, and accepted (inclusive of earnest or fortuitous nods to rationality, critique, and continual self-reflection). Value-relativists that are not nihilists, for example, can participate in and form traditions if they want others to accept their position and form a consensus communicated across generations. It is counterintuitive for a nihilist, paganist, Marxist, pragmatist, critical theorist, or rationalist to deny that as many people as possible should, over time, hold their position. The possibility of a plurality of radically divergent paganists in proximity to one another, for example, requires that each does not (or does not succeed if they try) destroy others different from themselves. If a paganist community holds what it considers a preferable philosophy, it would seem preferable that as many people as possible hold and practice its philosophy. For that to be the case, each successive generation would engage in tradition-formation and maintenance with the intent of having its values survive in practice across generations, even if the community did not engage in proselytizing.

It is not unusual for nihilists with various approaches to refer to the works of other nihilists as commendable; it is also not unusual for postmodernists to analyze the same authors as exemplars of modernity or the emergence of postmodernity. For nihilism to be intrinsically self-critical, it would be necessary for it to include a claim that its archetypes and reference sources are used in the process of making and remaking; a process that cannot combat its own conservatism. An argument for nihilism can be offered that does not rely on references to earlier texts, even if it gave credence to earlier authors and argument forms that provide support. However, the form of legitimation that characterizes tradition—symbols that function at their best when they are useless—would continue to be the subtext by which the argument for nihilism surreptitiously gained unintentional warrant—the stage is already set because a sense of continuity is easily imagined by virtue of an admittedly disjointed history. Nihilists, unable to combat their own conservatism or live in a world that has not already set the stage, cannot act toward themselves the way they want persons to act toward the world—as agents of sheer relativity living through sheer relativity. The discursive formations of nihilism form a tradition even if, counterintuitively, nihilists are not interested in perpetuating their philosophy. That is, the discursive formations of nihilism, if understood as forming a tradition, do not escape the conservatism its content vies against.[41]

Tradition and its derivations should be *A Preface to a Twenty-Volume Suicide Note*.[42] At least we would know whether we were about to witness the performance of a good horror movie or another philosophy of terror—inhabited by categorically impossible beings—possibly good models for vicarious identity but scary beings otherwise. If they were *A Preface to a Twenty-Volume Suicide Note*, this might be of some small aid in deciding to live as if, rather than as though, we were agents; acting as if, rather than as though, the totality of possible conscious life were already manifest in existing or historically pristine contrivances, gadgets, and doohickeys.

Purdue University

NOTES

1 Pascal Boyer, *Tradition as Truth and Communication* (Cambridge: Cambridge University Press, 1990), p. 3.

2 Eric Hobsbawm & Terence Ranger (eds.), *The Invention of Tradition* (Cambridge: Cambridge University Press, 1983), p. 4; also see George Allan, *The Importances of the Past* (Albany: State University of New York Press, 1986), p. 156.

3 Boyer, *Tradition as Truth and Communication*, p. 117.

4 Magili S. Larson, *The Rise of Professionalism* (Berkeley: University Press of California, 1977), p. 9.

5 Allan, *The Importances of the Past*, p. 200.

6 See for example Wolf Lepenies, " 'Interesting Questions' in the History of Philosophy and Elsewhere," in R. Rorty, J. B. Schneewind, & Q. Skinner (eds.), *Philosophy in History* (Cambridge: Cambridge University Press, 1986), pp. 141–72.

7 Allan, *The Importances of the Past*, p. 242.

8 See Jacques Derrida, *Writing and Difference* (Chicago: University of Chicago Press, 1978).

9 Richard Rorty, *Philosophy and the Mirror of Nature* (Princeton, N.J.: Princeton University Press, 1979).

10 See David Hollinger, *The American Intellectual Tradition* (New York: Oxford University Press, 1989).

11 See Edward W. Said, *Orientalism* (New York: Pantheon Books, 1978), and Stanley Diamond, *Culture in History* (New York: Columbia University Press, 1960).

12 See Marshall Hodgson, *The Venture of Islam* (Chicago: University of Chicago Press, 1974); also Clifford James, *The Predicament of Culture: Twentieth-Century Ethnography, Literature, and Art* (Cambridge, Mass.: Harvard University Press, 1988).

13 See Paulin Hountondji, *African Philosophy: Myth and Reality* (Bloomington: Indiana University Press, 1983), particularly his critique of ethnophilosophy, and Claude Levi-Strauss, *The Savage Mind* (Chicago: Chicago University Press, 1966); also see Boyer, *Tradition as Truth and Communication*. For arguments that rely on trad but are concerned with starting points and communication between trads, see H. J. Gadamer, *Philosophical Hermeneutics*, tr. David E. Linge (Berkeley: University of California Press, 1976).

14 Placide Tempels, *Bantu Philosophy* (Paris: Presence Africaine, 1959); also see Deusdedit Nkurunziza, *Bantu Philosophy* (New York: Lang, 1989).

15 By the "invention" approach to tradition I mean the approach taken by the following: Hobsbawm & Ranger, *The Invention of Tradition;* V. Y. Mudimbe, *The Invention of Africa* (Bloomington: Indiana University Press, 1988); Christian Delacampagne, *L'Invention de Racisme: Antiquité et Moyen Age* (Paris: Fayard, 1983); Roy Wagner, *The Invention of Culture* (Chicago: University of Chicago Press, 1975); Werner Sollors (ed.), *The Invention of Ethnicity* (Oxford: Oxford University Press, 1989); Denys Hay, *Europe: Emergence of an Idea* (Edinburgh: Edinburgh University Press, 1968); & Allan, *The Importances of the Past*. For the importance of reiteration, repetition, causal criteria of truth, and rituals as the conveyors of tradition, see Boyer, *Tradition as Truth and Communication*.

16 Hobsbawn & Ranger, *The Invention of Tradition,* p. 1.

17 See Patricia Williams, *Alchemy of Race and Rights* (Cambridge, Mass.: Harvard University Press, 1991); & George Soros, *Alchemy of Finance* (New York: Simon & Schuster, 1987).

18 See Richard Shenkman, *Legends, Lies & Cherished Myths of American History* (New York: Harper & Row, 1989).

19 Benedict Anderson, *Imagined Communities* (London: Verso, 1983), p. 145. For ideas of community and agency, see L. Harris, "Historical Subjects and Interests: Race, Class, and Conflict," in Michael Sprinkler et al. (eds.), *The Year Left* (New York: Verso, 1986), pp. 91–106; & "Columbus and the Identity of the Americas," *The Annals of Scholarship,* 1992.

20 Ladislav Holy, *Kingship, Honour and Solidarity* (Manchester: Manchester University Press, 1989), p. 125.

21 I borrow this term from James' *Predicament of Culture*.

22 James, *The Predicament of Culture,* p. 268.

23 See Richard Nisbett and Lee Ross, "Judgmental Heuristics and Knowledge Structures," in Hilary Kornblith, *Naturalizing Epistemology* (Cambridge: Massachusetts Institute of Technology Press, 1985), 195; Richard Nisbett and Lee Ross, *Human Inference* (Englewood Cliffs, N.J.: Prentice-Hall, 1985), pp 17–42; Daniel Kahneman, Paul Slovic, & Amos Tversky, *Judgment Under Uncertainty* (Cambridge: Cambridge University Press, 1982).

24 Noël Carroll, *The Philosophy of Horror or Paradoxes of the Heart* (New York: Routledge, 1990), p. 206.

25 This distinction does not deny the existence of akratic action. Someone can genuinely believe in the existence of a monster in a movie, believe that the monster in the movie is immediately before them, be genuinely scared, and sit through the movie although their fear has not made them immobile. Akratic actions do not, however, generally characterize people confronted with terror or the immanent likelihood that it will be directed at them.

26 Kwasi Wiredu, *Philosophy and an African Culture* (Cambridge: Cambridge University Press, 1980).

27 The analogy with parasitism is intended to suggest that parasites can be more or less harmful, and more or less dependent, on a host; conversely, a host can more or less benefit from a parasite. The relation is unstable and elastic, depending on the nature of the host and the parasite.

28 Franz Fanon, *Wretched of the Earth* (New York: Grove Press, 1963). For an interesting counterpoint to Fanon as well as a good deal of invention literature, see Edward W. Blyden, *Christianity, Islam and the Negro Race* (1887) (Edinburgh: Edinburgh University Press, 1967).

29 Blyden, *Christianity, Islam, and the Negro Race;* Mudimbe, *Invention of Africa*.

30 Alasdair C. MacIntyre, *After Virtue* (Notre Dame, Ind.: University of Notre Dame Press, 1981), pp. 214–18.

31 My conception of lived experience is closer to Dewey's and its importance is informed by Alain Locke; it is not intended as a paraphrase of MacIntyre's view of a living tradition.

32 See David-Hillen Ruben, "The Existence of Social Entities," *Philosophical Quarterly* 34:129 (Oct. 1982), 295–310.

33 Gustavus Vassa, *Equiano's Travels* (London: Heinemann, 1967); David Walker & Henry H. Garnet, *Walker's Appeal & Garnet's Address to the Slaves of the United States of America* (Salem, N.H.: Ayer, 1969); Alexander Crummell, *Africa and America: Addresses and Discourses* (Miami: Mnemosyne Publishing Co., 1969).

34 John J. McDermott, *Culture of Experience* (New York: New York University Press, 1976).

35 For an example of the distinction between serf and slave, see Peter Kolchin, *Unfree Labor* (Cambridge, Mass.: Harvard University Press, 1987).

36 See, for example, Lucius Outlaw, "African American Philosophy," *Social Science Information* 26:1 (1987), 75–97; & William R. Jones, "The Legitimacy and Necessity of Black Philosophy," *Philosophical Forum,* 9:2–3 (Winter–Spring 1977–78) 149–60. For a discussion of my conception of the history of black philosophy, see Leonard Harris, "The Lacuna Between Philosophy and History," *Journal of Social Philosophy* XX:3 (Winter 1989), 109–14; for a critique of my view, see Paul Jefferson, "The Question of Black Philosophy," *Journal of Social Philosophy* XX:3 (Winter 1989) 99–109. For an interesting discussion of identity, see David B. Wong, "On Flourishing and Finding One's Identity in Community," *Midwest Studies in Philosophy* XIII (1988):324–41.

37 Leonard Harris, *Philosophy Born of Struggle* (Iowa: Kendall Hunt Publishing Company, 1983).

38 Leonard Harris, *The Philosophy of Alain Locke* (Philadelphia: Temple University Press, 1989).

39 For examples of the way African Americans have been, in practice and conception, excluded from the moral community, see Trudier Harris, *Exorcising Blackness* (Bloomington: Indiana University Press, 1984), & Orlando Patterson, *Slavery and Social Death* (Cambridge, Mass.: Harvard University Press, 1982).

40 This view of jazz traditions is analogous to traditions of particle physics, i.e., traditions of transitivity in search of the primordial such that the primordial is a subject for continual revaluation.

41 For a view of nihilism as banal, dogmatic, and a philosophy that makes serious ethical questions a matter of aesthetic taste, see Karen L. Carr, *The Banalization of Nihilism* (Albany: State University of New York Press, 1992).

42 See Amiri Baraka, *A Preface to a Twenty-Volume Suicide Note: The Music* (New York: Morrow, 1987).

TWO TRADITIONS IN AFRICAN AMERICAN POLITICAL PHILOSOPHY

BERNARD BOXILL

The history of African American political thought can be divided into two great traditions—the assimilationist and the separatist. The assimilationist tradition maintains that a society in which racial differences have no moral, political, or economic significance—that is, a color-blind society—is both possible and desirable in America.[1] The separatist tradition denies this, some separatists maintaining that a color-blind society in America is not possible, others maintaining that it is not desirable.

Sometimes the differences between the traditions are only strategic, as, for example, where an ostensibly separatist theory recommends self-segregation as a means to eventual assimilation. Sometimes, however, the differences are profound, stemming from conflicting philosophical views about morality and human nature. I will illustrate this thesis by comparing the theories of the separatist Martin Delany, and the assimilationist Frederick Douglass, both of the nineteenth century.

DELANY

Delany's separatism depends on his explanation of the enslavement of Africans by Europeans in America, and on his account of the consequences of that enslavement.

Delany's explanation of African enslavement is set out in his book, *The Condition, Elevation, Emigration and Destiny of the Colored People of The United States,* and can be summarized as follows: the Europeans who first arrived in America were "not of the common people, seeking in a distant land the means of livelihood, but moneyed capitalists, the grandees and nobles."[2] To take full advantage of the opportunities America offered, they decided to enslave another class. Two obvious alternatives occurred to them, the Indians they found in America, and their own subservient class in Europe. But neither class was satisfactory. On the one hand, while the Indians were sufficiently "foreign" to their "sympathies"[3] to be exploited harshly without undue psychological penalty, they were "wholly unaccustomed to labor," and being "unable to withstand the hardships,"[4] died in great numbers. Besides, they had such meager skills in mining and agriculture that enslaving them was often hardly profitable.[5] On the other hand, while European workers had the requisite skills, they were not sufficiently foreign to the sympathies of their masters to be exploited with the severity which conditions in the New World demanded. Finally the Europeans decided to enslave Africans. Africans were an "industrious people, cultivators of the soil,"[6] and had "long been known to Europeans . . . as a long-lived, hardy race, subject to toil and labor of various kinds, subsisting mainly by traffic, trade, and industry. . . ." Moreover, they also possessed "distinctive characteristics" like "color" and "character of hair" which strongly marked them off from Europeans and made them "as foreign to the sympathies" of the Europeans as Indians. . . ."[7] This combination of characteristics sealed their fate. From the point of view of the Europeans they were "the very best class that could be selected" for enslavement in America,[8] and they were accordingly captured and brought there for this purpose.

The most striking aspect of this argument is the omission of any mention of morality as a possible constraint on the Europeans' desire to enslave Africans. Delany never even suggests that Europeans had to overcome their moral inhibitions against slavery in order to make slaves of Africans. This was not because he thought that Europeans were especially immoral; it was because he thought that most people were little restrained by moral considerations when they were dealing with those weaker than themselves. Thus he denounced moral suasion as a way for blacks to win their liberty, and disparaged black claims of moral equality as "useless," "nonsense," and "pitiable mockery," "*until*" black men and women attained "to a position" above doing the "drudgery" and "menial" work of whites.[9] In taking this stance Delany knew that he was swimming against the stream. The dominant school of abolitionists led by William Lloyd Garrison, and including Delany's friend Frederick Douglass, emphasized moral suasion. And this emphasis seemed good strategy. Europeans had long discontinued the practice of slavery among themselves, and their philosophers condemned it as the crowning injustice; in the words of John Locke, it was a "vile and miserable estate."[10] But evidently relying on his own observations of the way Europeans treated Africans, Delany remained skeptical of the constraints of morality.

Delany thought that when the strong can profit from mistreating the weak, the only hope for the weak is the sympathy of the strong. But sympathy spared only some of the weak. According to Delany sympathy moves the strong to select as the objects of exploitation and oppression those who "differed as much as possible, in some particulars, from themselves. This is to ensure the greater success, because it engenders the greater prejudice, or in other words, elicits less interest on the part of the oppressing class, in their favor.''[11]

Two points about Delany's account of sympathy are especially important. First the absence of sympathetic ties is not in itself a motive for aggression. It only removes the constraints on aggression when aggression serves self-interest. Thus Delany specifically denied that it was ''on account of hatred to his color, that the African was selected as the subject of oppression.''[12] He insisted that Africans were enslaved because this served the self-interest of Europeans; the difference in color between Africans and Europeans only dampened European sympathy for Africans. He even believed that the powerful would help the weak who were foreign to their sympathies when doing so served their self-interest. Thus he argued that both England and France would support his project for creating an African state and developing the resources of the continent because ''they would have everything to gain from such an adventure, the opening of an immense trade being the consequence.''[13]

The second important point about Delany's account of sympathy concerns those apt to be bound by sympathetic ties. David Hume thought that these ties mainly depended on the degree of contiguity and familiarity between the persons involved; thus he wrote in the *Enquiry* that ''sympathy with persons remote from us [is] much fainter than that with persons near and contiguous,'' and in the *Treatise* that, concerning the attention we give to others, '' 'tis only the weakest which reaches to strangers and indifferent persons.''[14] In particular, he did not remark that the strength of sympathetic ties also seemed to depend on the degree of resemblance between the persons involved, although his cruel and dismissive disparagement of ''negroes'' suggests that this dependence may not be insignificant.[15] Delany could not have failed to appreciate this fact about how our sympathies run. He saw every day that white sympathy for black misfortune was faint and weak, though the races were, by that time, no longer strangers to, nor remote from, one another. The explanation for this poor showing of sympathy, he maintained, lay in the obvious physical differences in appearance between whites and blacks. ''Being distinguished by our complexion,'' he wrote, ''we are still singled out—although having merged in the habits and customs of our oppressors.''[16]

Faced with this overwhelming and recalcitrant prejudice, Delany recommended the complete emigration of blacks from America. ''A new country and a new beginning,'' he declared, ''is the only true, rational, politic remedy for our disadvantageous position.''[17]

This recommendation was based on the assumptions about morality and human motivation that he had used to explain African enslavement. These assumptions not only explain why Europeans enslaved Africans, they also severely limit the options for black elevation. For example, his view that the moral demands the weak make against the strong are ''pitiable mockery'' clearly rules our moral suasion as a means of black elevation. Similarly, while his argument that Europeans enslaved Africans partly because Africans had economically valuable skills and were markedly different from them in physical appearance implies that Europeans would stop enslaving Africans if Africans became similar in appearance to Europeans, or lost the skills and qualities that made enslaving them profitable, neither of these possibilities offered any basis for hope. The first was evidently unachievable. As Delany noted, blacks could dress like whites and acquire their habits, but they could not become physically similar to whites. The second failed for a different reason. While it was achievable, it would end in disaster. It would put Africans in America in danger of genocide.[18] The fate of the Indians attested to this. But Delany's assumptions left at least one possibility for black salvation. If it was in the nature of things that Africans would always be liable to abuse of one sort or other by Europeans, they could nevertheless avoid abuse by going beyond the reach of Europeans.

Unfortunately this alternative also suffered from fatal drawbacks. The first was obvious. Slaves could not emigrate; their masters were not prepared to let them out of their clutches. The second was less obvious, and in a way more disturbing. Free blacks, those who could emigrate if they wanted to, did not want to emigrate. As Delany admitted, his proposals for emigration to Mexico, California, and South America were ''always hooted at, and various objections raised: one on account of distance, and another that of climate.''[19] He could not have been surprised. His theory of the consequences of slavery suggested that it was predictable that his proposals would meet with this response.

According to that theory, the major consequence of slavery was that many blacks became reconciled to their condition, and even came to love their masters. ''The slave,'' Delany wrote, ''may become a lover of his master, and learn to forgive him for continual deeds of maltreatment and abuse.''[20] Because he placed the highest value on freedom (''We had rather be a Heathen freeman, than a Christian slave,'' he declared[21]) Delany deplored and mourned this consequence of slavery, and called it ''degradation.''[22] Delany explained that this consequence of slavery was a result of the mind's adaptability. ''A continuance in any position,'' he wrote, ''becomes what is termed ''Second Nature''; it begets an adaptation and reconciliation of mind to such position.''[23] Delany evidently believed that this principle held true for animal nature in general, explaining why both the ''lofty-soaring Eagle'' and the slave may be tamed to their confinement and learn to love it.''[24] Delany also believed that this adaptation of mind went deep, and was passed on from parent to child. ''The degradation of the slave parent,'' he observed grimly, ''has been entailed upon the child, induced by the subtle policy of the oppressor . . . until it has become almost a physiological function of our system, an actual condition of our nature.''[25] Indeed, he believed that this degradation persisted among free blacks driving them to seek the domination and authority of whites although this invariably meant accepting positions as menials and servants. ''We have dwelt much upon the menial position of our people in this country,'' he lamented, ''because there is a seeming satisfaction and seeking after such positions manifested on their part. . . .''[26]

But if his theory of the consequences of slavery implied that free blacks would not want to stray far from whites, it also implied that they would balk at emigration. Delany understood this. He pointed out that many of those who objected to emigration to Mexico and South America, complaining that these regions were too hot and too far away, had apparently no objection to going to either place if they could go as servants to whites. They ''engage themselves to their white American oppressors—officers in the war against Mexico,'' he observed, where ''in the capacity of servants,'' they endured not only the climate of that country, but risked also the ''dangers of the battlefield.''[27] Had the Americans ''taken Mexico,'' Delany concluded ruefully, ''no people would have flocked there faster than the colored people of the United States.''[28]

Delany had evidently arrived at an impasse. On the one hand, emigration was one clear path to black salvation; on the other hand blacks either could not or would not take this path to their salvation. Somehow Delany had to find a way around this impasse. His solution is in his revised strategy in the appendix to his book.

While emigration was still the most important part of the revised strategy, there were three important changes. First, the revised strategy called on only a section of the people to emigrate, instead of all freemen, only ''enlightened freemen,''[29] or ''colored adventurers.''[30] Second, the revised strategy urged the selected emigres to go to a different place, instead of Central and South America, the ''Eastern Coast of Africa.''[31] Finally the revised strategy set them a different task once they reached their destination: instead of merely becoming useful and prosperous citizens of already existing nations, they were to create a great and powerful black nation.

It is tempting to suppose that Delany's revised strategy called on only ''enlightened freemen'' and ''colored adventurers'' to emigrate because he had given up on the majority of the freemen as too degraded to see that the only path to their elevation was emigration. But this would not explain the other two innovations in the revised strategy, the new destination and the new task. The change of destination is especially puzzling. In the body of the book, Delany had argued at length, and with every show of conviction, that Central and South America were far better places for black Americans to emigrate to than was Africa. Answering his own question, ''Where shall we go?'', he answered, ''We must not leave this continent: America is our destination and our home'';[32] and again, ''Upon the American continent we are determined to stay, in spite of every odds against us.''[33] Why then the sudden change to Africa?

The answer to this question is that Delany had shifted to a second strategy to secure black elevation. This strategy was also based on the fundamental assumptions of his philosophy. As we have seen, these assumptions imply that the weak who are foreign to the sympathies of the strong can avoid exploitation by the strong if they can get beyond the reach of the strong. But they also imply that these same weak can avoid exploitation by the strong if they become strong.

Consistently with this strategy, Delany was an early advocate of black power. More particularly, perceiving wealth as a source of power, and capitalist development as a means to wealth, he was also an early advocate of black capitalism. But he saw too that the odds did not favor the success of black capitalism in America. As he put it, ''To compete now with the mighty odds of wealth, social and religious preferences, and political influences of this country, at this advanced stage of its national existence, we may never expect.''[34] It was the hopelessness of the strategy of acquiring power in the U.S. which drove Delany unwillingly to the strategy of mass emigration. When that strategy also showed every prospect of failing, Delany returned to the strategy of black power, but with a twist. Seeing that the odds were against black power in the U.S., he concluded logically that it had to be developed outside the U.S. This left two questions: Where was black power to be developed, and how was it to be developed? Black power could not be developed just anywhere; a suitable place had to have the necessary economic potentialities, and, of course, an overwhelmingly black population. And, however black power was to be developed, it could not require mass black emigration from the U.S., for as we have seen Delany knew that this was not in the offing.

After surveying the options, Delany decided that the best place to develop black power was Africa. He came to this decision without any sentimental appeal to the idea of Africa as the fatherland of black people. The facts he appealed to were all directly related to the aim of finding a place where black power could be secured—Africa's vast size, and its agricultural, mining, and commercial possibilities. Delany also believed that Africa's climate discouraged white settlement, making it a special reserve for black people. In his opinion it was a ''physiological fact'' that black people could ''bear more different climates than the white race,'' and in particular that they could work and flourish in the warm climate of Africa where the white race became ''perfectly indolent, requiring somebody to work for them.''[35] Finally the choice of Africa as the place to develop black power also made mass black emigration from the U.S. unnecessary, for Africa's population was overwhelmingly black.

DOUGLASS

The most conspicuous disagreement between Delany and Douglass was on the issue of emigration as a strategy for black elevation. Douglass rejected that strategy.[36] His main objection was that it falsely assumed that, "there is no hope for the Negro here. . . ."[37] Part of the reason for his optimism was that, unlike Delany, he was convinced of the efficacy of moral suasion.

Douglass thought that morality was justified by certain facts about human nature. In particular, he believed that people have human rights because of their human nature. This was a crucial move. Since all people equally have human nature, it enabled Douglass to conclude that all people—blacks included—equally have human rights. Here is how he put it:

> Human rights stand upon a common basis; and by all the reason that they are supported, maintained and defended, for one variety of the human family, they are supported, maintained and defended for all the human family; because all mankind have the same wants, arising out of a common nature."[38]

Douglass also maintained that human nature was plainly or self-evidently possessed by all people—blacks pointedly not excepted. That was the point he was making when he wrote that "common sense itself is scarcely needed to detect the absence of manhood in a monkey, or to recognize its presence in a Negro."[39] This too was a crucial move. It enabled Douglass to conclude that, once the case for human rights was made, there was no need for independent argument to claim that blacks had human rights. As he put it, the Negro is "at once self-evidently a man, and therefore entitled to all the rights and privileges which belong to human nature."[40]

Douglass's claims on the self-evidence of human nature and human rights indicate that he had been deeply affected by the Declaration of Independence. The opening words of the Declaration read, "We hold these truths to be self-evident, that all men are created equal; that they are endowed by their Creator with certain inalienable rights." Given the influence of John Locke on the writers of the Declaration of Independence, it is not surprising that Douglass's claims about the self-evidence of human nature and human rights bear a striking resemblance to claims advanced by Locke. Locke not only maintained that the law of nature is "evident" or "plain,"[41] he also suggested that this was because human beings plainly shared a common humanity. Thus Locke argued that nothing is "more evident, than that creatures of the same species and rank promiscuously born to all the advantages of Nature, and the use of the same faculties, should also be equal one among the other with subordination or subjection.''[42] And, even more unmistakenly, citing the ''judicious Hooker'' with approval, he wrote ''This equality of men by nature the judicious Hooker looks upon as so evident in itself . . . that he makes it the foundation of that obligation to mutual love amongst men, on which he builds the Duties they owe one another, and from whence he derives the great Maxims of Justice and Charity.''[43] As I shall suggest, it was the influence of Lockean moral theory on Douglass that determined in large measure his confidence in moral suasion and consequently his hope for blacks in the United States. But Douglass was no pedestrian Lockean. His politics is more egalitarian and democratic than Locke's, and his account of oppression or tyranny more subtle and sophisticated. In addition, Douglass's conception of human nature was different from Locke's, and this put him in a position to provide an account of revolt and rebellion that Locke's theory of politics needed, but which Locke himself never attempted to produce.

Douglass's conviction that all persons, including blacks, self-evidently have human rights put him in a position to reject Delany's view that moral appeals by the weak to the strong are pointless, out-of-place, and probably nonsensical and delusive. If blacks self-evidently possess human rights, it can hardly be out-of-place or nonsensical or delusive for them to protest the violation of these rights. It may also not be pointless. For if blacks self-evidently possess human rights, appealing to the world to help stop the violation of these rights will not fall on deaf ears, and is likely even to shame the violators into desisting.[44]

Douglass's view that all persons self-evidently have human rights also gave him reason to reject Delany's suggestion that the slave and the oppressed readily become reconciled to their positions, and consequently degraded. For Douglass's view not only claims that everyone equally has human rights, it also suggests that everyone—the oppressed and the enslaved included—is likely to see that everyone equally has human rights. But if the oppressed and the enslaved see that everyone equally has human rights, they will see that they themselves have human rights. Assuming that human rights include rights not to be enslaved or oppressed, it follows that the oppressed and enslaved will hardly believe that they suffer no wrong in being enslaved and oppressed. But if they do not believe that they suffer no wrong in being enslaved and oppressed, they will hardly be reconciled to being enslaved and oppressed.

This result is significant enough, but it has important consequences that Douglass used to further strengthen his case for the efficacy of moral suasion. Given that the enslaved and oppressed are very likely to feel wronged by, and therefore resentful of, their enslavement and oppression, it follows that they will have a tendency to resist those who enslave and oppress them. This implies that successful enslavers and oppressors must have devised strategies for crushing that tendency. As Douglass knew for the case of black slavery these strategies involved the infliction of pain or violent death when the slaves showed any sign of dissatisfaction with their condition. To his mind this proved that slavery was not only cruel, but that it was necessarily cruel. Thus, after detailing the cruelties of slavery he concluded that, "it is necessary to resort to these cruelties, in order to make the slave a slave, and to keep him a slave. . . . The slaveholder feels this necessity. I admit this necessity."[45] And he used slavery's unavoidable cruelties to strengthen his moral campaign against it, displaying and recounting them in order to engage the sympathies of an otherwise disinterested world, and to impel it thereby to see that slavery violated self-evident human rights, and therefore should be abolished.

Quite early in his career, however, Douglass began to have doubts about the efficacy of this campaign. The immediate cause of these doubts was probably that the campaign was making little headway against slavery. But they also reflected Douglass's growing awareness that the idea that everyone self-evidently has human rights may not have all the consequences it seemed to have promised. If the sympathies of the world have to be engaged in order to make it see that slavery violated self-evident human rights, then it seems that the mere self-evidence of these rights does not guarantee that a great many people will not ignore their known violation. And an even more sobering limitation should have been evident from the first. The recalcitrance of the slavemasters, their self-righteous denials of wrongdoing, and most of all, the apparent equanimity many of them displayed when confronted with their wickedness, suggests that even if it is self-evident that everyone has human rights, some people may still fail to see, or at least may still refuse to see, that some other people have human rights.

These sobering reflections could have moved Douglass to abandon the idea that everyone self-evidently has human rights. Instead he argued that people could be blind to, or uncaring of, others' human rights, despite the fact that it is self-evident that everyone has human rights. This was Locke's position too. Locke maintained that the plainness of the "law of nature" was consistent with people being ignorant and disrespectful of it. According to Locke, "though the Law of Nature be plain and intelligible to all rational creatures; yet men being biassed by their interest, as well as ignorant of study for it, are not apt to allow of it as a Law binding to them in the application of it to their particular cases."[46]

Locke drew egalitarian consequences from his view. He argued that it helped to protect people against those who affected to be "Masters." According to Locke, "those who affected to be Masters" tended to claim that "general propositions that could not be doubted of, as soon understood" were "innate"; since innate propositions were supposed to be stamped on the mind, and known without any effort or study, the object was to take subjects "off from the use of their own reason and judgment, and put them upon believing and taking" things on trust. "In which posture of blind credulity," Locke continued, "they might be more easily governed by, and made useful to some sort of men, who had the skill and office to principle and guide them.''[47] Locke thought that his view saved people from such blind credulity because it insisted that they have to ''study'' the law of nature in order not to be ''ignorant'' of it, and consequently encouraged them to use their reason.

But the idea that people have to study and apply their faculties in order to know the law of nature, though that law is plain, offers obvious opportunities for the elitist. Locke seized these opportunities. Thus, in his *Questions Concerning the Law of Nature,* after maintaining that ''there exists a law of nature knowable by reason,'' and that ''reason is granted to all by nature,'' he allowed that ''it does not follow necessarily from this that it is known to each and all,'' concluding eventually that on the question of morality ''we must consult not the majority of mankind, but the sounder and more perceptive part.[48]

Locke was aware that governments often deliberately tried to keep people ignorant. In certain countries, he notes, even those with enough money and leisure to discover the truth are prevented from doing so because they are ''cooped in close, by the Laws of their countries, and the strict guard of those, whose interest is to keep them ignorant. . . .''[49] But he did not extend this excuse for ignorance to the laboring classes generally or to slaves. Thus he maintained that '' 'Tis not to be expected that a Man, who drudges on, all his life, in a laborious trade, should be . . . knowing in the variety of things done in the world,'' and that a ''great part of Mankind,'' is confined to this drudgery ''by the natural and unalterable state of things in this world.''[50]

Douglass describes similar causes of moral ignorance in the slave institution. ''To enslave men,'' he noted, ''it is necessary to have their minds occupied with thoughts and aspirations short of the liberty of which they are deprived''[51]; if a slave ever ventures ''to vindicate his conduct when harshly and unjustly accused,'' or suggests ''a better way of doing a thing, no matter what,'' then he must be whipped for being ''impudent'' and ''officious.''[52] Slaves were ''trained from the cradle up, to think and feel that their masters are superior, and invested with a sort of sacredness,'' so that ''there are few who can outgrow or rise above the control which that sentiment exercises.''[53] The moral outrage that imbues these remarks contrasts strikingly with Locke's cool discussion and suggests that Douglass was making more egalitarian use of Locke's theory than Locke himself did.

And Douglass noticed a cause of moral ignorance that Locke never dreamed of. While Douglass maintained that greed and selfishness were the first causes of the slavemasters' moral blindness, he suggested that they found another excuse to remain blind if their slaves submitted. According to Douglass, ''the very submission of the slave to his chains is held as evidence of his fitness to be a slave; it is regarded as one of the strongest proofs of the divinity of slavery, that the Negro tamely submits to his fetters.''[54]

These considerations indicate that although Douglass never ceased to insist on the moral equality of oppressor and oppressed, he also came to concede that greed, selfishness, exhaustion, fear, a preoccupation with other things, and the responses of the oppressor and oppressed to their relative positions could blind them to that equality. This may seem to imply that the mature Douglass would have to endorse Delany's view that moral suasion is ineffective and irrelevant to the abolition of slavery. Nothing could be further from the truth. Although Douglass did begin to supplement moral suasion with appeals for slave rebellion, he did so mainly because he believed that resistance was a form of moral suasion.

This belief follows logically from his view that the slave who submitted provided his enslavers with a ''proof'' that he was fit to be a slave. Douglass was clear that this ''proof'' was bogus. He believed that the right to liberty that slavery violated was self-evident because it was based on self-evident facts of human nature. As he declared, ''The existence of this right [the right to liberty] is self-evident. It is written upon all the powers and faculties of man.''[55] Now one of these powers and faculties was the desire for liberty. Although Douglass denied that the slave ever lost this desire, or consequently his right to liberty, he allowed that punishment for seeking liberty could persuade the slave not to seek liberty, and that the unremitting harassment, pain, and exhaustion the slave was subjected to could distract him from the very thought of liberty. ''When I was looking for the blow about to be inflicted on my head,'' Douglass confessed, ''I was not thinking of my liberty; it was my life.''[56] Thus the constant cruelty heaped on the slave served a purpose that was deeper than merely frightening him into submission. It also distracted him from the main desire that would otherwise move him to resist. Moreover, because the submissive or distracted slave failed to display the desire for liberty that was the basis of the right to liberty, his behavior gave his masters the semblance of an argument that they were justified in enslaving him. But it was only the semblance of an argument, and the slavemasters were dishonest and self-deceived in seizing on it. They knew very well why the slave failed to display a desire for liberty, and that it did not mean that he did not desire liberty. Still Douglass allowed that the argument was psychologically compelling especially to those who wanted to believe that it was sound—at one point he said it was ''human nature''[57] to be persuaded by it—and consequently that the best response to it was for the slave to resist. ''Resistance,'' he concluded, ''is, therefore wise as well as just.''[58]

The crucial point in the above discussion is that Douglass recommends resistance not simply because it may force the slavemasters to give up slavery, but because it denies them the semblance of a rational justification for slavery, and therefore moves them to give up slavery because they have less excuse to question the moral equality of the slave. Consequently, for Douglass, resistance can be a means to the moral regeneration of enslavers and so a form of moral suasion. And Douglass believed that slave resistance would help to make the slavemasters acknowledge the slave's moral equality in another way, viz., through arousing his fear. As he put it, "something must be done to make the slaveholders feel the injustice of their course. We must . . . as John Brown, Jr., has taught us this evening, reach the slaveholders' conscience through his fear of personal danger."[59]

But if the slave's submission could seduce the slavemaster into believing that the slave was his moral inferior, it could also seduce the slave into believing the same thing. Douglass understood this. That is why he thought that resistance was a particularly valuable kind of moral suasion. For he believed that just as it could help clear the slavemaster's moral vision, it could also help clear the slave's moral vision. The view is graphically presented in his account of the results of his fight with Covey, the slavebreaker. Covey, Douglass relates, had succeeded in breaking his spirit through whippings, starvation, and overwork. Finally, in desperation, Douglass fought back. He recalled that this produced a profound moral change in him. "It rekindled in my breast the smouldering embers of liberty. It . . . revived a sense of my own manhood. I was a changed being after that fight. I was nothing before—I was a man now. It recalled to life my crushed self-respect, and my self-confidence, and inspired me with a renewed determination to be a free man."[60]

Whatever their force, these views would have only a theoretical significance if the slave was unlikely to resist. But Douglass's assumptions about human nature suggested that slave resistance could not be put off indefinitely.

The crucial assumption has already been noted. Douglass believed that the human desire for liberty that was the basis of the right to liberty was powerful and almost ineradicable.[61] In his view this desire persisted even if the slave failed to see the self-evident fact that he had a right to liberty. Thus although Douglass yielded to the possibility of the degraded slave, he utterly rejected the possibility of the happy slave.[62] Further he was also clear that cruelty could only distract people from their desire for liberty, not extinguish it. As he put it, "as soon as the blow was not to be feared, then came the longing for liberty."[63] Douglass believed that the cruelty necessary to distract the slave from his desire to be free would eventually combine with his unhappiness for the loss of his freedom and overcome his fear of the only escape—death. At this point, having nothing to lose, the slave would fight back, and in fighting back, would, if Douglass's claims about the morally regenerative nature of resistance are true, regain the sense of his moral equality. This indeed was the route of Douglass's own moral rebirth. As he put it, citing the cause of the fight with Covey, "I had reached the point at which I was not afraid to die."[64]

ASSESSMENTS

In this essay I have tried to show by a discussion of the views of Delany and Douglass that the disagreement between separatism and assimilationism need not be only over strategies, but may also stem from profoundly different views about morality and human nature. Delany emphasized the enduring role of self-interest and sympathy in human affairs, and deemphasized the role of morality. Douglass on the other hand allowed the salience of self-interest and sympathy in human affairs, but also gave a potentially decisive role to morality because he believed that human beings all had the rational insight to see their self-evident moral equality. In this concluding section I comment on the relative merits of these competing views by considering how they deal with the bane of blacks in America—racism.

Racism presupposes a definition of race. According to that definition a race is a group of people who resemble each other with respect to several conspicuous, normally invariant, not readily disguised, physical, and biologically inherited features such as hair type, facial features, and especially skin color.

Some well-meaning people have tried to refute racism by arguing that there are no races. Usually their arguments simply substitute racism's definition of race with a new definition so designed that no group of people could be a race. This is not refuting racism, it is changing the subject.

Usually these same well-meaning people also argue that racism's definition of race is not scientifically useful. They are right because racists tend to make false claims about the races, typically that racially different people inherit different psychological traits and mental abilities. But these false claims are not essential to racism. They usually would not justify the racist's behavior even if they were true. For example, during the period of slavery, Europeans said that Africans were inherently slow-witted and servile. These claims were false, but even if they were true, they would not have justified the "middle passage," and the routine brutality of plantation slavery, notwithstanding the harsh standards of that harsh period. A contemporary example concerns the race/IQ dispute. Some authors affirm that the difference between the average IQ of blacks and whites is biologically determined. The evidence hardly justifies their confidence, but even if it did, discrimination on the basis of race would not be justified. Justice and fairness would still demand that individuals be judged on their merits.

It is illuminating to compare racism to egoism. The egoist often has false beliefs about himself and others which, were they true, would sometimes justify the partiality he shows to himself. But even if he is disabused of these false beliefs, he usually does not stop being unfairly partial to himself. He usually persists in this however clearly he sees himself and others. The racist tends to behave in a somewhat similar fashion. He often has false beliefs about the races, but he tends to persist in being unfairly partial to his race even if he is forced to give up these beliefs.

This suggests that the real reason the racist makes false claims abut the races is not to justify his behavior. My suggestion is that it is to express his contempt and distrust of races other than his own, to encourage the members of his own race to share that contempt and distrust, and to tighten the bonds between them. Thus the false claims associated with racism should not be thought of as parts of racism, but rather as among its causes; and not as informative but rather as expressive.

This point is worth emphasizing because the view that the false claims associated with racism are part of racism implies that racism would vanish if people stopped believing these false claims. This mistaken idea underestimates the persistence of racism. Persuading people of the truth about the races is the easy part in the fight against racism. The hard part is to persuade them not to be unfairly partial to members of their own race.

The importance Delany gives to sympathy in human affairs helps to explain why this is so. Sympathy moves us to identify with others, to be gladdened at their good fortune, and saddened at their misfortune. But, as Delany warned, sympathy is selective. It tends to move us to identify with those we think are most like us; that is, those in whom we notice a considerable resemblance. What this resemblance will be varies. It may be subtle, and it may not even be literally noticed, for it may exist only in the imagination of the beholder. But it is usually a real resemblance, and one that is not only real but also conspicuous, inborn, and invariant. This is so for the fairly obvious reason that, all else equal, average people will notice resemblances rather than imagine them; and, almost by definition, will more easily notice resemblances that are conspicuous, invariant and not readily disguised, rather than those that are subtle, variable, and readily disguised. But, as we have seen, the resemblances between those of the same race are conspicuous, invariant, and not readily disguised. Consequently, all else equal, most people will tend to identify with those of their own race, or will be more easily persuaded to identify with those of their own race rather than with those of other races.

Delany's theory therefore implies that people tend to be racists or that they are easily persuaded to be racists, and suggests what must be done to prevent this tendency from leading to their degradation, given the force of self-interest. Like Thomas Hobbes, that other great realist, who accepted the overwhelming egoism of human beings and tried to show how they could nevertheless have peace,

Delany accepted the marked liability to racism among human beings, and tried to show how they could nevertheless avoid degradation. Where Hobbes recommended a sovereign, Delany recommended an equality of racial groups. The people who object to Hobbes will object to Delany too. They will protest that he takes too cynical, and indeed, too pessimistic a view of human nature. They find it far more agreeable to maintain with Frederick Douglass that human nature has a higher side, rationality, which can be used to expand our imaginations, and enable us to identify with the whole human race. They are right, of course. We are morally equal, we can eventually come to see this, and the best society would rest on that shared insight. The question is whether it is in the offing. Delany warns us that the incredible proclivity of the human race to racism suggests that it is not.

University of North Carolina

NOTES

1 Obviously I am following Richard Wasserstrom's famous account of color-blindness in "On Racism and Sexism," in *Today's Moral Problems* (New York: Macmillan, 1979).

2 *The Condition, Elevation, Emigration and Destiny of the Colored People of the United States* (Salem, Mass.: Ayer Publishing Company, 1988), p. 51.

3 Delany, *Colored People of the United States,* p. 22.

4 Delany, *Colored People of the United States,* p. 20.

5 Delany, *Colored People of the United States,* p. 62.

6 Delany, *Colored People of the United States,* p. 53.

7 Delany, *Colored People of the United States,* p. 22.

8 Delany, *Colored People of the United States,* p. 22.

9 Delany, *Colored People of the United States,* p. 43.

10 John Locke, *Two Treatises of Government* (Cambridge: Cambridge University Press, 1988), Bk. I, Ch. I, p. 142.

11 Delany, *Colored People of the United States,* p. 22.

12 Delany, *Colored People of the United States,* p. 22.

13 Delany, *Colored People of the United States,* p. 212.

14 David Hume, *Enquiries concerning Human Understanding and concerning the Principles of Morals* (Oxford: Clarendon Press, 1975), p. 229; *A Treatise of Human Nature* (Oxford: Clarendon Press 1978), Bk. III, Pt. II, p. 488.

15 See his "Of National Characters," in *David Hume: Essays, Moral, Political and Literary* (Indianapolis: Liberty Press, 1985) p. 208.

16 Delany, *Colored People of the United States,* p. 209.

17 Delany, *Colored People of the United States,* p. 205.

18 Some contemporary authors fear that the danger exists today. See William A. Darity, "The Managerial Class and Surplus Population," *Society* 21:1, (Nov./Dec. 1983), 54–62.

19 Delany, *Colored People of the United States,* p. 184.

20 Delany, *Colored People of the United States,* p. 207.

21 Delany, *Colored People of the United States,* p. 181.

22 Delany, *Colored People of the United States,* p. 207.
23 Delany, *Colored People of the United States,* p. 207.
24 Delany, *Colored People of the United States,* p. 207. Compare Rousseau; according to him, ''Slaves lose everything in their chains, even the desire to be rid of them. They lose their servitude.'' J. J. Rousseau, *On the Social Contract,* Judith R. Masters (New York: Saint Martin's Press, 1978) Book I, Chapter II, p. 48. The more easily a writer thinks degradation occurs the more radical are his proposals for reform. Delany is no exception.
25 Delany, *Colored People of the United States,* p. 48.
26 Delany, *Colored People of the United States,* p. 197.
27 Delany, *Colored People of the United States,* pp. 184–85.
28 Delany, *Colored People of the United States,* p. 185.
29.Delany, *Colored People of the United States,* p. 213.
30 Delany, *Colored People of the United States,* p. 211.
31 Delany, *Colored People of the United States,* p. 211.
32 Delany, *Colored People of the United States,* p. 171.
33 Delany, *Colored People of the United States,* p. 173.
34 Delany, *Colored People of the United States,* p. 205.
35 Delany, *Colored People of the United States,* p. 214.
36 Only once, in 1861, did Douglass ever seriously entertain the possibility that emigration was a means to black elevation, when he planned to visit Haiti to see whether it was a suitable destination. *Douglass' Monthly,* Jan. 1861. This should be distinguished from his endorsement of emigration out of the South to ''other parts of the country'' in 1886. See *The Life and Writings of Frederick Douglass,* ed. Philip S. Foner, Volume 4 (New York: International Publishers, 1975), pp. 437–38.
37 Howard Brotz (ed.), *Negro Social and Political Thought 1850–1920* (New York: Basic Books, 1966), p. 329.
38 Brotz, *Negro Social and Political Thought,* p. 307.
39 Brotz, *Negro Social and Political Thought,* p. 291.
40 Brotz, *Negro Social and Political Thought,* p. 130. I have explored the implications of this in ''Dignity, Slavery and the 13th Amendment,'' in Michael Myer and William Parent (eds.), *Human Dignity, the Bill of Rights and Constitutional Values* (Ithaca: Cornell University Press, 1992).
41 Locke, *Two Treatises,* Bk. II, Ch. II, Sects. 4, 5, 6, 11, 12, etc.
42 Locke, *Two Treatises,* Bk. II, Ch. II, Sect. 4.
43 Locke, *Two Treatises.*
44 *Life and Writings of Frederick Douglass,* Vol. I, p. 136, 147, 162–64.
45 *Life and Writings of Frederick Douglass,* Vol. I, p. 157.
46 Locke, *Two Treatises,* Bk. II, Ch. IX, Sect. 124, p. 351.
47 John Locke, *An Essay Concerning Human Understanding,* (Oxford: Oxford University Press, 1975), Bk. I, Ch. IV, Sect. 24, pp. 101–2.
48 John Locke, *Questions concerning the Law of Nature,* Robert Horwitz, Jenny Strauss Clay, Diskin Clay (Ithaca: Cornell University Press, 1990), pp. 109, 111. See also page 119 where Locke maintains that we know the law of nature by the ''light of nature,'' which means that the Law of Nature is a ''truth whose knowledge man can, by the right use of those faculties with which he is provided by nature . . . tain by himself and without the help of another.'' On pages 135 and 137, however, he notes that the law of nature is ''not so easily apprehended'' and ''very few'' know it.
49 Locke, *Essay concerning Human Understanding,* Bk. IV, Ch. XX, p. 708.

50 Locke, *Essay concerning Human Understanding,* p. 707–8. No doubt this was supported by his theory of property which justified vast inequalities.
51 Frederick Douglass, *My Bondage and My Freedom,* (New York: Dover, 1969), p. 253.
52 Douglass, *My Bondage and My Freedom,* p. 260.
53 Douglass, *My Bondage and My Freedom,* p. 251.
54 *Life and Writings of Frederick Douglass,* Vol. 2, p. 534. See also page 287 where he wrote that the slave's submission "becomes an argument in the mouths of the community, that Negroes are, by Nature, only fit for slavery; that slavery is their normal condition."
55 *Life and Writings of Frederick Douglass,* p. 140.
56 *Life and Writings of Frederick Douglass,* Vol. 1, p. 157.
57 *Life and Writings of Frederick Douglass,* p. 157.
58 *Life and Writings of Frederick Douglass,* Vol. 2, p. 534.
59 *Life and Writings of Frederick Douglass,* p. 534–35.
60 *Life and Times of Frederick Douglass: The Complete Autobiography* (New York: Collier Books, 1962), p. 143. See also *Life and Writings of Frederick Douglass,* Vol. 3, pp. 342–43. I have tried to assess the force of this argument and given a more thorough account of the relationship between Locke and Douglass in "Radical Implications of Lockean Moral Theory: The Case of Frederick Douglass," read at the American Philosophical Association, Pacific Division Meeting, San Francisco, April 1991.
61 *Life and Writings of Frederick Douglass,* Vol. 2, p. 140.
62 *Life and Writings of Frederick Douglass,* Vol. 2, p. 140.
63 *Life and Writings of Frederick Douglass,* Vol. 1, p. 157.
64 *Life and Times of Frederick Douglass,* p. 143.

MODERNITY AND INTELLECTUAL LIFE IN BLACK

FRANK M. KIRKLAND

In his essay, "Toward a Future That Has No Past," Orlando Patterson draws the following conclusion about blacks of the Americas or the New World diaspora:

> The Blacks now face a historic choice. To survive, they must abandon their search for a past, must indeed recognize that they lack all claim to a distinctive cultural heritage, and that the path ahead lies not in myth making and in historical reconstruction, which are always doomed to failure, but in accepting the epic challenge of their reality. Black Americans can be the first group in the history of mankind who transcend the confines and grip of a cultural heritage, and in so doing, they can become the *most truly modern of all peoples*—a people who feel no need for a nation, a past, or a particularistic culture, but whose style of life will be a rational and continually changing adaptation to the exigencies of survival at the highest possible level of existence.[1]

Patterson believes that blacks throughout the Americas can assume this challenge in becoming "the most truly modern of all peoples" because "they do not have a sense of the past," "do not have a sense of [the] historic."[2] Although he concedes that this challenge may be a colossal one, he nonetheless claims that blacks should assume it, since they "have already made the major sacrifice for its performance—the loss of their history."[3] Furthermore, blacks should assume the challenge, he adds, "for otherwise they are lost."[4]

Patterson rightly admits that blacks' not having a sense of the past is not equivalent to blacks' not having a past at all, but rather to their past having no significance for their future-oriented present. The sense of the past to which Patterson refers is the impact of slavery's legacy and of African cultural remnants on blacks of the diaspora. With minor qualification Patterson believes that the "slave experience has little relevance for the present either as a collectively shared memory binding all the black peoples of the Americas or as a socio-historical continuity shared by them all."[5] He further maintains that African cultural remnants are only a small segment of any black community in the Americas and have disappeared to a large extent as a consequence of modern societal dislocations wrought by liabilities of and changes in capitalist economic organization.[6]

Moreover, Patterson argues that the choice of blacks to become the "most truly modern of all peoples," i.e., to move toward a future without a past, would be concomitant with their adoption of a rationally methodical form of conduct suitable to the formation of capital, to the development of productive forces, to the extension of rights of political participation, and to the expansion of administrative bureaucracy—all elements representative of *societal* modernity.

But therein lies the difficulty. Patterson wants to talk about blacks being "the most truly modern of all people" in *cultural* terms. Yet he conflates the conduct of what would make blacks *culturally* modern with the conduct mentioned above that makes them *socially* modern and that enables them to deal successfully with the effects of the modern societal imperative of capitalist economic organization. This conflation has extraordinary ramifications for how Patterson understands *premodern* black culture given his thesis. He reduces premodern black culture to the ghetto-specific milieu of the "culture of poverty," and he outlines the sociopsychological disposition and the rationally methodical form of conduct blacks need to assume to make the turn away from the culture of poverty to cultural modernity. In this context, cultural modernity means, for Patterson, blacks acting in ways that leave them relatively immune from the liabilities of capital.

Patterson ascribes the "culture of poverty" to blacks throughout the diaspora, contending that it characterizes the underlying yet spurious premodern cultural unity amongst them. For Patterson, black cultural arrangements

> almost all stem from the imperatives of urban poverty. The "black family," "black speech," "black lifestyles" are in no way distinctively black, but are simply lower class. . . . Thus, at the very point where blacks . . . approach a kind of cultural identity, they cease to be black in any meaningful cultural sense of that term. The culture of poverty, which is a poverty of culture, is fast becoming the lot of all black Americans, whether through necessity or by choice; black culture increasingly is "black" only in name.[7]

Since Patterson regards a culturally autonomous heritage of blacks of the diaspora as something of a myth and construes the "culture of poverty" as symbolically and materially impoverished as a culture, it is not surprising that he frames blacks' turn to modernity as one of sheer choice, a choice that can never be rationally motivated by the patterns of meaning available in their own cultural heritage. The choice can be rationally motivated only by the exigencies of capital.

Unlike, for example, Max Weber, who is able to trace the pulse of cultural modernity in the west (a process of disenchantment) through the west's own cultural forms of "religious world-rejection," Patterson cannot find a pulse of modernity beating at all in the cultural tradition of blacks. If blacks are to sustain a lifestyle ethically adequate to modernity, according to Patterson, they must surrender the use of their cultural tradition for interpreting themselves and the world. Although Weber could and did argue that cultural modernity in the west entails a radical break from the binding authority of its cultural tradition, he could and did demonstrate how that break was *rationally motivated* by the patterns of meaning of the west's cultural heritage. On the other hand, Patterson argues for modernity in black, if I may so speak, to break with its cultural tradition *while denying there is any aspect of the black cultural heritage able to provide a rational motive for such a break.*

I shall desist from discussing Patterson's claims any further. What I intend to do in the remainder of this essay, however, is give an account of blacks' culturally distinctive acquiescence to modernity—to explicate modernity in black. My focus will be on African-American intellectuals' confrontation with modernity. My main concern is not to refute Patterson's claims but to offer a portrait other than his, in which a cultural modernity in black is plausible and is a matter of serious interest to African-American intellectuals.

The essay consists of four parts. Part One examines DuBois' text, "The Talented Tenth," one of the first African-American texts to delineate systematically the role of African-American intellectuals. In this part, I shall distinguish briefly the talented tenth of the slave experience from that of modernity. Parts Two, Three, and Four can best be described as case studies representing variants of the talented tenth of modernity. The second and third parts deal with Alexander Crummell and Booker T. Washington respectively, each advocating in their distinctive ways the impact of modernity on African-American forms of life. The fourth part returns to Du Bois and delves into *The Souls of Black Folk* for what I argue should be the paradigmatic way of defining modernity for and in the light of those forms of life.

RETHINKING DU BOIS' "THE TALENTED TENTH"

Du Bois' essay, "The Talented Tenth," sets the tenor for assessing the African-American intellectual enterprise. It tellingly argues for what can be construed as a historical rule for the cultural progress of African-Americans and, in so arguing, defines the carriers of that cultural progress. For Du Bois, the historical rule is that the cultivation of vividly conceived ideals of the cultural group or race is dependent upon and embodied in that group's talented tenth.[8]

Du Bois treats historical realities as sites for the emergence of values, because he anchors his historical studies of cultural phenomena or groups in a value theory. This is an aspect of Du Bois' position that has largely been neglected.[9] By tailoring a value theory to the requirements of an historical social science, history becomes for Du Bois the unfolding of values—what Du Bois calls "race ideals'' or ''race spirit.'' These ideals make claims or demands upon members of a race, whose responses to them are judgments, value judgments, a race's ''message'' in the words of Du Bois. Value judgments can be expressed and discussed cognitively, in contrast to mere feelings which are indeterminate and incommunicable. They constitute motivations for action and are to govern the actions, discursive and otherwise, of members of a cultural group. Yet, for Du Bois, they are mediated historically. So history becomes for Du Bois the unfolding of values or race ideals, not simply of events, and historical individuals become those who evaluate and realize values, taking a cognizant position toward them while, at the same time, being motivated by them.

One of the three tasks Du Bois' essay assumes is an historical demonstration of the exceptional qualities of the talented tenth, whose vocation is the intellectual, educational, and moral development of the group to which they historically and culturally belong. Since Du Bois charts this vocation in historical terms, he is compelled to address its origins and objectives. And since this vocation points to some conception of action, the reference point for action cannot be African-American culture as a whole, but historical individuals of that culture. For a culture is not a purposive agent; at best it serves a purpose guaranteeing the likelihood of meaningful action.

The objectives of the talented tenth's vocation as well as its coordination of action undergo change historically. On a prima facie level, Du Bois identifies members of the talented tenth in terms of historical epochs, viz., the talented tenth of the Colonial/Revolutionary War Era, of the Abolitionist Era, of the Reconstruction Era, and of the 20th-Century/Modern Era.[10] But the more substantial demarcation lies in Du Bois' differentiation of the talented tenth in terms of the objective of its vocation. Whereas the objectives through the first three epochs are the abolition of slavery and the transformation of enslaved Africans into free human beings with political rights, the objectives of the fourth involve the preparation of African-Americans for entrance into the modern age by eliminating the disparaging and retarding effects of slavery and racism, viz., illiteracy, poverty, and the overall disruption of the ethical life of African-Americans.[11]

Legal emancipation from enslavement and the institutionalization of intellectual life within the African-American setting (post-1865) constitute for Du Bois the threshold of an African-American modernity. Frances E. W. Harper initially sketches the notion of an African-American modernity in the following statement.

> We have had a mournful past in this country, enslaved in the South and proscribed in the North; still it is not best to dwell too mournfully upon ''by gones.'' If we have had no past, it is well

> for us to look hopefully to the future—for the shadows bear the promise of a brighter coming day; and in fact, so far as the colored man is concerned, I do not feel particularly uneasy about his future.[12]

Alexander Crummell echoes these sentiments more strongly in the idea of a moral obligation of educated black men and women in his address "The Need of New Ideas and New Aims":

> The *duty* [of educated black folks] lies in the future. . . . [Yet] there is an irresistible tendency in the Negro mind in this land to dwell morbidly and absorbingly upon the servile past. . . . Duty for today, hope for the morrow, are ideas which seem oblivious to even leading minds among us. . . . What I would fain have you guard against is not the memory of slavery, but the constant recollection of it, as the commanding thought of a new people, who should be marching on to the broadest freedom in a new and glorious present, and a still more magnificent future.[13]

This focus on the future distinguishes the talented tenth of the modern age from those of the slave experience. The talented tenth of modernity advance the notion that African-Americans need to develop their cognitive and expressive capacities for the sake of enabling them to disconnect the boundaries of their hopes and expectations from the context of their experience past and present. Crummell gives evidence for this claim in his distinction between memory and recollection:

> memory . . . is a passive act of mind . . . the necessary and unavoidable entrance, storage, and recurrence of facts and ideas to consciousness. Recollection . . . is the actual seeking of the facts, the endeavor of the mind to bring them back to consciousness. The natural recurrence of the idea or the fact of slavery is that which cannot be faulted. What I object to is the unnecessary recollection of it.[14]

It appears, then, that for the talented tenth of modernity the African-American's openness to the novelty of the future hinges in some fashion on a severance from the legacy of slavery. This is made clear through the signal concept of modernity in the African-American tradition, viz., the New Negro.

CRUMMELL, MODERNITY, AND RACE

I have used the notion of modernity without developing it more adequately. As implied above, modernity is that world view, arising out of the European Enlightenment, enabling a person's sociopsychological disposition to be open to the future and shaping the conviction that a person's hopes and expectations need not be anchored in the context of her previous experience.[15] Another pertinent sense of modernity is that of an epoch wherein legitimate structures of human interaction are those informed by a conception of the person whose social significance is no longer defined by natural determinations such as race, sex, etc., but by a person's self-determination.

The first sense engenders the belief that the future cannot be a source or a locus of dissatisfaction or discontent, especially when laden with utopian conceptions concerning civilization as the goal state of material and social progress and racial/cultural uplift. Crummell's subscription to this view motivated his critique of what he understood as a common tendency amongst African-Americans, viz., "dwelling morbidly and absorbingly upon the servile past." African-Americans' constant recollection of the slave experience, Crummell argued, would result in their "arrested development" intellectually, morally, socially, and materially. So the first sense leads him to put forward his conception of what distinctively constitutes modernity in African-American life.

However, as Crummell himself notes, his views "were met with emphatic and most earnest protest" by Frederick Douglass. Douglass "urged his hearers to a constant recollection of the slavery of their race and of the wrongs it had brought upon them."[16] He believed that the abolition of slavery was sufficient for preparing African-Americans' entrance into the future and that there was no specific moral duty lying particularly in the future, as Crummell maintained, for African-Americans to assume. Douglass never systematically tied the need for the recollection of the slave experience to the need to be open to the future or to the need for a collective racial endeavor toward sociocultural solidarity, refinement, and uplift. For Douglass, "free the slaves and leave them alone"; they did not require any extraordinary educational effort for entrance into the modern world. "There is nothing the matter with the Negro whatever; he is all right. Learned or ignorant, he is all right."[17] There was for Douglass no specific moral duty pertinent simply to the future, since his primary intellectual focus was on the elimination and prohibition of slavery and of any other pernicious social arrangement which would destroy the possibility of morality itself, viz., the preservation of humanity as having intrinsic worth in our own person and in others.

Crummell's original insight was to recognize that, for African-Americans, moral duty had to extend beyond preserving the intrinsic worth of moral or natural personhood to prescribing positive ends cognate to the well-being and happiness of African-Americans. This insight is reflected in Crummell's position that African-Americans needed to establish their own art, science, philosophy, and scholarship as well as their own manufactures, business enterprises, and symbols of power in order to make evident their contribution to American culture and global civilization.[18] The well-being and happiness of African-Americans could be realized, Crummell believed, once this contribution was established through the racial solidarity and collective effort amongst African-Americans in those and various other fields of endeavor. Crummell's position thus entailed that

African-Americans display a moral fidelity to their own particular social community, and that they recognize their ethical sensibility as (a) embodied in their own forms of cultural life, (b) justified in terms of the ends cognate to them, and (c) occasioned and maintained by the kinds of ethical sustenance those forms afford. Deprived of those forms, an African-American ethical sensibility would be unlikely to flourish.

These three points comprise the ethical ambit of what is called racial/cultural nationalism defined usually in terms of a kind of allegiance to a particular racial/cultural group which only those sharing membership in that group can display. Racial/cultural nationalism does not in principle convey an unreflective or unthinking allegiance to one's own particular group. Rather it reflects a particular regard not only for one's own group but, more importantly, for the excellences, accomplishments, and ends of one's own group. On these grounds, Crummell could contend that the fidelity of African-Americans to their forms of life is a prerequisite for their ethical sensibility, and that the ends cognate to the African-American forms of life would be, in the main, the cardinal virtues of their ethical sensibility.

Nevertheless, Crummell was well aware that the three points were not sufficient to sustain the ethical sensibility of that nationalism. Since a racial/cultural nationalist would have to evince a fidelity to her racial/cultural group that would be in a number of ways unqualified and unconditional, Crummell recognized that such a fidelity might lead her to refrain from examining those ends or practices and, as a consequence, to accept them regardless of whether they were rationally justifiable or not.

To circumvent this problem, Crummell exempted from self-criticism the unconditional fidelity to racial/cultural solidarity by construing African-American forms of life not in terms of their current sociocultural state but in terms of a project, an undertaking he called "civilization." Civilization was, Crummell believed, a projection of African-Americans producing in solidarity the intellectual, material, and spiritual objectifications of their race—"noble thought, grand civility, a chaste and elevating culture, refinement"[19] and economic self-sufficiency. This projection had its realization in the future, and African-Americans, particularly intellectuals, had a moral responsibility to bring this projection of civilization into being for themselves.

Central here is Crummell's obligatory distinction between the currency of African-American forms of life and their projection as civilization. For Crummell, African-Americans have an *unconditional* ethical allegiance to the racial/cultural solidarity exemplified in the project of civilization. At the same time, their ethical allegiance to their current sociocultural forms of life would be *conditional* upon those forms' compatibility with advancing and promoting that project rather than thwarting and nullifying it. Only fidelity to the project is unconditional, because civilization occasions the commitment of African-Americans to link their forms of life with a future solidarity and self-sufficiency which is their responsibility to realize. Fidelity to current forms of African-American life would be open to self-criticism only if those current forms backslide from or, even worse, repudiate the project.

Yet the admission that a fidelity to one's racial/cultural group does not preclude rational self-criticism still does not forestall a major obstacle to Crummell's position. As stated earlier, Crummell's focus is on the development of African-American sociocultural resources for the sake of shaping and enhancing the sociopsychological disposition of African-Americans for entrance into the modern world. Such a development would require African-Americans to disconnect their openness to the future, their hopes and expectations, from the context of their past and present experiences. In taking this position, Crummell must affirm that current forms of African-American life cannot and ought not take their bearings from criteria supplied by African or African-American forms of life in previous epochs. In short, African-American forms of life in *modernity* ought continually to break with their past.

But here lies the rub. Crummell requires something that confers a distinctive mark on African-Americans, serving as both the motive for assuming the project of civilization and as the feature for identifying them as that group whose project this is. Usually a group's acknowledged historical past serves as the mark that has already bestowed upon a group its own sociocultural identity. However, given Crummell's position of severing the future from the past and his claims about the symbolic and material poverty of both African culture and the slave experience, it is quite clear that he needs something other than the historical past of African-Americans to serve as the distinctive mark of their sociocultural identity.

What provides that mark for Crummell is *race,* but understood as a ''homogeneous population of one blood, ancestry, and lineage'' established by divine provenance.[20] Crummell lays out a position in which race, analogically employed, determines a peculiar action-generating fidelity to or regard for a particular group, a fidelity that moves providentially with biological descent and sociopsychological integration.[21] In Crummell's eyes, sustaining this providentially inspired racial impulse is required for African-Americans to avoid distractions, like remembrance of the slave experience, and to consummate their own cultural uplift and solidarity in the project of civilization. On this note, race and modernity become problematically linked in a twofold way.

First, by linking race and modernity, Crummell seems to contradict the other sense defining modernity—that race or any other natural determination cannot legitimately inform modern structures of human interaction. Under the auspice of modernity, participation in civil society can be neither legitimately extended to nor legitimately denied persons on the basis of their possessing some natural characteristic (race, sex, ancestry, etc.) putatively endowed with social significance positive or otherwise.[22] Indeed Douglass affirmed this precept and used it to support his claim that a race-specific moral duty or fidelity was nonsense as well as pernicious.[23] Crummell never disavowed this precept. He simply offered an account affirming the moral obligation for African-Americans to develop what is distinctive and commendable in their culture and to promote their cultural worth, while maintaining that different racial/cultural groups can subscribe to a common conception of justice and participate peacefully in civil society. Now such an account is not necessarily incompatible with modernity's precept regarding race so long as the sentiments expressed do not convey a racial chauvinism. Crummell's discourse unfortunately took a chauvinist turn because of his concern that African-Americans not leave their moral and cultural ties too open to dissolution by interracial sexual encounters.

Second, the theoretical difficulties attached to the race-modernity linkage arise from Crummell's attempts to make the notion of race the primary locus of a group's cultural content, norms, and patterns of identification. This is not novel to Crummell, but represents the musings of many 19th-century intellectuals who discussed race in the tradition of *Volksgeistphilosophie*. Race as a natural determination becomes laden (1) with cultural content whose transmission conveys a group's "local knowledge," (2) with cultural norms whose transmission establishes a group's solidarity, and (3) with cultural patterns of identification whose transmission informs a group's socialization process. All these elements, the codes of culture so to speak, are spuriously regarded as being generated through providential inspiration and transmitted through biological descent. And since Crummell woefully devalued the premodern cultural codes of African and African-American forms of life, he could never comprehend the spuriousness of making race the primary locus of a group's cultural codes.

Crummell, then, cannot establish the distinctiveness of modern African-American forms of life, because he cannot conceptually allow them to be informed by their past and he regards the cultural codes of premodern African and African-American forms of life as materially and symbolically deficient. He is thus left with an apocryphal notion of race to do the conceptual work, a notion failing theoretically to establish modernity in black. Not surprisingly, then, Crummell continually turns to the cultural codes and language of modern British society as the standard African-Americans should emulate in their project of civilization.[24] His inability to provide an intellectually distinctive conception of modernity in African-American life does not, however, halt the theoretical enterprise of formulating such a conception. Indeed, Crummell's most famous protégé would provide, I believe, the most cogent formulation of what distinctively constitutes modernity in African-American life. This formulation is pithily conveyed in the words: ''The problem of the 20th century is the problem of the color line.'' Or, as I shall restate it, the problem of modernity is the problem of color line.

Crummell's protégé, W. E. B. Du Bois, wrote arguably the canonical text in the African-American intellectual tradition, *The Souls of Black Folk* (SBF), a text that at the time of its publication in 1903 was highly controversial but that, nevertheless, remains even today masterly and singularly paradigmatic in its interpretation of African-American life. The controversy surrounding it at the time of its publication stems from its trenchant critique of Booker T. Washington. These two themes are strongly interwoven because in SBF Du Bois tries to come to terms explicitly with the sense of historical and temporal awareness pertinent to modern African-American forms of life. And it is clear from that text, especially in connection with Du Bois' ''The Talented Tenth,'' also published in 1903, that he unequivocally rejects Washington's sentiments on this issue, sentiments that black and white people regarded as carrying the day. Since Washington's sentiments on modernity are important for an appreciation of Du Bois, let me discuss them next.

WASHINGTON, MODERNITY AND THE SCHOOL OF SLAVERY

Washington never expressly affirms the notion of modernity in African-American life as a continual breaking with its past in its orientation toward the future. However, the idea is strongly implicit in his autobiography, *Up From Slavery* (UFS), which narrates the story of the Tuskegee experiment out of which Washington's ''New Negro'' or the modern-day African-American emerges. Admittedly this appears puzzling—Washington gives credence to the notion of modernity in an autobiography, whose literary form involves recourse to the past (not a break with it) to address one's future orientation. Nevertheless, that credence is revealed in UFS through his understanding of the slave experience and of the need for an accommodationist politics. My concern, however, is not with the reliability of his evidence about slavery or with the integrity of his politics. It is simply with how they contribute to his understanding of the notion of modernity in black.

In UFS, Washington gives an account of his past in which he throws off, after Emancipation, the ''psychological'' manacles of slavery, acquires an education, develops a plan for the social uplift and improvement of African-Americans on the basis of it, and becomes a politically powerful figure by virtue of the plan's successful implementation. This account reflects his view that African-Americans need to work upward from slavery and into modern civil society by their own efforts, and that they require social tranquility to engage in the project of civilization, understood primarily in terms of economic and material advancement. For social tranquility, African-Americans would pay the price of acquiescence in segregation, recognizing that ''agitation of questions of social equality [was] the extremest folly.''[25] So, according to Washington, ''in all things that are purely social we [black and white people] can be separate as the fingers, yet one as the hand in all things essential to mutual progress.''[26]

This is a heavy sociopsychological and sociocultural price to pay for entrance without harm into modern civil society. But this price is set by how he understands the slave experience and by what he takes to be the sociopsychological disposition of African-Americans in the aftermath of slavery. Despite the fact that he condemns on straightforward moral grounds the wholesale cruelty, deprivation, and horror of slavery and racism, his discussion of slavery primarily takes the shape of an apology for slavery's *technically practical benefits,* e.g., mastery of some craft or acquisition of some skill. Indeed, *morally practical benefits,* like autonomy, dignity, and personal well-being, do not ensue from the ''peculiar institution'' for the enslaved African. But Washington does not assess slavery solely as an *institution,* understood here as something sanctioned by norms, traditions, and cultural patterns of identification. On the contrary, he assesses slavery mainly as a *system,* understood here as a stable self-implementing mechanism.

As institution, slavery can be viewed only in terms of how masters and slaves orient their actions to one another under the auspice of normatively sanctioned force favoring the master and at the expense of the humanity of the slave. Moreover, one can address issues regarding the moral rightness of slavery; one can speak of attempts at self-understanding on the part of masters and slaves about their respective social situations and moral positions. On the other hand, as a system, slavery can be viewed only in terms of the functional network of the unintended consequences of masters' and slaves' actions. Their actions give rise to other actions unintended by them, which are functionally pertinent to the stability of slavery as a self-regulating mechanism. Here one's discourse about slavery is morally minimized, if not neutralized, because slavery is construed as a mechanism in which the actions of masters and slaves are functionally dependent upon one another without this being willed or known by them.[27]

Consider some of Washington's remarks concerning the slave experience. 1) He describes his white father's disavowal of him as his son by describing the man as ''simply another unfortunate victim which the Nation unhappily had engrafted upon it at the time.''[28] Notice Washington does not speak of his father's disavowal of him as intentional but as part and parcel of the system of slavery. 2) He rehearses his mother's theft of chickens to feed him and his siblings by portraying her as ''simply a victim of the system of slavery.''[29] Washington speaks of his mother's thievery as a functional consequence of the system. 3) On blacks' attitudes toward whites, he claims that ''as a rule . . . members of [his] race entertain no feelings of bitterness against the whites before and during the war. . . ."[30] Here Washington is asserting that the enslaved African's sentiments of moral outrage toward her master are "as a rule" out of place functionally in the system of slavery. The question of injustice as a functional rule pertinent to the machinery of slavery is never tendered because such a question raises matters dysfunctional to slavery.

These three remarks suggest that, by treating slavery as a system, Washington is able to view it as *subjectless*. On this view, no moral predicates can be ascribed to the agents within it, because the actions of masters and slaves are behavioral regularities part and parcel of the functioning of the system of slavery. So the actions of Washington's father and mother and the attitudes of blacks toward whites assume a functional significance according to their contribution to the stability of slavery as a system.

4) However, Washington does not remain locked into this viewpoint. He claims "notwithstanding the cruel wrongs inflicted upon us, the black man got nearly as much out of slavery as the white man did. The hurtful influences of the institution were not by any means confined to the Negro. . . . The whole machinery of slavery was so construed as to cause labor, as a rule, to be looked upon as a badge of degradation, of inferiority."[31] Here Washington purports that the system of slavery has yielded both positive and negative consequences which have had almost an equal impact on both blacks and whites. One of the negative consequences is that slavery has rendered labor an undignified activity. Yet one of the positive consequences pertinent to enslaved Africans, he claims, is that "ten million Negroes inhabiting this country, who themselves or whose ancestors went through the *school of slavery,* are in a stronger and more hopeful condition materially, intellectually, morally, and religiously than is true of an equal number of black people in any other portion of the globe."[32]

This notion of slavery as a "school" is prima facie at odds with slavery as a system, because Washington characterizes it as yielding morally practical benefits. This is not the case with slavery construed as a system. Moreover, in regard to this notion of "slavery as a school," Washington claims elsewhere that "we [African-Americans] went into slavery in this country pagans; we came out Christians. We went into slavery without a language; we came out speaking the proud Anglo-Saxon tongue. If in the providence of God the Negro got any good out of slavery, he got the habit of work."[33] When Washington speaks of "slavery as a school," he does so in terms of providence's influential workings on the system of slavery. African-Americans, who have gone through the "school of slavery," demonstrate for Washington "how providence so often uses men and institutions to accomplish a purpose," and his "faith in the future of [his] race in this country" is due to "providence which has already led [his] race through and out of the wilderness."[34] What are we to make of these claims?

Washington's use of providence enables him to establish, for the lack of a better expression, a "functional fit" between the morally and technically practical benefits of slavery. The question to ask then is what morally practical benefits are functionally congruent with the technically practical ones of slavery? For Washington, the "school of slavery" develops in enslaved Africans the mastery of some task and the willingness to work. More specifically, acquisition of some skill would be functionally coupled with self-discipline, diligence and generally acting in ways to secure the trust and confidence of their masters. The "school of slavery" would be for Washington a causally relevant factor in generating the capacity of African-Americans to engage in a kind of methodical conduct, an ascetic lifestyle combining active self-control with mastery of tasks and of one's social environment. The "school of slavery" inculcates in enslaved Africans habits that ultimately would be conducive and serviceable to the economic order of modern civil society. "Slavery as a school" would be a phase in the training and development of African-Americans, an economic and moral training ground for enslaved Africans who, once emancipated, would thereby be capable of contributing to the material advancement of civil society.

Washington's views are thus markedly different from Crummell's. Washington attaches the work of providence to the system of slavery and not to race as does Crummell. For this reason he gives slavery a positive significance that Crummell never could—as a factor contributing to African-Americans' project of civilization. According to Crummell, slavery produced servility and drudgery pure and simple, did not bear any civilizing tendencies, and was not part of any educational process whatsoever.[35] However, Washington, with his notion of "slavery as a school," seems to define modernity in black with a serviceable connection to a historical past. This stands in stark contrast to Crummell's view that modernity in black radically breaks with its past and thus cannot take its bearings from it.

However, this connection Washington makes between modernity in black and the "school of slavery" as its historical past rests on a great theoretical fault. A providentially wrought functional congruence between technical skills and moral qualities in the "school of slavery" is not an historically shaped experience. If "slavery as a school" is providentially influenced, then it is inexplicable historically and operates outside of or behind the awareness, in this case, of enslaved Africans. Rather it is a *counterfactual* device used by Washington to grasp the unintended consequences of the actions of enslaved Africans and ultimately to effect a certain perception of blacks by whites as well as by blacks toward themselves in modern civil society. Washington so submerges the historical character of the "peculiar institution" within the "school of slavery" that he has little, if any, way to express the horrors and improprieties of that institution. He has little, if any, way to articulate how the experience of enslaved Africans in the "peculiar institution" might have *structural* features resistant to any kind of "functional fit" between it and the "school of slavery." Since the counterfactual device of the "school of slavery" would have to preclude the historical experience of enslaved Africans, it would also have to preclude that slavery was experienced by Africans with notions enabling them at least to thoughtfully contrast, if not thoughtfully or actively resist, it with some conception of justice, the good life, and collective identity.

If my remarks here carry weight, then there is no singular manner in which the "school of slavery" can serve as a historical legacy for modern African-American forms of life or the "New Negro," to use Washington's term. It cannot be a cultural reservoir for an African's "local knowledge" of the slave experience; it cannot be a source for normatively binding social relations amongst enslaved Africans and between them and slave masters; it cannot be a milieu in which individual moral and technical competences are formed. Hence it contains neither sociocultural nor sociohistorical content which could inform or guide the future orientation of the "New Negro." Moreover, if Tuskegee institutionally develops the moral and technical skills providentially rendered through the "school of slavery," then it educationally prepares African-Americans for the modern world in such a way as to suppress the memory of slavery as the "peculiar institution" for African-Americans. The manner in which Tuskegee institutionally inculcates and develops moral habits and technical skills in the "New Negro" is itself insulated from the institutional legacy of slavery. So the education or intellectual enterprise of the "New Negro" comprising modern African-American forms of life would be directed practically to the future yet, contrary to Washington's belief, would be radically disconnected from a historical past due to Tuskegee's functional connection with the "school of slavery" and hence consequent suppression of slavery's institutional legacy.

"THE SOULS OF BLACK FOLK" AND THE TALENTED TENTH OF MODERNITY

Despite the criticism above, Washington's characterization of the "New Negro" would still meet the criterion drawn from Du Bois' "The Talented Tenth" concerning the talented tenth of modernity or "college-bred Negro." But in that essay Du Bois was highly critical of the "college bred Negro" emerging out of Tuskegee. It is usually claimed that the basis of the criticism hinged on Du Bois' belief that a liberal education had greater significance than a vocational one for African-Americans. I shall argue, however, that Du Bois' critique of Washington's "New Negro" has much less to do with the difference in significance of the two kinds of education than with the ability or inability to bear a sense of modernity distinctive of African-American forms of life.

One can take this tack only if one reads "The Talented Tenth" in the light of SBF. Furthermore, if this reading was accepted, then Du Bois' critique of Washington on what distinctively constitutes modern African-American forms of life would also extend to Crummell, his laudation of Crummell in SBF notwithstanding. For SBF is a peculiar treatise in which Du Bois rethinks the aspects of modernity in terms of the "problem of the color line." Despite the fact that Du Bois quite strongly conveys Crummellian views in SBF, he does theoretically address the issue of race and modernity in a way that Crummell could not.

Du Bois' term of art for the "color line" is "the Veil."[36] He means to suggest by it not just the next-to-impregnable barrier that segregates racially (personages, institutions, policies, doctrines, tragic and comic experiences make up this barrier) but also the fabric, so to speak, that conceals from white people an understanding of the legacy and currency of African-American forms of life wrought by it, viz., material poverty, stifled ambitions and diminished expectations on the one hand yet unwonted moral gallantry, melodious and resonant expressiveness, and irrepressible religious faith on the other. With the notion of "the Veil," Du Bois establishes a commonality amongst African-Americans not simply on race or ancestry but, more significantly, on segregation imposed by racism, on economic and formal educational impoverishment imposed by slavery, and on self-imposed moral and religious discipline strengthened by a music whose venerability is "far more ancient than the words."[37] Moreover, "the Veil" produces in African-Americans a sociopsychological and, as I shall demonstrate, sociohistorical disposition that Du Bois refers to as *double consciousness*.

Consider this hefty portion of SBF regarding the notion of double consciousness:

> After the Egyptian and Indian, the Greek and Roman, the Teuton and Mongolian, the Negro is a sort of seventh son, born with a veil, and gifted with a second-sight in this American world,—a world which yields him no true self-consciousness, but only lets him see himself through the revelation of the other world. It is a peculiar sensation, this double consciousness, this sense of always looking at one's self through the eyes of others, of measuring one's soul by the tape of a world that looks on in amused contempt and pity. One ever feels his twoness—an American, a Negro; two souls, two thoughts, two unreconciled strivings; two warring ideals in one dark body, whose dogged strength alone keeps it from being torn asunder. The history of the American Negro is the history of this strife—longing to attain self-conscious manhood, to merge his double self into a better and truer self. In this merging he wishes neither of the older selves to be lost. He would not Africanize America, for America has too much to teach the world and Africa. He would not bleach his Negro soul in a flood of white Americanism, for he knows that Negro blood has a message for the world. He simply wishes to make it possible for a man to be both a Negro and an American, without being cursed and spit upon by his fellows, without having the doors of opportunity closed roughly in his face.[38]

For Du Bois what distinguishes African-Americans from other cultural groups is this notion of double consciousness which is the result of "the Veil." He presents it in SBF both negatively and positively and gives it three related yet distinct senses, two lying on the negative side and the third lying on the positive. The first yet least prominent sense is double consciousness as *duplicitous,* in which "one looks at one's self through the eyes of others or measures one's soul by the tape of a world that looks on in amused contempt and pity." Here double consciousness leads one to a false self-interpretation constitutive of a false kind of life, thwarting an authentic self-presentation. It appears then to be a kind of *self-deception.* The second and most prominent sense is double consciousness as *dualistic* and *duellistic,* in which "the contradiction of double aims"[39] predominates. Here double consciousness produces disorientation, competing ideals, irreconcilable strivings, all of which yield a kind of *self-doubt.* The third sense is double consciousness as *dyadic,* which is not as prominent as the second, but which is in my opinion more significant. The dyadic sense of double consciousness represents for Du Bois the "merging of [an African-American's] double self into a better and truer self" without losing its twofold character of being both an African and an American. This dyadic sense of double consciousness yields for African-Americans, according to Du Bois, a true *self-consciousness,* coming with the rending of "the Veil" and enabling African-American forms of life to carry their "message" or cultural contributions to the world, to engage in the project of civilization.

The duplicitous and dualistic/duellistic senses of double consciousness are sociopsychological attitudes African-Americans can assume, and they do not define fixed personality types. The dyadic sense of double consciousness represents in contrast to the other two an ideal norm, because it is tied to the "rending of the Veil," portrayed by Du Bois as a distant, far-off event, portrayed on the premise of the conditional existence of an "Eternal Good."[40] Historically, however, "the Veil" did lift partially, temporarily, but it quickly and starkly came down as if it were never raised. Du Bois powerfully rehearses this history, and it serves in and throughout SBF as the background and condition for double consciousness and for what distinctively shapes for him modern African-American forms of life.

Du Bois presents this view most poignantly in the chapter "Of the Faith of Fathers" whose content bears striking resemblance to that found in "The Talented Tenth." The signal difference, however, is that instead of beginning historically with the intellectual talents of free African-Americans in the colonial era and tracing the use of those talents in the service of rectifying the plight of enslaved Africans, he starts with the African priest in the religious formation of an African ethical life. He then traces the leadership habits and the cultivation of the intellectual tendencies of African-Americans through the medium of religion, specifically through the resistances and revisions of African religions in their encounter with slavery and Christianity. This entails providing an historical account of African-American religion and its carriers from its African sources through its shaping on the plantation to its urban institutional arrangements as churches in the North. And Du Bois draws the conclusion that, despite the paucity of their numbers, "the chief influence" of free African-Americans, whose intellectual and ethical energies were directed toward the slavery question, "was *internal*—was exerted on the black world, and that there [they were] the ethical and social leader[s]."[41] This conclusion suggests that the mission of the talented tenth has African religious antecedents.

As I stated previously, freedom was the object of discourse for the talented tenth of the enslavement period, and their call for the abolition of slavery became identified with the salvation mission of African-American religion. With this identification, the talented tenth of the enslavement period was able to shift for African-Americans the idea of salvation and the interest in compensation from an other-worldly to a this-worldly orientation. "When Emancipation finally came, it seemed to the freedman a literal Coming of the Lord. . . . Joyed and bewildered with what came, he stood awaiting new wonders till the inevitable Age of Reaction swept over the nation and brought the crisis of today."[42]

This temporary rising and subsequent falling of "the Veil" defined for Du Bois the critical juncture of African-American religion, and they placed now on the talented tenth of modernity the intellectual difficulty and ethical burden of providing African-Americans answers to issues of compensation in this world for the inadequacy of and injustice done to their forms of life. Specifically this required the talented tenth of modernity to address African-Americans on issues regarding (a) the locus of salvation or compensation in the future of this world in which said future is now and (b) the connection between African-Americans' interest in salvation or compensation on the one hand and conceptions of what actions justify claims for compensation.

Focusing on the second part of (b) for a moment, if one were to raise the question to Crummell, Washington, and Du Bois regarding the question of what action must be taken, all of them would most likely say the following—African-Americans determining their own fate by satisfying the demands for clarity and consistency, both intellectually and morally, and translating them into their own conduct recognized by others. However, only Du Bois understood that this conception of action would also have to be conjoined with an awareness of the problems that "the Veil" and its rise and fall have wrought.

Of course, both Crummell and Washington recognized the horrors of slavery and racial segregation and were critical of them. But despite their recognition and criticism, their intellectual discourse never consolidated African-American cultural responses to the problems of "the Veil" with the above-mentioned kind of action needed to gain entrance into modern civil society. Their discourse did not and could not entertain the possibility that, given "the Veil," such entrance could be culturally problematic and historically empty. *In short, despite their patent differences, both Crummell's and Washington's acceptance of modernity's preponderance of the future over the past compels them to understand the relation between modernity and African-American forms of life as culturally and historically compatible.*

Repairing to SBF, Du Bois gives telling thought to the real possibility that if modernity's preponderance of the future over the past is not seriously rethought and revised, then the African-American entrance into modern civil society would be culturally unsatisfying and historically hollow. His revision does not entail giving weight to the past over the future, since he would not deny modernity's irreversible character. But he does give extensive consideration to the past of African-Americans and to augmenting the sense of the future vis-a-vis that past. This is exemplified in the following hefty passage on the impact of the rise and fall of "the Veil" for African-American religion.

> It is difficult to explain clearly the present critical stage of Negro religion. First, we must remember that living as the blacks do in close contact with a great modern nation, and sharing, although imperfectly, the soul-life of that nation, they must necessarily be affected more or less directly by all the religious and ethical forces that are today moving the United States. These questions and movements are, however, overshadowed and dwarfed by the (to them) all-important question of their civil, political, and economic status. They must perpetually discuss the "Negro Problem"—must live, move and have their being in it, and interpret all else in its light or darkness. . . . All this must mean a time of intense ethical ferment, of religious heart-searching and intellectual unrest. From the double life every American Negro must live, as a Negro and as an American, as swept on by the current of the nineteenth while yet struggling in the eddies of the fifteenth century—from this must arise a painful self-consciousness, an almost morbid sense of personality and a moral hesitancy which is fatal to self-confidence. The worlds within and without the Veil of Color are changing, and changing rapidly, but not at the same rate, not in the same way; and this must produce a peculiar wrenching of the soul, a peculiar sense of doubt and bewilderment. Such a double life, with double thoughts, double duties, and double social classes, must give rise to double words and double ideals, and tempt the mind to pretense or to revolt, to hypocrisy or to radicalism.[43]

For Du Bois, African-Americans participate "imperfectly" in modernity. This "imperfection" is due to the "Negro Problem," "the Veil," compelling African-Americans to live their lives, define their being, interpret everything, even their participation in a modern civil society, according to it. This circumstance engenders difficulties in the inner life (sociopsychological disposition) of African-Americans. This "imperfect" participation in modernity yields a historical and temporal awareness in African-Americans, self-consciously oriented toward their future yet self-consciously cognizant of their past. For Du Bois, such a self-consciousness for an African-American must be "painful" and must engender an "almost morbid sense of personality and a moral hesitancy fatal to self-confidence."

In the context of the citation above, self-consciousness is not an ideal norm, but is characteristic of two modes of double consciousness, each encompassing a kind of reflective historical awareness and yielding certain motivations to action. Here double consciousness is not the sociopsychological split between being an African and an American; rather it is the sociohistorical split between an African-American's reflective stance toward the past ("struggling in the eddies of the 15th century") and an African-American's reflective stance toward the future ("swept on by the current of the 19th century"). Self-consciousness is thereby the reflective awareness of the sociohistorical conflict of African-Americans being "Janus-headed," so to speak, regarding their historical legacy and their future-oriented currency, both shaped specifically by the temporary rise and subsequent fall of "the Veil."

Du Bois' discussion here of self-consciousness is tied inextricably to the talented tenth of modernity or the college-bred Negro: the two sociohistorical modes of double consciousness are exemplified within that group. At the end of the chapter "Of the Faith of Fathers," Du Bois speaks of these two modes of double consciousness as "two extreme types of ethical attitudes . . . between which the mass of the millions of Negroes, North and South, wavers."[44]

Du Bois is referring to the dilemma faced by the talented tenth of modernity in addressing the impact of "the Veil" on African-American participation in modern civil society. This dilemma splits the talented tenth of modernity in accordance with the two sociohistorical modes of double consciousness mentioned above. Bear in mind that this group subscribes to the view of modernity as a future without a past. Yet one segment of it, which Du Bois calls the "radical" mode of double consciousness,[45] interprets the rise and fall of "the Veil" as the key to understanding the future as a source of dissatisfaction and discontent for African-Americans. Not a future deferred but a future foreclosed.

The "radical" segment interprets this state of affairs as a gross betrayal and violation of the principles of modernity regarding race and the future. It rails against accepting the foreclosure of modernity to African-Americans, but its critique cannot rend "the Veil." Moreover, this "radical" segment views the past of African-Americans as *without* the cultural codes and resources redeeming African-American forms of life adequate to the modern world. Both the lack of success of its critique and the inability to draw from an African-American past have devastating consequences for this "radical" segment. These states of affairs, I believe, are what Du Bois has in mind when he claims that the "radical" segment, "conscious of [their] impotence and pessimistic, often become bitter and vindictive; and [their] religion, instead of a worship, is a complaint and a curse, a wail rather than a hope, a sneer rather than a faith."[46] In short, the "radical" segment of the talented tenth of modernity regards "the Veil" not only as foreclosing modernity to African-Americans but also as impoverishing the cultural resources of an African-American past which could provide motivations for action against "the Veil."

Du Bois calls the other segment of the talented tenth of modernity the "hypocritical"[47] mode of double consciousness. He views this group proffering a discourse that modernity need not be foreclosed to African-Americans *if* they tailor their form of life to conceal the legacy and currency of "the Veil." More succinctly, this segment promotes the idea that African-Americans can sustain an openness to the future and share in modern civil society, especially economically, on the condition that they acquiesce to suppressing, if not denying, the impact of "the Veil's" legacy and currency on them. The price for African-Americans sharing in modernity in this manner is, according to Du Bois, a "Lie."[48] In short, then, the "hypocritical" segment of the talented tenth of modernity does not regard "the Veil" as foreclosing modernity to African-Americans as long as they do not wittingly interpret their past and present forms of life in the light of it.

This exposition shows the talented tenth of modernity as a more differentiated lot than standardly conceived. Furthermore, it appears that there is more of a similarity than I have previously intimated between the sociopsychological modes of double consciousness (dualistic/duellistic and duplicitous) on the one hand and the sociohistorical modes (radical and hypocritical) on the other. However, the sociopsychological modes pertain to African-Americans whose life is *sunk* in double consciousness, while the sociohistorical modes refer to African-Americans who *lead* their life in a doubly conscious way. Nonetheless, the "radical" and "hypocritical" segments of the talented tenth of modernity or the "college-bred" or New Negro represent for Du Bois those African-American leaders who have accepted modernity's preponderance of the future or a future-oriented present over the past.

Du Bois does not explicitly designate a third segment of the talented tenth of modernity. But he does present himself as an exemplar amongst those African-Americans, different from the "radical" or the "hypocritical" segments, who are of "dawning self-consciousness," able, and seeking "to analyze the burden [they] bore upon [their] back, that deadweight of social degradation partially masked behind a half-named Negro problem."[49] He incessantly argues that "the Veil" and the consequences it wrought have extended into the modern world, and that the principles of modernity regarding race and the preponderance of the future over the past must be modified. He executes this modification in a non-serial but two-fold manner. First, on the basis of his treatment of the sorrow songs, he interprets the African-American past as itself once a future to be characterized now in terms of the hopes and expectations of enslaved Africans. Second, he represents the future-oriented present of African-Americans in terms of possibly experiencing a "second slavery,"[50] possibly "being reduced to semi-slavery,''[51] or possibly experiencing in the modern scene ''the wail of prisoned souls within the veil and the mounting fury of shackled men.''[52] Representing their future-oriented present in this fashion serves to engender in African-Americans, through recollection, the responsibility of also satisfying the hopes and dreams of previous generations. Let us examine more closely these two points.

Although Du Bois does not regard himself as possessing technical musical expertise on the sorrow songs, he does understand the modern scene as punctuated with meaning from these musical accomplishments. Repeatedly he construes the sorrow songs as a significant cultural resource of African-Americans. He characterizes them as the articulate yet veiled message of enslaved Africans to the world, dialectically expressing on the one hand ''death and suffering,'' ''trouble and exile,'' ''strife and hiding,'' and on the other hand ''an unvoiced longing toward a truer world,'' ''a hope—a faith in the ultimate justice of things.''[53] However, despite his description of them as ''the most beautiful expression of human experience born this side of the seas,''[54] Du Bois raises a question that focuses on them less as aesthetic remnants of African or of plantation culture than as signalling unfulfilled hopes, crushed expectations, and deferred dreams of those who crooned them. He asks whether the hope expressed in these songs rings true, whether such a hope is justified.[55] This question offers a clue to the manner in which he interprets the African-American past. The sorrow songs lead him to represent that past as itself once a future, since the songs conveyed that future in terms of the hopes and expectations of enslaved Africans, hopes and expectations that were suppressed and went unfulfilled. For Du Bois, they delineate a future past in which the possibility of enslaved Africans' extending the bounds of their expectations and innovations in a utopian manner is nullified.

This future past of enslaved Africans, according to Du Bois, has increasingly led those on the modern scene in the west to assume, if not unabashedly claim, that the probationary period of enslaved Africans and their heirs for entering the modern world is now over, because they have demonstrated their improficiency and are thus unworthy of redemption. For Du Bois, ''such an assumption is the arrogance of peoples *irreverent toward Time* and ignorant of the deeds of men.''[56] This ''irreverence toward Time,'' I believe, is an attitude shaped by ''the Veil,'' an attitude that the future past of enslaved Africans, i.e., the history of African-Americans, is a *terra incognita* and a *tempus incognitum*. In effect, this ''irreverence toward Time'' signifies ''the Veil''-shaped view that, for African-American forms of life, history is an empty and shapeless continuum and is incapable of serving as an alembic as it does for other cultural forms of life.

Du Bois' interpretation of the sorrow songs is intended to undermine this view. Shackled to the historical continuum of drudgery, fatalism, and sheer survival and thereby deprived of the calling to a good and just life, enslaved Africans, according to Du Bois, projected these melodies in tones hopeful toward bringing this continuum to a halt, if only for a fleeting moment. And in that moment, when this continuum is briefly punctuated, their songs soberly conveyed the hopeful message that "men will judge men by their souls not by their skins,"[57] a message sociopsychologically and socioculturally innovative with respect to an historical continuum endlessly pressing forward, marked by the denial of social justice. The sorrow songs are for Du Bois the aesthetic and moral precinct in which the hopes and expectations of enslaved Africans are problematically coupled with the temporal aspects of modernity, because they give expression to how enslaved Africans briefly yet repeatedly *disconnected their hopes and expectations from this continuum but without satisfaction or fulfillment.*

Du Bois also counters the "irreverence of Time" with his representation of a future-oriented present as the possible experience of a "second slavery." Throughout SBF, he incessantly invokes the representation of enslavement to delineate the social condition of post-Emancipation African-Americans. His claim about a "second slavery" can be supported by a number of events of which he was well aware. For example, in the decade prior to the publication of SBF, the fourth major race riot in New York City had occurred, 1,665 African-Americans had been lynched, and "law courts became the almost universal device of reenslaving blacks,"[58] as exemplified by the Supreme Court decisions of *Plessy vs. Ferguson* (1896) and *Williams vs. Mississippi* (1898) which legalized racial segregation and black disfranchisement respectively.[59]

In the context of modern African-American forms of life, Du Bois' discussion of a "second slavery" triggers, even today, the view of the future-oriented present of African-Americans as a continuation of previous enslavement, thereby leading to their characterization, if not disparagement, as "perpetual victims," to use the current argot. This view has been subject to a good deal of criticism by the likes of Zora Neale Hurston, George Schuyler and, more recently, Shelby Steele, all of whom would in their various ways claim that such a view mortgages the sense of future happiness amongst African-Americans and encumbers their disposition to make or take opportunities for individual advancement. Du Bois' depiction of the future-oriented present of African-Americans in terms of a "second slavery" does lend itself to this view. But it primarily reflects his belief that the past of African-Americans cannot be allowed to descend so far below the surface of their future-oriented present as to be ultimately ignored.

At the crux of the notion of a "second slavery" is the expansion of African-Americans' future-oriented present as a locus for the retrieval of their tradition through recollection. Du Bois employs it to argue that African-Americans in a future-oriented present cannot accept the realization of modernity without recognizing that it has been (and can continue to be) bought with the irreparable injustice and misery inflicted on past generations of enslaved Africans. The two principles of modernity—the future as a locus free of discontent while open to novelty and as an epoch for structures of interaction inclusive of all persons regardless of race—are sullied, violated for African-Americans. What engenders the violation can be neither cleansed nor purged. Usually one intellectually discredits this breach by counterfactually extending those principles to past generations of enslaved Africans. But Du Bois does not take that route, because the counterfactual extension fosters the view that the violation and its cause can now in the future-oriented present be made moot, fall into oblivion, and be forgotten. He wants to insure against that possibility, since he seeks a way for African-Americans to achieve some kind of virtual compensation for the breach.

Only through recollection can African-Americans of a future-oriented present virtually compensate for the violation of the principles of modernity. For Du Bois, recollection pries loose from the continuum of past horrors fleeting revelations of enslaved Africans punctuating it with forms of expression that rendered their hopes and expectations of what counted as good and just reflectively transparent albeit constantly unfulfilled. It enables African-Americans to highlight fragments torn from the past and define them as motives for rending "the Veil"; it enables them to conceive themselves as breaking the repetition of unfulfilled expectations regarding what counts as good and just in their future-oriented present. Without it, they fall victims to the "irreverence toward Time" and to the "ignorance of the deeds of men," succumbing to a complacency of mind regarding a past that goes unredeemed and a future-oriented present that lends itself to being forgotten.

This is why modernity in black, for Du Bois, is not the African-American experience of progress and uplift that gives to the hopes and expectations of African-Americans a radically novel quality immune from discontent and open to utopian conceptions. It involves tempering the future-oriented present of African-Americans with the "sobering realization of the meaning of progress,"[60] and this comes with what he calls the "change of the child of Emancipation to the youth with dawning self-consciousness, self-realization, self-respect."[61] Du Bois' conception of a future-oriented present entails the retrieval of slavery's institutional legacy not as a moment of some sociocultural developmental scheme, but as a moment accorded significance in and for such a present. That retrieval is meant to provoke those endowed with "dawning self-consciousness" in a future-oriented present to recognize that the transmitted testimony of a future past is a matter of their own utmost practical concerns lest it give way to vanishing irretrievably. The transmitted content of the future past of enslaved

Africans lays a claim on those endowed with "dawning self-consciousness" and with "some faint revelation of [their] power, of [their] mission"[62] to stand in compassionate solidarity with previous generations of enslaved Africans.

Modernity in black is further "sobered" by a "more careful adjustment of education to real life [and a] clearer perception of the Negroes' social responsibilities."[63] Given my discussion so far, this signifies for Du Bois that black institutions of higher learning, regardless of their liberal or vocational status, must inculcate in African-Americans an historical awareness, which mitigates the preponderance of an ever developing future-oriented present over the contents of the past. Such an awareness treats the African-American past as the horizon of enslaved Africans' unfulfilled expectations and the African-American future-oriented present as retrospectively experiencing embers of hope in response to currently urgent tasks (poverty, illiteracy, continuing racial discrimination, etc.). In this historical awareness are laced two themes for Du Bois: first, that the African-American tradition is established no more by "the Veil"-formed drudgery, gaucherie, and solecism than by its own cultural codes, and second, that each new generation of "college-bred Negroes" bears the responsibility intellectually and ethically not only for future generations of African-Americans but also for the tragically endured fate of prior generations of enslaved Africans.

Like Crummell and Washington before him, Du Bois recognizes that the college-bred or New Negro is subject to the burden of the future of preparing African-Americans for entrance into modern civil society. But whereas for the former two, the New Negro is summoned to historically responsible action which overrides either anything in the past of African-Americans or how that past is construed, Du Bois advocates the position that the New Negro's or talented tenth's openness to future alternatives and innovations, its future-oriented responsibility, also covers past epochs delineated in terms of hopes and expectations. For Du Bois, then, modernity in black concentrates on the talented tenth's responsibility for meeting the pressures of the future which are now augmented, through recollection, with a future past unfulfilled.

From the foregoing discussion, we can now delineate why the problem of modernity is the problem of the color line. Whereas modernity in the west fosters the belief that a future-oriented present, severed from any sense of an historical past, can yield culturally distinctive and progressive innovations, modernity in black promotes the conviction that a future-oriented present can be the fortunate occasion in which culturally distinctive innovations are historically redemptive of a sense of past. No African-American innovation or novelty in a future-oriented present can be culturally progressive or uplifting if it is not historically redemptive at the same time. *Modernity in black thus retrieves a sense of the past not to be subject to its binding authority, but rather to deliver it from a silent oblivion threatening to deprive it of any novel role it could assume in a future-*

oriented present, in the light of the "need of new ideas and new aims," if I may here use the words of Crummell.

This threat compels Du Bois to entertain the thought that modernity for African-Americans could yield a freedom without cultural renascense or a prosperity without freedom, in short an emancipation without happiness as signalled by the rise and fall of "the Veil."[64] This idea of a meaningless emancipation looms large for Du Bois, unlike his predecessors or contemporaries. Douglass, for example, would regard an African-American cultural renascence as an insignificant venture in the light of rending "the Veil," and hence could affirm wittingly a freedom without cultural fulfillment. Crummell would advocate an African-American cultural renascence in the light of rending "the Veil," but would believe that African-American patterns of meaning were symbolically deficient and that such a renascence would require patterns of meaning outside of African-American culture. Hence, despite his advocacy, Crummell could affirm unwittingly a freedom without cultural fulfillment. Washington would claim that an African-American economic renascence would be compatible with "the Veil" since he would believe that the slave experience had engendered patterns of meaning conducive for economic success. Hence Washington could affirm a prosperity without freedom (whether wittingly or unwittingly I shall leave to the reader).

Modernity in black rings paradoxically in these accounts, save for Douglass', in which it is without sense. Du Bois' SBF undoes the paradoxical character of these accounts while countering the possibility of a meaningless emancipation. Here he is concerned that, even in the context of emancipation or modernity in the west, African-Americans could still find themselves depleted of semantic content necessary to interpret their forms of life as something meaningful and good.[65] African-American cultural innovation and progress are measured by the extent to which they are historically redemptive and thus bring to awareness elements wrested from the past, placing African-Americans in a future-oriented present in a critical position. They are at odds with what counts as cultural innovation and progress in the west, because those elements of the African-American past have been jettisoned from or ignored within that modern context. Consequently, in the modern western setting, African-American cultural innovations can be assessed only by mortgaging any historically redemptive and therewith distinctive capacity they may have possessed. They would be innovations on which elements of an African-American past have no claim, and which would dispense with the importance of African-Americans' retrieving their past.

Nonetheless, many have argued *contra* Du Bois that modernity in the west resolves the problem of the color line. Under its auspices, civil, legal, and moral forms of interaction cannot in principle be legitimately informed by race as a natural determination. Du Bois never denied this. Yet he also recognizes that these forms of interaction always presupposes the ethical and historical identities of the individuals involved, even though these forms are not rendered legitimate by an appeal to any specific ethical and historical identity. They are made legitimate through the reciprocally recognized self-determination of those individuals, and their ethical and historical identities are at work only insofar as they give concrete content to an otherwise abstract notion like self-determination.

What Du Bois wants to subvert is the allegation that African-Americans employ "race" only as a natural determination and not as a component of an ethical/historical identity fashioned in accordance with their self-determining capacity. But even if successful, he knows that race as an ethical/historical identity does not itself establish the structure of social interaction. Rather the reciprocally recognized self-determination of individuals provides the structure within which their ethical/historical identities are operative in social interaction. If the ethical/historical identities of individuals were to establish the structure of interaction, they would enjoin those individuals to act on obligations and fidelities rooted in the norms and traditions of their respective racial/cultural group, fidelities that would not necessarily command mutual respect.

The exercise of self-determination reflects the autonomy of one's personhood *and* it individuates through the appropriating of an ethical/historical identity in a context with others likewise exercising self-determination. Here interaction comprises not simply the relation between individuals with different ethical/historical identities but the relation between similarly self-determining yet distinct ethical/historical individuals. Respect for one's ethical/historical identity on the part of others come from the recognition that straightforwardly accompanies the exercise of self-determination. Regardless of being either a part or the whole of one's ethical/historical identity, race is, to use Du Bois' term, "conserved" yet always open to revision in that reciprocally recognized exercise. Although the principle of this exercise has its origins in Europe, it is not distinctly European, because its validity cannot be measured by its point of origin. But within the context of modernity in the west, the principle's validity has been so measured. Consequently, the principle itself has been comprehended along European ethical/historical lines, blocking the construction of ethical/historical identities of Africans and African-Americans through self-determination. This is why Du Bois works out a cultural modernity in black.[66]

In conclusion, my discussion stayed clear of interpreting the talented tenth of modernity in terms of class stratification, not because I believe that approach is wrong, but because I wanted to consider the talented tenth of modernity in terms of double consciousness. My reading gives the talented tenth of modernity a philosophically idealist rather than an economically materialist stance. It shows a much greater segmentation within the talented tenth of modernity itself, a segmentation that heretofore has not been articulated, an understanding of which can provide a better appreciation of the task, I believe, Du Bois set for this group, viz., inculcating in African-Americans that cultural uplift and progress must be historically redemptive.

This task, I believe Du Bois would assert, is best executed by that segment of the group that is of "dawning self-consciousness." Being clear about this segmentation enables one to better counter the disparaging critiques of the talented tenth of modernity registered by the likes of Carter G. Woodson, Zora Neale Hurston, C. L. R. James, E. Franklin Frazier, Nathan Huggins, and even Du Bois himself, because it opens up, I would claim, different schemes for construing the theory/practice relationship within the African-American tradition. But these are matters for future consumption. Even the matters addressed in this essay are only an appetizer, since I have stopped the analysis historically at 1903 and have neither presented nor subjected to criticism systematically the reflections of African-American women intellectuals on the question of modernity.[16] Nevertheless, for these issues, the skillet has just been "greased."

Hunter College and Graduate Center, City University of New York

NOTES

1 Orlando Patterson, "Toward a Future That Has No Past: Reflections on the Fate of Blacks in the Americas," in *The Public Interest,* No. 27 (Spring 1972), pp. 60–61.

2 Patterson, "Toward a Future That Has No Past," p. 45.

3 Patterson, "Toward a Future That Has No Past," p. 62.

4 Patterson, "Toward a Future That Has No Past," p. 62.

5 Patterson, "Toward a Future That Has No Past," p. 46.

6 Patterson, "Toward a Future That Has No Past," pp. 50–59.

7 Patterson, "Toward a Future That Has No Past," p. 55.

8 W. E. B. Du Bois, "The Talented Tenth," in *Du Bois: Writings,* ed. Nathan Huggins (New York: The Library of America, 1986), pp. 842–61.

9 Du Bois' position is, I believe, influenced by his reading of and association with Max Weber, who argued for the importance of connecting historical sociology with a theory of value. While at the University of Heidelberg, Du Bois was a student of Weber, and while in Atlanta in 1904, Weber visited Du Bois and solicited an essay from him entitled "Die Negerfrage in den Vereinigten Staaten." It was published in Weber's journal *Archiv für Sozialwissenschaft und Sozialpolitik* in 1906.

10 Du Bois, "The Talented Tenth," pp. 842–46.

11 Houston Baker has also raised this point in his monograph *Modernism and the Harlem Renaissance* (Chicago: University of Chicago Press, 1987).

12 See a "Letter to Col. Hinton, 1867," in *A Brighter Coming Day: A Frances Ellen Watkins Harper Reader,* ed. Frances Smith Foster (New York: The Feminist Press at CUNY, 1990), p. 124.

13 Alexander Crummell, *Africa and America: Addresses and Discourses* (Miami: Mnemosyne Publishing Company, 1969), pp. 13, 14, and 18.
14 Crummell, *Africa and America,* p. 18.
15 Cf. Reinhart Koselleck, *Futures Past: On the Semantics of Historical Time* (Cambridge: MIT Press, 1985), pp. 267–270.
16 Crummell, *Africa and America,* p. iv.
17 Frederick Douglass, ''Why Is the Negro Lynched,'' in *The Life and Writings of Frederick Douglass,* Vol. 4, ed. Philip S. Foner, (New York: International Publishers, 1950), p. 518.
18 Alexander Crummell, ''Civilization, The Primal Need of the Race,'' *American Negro Academy Occasional Papers,* No. 3 (Washington, D.C.: The American Negro Academy, 1898).
19 Crummell, ''Civilization,'' p. 6.
20 Alexander Crummell, ''The Race Problem in America,'' in *Africa and America: Addesses and Discourses,* p. 48.
21 Crummell, ''The Race Problem,'' p. 46.
22 Cf. G. W. F. Hegel, *The Philosophy of Right,* trans. T. M. Knox (New York: Oxford University Press, 1967).
23 Cf. Frederick Douglass, ''The Nation's Problem,'' in *Negro Social and Political Thought, 1850–1920: Representative Texts,* ed. Howard Brotz (New York: Basic Books, 1966), pp. 311–28.
24 Cf. Alexander Crummell, ''The English Language in Liberia,'' in *The Future of Africa* (New York: Scribner, 1862), pp. 9–57. Also cf. Alexander Crummell, ''The Attitude of the American Mind Toward the Negro Intellect,'' *American Negro Academy Occasional Papers,* No. 3 (Washington, D.C.: The American Negro Academy, 1898), pp. 12–16.
25 Booker T. Washington, *Up From Slavery,* in *Three Negro Classics* (New York: Avon Books, 1965), p. 149.
26 Washington, *Up From Slavery,* p. 148.
27 I make use of Habermas' conceptual distinction between ''lifeworld'' and ''system'' to inform for the most part my distinction between slavery as an ''institution'' and as a ''system.''
28 Washington, *Up From Slavery,* p. 30.
29 Washington, *Up From Slavery,* p. 31.
30 Washington, *Up From Slavery,* pp. 35–36.
31 Washington, *Up From Slavery,* pp. 37–38.
32 Washington, *Up From Slavery,* p. 37.
33 Booker T. Washington, *Black-Belt Diamonds: Gems from the Speeches, Addresses, and Talks to Students of Booker T. Washington,* selected and arranged by Victoria Earle Matthews (New York: Negro Universities Press, 1969), pp. 8, 9, 10.
34 Washington, *Up From Slavery,* p. 37.
35 Cf. Alexander Crummell, ''The Dignity of Labor and Its Value to a New People,'' in *Africa and America: Addresses and Discourses,* p. 71.
36 W. E. B. Du Bois, *The Souls of Black Folk,* in *Three Negro Classics* (New York: Avon Books, 1965).
37 Du Bois, *The Souls of Black Folk,* p. 380.
38 Du Bois, *The Souls of Black Folk,* pp. 214–15.
39 Du Bois, *The Souls of Black Folk,* p. 215.
40 Du Bois, *The Souls of Black Folk,* p. 387.
41 Du Bois, *The Souls of Black Folk,* pp. 344–45.
42 Du Bois, *The Souls of Black Folk,* p. 345.
43 Du Bois, *The Souls of Black Folk,* pp. 345–46.
44 Du Bois, *The Souls of Black Folk,* p. 348.

45 Du Bois, *The Souls of Black Folk,* p. 346.
46 Du Bois, *The Souls of Black Folk,* p. 346.
47 Du Bois, *The Souls of Black Folk,* p. 346.
48 Du Bois, *The Souls of Black Folk,* p. 347.
49 Du Bois, *The Souls of Black Folk,* p. 218.
50 Du Bois, *The Souls of Black Folk,* p. 220.
51 Du Bois, *The Souls of Black Folk,* p. 250.
52 Du Bois, *The Souls of Black Folk,* p. 272.
53 Du Bois, *The Souls of Black Folk,* pp. 380, 382, and 386.
54 Du Bois, *The Souls of Black Folk,* p. 378.
55 Du Bois, *The Souls of Black Folk,* p. 386.
56 Du Bois, *The Souls of Black Folk,* p. 386.
57 Du Bois, *The Souls of Black Folk,* p. 386.
58 Du Bois, *The Souls of Black Folk,* p. 330.
59 Cf. Rayford W. Logan, *The Negro in American Life and Thought: The Nadir, 1877–1901* (New York: Dial, 1954), pp. 97–116. Also cf. James Weldon Johnson, *Along This Way* (New York: Viking Press, 1969), p. 158.
60 Du Bois, *The Souls of Black Folk,* p. 219.
61 Du Bois, *The Souls of Black Folk,* p. 218.
62 Du Bois, *The Souls of Black Folk,* p. 218.
63 Du Bois, *The Souls of Black Folk,* p. 219.
64 Although I cannot delve into this matter here, the actual phenomenon within African-American history of an emancipation without meaning or fulfillment motivates my reading of Du Bois' SBF in terms of the reflections of Walter Benjamin, especially his texts *Die Ursprung des deutschen Trauerspiels* and the *Passagen-Werk.*
65 This sentiment is brought home in a remark by Du Bois in "Of the Meaning of Progress." He states, "The mass of those to whom slavery was a dim recollection of childhood found the world a puzzling thing: it asked little of them, and they answered with little, and yet it ridiculed their offering." Cf. *The Souls of Black Folk,* p. 258.
66 Kwame Anthony Appiah and Bernard Boxill interpret the intellectual career of Du Bois' thought on race in the light of his Crummellian-inspired essay "The Conservation of the Races" (1897), in which Du Bois argues for treating race *solely* as a notion expressing ethical and cultural difference and not as one expressing biological difference. Both argue that Du Bois was unable to give warrant to his claim since all attempts to treat race as a notion expressing cultural difference either required falling back onto a scientifically invalidated biological notion (Appiah) or yielded certain paradoxes if the cultural notion were to be separated from the burdens of racism (Boxill). I have argued, however, that in SBF Du Bois discusses the cultural notion of race in the light of "the Veil," thereby not separating it from the pressures of racism, and therewith meeting Boxill's objection. Du Bois' position in SBF on this matter is consistent with that expressed in *Dusk of Dawn* (1940), and it signals his theoretical break with Crummell on this point.

However, Appiah would not see this position meeting his objection, because he believes that, if one employs the cultural notion of race, one can never eschew the appeal to the biological notion which leads to identifying and differentiating groups according to ungrounded essentialist traits. So, for Appiah, the cultural idea that "being (partially) descended from black people makes one 'really' [essentially] black in ways that have ethical consequences" rests on false beliefs about the underlying biology.

Let me take a less metaphysical than hermeneutic/pragmatic perspective. Granting everything that the modern biological sciences have said against the notion of race expressing biologically significant identities and differences amongst groups, it is still possible for this scientific accomplishment not to permeate or feed back into the social reality. (For instance, it has long since been an astronomical truism that the sun neither rises nor sets but, as we know, that truism has not permeated or disturbed our palpable knowledge and aesthetic appreciation of what we refer to as sunrises and sunsets.) The scientific achievement invalidating the notion of race has not effectively permeated the social reality due to the recalcitrant social phenomenon of racism and its historical legacy.

Under these circumstances, the notion of race cuts across three areas of the social reality—culture, language, and the body (and not just the body simply as "living organism")—which institutionalizes cogent yet controvertible beliefs about race as a significant component of one's ethical identity. Cogent because socially based palpable knowledge about race is disclosed as rational only against the social background of which the legacy (and currency) of racism is a part. Controvertible because the cogency of those beliefs about race rests on reasons that are assailable and subject to modification as the social reality changes over the long term. So one could say that the cultural idea that being (partially) descended from black people makes one "really" (palpably) black in ways that have ethical consequences rests on cogent yet controvertible beliefs about race arising out of the social reality. See the following: Anthony Appiah, "The Uncompleted Argument: Du Bois and the Illusion of Race," in *Critical Inquiry,* Vol. 12, No. 1, Autumn 1985, pp. 21–37; Anthony Appiah, "The Conservation of 'Race,' " in *Black American Literature Forum,* Vol. 23, No. 1, Spring 1989, pp. 37–60; Anthony Appiah, " 'But Would That Still Be Me?': Notes on Gender, 'Race,' Ethnicity As Sources of Identity" in the *Journal of Philosophy,* Vol. 87, No. 10, October 1990, pp. 493–99; Bernard Boxill, *Blacks and Social Justice* (Totowa: Rowman & Allanheld, 1984), pp. 173–85; Alain Locke, "The Concept of Race as Applied to Social Culture" and "The Contribution of Race to Culture," in *The Philosophy of Alain Locke: Harlem Renaissance and Beyond,* ed. Leonard Harris (Philadelphia: Temple University Press, 1989), pp. 187–99 and 201–6.

67 To this end I have learned a great deal from the approach of Hazel Carby's *Reconstructing Womanhood: The Emergence of the Afro-American Novelist* (New York: Oxford University Press, 1987).

DU BOIS ON THE INVENTION OF RACE

TOMMY L. LOTT

In his well-known address to the newly founded American Negro Academy, W. E. B. Du Bois entertained the question of the fate and destiny of African-Americans as a group, asking somewhat rhetorically, "Does my black blood place upon me any more obligation to assert my nationality than German, or Irish or Italian blood would?"[1] His answer was that it is "the duty of the Americans of Negro descent, as a body, to maintain their race identity."[2] The argument he advanced to support this claim has sometimes been understood to suggest that African-Americans as a group are obligated to maintain and perpetuate their culture in order to retain their authenticity.[3] We should resist, however, becoming overly focused on this aspect of Du Bois's view, for it is fairly clear, on even the most cursory reading of his essay, that he was not particularly concerned with the African past as a standard for measuring the authenticity of African-American culture. Indeed, he proposed to resolve the dilemma of African-American double consciousness by appealing to a revisionist analysis of the concept of race that eschews a biological essentialist account of race identity.

One very good reason, frequently cited by commentators, for supposing that Du Bois was primarily concerned with the question of authenticity is his repeated criticism of African-Americans striving for "self-obliteration," seeking "absorption by the white Americans," or pursuing "a servile imitation of Anglo-Saxon culture."[4] Although there certainly was a concern with authenticity expressed in Du Bois's remarks, I believe that it is somewhat misleading to take this to have been his primary motivation for raising these issues, for there is a very important reason why such issues were not in the foreground of his discussion of race, and why they do not figure into his argument regarding the obligation of African-Americans to maintain their race identity. Hence, I shall present a reading of Du Bois's essay, that, with regard to the question of race identity, deviates from several recent interpretations.[5]

Du Bois's argument for the claim that African-Americans are obligated to retain their race identity is connected with his early view of the role of culture in the African-American quest for social equality.[6] In particular, he maintained that the cultural integrity of African-Americans is crucial for their gaining acceptance as social equals. The view Du Bois stated in 1897 displays the late nineteenth-century historical context of African-American social thought; consequently, many features of the argument he presented can be found in the writings of his contemporaries. By contextualizing his argument I aim to show that he presented a notion of race that was in keeping with his own version of a race uplift theory of social change. According to my interpretation, his revisionist account represents a view of race identity that accorded with the prevailing African-American social philosophy at the turn of the century. I will begin with a brief discussion of his definition of race, followed by a sketch of some of the historical sources from which he may have drawn certain ideas to develop his argument for the duty of African-Americans to retain their race identity. I want to defend the plausibility of Du Bois's sociohistorical view of race identity against several, quite damaging, criticisms and thereby salvage the major thrust of his argument.

A REVISIONIST CONCEPT OF RACE

With the aim of presenting an account tailored to fit his theory of social change, Du Bois proposed the following definition of race,

> It is a vast family of human beings, generally of common blood and language, always of common history, traditions and impulses, who are both voluntarily and involuntarily striving together for the accomplishment of certain more or less vividly conceived ideals of life.[7]

Unless we bear in mind why Du Bois was motivated to write about African-American identity, his definition of race will seem quite implausible, especially his stipulation that a racial group must *always* share a common history, traditions, and impulses, but need not always share a common blood or language. The reason Du Bois's proposal seems implausible is because he meant to implicitly contest the way the received view, which places a greater emphasis on common blood, has been socially constructed. Unfortunately, the insight that underlies his definition is diminished by the twofold nature of his account, an account which involves both a deconstruction of the received view as well as a reconstruction of his alternative conception.

Du Bois opened his essay with the statement that African-Americans are always interested in discussions regarding the origins and destinies of races because such discussions usually presuppose assumptions about the natural abilities, and the social and political status of African-Americans, assumptions that impede African-American social progress. He noted that the undesirable implications of some of these assumptions have fostered a tendency for African-Americans "to deprecate and minimize race distinctions."[8] He took himself to be giving voice to their aspiration for social equality by advancing a conception of African-Amcricans that would allow a discussion of racial distinctions while accommodating the tendency of African-Americans, under the dominating influence of racism, to want to minimize references to physical differences in such discussions.

Du Bois was interested in formulating non-biological criteria for a definition of race mainly because he wanted to provide a more adequate ground for the group identity he considered a crucial component in the African-American's social agenda. He made this clear when, with the reference to the idea of race in general, he spoke of "its efficiency as the vastest and most ingenious invention for human progress."[9] He suggested that, following the success model of other groups, African-Americans must *invent* a conception of themselves that will contribute to their social elevation as a group. His revisionist notion of race was therefore proposed at the outset of something African-Americans must self-consciously adopt for political purposes. We can notice that he did not fail to acknowledge the social construction of the concept of race when, in his citation of the eight distinct racial groups, he qualified his reference to them with the phrase "in the sense in which history tells us the word must be used."[10] What shows us that he aimed to deconstruct the received view, however, is the way he juxtaposed his sociohistorical concept of race with what he referred to as "the present division of races," viz., the scientific conception of the three main biological groups; for he goes on to point out that biology cannot provide the criteria for race identity because, historically, there has been an "integration of physical differences."[11] This fact leads him to conclude that what really distinguishes groups of people into races are their "spiritual and mental differences."[12]

Some of Du Bois's readers have rejected his sociohistorical definition of race in favor of a definition based on physical differences.[13] What Du Bois's detractors tend to overlook, however, is the fact that his definition does not deny the obvious physical differences that constitute race, nor does his discussion of race display any special commitment to the sociohistorical view he sets forth. A close reading will reveal that he only meant to deny the *viability* of a strictly biological account of race, and, furthermore, to assert that an empirical study of history will show this to be the case. Based on his own survey of anthropological findings, he tells us that when different groups of people came together to form cities,

> The larger and broader differences of color, hair and physical proportions were not by any means ignored, but myriads of minor differences disappeared, and the sociological and historical races of men began to approximate the present division of races as indicated by physical researches.[14]

The aim of Du Bois's deconstruction of the concept of race was to create a means of employing the prevailing definition of race based on genetics, i.e., to allow him to continue speaking of "the black-blooded people of America," or the "people of Negro blood in the United States," while at the same time leaving room for him to question any undesirable implications of such definitions, i.e., to override definitions that imply that the physical differences which typically characterize the various races somehow justify social inequality.

THE AFRICAN-AMERICAN CULTURAL IMPERATIVE

But what bearing does Du Bois's revised notion of race have on his argument for the claim that African-Americans have a duty to retain their race identity? As Boxill has noted, one important reason Du Bois cites to support this imperative is that African-Americans have a distinct cultural mission as a racial group.[15] On behalf of the Negro Academy, Du Bois asserted that, "We believe that the Negro people, as a race, have a contribution to make to civilization and humanity, which no other race can make."[16] But what exactly is this unique contribution? I am not sure whether Du Bois had an answer to this question. He weakly stated that African-Americans are "a nation stored with wonderful possibilities of culture," which suggests that they do not yet have any such cultural contribution to make. He then goes on to speak of "a stalwart originality which shall unswervingly follow Negro ideals."[17] And, although he makes passing references to "Pan-Negroism" and the "African fatherland," at no point does he advocate reclaiming any African cultural retentions.[18] Instead, he prefers to tell us that "it is our duty to conserve our physical powers, our intellectual endowments, our spiritual ideals."[19]

What then did Du Bois mean when he spoke of the duty of African-Americans to conserve their race identity in order to make a cultural contribution? His view of what constitutes African-American culture seems especially problematic when we consider some of his remarks regarding African-American identity. He states that,

> We are Americans, not only by birth and by citizenship, but by our political ideals, our language, our religion. Farther than that, our Americanism does not go. At that point, we are Negroes, members of a vast historic race that from the very dawn of creation has slept, but half awakening in the dark forests of its African fatherland.[20]

If African-Americans share the same language, religion, and political ideals with other Americans there does not seem to be much left for them to uniquely contribute to American culture.[21] Although, in some places, Du Bois spoke of the African-American's special mission in terms of a distinct cultural contribution he seems to have had more than simply culture in mind. I suspect that he really meant to speak of a *political* mission that culture in some way enables African-Americans to carry out. This is suggested, for instance, by his remarks regarding "that black to-morrow which is yet destined to soften the whiteness of the Teutonic to-day."[22] What Du Bois may have meant here is simply that, through the establishment of a culturally pluralistic society, white cultures will no longer dominate. Instead, social equality will be fostered through a cultural exchange between the various races.

If we consider Du Bois's sociohistorical definition of race, along with his belief that African-Americans have a special mission, his rejection of biological essentialism and his failure to make use of the idea of African cultural retentions, begin to appear quite troublesome.[23] For, as Appiah has keenly observed, his talk of Pan-Negroism requires that African-Americans and Africans share something in common other than oppression by whites.[24] This lacuna in Du Bois's argument can be explained to some extent by considering the *tentative* nature of the duty of African-Americans to conserve their race identity. According to Du Bois, this duty lasts only "until this mission of the Negro people is accomplished."[25] These remarks imply that the special mission of African-Americans has more to do with their struggle for social equality than with their making a cultural contribution; once social equality has been achieved, this duty no longer exists. We can see the explicitly *political* nature of this mission clearly expressed in the following remarks:

> (African-Americans) must be inspired with the Divine faith of our black mothers, that out of the blood and dust of battle will march a victorious host, a mighty nation, a peculiar people, to speak to the nations of earth a Divine truth that shall make them free.[26]

Although the imperative to make a cultural contribution has more to do with politics than with culture, there is nonetheless a link between them, for African-Americans must be inspired "out of the blood and dust of battle" to produce a unique culture that will contribute to world civilization. What makes African-American culture unique is its hybrid genesis within the context of racial oppression in America. The need for African cultural retentions is diminished given that the culture forged out of this experience will enable African-Americans to assume a role of political leadership among other black people. Du Bois's argument for the claim that African-Americans have a duty to conserve their race identity is backward-looking in the sense that it makes reference to the historical oppression of African-Americans, as a diaspora group, as a ground for this duty. His argument is forward-looking in the sense that it foresees an end to this oppression and, hence, an eventual release from the imperative.

NINETEENTH-CENTURY AFRICAN-AMERICAN SOCIAL THOUGHT

Some commentators have invoked biographical facts about Du Bois's own racial background to explain why he wanted to advance a sociohistorical account of race.[27] While it is not unfair to see this as an important factor influencing his thinking about race, it is a plain misunderstanding to suppose that the reconstruction Du Bois proposed was wholly original. When we consider his argument within the context of African-American social thought at the turn of the century, certain quite noticeable details strongly indicate the influence of his contemporaries. He alludes to many concerns that had been expressed on both sides of the perennial separatist-integrationist debate by combining, under his own concept of cultural pluralism, certain tenets drawn from various doctrines of earlier emigrationist-assimilationist thinkers such as Blyden and Douglass. By far one of the most abiding and dominant influences on his thinking was clearly Booker T. Washington. We can notice the traces of some of Du Bois's nineteenth-century influences by paying careful attention to certain ideas that crop up in his essay.

According to Wilson J. Moses, Du Bois's argument in "The Conservation of Races" was directly influenced by Alexander Crummell, whose inaugural address to the Negro Academy expressed a similar preoccupation with the idea of "civilization" as a means of social elevation.[28] Crummell, along with other nineteenth-century activists such as Henry Highland Garnet and Martin Delany, was prominent among the supporters of the African Civilization Society. The goals and values of nineteenth-century African-American nationalism were often situated in arguments regarding the development of "civilization" as a means of group elevation. With an eye to the place of African-Americans in a world civilization, Du Bois seems to reflect Blyden's earlier call of providence in his talk of an "advance guard" of African-Americans who must "take their just place in the van of Pan-Negroism."[29] Appiah has suggested this reading, perhaps inadvertently, in characterizing Du Bois's remarks regarding the African-American message for humanity as deriving from God's purpose in creating races.[30] The claim Du Bois makes here regarding the leadership role of African-Americans vis-a-vis other black people in Africa and the diaspora seems to capture the gist of Blyden's argument for emigration, although emigration was a proposal that Du Bois never embraced.

Despite the fact that his mention of "Pan-Negroism" presages the Pan-Africanism he would later adopt, Du Bois seems to have believed in 1897 that the uplift of Africa, and black people everywhere, could best be brought about by African-Americans pursuing cultural self-determination in America. Of course, the problem this poses for his sociohistorical account of race is that African-American and African cultures are significantly different. The idea of

"Pan-Negroism" he derived from that account, i.e., "Negroes bound and welded together," failed to recognize the important cultural differences among the various groups of African and African diaspora people.[31]

By contrast with Blyden's African nationalism, Frederick Douglass saw ex-slaves as Americans. He believed that, once African-Americans were educated and allowed to demonstrate their equality with whites, assimilation into the American mainstream would someday be possible. In some of his remarks, Du Bois avers to Douglass's view that slavery had severely damaged the dignity and sense of self-worth of African-Americans. He maintained that the first step toward social equality will be "the correction of the immorality, crime and laziness among the Negroes themselves, which still remains as a heritage from slavery."[32]

Under the legal segregation that followed slavery Douglass's assimilationist view found a new expression in the philosophy of Booker T. Washington. Washington's strategy for changing the socioeconomic conditions of African-Americans was to appeal to the self-interest of whites. He gave priority to economic development as a key to the elevation of African-Americans as a group. Rather than demand social equality, Washington believed it would gradually come with the economic progress of the group. Notwithstanding their much-heralded disagreement over the role of political agitation, Du Bois seems to have accepted certain aspects of Washington's strategy. Along with Washington, for instance, Du Bois advocated social separation from whites "to avoid the friction of races."[33] And Du Bois's assertion that "No people that laughs at itself, and ridicules itself, and wishes to God it was anything but itself ever wrote its name in history" seems to be a rewording of Washington's famous statement at the Atlanta Exposition that "No race that has anything to contribute to the markets of the world is long, in any degree, ostracized."[34] Both claims are reminiscent of Douglass's earlier concern with the self-esteem of African-Americans as a group. Unlike Washington, however, Du Bois placed a greater emphasis on the cultural status of African-Americans. He argued against "a servile imitation of Anglo-Saxon culture" on the ground that African-Americans have a unique cultural contribution to make and that to accomplish this they must not assimilate.[35] For Du Bois, social equality would be attained through the distinctive cultural achievements of African-Americans, who must retain their race identity in order to accomplish this.

When we consider Du Bois's idea of African-Americans gaining social equality through their cultural achievements we must not overlook some of the earlier proponents of this suggestion, viz., members of the various literary societies in the early part of the nineteenth century and the New Negro literary movement at the beginning of the 1890s.[36] Maria W. Stewart followed David Walker in the tradition of advocating moral uprightness as the basis for elevating the race, a tradition which was perpetuated throughout the nineteenth century by various African-American voluntary associations.[37] We can notice the sense of a mission, for instance, in Anna Julia Cooper's advocacy of an African-American literature "to give the character of beauty and power to the literary utterance of the race."[38] In this vein then we should understand Du Bois's statement that "it is our duty to conserve our physical powers, our intellectual endowments, our spiritual ideals." His somewhat vague proposition here emanated from a history of ideas that assigned a specific role to culture in the elevation of African-Americans as a group.

Indeed, as a cornerstone of many turn-of-the-century theories of social change, the African-American cultural imperative created a strong expectation that educated African-Americans would employ their intellectual resources in the service of race uplift. On the assumption that culture and politics must coincide, Frances E. W. Harper and Pauline E. Hopkins presented arguments in their novels for the obligation of the black elite, viz., mulattoes, to refrain from marrying whites, or passing, and instead devote themselves to the betterment of African-Americans as a group.[39] They aimed to influence some members of the group to remain loyal and to assume responsibility for elevating other members by arguing that there is a special duty requiring a sacrifice of social privilege. Du Bois seems to have heeded their teachings when he spoke against the loss of race identity in "the commingled blood of the nation," and when he raised the question "is self-obliteration the highest end to which Negro blood dare aspire?"[40]

The duty to conserve African-American race identity so as to develop a distinct culture derives from an historical context in which the oppression of African-Americans as a group obtains. Under such conditions the function of culture is to resist oppression. Even if we accept the idea that African-Americans are, in some sense, collectively obligated to resist oppression we might still wonder whether they are, for this reason, obligated to conserve their race identity so as to develop a distinctive culture. With regard to the oppression experienced by African-Americans it seems that, for Du Bois, the right of resistance is tantamount to the right of cultural self-determination. Although African-Americans are, perhaps collectively, obligated to resist oppression in the sense that every African-American has a *right* not to acculturate into the American mainstream, this does not establish that African-Americans have a *duty* to conserve a distinctive culture.[41]

RACE, ETHNICITY, AND BIOLOGY

When Du Bois defines race in terms of sociohistorical, rather than biological, or physical, criteria he seems to have blurred an important distinction between race and ethnicity, where the former is understood to refer to biological characteristics and the latter refers chiefly to cultural characteristics.[42] Several commentators have taken him to task for lapsing into this confusion. Their criticisms, however, seem to presuppose that people can be divided into biologically distinct racial groups that develop in relative isolation. Du Bois's contention was that this ideal-type model of racial and ethnic groups lacks empirical validity, for sociohistorical factors have a greater significance for understanding the essentially *political* genesis, structure, and function of such groups.

Appiah, for instance, objects to Du Bois's sociohistorical definition on the ground that a group's history or culture *presupposes* a group identity and, therefore, cannot be a criterion of that group's identity.[43] He attempts to refurbish Du Bois's talk of a common history by adding a geographical criterion such that a group's history is to be understood as (in part) the history of people from the same place. This move, however, seems needless on two counts. First, Du Bois makes clear that an important part of the history of African-Americans is their African past, and since he had little concern with cultural retentions, his point was largely a matter of geography. Secondly, as a criterion of group identity, geography does not add much, given that there are racially and culturally diverse people in various locations.

A similar objection has been raised by Boxill who points out that it is simply false to maintain that every black American shares a common culture. Instead, Boxill offers a physical definition of race that is reflected in the way the racist classifies people into races, whether they share a common culture or not:

> I propose that, insofar as black people are a race, they are people who either themselves look black—that is, have a certain kind of physical appearance—or are, at least in part, descended from such a group of people.[44]

Boxill, however, is a bit too hasty in his dismissal of the obvious fact that the American system of classification, constructed on the basis of a racist ideology, breaks down when people of mixed blood do not neatly fit into the prescribed racial categories. He makes reference to the notion of "passing" to show that, with regard to people of mixed blood, a physical definition of race still offers the best account. But he overlooks the fact that this notion is fairly limited to the United States and perhaps to similar societies with a majority white population.[45] Moreover, as I shall indicate shortly, many times the practice of racism, which informs Boxill's definition, seems to conveniently disregard the biological criteria he takes to be essential.

The best way to meet the objection that a definition of race based primarily on sociohistorical criteria confuses race with ethnicity is to accept it. In the United States the alleged confusion seems to have become a matter of institutionalized practice. College application forms, for instance, frequently display some such confusion when under the ethnic identity category they list *racial* designations such as ''black'' and ''white'' along with *ethnic* designations such as ''Japanese'' and ''Hispanic.'' It becomes clear that such a system of racial and ethnic classification is constructed for political purposes when we take note of certain combined categories such as ''Hispanic, not black.''[46] As primarily a linguistic designation, the term ''Hispanic'' can apply to groups of people who consider themselves white, black, or mixed-blood. Why then is there a need for a special category which designates a racial distinction that only singles out black people?

The idea that various notions of race have been constructed by racists for political purposes was well recognized in nineteenth-century African-American social thought. In his 1854 essay, ''The Claims of the Negro Ethnologically Considered,'' Douglass accused the slaveholders of seeking a justification in science for the oppression of slaves. He pointed out that by engaging arguments that amount to ''scientific moonshine that would connect men with monkeys,'' they wanted ''to separate the Negro race from every intelligent nation and tribe in Africa.'' Douglass surmised that ''they aimed to construct a theory in support of a foregone conclusion.''[47]

A similar accusation was published anonymously in 1859 in an article in the *Anglo-African Magazine*. The author begins with the claim that there is no pure unmixed Anglo-Saxon race, arguing that all whites with ethnic backgrounds (even with Egyptian blood) still claim to be Anglo-Saxon. The author then refers to the construction of the Anglo-Saxon race as ''a legendary theory.''[48] The underlying racism of this theory, which relies on the Bible, is exposed by raising the question: if the curse of Canaan is used to prove that black blood is contaminated, what about the curse that marked out Anglo-Saxons for slavery? According to the author, Noah's curse did not point specifically to black people since Cush and Canaan were both sons of Ham. Ethnologists who use Biblical references to establish racial distinctions that imply black inferiority employ ''a curious chain of evidence,'' for there is no African race, i.e., no group with pure African blood. The author reduces to absurdity the Biblical evidence for this belief, according to which:

> First, Abyssinians belong to a white race.
> Secondly, Ethiopians were the same as the Abyssinians.
> Lastly, the Negroes were Ethiopians.[49]

The conclusion drawn from this *reductio* argument was that Negroes (Ethiopians) belong to the white race. The author's purpose in presenting this argument seems to have been to urge that all racial terms be treated as misnomers.

These nineteenth-century discussions of race indicate two of the most important factors underlying Du Bois's deconstruction of the biological concept of race, viz., racism and intermingling. Although the identity of every racial or ethnic group will involve both (a) physical or biological criteria and (b) cultural or sociohistorical criteria, whether, in any given society, (a) gains precedence over (b) seems to be a matter of politics, i.e., racism. But even in societies such as the United States where biological criteria have gained precedence, the fact of intermingling has rendered any attempt to establish rigid biological racial classifications problematic. When we consider groups such as Chicanos, Amerasians, or Cape Verdians it becomes clear that ethnic designations are needed to accommodate interminglings that have resulted in the creation of group identities that are based almost entirely on sociohistorical criteria.[50]

THE DILEMMA OF BIOLOGICAL ESSENTIALISM

One major shortcoming of Du Bois's sociohistorical concept of race is that it fails to make clear how, in the face of racism, African-Americans are supposed to invent, or reconstruct, a concept of black identity that will contribute to the progress of the group. Racism is firmly grounded in scientific thinking regarding biologically determined racial types such that, for conceptual reasons, it seems undeniable that there are fundamentally yellow, black, and white people, despite any other ethnic, or cultural, designation that applies to them.[51] As Appiah has noted, Du Bois's proposal to replace the biological concept of race with a sociohistorical one "is simply to bury the biological conception below the surface, not to transcend it."[52] What is at issue, however, is whether the rigid dichotomy between race and ethnicity is tenable. Du Bois introduced sociohistorical criteria as a way to give an account of African-American group identity without presupposing this dichotomy. His insight was to draw from the history of racial intermingling in the United States both an objection to the biological essentialism of scientific classifications, as well as a ground on which to reconstruct African-American group identity in a social context dominated by a racist ideology.

With regard to the political aspect of Du Bois's reconstructionist project there is a dilemma posed by the ideological competition between Pan-African nationalists and Pan-Indian nationalists, both of whom have made appeals for unity to the same mixed-blood populations.[53] Each nationalist group wants to lay claim to much of the same constituency as rightfully belonging to it, and each would justify this claim by reference to the relevant biological ancestry. Their respective injunctions regarding group loyalty make use of this essentialized conception of group membership for political purposes. In keeping with the biology inherent in their respective appeals for group loyalty, persons mixed with both African and Indian ancestry are asked to identify with the group that best represents their physical appearance.[54]

It is worth noting that the nationalist's motivation for establishing such rigid biological criteria for group membership is strictly political. Since black people and Indians are oppressed on the basis of race, rather than culture, the nationalists are rightfully inclined to seek to reconstruct the group identity of black people, or Indians, on strictly racial grounds. Du Bois, of course, recognized this and sought to achieve the same political ends as the nationalists, but without invoking the biological categories handed down from scientific racism. He wanted to accommodate the fact that intermingling had become an important feature of the history of African-Americans as a group. For Du Bois, then, group loyalty need not rely on a biological essentialism, given that most African-Americans are of mixed blood. As a criterion of group identity, he proposed to give culture a greater weight than physical characteristics.

The way biology is used to rationalize the American system of racial classification gives rise to an interesting puzzle regarding the dichotomy between race and ethnicity. Consider, for instance, the case in which two siblings are racially distinct, in some genetic sense, but have the same physical characteristics, as when a white male has offspring by both a black and a white female.[55] We can speak of the offspring as being racially distinct on wholly genetic grounds, given that one child has two white parents and the other is of mixed parentage. The fact that this particular genetic difference should matter with regard to racial classification suggests a reason for the belief that race and ethnicity are not interchangeable concepts, viz., only the offspring of two white parents can be considered white.[56]

This particular application of biological criteria becomes much more problematic, however, when the practice of tracing genetic background fails to neatly correlate with the practice of using physical characteristics as a basis for racial classification. We can see this problem by considering an example that involves a multiracial ethnic group that overlaps both black and white racial categories. Suppose that the female offspring of black/white mixed-blood parents has the same physical characteristics as the male offspring of non-black Hispanic parents, and further that they marry and have two children (a boy and a girl) who both, in turn, marry whites. Both are genetically black due to their mother's mixed blood, but since the girl no longer has a Spanish surname her children will be classified as white, while her brother's children will be classified as Hispanic. What this shows, I think, is not only that concepts of race and ethnicity are sometimes interchangeable, but also that, for sociological reasons, at some point genetics frequently drops out of consideration as a basis for racial classification.[57]

We might wonder whether the emphasis Du Bois placed on sociohistorical criteria avoids the nationalist dilemma that arises on the biological essentialist account. Suppose that there are two persons with the same racial and cultural profile, i.e., each is of mixed heritage (with one black parent), each has the physical characteristics of a white person, and each has been acculturated into a white community. What if one decides to adopt a black identity despite her white cultural background? Can her newly acquired consciousness allow her to transcend her cultural background? Given the American system of racial classification, based on genetics, she is entitled to claim a black identity, something which seems to be ruled out on strictly sociohistorical grounds.[58]

In many cases where members of multiracial ethnic groups seem to have pretty much adopted some version of Du Bois's sociohistorical criteria for their own group identity we can notice that the race-culture ambivalence engendered by the American system of racial classification is frequently resolved along cultural lines. For black Latinos, such as Puerto Ricans, Cubans, or Dominicans, language exerts an overriding influence on their group identity. Persons with black ancestry who have acculturated into these Latino groups would, in many instances, be more inclined to identify with people who share their cultural orientation than with people who share their physical characteristics, despite a great deal of pressure from the dominant society to abide by the prescribed racial classifications.[59]

Du Bois has been taken to task for giving insufficient attention to the cultural differences among different groups of black people in various parts of the world. Indeed, his sociohistorical notion seems to break down when applied to culturally distinct groups of black people. But if in many cases culture gains precedence over race as a basis for group identity, he must have thought that there is something universal, or essential, in the cultures of all the various black ethnic groups, viz., a common history of oppression. Appiah has objected to Du Bois's sociohistorical essentialism by pointing out that it fails to uniquely apply to black people, for African-Americans share a history of oppression with many groups other than Africans or diaspora black people. This objection must be questioned, for I do not think it does much damage to Du Bois's suggestion that a commonly shared history of oppression provides a basis for African-American identity and for Pan-African unity.

What Du Bois was after with his reconstructed notion of race is best exemplified by considering its application to Jews. Membership in this group is determined mainly, but not exclusively, by a blood relationship (i.e., matrilineal descent) with other members of the group.[60] Yet Jews are represented in all three of the biological races, most likely as a result of having intermingled.[61] Jewish identity does not seem to be strictly a matter of culture, i.e., religion, or language, for during the Inquisition many people who were Jewish "by birth" were forced to convert to Catholicism (hence the term "Jewish Catholic"), and, presently, there are many individuals who have chosen not to learn Hebrew, or to practice a religion, yet in both cases they would still be considered Jews, and by and large they would themselves accept this designation. What then is essential to having a Jewish identity?

One very important factor which plays a major role in the construction of Jewish identity is the history of oppression commonly shared by Jews of all races and cultures.[62] With regard to this oppression there is a sociohistorical continuity to the consciousness which unifies the group that is perpetuated by the persistence of antisemitism. Moreover, this consciousness seems to extend uniquely throughout the Jewish diaspora and, since the holocaust, has provided a rallying call for the maintenance of a homeland in Israel. What is important to notice in this regard is that contemporary Zionists in Israel have been accused of racism toward non-Jews, while antisemitism directed toward Jews seems to be virtually identical with other varieties of racism.[63] What this shows, I think, is that there seems to be some sense in which racist practices can be attributed to a multiracial ethnic group, and equally, a sense in which such groups can be considered the victims of racism.

In considering how Du Bois's reconstructed notion of race can be applied to multiracial ethnic groups we must not assume that this is always by virtue of intermingling in the sense of some form of racial amalgamation. In both the United States and in Latin American societies where so-called "miscegenation" has occurred, the mixed-blood populations are largely the result of involuntary sexual contact between white masters and their slaves.[64] In this historical context racism toward ex-slaves and their offspring has produced a value system such that "whitening" has become the racial ideal.[65] Although this is, understandably, a dominant tendency among oppressed Third World people generally, we must not allow the influence of racism to blind us to a quite different sense in which racial identities have been constructed.

Consider, for instance, the fact that British colonialists sometimes referred to the natives of India and Australia as "blacks" and "niggers." Pan-African nationalism may very well be viewed as a response to colonialism, but can it therefore be restricted to groups of people of black African origin? There seems to be a clear sense in which people who are not of black African descent share a common oppression with black Africans and diaspora black people. In Australia there has developed a black consciousness movement among the aboriginals, who have appropriated a black identity heavily influenced by the sixties Civil Rights struggle in the United States.[66] In England the term "black" is often used politically to include people of both West Indian and Asian descent. The reason for this development is that the Asian immigrant populations from Pakistan and India are politically aligned (in a way that is temporary and strained at times) with the West Indian immigrant population. The basis for the formation of this multiracial coalition under the rubric "black people" is the common history of oppression they share as ex-colonial immigrant settlers in Britain.[67]

The extension of the racial term ''black'' to non-African people in Australia, as well as to Asians in contemporary Britain, provides some indication that there is a sense in which a racial concept can be reconstructed to extend to a multiracial group that has not intermingled in the sense of having mixed blood.

Du Bois's proposal regarding group identity requires an adjustment in the biological essentialist criteria to account for intermingling in the sense of racial amalgamation, but what about multiracial group coalitions? By shifting the emphasis to sociohistorical consciousness he wanted to modify the biological requirement (influenced by scientific racism) to specify only a vague blood tie. Given the fact of racial amalgamation in the United States, he rightly maintained that African-American identity can only reside in sociohistorical consciousness. It is far from clear that he would have embraced all that this implies, viz., that sociohistorical consciousness figures into the social formation of racial and ethnic groups on the model of multiracial group coalitions as well.

RACISM AND COLOR STRATIFICATION

What if a peculiar sort of cultural exchange were to suddenly occur such that the sociohistorical consciousness that once resided in the biological group now known as ''black people'' also begins to manifest itself in the biological group now known as ''white people''? Suppose further that, at some time in the future, the former group is exterminated (by genocide) or disappears (through amalgamation), and that the latter group inherits this consciousness. To what extent do we continue to apply the term ''black people''? It seems that on Du Bois's account some such transference of consciousness would be allowed as long as there is, perhaps, a blood tie (say, ''traceable'') and the inheritors have a sociohistorical connection with their ancestors. If we treat Du Bois's stipulation regarding common blood as inessential it seems that his sociohistorical criteria provide a sufficient ground on which to establish the black identity of this biological white group.[68]

While it may appear odd to speak of ''white African-Americans,'' such an expression could conceivably be applied in some sense that parallels the present usage of the expression ''black Anglo-Saxons,'' which does not seem odd.[69] In each instance the respective expression would be applied by virtue of a transference of consciousness from one biological group to another, even when there is no blood tie between them. The reason that the expression ''white African-American'' may seem odd is because in the United States the concept of race applies strictly to blacks and whites in the sense that ''traceable ancestry'' really means that to be white is to have *no* non-white ancestry and to be black is to have *any* black ancestry. With few exceptions we can safely assume that there will be only a one-way transference of consciousness, i.e., black people will acculturate into the dominant white mainstream.[70]

It would be a mistake, however, to rule out entirely the possibility of a group of white people appropriating something very much akin to the racial consciousness of African-Americans. In 1880 Gustave de Molinari documented his observation that the English press "allow no occasion to escape them of treating the Irish as an inferior race—a kind of white negroes."[71] What is most interesting about this instance of bigotry by one white ethnic group directed toward another is that it was justified by appealing to the same scientific racism used to justify the oppression of black people, i.e., the idea that the Irish were a lower species closer to the apes. Moreover, presently in Northern Ireland, Irish Catholics are sometimes referred to by Protestants as "white niggers"—and, in turn, have appropriated and politically valorized this appellation. The link between African-Americans and, say, black South Africans is largely sociohistorical such that an important feature of African-American identity includes a commonly shared history of oppression, but only in this attenuated sense. Similarly, there is no reason to suppose that Irish Catholic identity could not conceivably include, as fellow colonial subjects, a commonly shared history of oppression, in this attenuated sense, with African-Americans and black South Africans.[72]

The oddness of the concept of "white Negroes" or "white African-Americans" is a result of a special norm that places black people into a rock bottom category to which others can be assimilated for political purposes.[73] The simianized portrayal of Irish Catholics figures into their oppression and degradation in a fashion similar to the function of such portrayals of African-Americans. What must be noted, however, is that black people are the paradigm for any such category.[74] This indicates that racism is an ideology regarding the superiority of white people and the inferiority of nonwhite people. Du Bois made reference to the fact that this color spectrum is defined mainly by the black and white extremes. Although certain white ethnic groups, such as the Irish and the Jews, have experienced their own peculiar brand of racial oppression by other whites, they are not above engaging in racial discrimination against blacks.

The most telling criticism of Du Bois's attempt to reconstruct an African-American identity in terms of culture, rather than biology or physical characteristics is the fact that so much racism is based on color discrimination.[75] Unlike most racial and ethnic groups, for black people physical characteristics are more fundamental than cultural characteristics with regard to racism. It is for this reason that black Jews experience discrimination by other Jews, or that there is a need to distinguish black Hispanics from all others.[76] Racism based on color indicates that black people occupy an especially abhorrent category such that even hybrid groups that include mulattoes discriminate against them.[77]

Although certain considerations regarding the intermingling of different racial and ethnic groups motivated Du Bois's revision of the notion of race his main concern was with the impact of racism on African-American group identity. He aimed to address the problem of color discrimination within the group by providing a concept of race that would bring African-Americans of different colors together.[78] To the extent that color was an indication of class position among African-Americans he also dealt with the issue of group pride by rejecting the extremely divisive assimilationist racial ideal. He challenged the assimilationist doctrine of "whitening" by formulating the criteria of group identity in non-biological terms, a strategy designed to include African-Americans on both ends of the color spectrum. Group elevation does not require amalgamation and self-obliteration. Instead, social progress for African-Americans requires a conservation of physical characteristics (already multiracial) in order to foster cultural development. The strength of a group lies in its cultural integrity, which has to be situated in a dynamic historical process, rather than in a biologically fixed category.

San Jose State University

NOTES

My research for this essay was partially supported by a Ford Postdoctoral Fellowship, 1989–90, and by a grant from Stanford University, 1991, hereby gratefully acknowledged.

1 W. E. B. Du Bois, "The Conservation of Races," in Howard Brotz (ed.), *Negro Social and Political Thought, 1850–1920* (New York: Basic Books, 1966), p. 491. All subsequent references to Du Bois will be to this work unless otherwise indicated.
2 Du Bois, p. 491.
3 Bernard R. Boxill, *Blacks and Social Justice* (Totowa, N.J.: Rowman & Allanheld, 1984), p. 180.
4 Du Bois, p. 488.
5 Joseph P. DeMarco, *The Social Thought of W. E. B. Du Bois* (Lanham, Md.: University Press of America, 1983), pp. 31–62; Boxill, *Blacks and Social Justice,* pp. 173–85; Anthony Appiah, "The Uncompleted Argument: Du Bois and the Illusion of Race" in Henry L. Gates, Jr. (ed.), *"Race," Writing, and Difference* (Chicago: University of Chicago Press, 1985), pp. 21–37.
6 In this essay I do not take on the larger task of comparing Du Bois's claims in "The Conservation of Races" with modifications that appeared in his later writings. For useful analyses in this regard see the above cited works by DeMarco and Appiah.
7 Du Bois, p. 485.
8 Du Bois, p. 485.
9 Du Bois, p. 485.
10 Du Bois, p. 485.
11 Du Bois, pp. 486–87.
12 Du Bois, p. 486.
13 Boxill, *Blacks and Social Justice,* p. 178; Appiah, "The Uncompleted Argument," p. 28.
14 Du Bois, p. 487.
15 Boxill, *Blacks and Social Justice,* p. 183.
16 Du Bois, p. 491.
17 Du Bois, p. 488. Du Bois leaves open the question of whether Egyptian civilization was "Negro

in its origin'' and stresses that ''the full, complete Negro message of the whole Negro race has not as yet been given to the world'' (p. 487).

18 Du Bois, pp. 487 & 489.

19 Du Bois, p. 489.

20 Du Bois, p. 489. Du Bois's reference to Negroes in Africa as having ''slept, but half awakening'' reflects his lack of knowledge of African history at this early stage of his career. He later wrote the following about his reaction to Franz Boas's 1906 Atlanta University commencement address on the topic of black kingdoms south of the Sahara: ''I was too astonished to speak. All of this I had never heard. . . .'' *Black Folk: Then and Now* (New York: Henry Holt, 1939), p. vii.

21 Du Bois cites the fact that African Americans have given America ''its only American music, its only American fairy tales, its only touch of pathos'' (p. 489). Later Du Bois spoke of African-American music as ''the greatest gift of the Negro people.'' *The Souls of Black Folk* (New York: Fawcett World Library, 1961), p. 181.

22 Du Bois, p. 489.

23 In a much later work Du Bois rejects what he calls ''the physical bond'' but goes on to assert that ''the real essence of this kinship is its social heritage of slavery.'' *Dusk of Dawn: An Essay Toward an Autobiography of a Race Concept* (New York: Schocken, 1968), pp. 116–17, quoted in Appiah, ''The Uncompleted Argument,'' p. 33.

24 Appiah, p. 32.

25 Du Bois, p. 491.

26 Du Bois, p. 489.

27 DeMarco, *Social Thought of W. E. B. Du Bois,* p. 33; Appiah, ''The Uncompleted Argument,'' p. 27.

28 Wilson J. Moses, *Alexander Crummell: A Study of Civilization and Discontent* (Oxford: Oxford University Press, 1989), p. 262. With regard to the notion of ''civilization'' Du Bois's European influences must also be acknowledged. Bernard W. Bell maintains that although there is no documentary evidence of his having read Herder ''it is unlikely that Du Bois remained untouched by the spirit and thought of Herder, Goethe, and Rousseau.'' *Folk Roots of Contemporary Afro-American Poetry* (Detroit: Broadside Press, 1974), p. 23. For a discussion of Du Bois's known academic influences see Francis L. Broderick, ''German Influence on the Scholarship of W. E. B. Du Bois,'' *Phylon* 19 (December 1958) and ''The Academic Training of W. E. B. Du Bois,'' *Journal of Negro Education* 27 (Winter 1958).

29 Du Bois, p. 487.

30 Appiah, ''The Uncompleted Argument,'' p. 25.

31 Du Bois did acknowledge that ''The term Negro is, perhaps, the most indefinite of all'' and applies to a wide variety of people, but he does not hesitate to override this consideration with remarks such as ''200,000,000 black hearts beating in one glad song of jubilee'' (pp. 486–87).

32 Du Bois, p. 491.

33 Du Bois, p. 488.

34 Du Bois, p. 489; Booker T. Washington, ''Atlanta Exposition Address'' in Brotz, *Negro Social and Political Thought,* p. 359. Du Bois seems even closer to Washington when he implores the Academy to ''continually impress the fact upon the Negro people that . . . they MUST DO FOR THEMSELVES . . . that a little less complaint and whining, and a little more dogged work and manly striving would do us more credit and benefit than a thousand Force or Civil Rights bills'' (p. 490).

35 Du Bois, p. 488.

36 See Dorothy Porter, ''The Organized Educational Activities of Negro Literary Societies, 1828–1846,'' *Journal of Negro Education* 5 (October, 1936), pp. 556–66.

37 See C. M. Wiltse (ed.), *David Walker's Appeal* (New York: Hill and Wang, 1965); Maria W.

Stewart, "An Address Delivered Before the Afric-American Female Intelligence Society of America" and "Mrs. Stewart's Farewell Address to Her Friends in the City of Boston" in Marilyn Richardson (ed.), *Maria W. Stewart, America's First Black Woman Political Writer* (Bloomington: Indiana University Press, 1987); Howard H. Bell, "National Negro Conventions of the Middle 1840's: Moral Suasion vs. Political Action," *Journal of Negro History* 42 (October, 1957), pp. 247–60; Howard H. Bell, *A Survey of the Negro Convention Movement 1830–1861* (New York: Arno Press, 1969).

38 W. H. A. Moore, "The New Negro Literary Movement," *AME Church Review* 21 (1904), p. 52.

39 Cf. Frances E. W. Harper, "Iola," and Pauline E. Hopkins, "Sappho," in Mary Helen Washington (ed.), *Invented Lives* (New York: Anchor, 1987), pp. 87–129. For a discussion of why some African-Americans choose to pass see James E. Conyers and T. H. Kennedy, "Negro Passing: To Pass or Not to Pass," *Phylon* 25, 3 (Fall 1963), pp. 215–23, and Virginia R. Domínguez, *White by Definition* (New Brunswick, N.J.: Rutgers University Press, 1986), pp. 200–204.

40 Du Bois, p. 488.

41 Cf. Boxill, *Blacks and Social Justice,* p. 185.

42 For a discussion of the rather tenuous racial basis for ethnicity see R. B. LePage and Andree Tabouret-Keller, *Acts of Identity: Creole-Based Approaches to Language and Ethnicity* (Cambridge: Cambridge University Press, 1985), pp. 207–49. Lucius Outlaw has argued a similar line regarding the social construction of race and ethnicity. See his "Toward a Critical Theory of 'Race' " in David T. Goldberg (ed.), *Anatomy of Racism* (Minneapolis: University of Minnesota Press, 1990), pp. 58–82.

43 Appiah, "The Uncompleted Argument," p. 27. In this regard Du Bois may have followed the view of Herder. According to Herder, "[Races] belong not, therefore, so properly to systematic natural history, as to the physico-geographical history of man." F. McEachran, *The Life and Philosophy of Johann Gottfried Herder* (Oxford: Clarendon Press, 1939), p. 298, cited in Cedric Dover, "The Racial Philosophy of Johann Herder," *British Journal of Sociology* Vol. 3, 1952, p. 125. See also Vernon J. Williams, Jr., *From A Caste to A Minority: Changing Attitudes of American Sociologists Toward Afro-Americans, 1896–1945* (New York: Greenwood Press, 1989), pp. 86–87.

44 Boxill, *Blacks and Social Justice,* p. 178.

45 For an historical account of racial classification see Michael Banton, "The Classification of Races in Europe and North America: 1700–1850," *International Social Science Journal* 111 (February 1987), pp. 45–60. According to Robert E. Park, "In South America and particularly in Brazil, where Negroes and mixed bloods constitute more than 60 per cent of the population, there is, strictly speaking, no color line . . . [although] the white man is invariably at the top, and the black man and the native Indian are at the bottom." *Race and Culture* (Glencoe, Ill.: Free Press, 1950), p. 381. Similarly, Julian Pitt-Rivers reports that "A man who would be considered Negro in the United States might, by traveling to Mexico, become *moreno* or *prieto,* then *canela* or *trigueno* in Panama, and end up in Barranquilla white." "Race, Color, and Class in Central America and the Andes" in John Hope Franklin (ed.), *Color and Race* (Boston: Houghton Mifflin Co., 1968), p. 270. With reference to black people of lighter skin Philip Mason tells us that " 'The white man' in Jamaica sometimes means a well-to-do person who behaves as though he came from Europe and would often not be classed as 'white' in the United States." "The Revolt Against Western Values" in Franklin (ed.), *Color and Race,* p. 61.

46 See the California State University and University of Massachusetts Application Forms, 1991–92. For a discussion of the definitions of affirmative action categories see David H. Rosenbloom, "The Federal Affirmative Action Policy" in D. Nachimias (ed.), *The Practice of Policy Eval-*

uation (New York: Saint Martin's Press, 1980), pp. 169–86, cited in Dvora Yanow, "The Social Construction of Affirmative Action and Other Categories," a paper presented at the Fifth National Symposium on Public Administration Theory, Chicago, April 9–10, 1992. For a discussion of the political implications of treating the concepts of race and ethnicity as interchangeable see Michael Omi and Howard Winant, *Racial Formation in the United States: From the 1960s to the 1980s* (New York: Routledge & Kegan Paul, 1986), pp. 14–37.

47 Frederick Douglass, "The Claims of the Negro Ethnologically Considered" in Brotz, *Negro Social and Political Thought,* p. 250.

48 S. S. N., "Anglo Saxons and Anglo Africans," *The Anglo African Magazine,* Vol. 1, 1859 (New York: Arno Press, 1968), p. 250.

49 "Anglo Saxons," p. 250.

50 According to Margot Pepper, "Although *Chicano* has been misused to identify all Mexican Americans, it actually refers to a specific political and cultural attitude; it is not an ethnic category." "Resistance and Affirmation," *San Francisco Guardian* (June 26, 1991), p. 33. Velina Hasu Houston, president of the Amerasian League, informs us that "The term (*Amerasian*) referred to all multiracial Asians, whether their American half was Anglo, African American or Latino." "Broadening the Definition of Amerasians," *Los Angeles Times* (July 11, 1991), p. E5. Cape Verdians are a mixed Portuguese/African group who speak a creole language, but, in Massachusetts, are not classified as either black or Hispanic.

51 Cf. Ruth Benedict and Gene Weltfish, *The Races of Mankind,* Public Affairs Pamphlet No. 85 (September 1980), p. 8.

52 Appiah, "The Uncompleted Argument," p. 34. DeMarco suggests that Du Bois may have believed that the original world population was divided into the three different races, since he "characterized the growth of racial units as one which proceeds from physical heterogeneity to an increasing physical homogeneity." DeMarco, *Social Thought,* p. 41. Arnold Rampersad, however, has pointed out that by 1915 Du Bois shifted more toward a common ancestry view. *The Art and Imagination of W. E. B. Du Bois* (Cambridge, Mass.: Harvard University Press, 1976), pp. 230–31.

53 Cf. Robert A. Hill and Barbara Bair (eds.), *Marcus Garvey Life and Lessons* (Berkeley: University of California Press, 1987), p. 206, and V. R. H. de la Torre, "Indo-America" and "Thirty Years of Aprismo" in *The Ideologies of the Developing Nations* (New York: Simon and Schuster, 1972), pp. 790–800.

54 In 1885, Croatan Indians in Robeson County, North Carolina, sought to distinguish themselves from African-Americans, with whom they had mixed, by getting the legislature to pass laws that made them the final judges on questions of genealogy. They adopted the pragmatic definition," an Indian is a person called an Indian by other Indians." Guy B. Johnson, "Personality in a White-Indian-Negro Community," in Alain Locke and Bernhard J. Stern (eds.), *When Peoples Meet* (New York: Progressive Education Association, 1942), p. 577.

55 See, for instance, Jean Fagan Yellin (ed.), Harriet Jacobs, *Incidents in the Life of a Slave Girl* (Cambridge, Mass.: Harvard University Press, 1987), p. 29.

56 In the mid-seventeenth century, Virginia enacted legislation that stipulated that children born of a black woman would inherit her status, even when the father was white. This measure allowed slaveholders to literally reproduce their own labor force. See Paula Giddings, *When and Where I Enter* (New York: Bantam, 1985), p. 37. Marvin Harris argues that the difference between the United States and Latin America in applying this rule of descent must be understood in terms of it being "materially advantageous to one set of planters, while it was the opposite to another." *Patterns of Race in the Americas* (New York: W. W. Norton, 1964), p. 81.

57 Indeed, in many cases where phenotypical characteristics are ambiguous with regard to an individual's genotype, self-identification (i.e., cultural criteria) becomes more of a possibility. C.

Eric Lincoln informs us that ''Reliable estimates on the basis of three hundred and fifty years of miscegenation and passing suggest that there are several million ''Caucasians'' in this country who are part Negro insofar as they have Negro blood or Negro ancestry.'' ''Color and Group Identity in the United States,'' in Franklin (ed.), *Color and Race*, p. 250. To see that the issue of genetic heritage is mostly a matter of politics we need only consider the fact that the Louisiana state legislature recently repealed a 1970 statute that established a mathematical formula to determine if a person was black. The ''one thirty-second rule'' was changed to ''traceable amount.'' Frances Frank Marcus, ''Louisiana Repeals Black Blood Law,'' *New York Times* (July 6, 1983), p. A10. For a detailed historical account of the politics surrounding the Louisiana law see Domínguez, Chapters 2 & 3. When Hawaii became a United States Territory in 1990 the ''one thirty-second rule'' was lobbied against by five large landholding companies. For economic reasons they favored the present law which requires 50% native blood to be eligible for a land grant. See Timothy Egan, ''Aboriginal Authenticity to Be Decided in a Vote,'' *New York Times* (January 1, 1990), p. A12.

58 See the discussion of Hansen's Law by Werner Sollors in his *Beyond Ethnicity: Consent and Descent in American Culture* (New York: Oxford University Press, 1986), pp. 214–221. For a discussion of its application to Louisiana creoles see Domínguez, Chapter 7.

59 Boxill's definition of black people cannot accommodate such cases for he would insist on phenotype and descent as overriding factors such that black Latinos who operate with a primarily *cultural* identity must be viewed as in some sense ''passing.''

60 According to Israel's Law of Return anyone born to a Jewish mother who has not taken formal steps to adopt a different religion has the right to become a citizen of Israel.

61 Cf. Benedict and Weltfish, *The Races of Mankind,* p. 10; Abram Leon Sachar, *A History of the Jews* (New York: Alfred A. Knopf, 1979), p. 250.

62 According to Louis Wirth, ''What has held the Jewish community together in spite of all disintegrating forces is . . . the fact that the Jewish community is treated as a community by the world at large.'' ''Why the Jewish Community Survives'' in Locke and Stern (eds.), *When Peoples Meet,* p. 493.

63 Cf. Peter Singer, ''Is Racial Discrimination Arbitrary?,'' *Philosophia* 8, 2–3 (November 1978), p. 185. See also Edward W. Said, ''Zionism from the Standpoint of Its Victims'' in Goldberg *Anatomy of Racism,* pp. 210–46.

64 Webster's dictionary emphasizes the fact that this term applies primarily to marriage or interbreeding between whites and blacks.

65 See Thomas E. Skidmore, ''Racial Ideas and Social Policy in Brazil, 1870–1940,'' in Richard Graham (ed.), *The Idea of Race in Latin America, 1870–1940* (Austin: University of Texas Press, 1990), pp. 7–36; and Parks, *Race and Culture,* p. 385.

66 For an account of the aboriginal struggle for social equality in Australia, see Roberta B. Sykes, *Black Majority* (Victoria, Australia: Hudson Publishing, 1989).

67 Consider, for instance, the following quote: ''Now, a comment about the title of the book and why we have chosen the term 'black population.' What the immigrants from New Commonwealth and Pakistan (NCWP) and their children born have in common is the material consequences and, in very many cases, the direct experience of discrimination. Discrimination, as the studies, by Political and Economic Planning (PEP) have demonstrated, is based upon colour. Hence, the reference to Britain's black population. It can, of course, be argued that some immigrants and their children do not and would not want to be labelled as *black*. That is not denied, but the defence of this terminology in this context lies with the fact that, irrespective of their own particular beliefs, experiences and the wide range of cultural variations, racism and racial discrimination is a crucial determinant of their economic and social situation.'' The Runnymede Trust and The Radical Statistics Race Group, *Britain's Black Population* (London:

Heinemann Educational Books, 1980), p. xii. See also Kobena Mercer, " '1968': Periodizing Postmodern Politics and Identity," in Lawrence Grossberg, Cary Nelson, Paula Treichler (eds.), *Cultural Studies* (New York: Routledge, 1992), pp. 424–38; Frank Reeves, *British Racial Discourse* (Cambridge: Cambridge University Press, 1983), p. 255; Lionel Morrison, *As They See It* (London: Community Relations Commission, 1976), pp. 35–49; Brian D. Jacobs, *Black Politics and Urban Crisis in Britain* (Cambridge: Cambridge University Press, 1986), pp. 41–62; Paul Gilroy, *"There Ain't No Black In The Union Jack"* (London: Hutchinson, 1987).

68 In *Worlds of Color,* written near his ninetieth birthday, Du Bois gave the following description of Jean Du Bignon: "a 'white Black Girl' from New Orleans; that is, a well educated young white woman who was classed as 'Colored' because she had a Negro great-grandfather." *Worlds of Color* (Millwood, N.Y.: Kraus-Thomson, 1976), p. 9. It should be noted here that Du Bois seems to have inconsistently treated his own blood tie with his Dutch ancestors as inessential. Most likely this was due to his *cultural* identification with black people, as well as with his tacit commitment to the "census" definition of a black person—viz., that a black person is a person who "passes" for a black person in the community where he lives. See Parks, *Race and Culture,* p. 293.

69 In the nineteenth-century black Americans sometimes referred to themselves nonpejoratively as "Anglo-Africans." With a similar reference to a white cultural influence Nathan Hare's book, *The Black Anglo Saxons* (New York: Collier Books, 1965), was offered as a criticism of the assimilationist mentality of certain segments of the black middle class.

70 One notable exception is the white rap group, *Young Black Teenagers,* who explain their appropriation of this title (along with tunes such as "Proud to Be Black" and "Daddy Kalled Me Niga Cause I Likeded To Rhyme") as an expression of their having grown up in a predominately black youth culture in New York City. See Joe Wood, "Cultural Consumption, From Elvis Presley to the Young Black Teenagers," *Village Voice Rock & Roll Quarterly,* pp. 10–11.

71 Quoted in L. Perry Curtis, Jr., *Apes and Angels: The Irishman in Victorian Caricature* (Washington, D.C.: Smithsonian Institution Press, 1971), p. 1.

72 In his very interesting documentary film, *The Black and the Green,* Saint Claire Bourne explores the theme of black consciousness in the Irish Catholics' struggle for social equality.

73 See Norman Mailer's "The White Negro" in his *Advertisements for Myself* (New York: Andre Deutsch, 1964).

74 Kobena Mercer cites a passage from Arthur Rimbaud's "A Season in Hell" (1873) in which the claim is made: "I am a beast, a Negro." Mercer, " '1968,' " p. 432.

75 With regard to his discussion of Du Bois's concept of race, Anthony Appiah was sharply criticized by Houston Baker for downplaying the role of color discrimination in everyday affairs. See his "Caliban's Triple Play" in Gates (ed.), *"Race," Writing, and Difference,* pp. 384–85, and Appiah's reply "The Conservation of 'Race'," *Black American Literature Forum,* Vol. 23, No. 1 (Spring 1989), pp. 37–60.

76 Cf. Morris Lounds, Jr., *Israel's Black Hebrews: Black Americans in Search of Identity* (Washington, D.C.: University Press of America, 1981), pp. 209–13.

77 Cf. Ozzie L. Edwards, "Skin Color as a Variable in Racial Attitudes of Black Urbanites," *Journal of Black Studies,* Vol. 3, No. 4 (June, 1972), pp. 473–83; Robert E. Washington, "Brown Racism and the Formation of a World System of Racial Stratification," *International Journal of Politics, Culture, and Society,* Vol. 4, No. 2, 1990; Lincoln, "Color and Group Identity," pp. 249–63.

78 With regard to the "self-questioning," "hesitation," "vacillation," and "contradiction" faced by mulattoes Du Bois remarked that "combined race action is stifled, race responsibility is shirked, race enterprises languish, and the best blood, the best talent, the best energy of the Negro people cannot be marshalled to do the bidding of the race" (p. 488).

XENOPHOBIA AND KANTIAN RATIONALISM[1]

ADRIAN M. S. PIPER

Contemporary Kantian ethics has given a wide berth to Kant's analyses of reason and the self in the *Critique of Pure Reason*.[2] Perhaps this can be ascribed to P. F. Strawson's influential fulminations against Kant's transcendental psychology in *The Bounds of Sense*.[3] Strawson's view was an expression—one of many—of a postwar behaviorist sensibility, for which the best conceptual analysis of interior mental life was no analysis at all. In recent years this sensibility has become increasingly anachronistic, both in ethics and in philosophy of mind, and is in need of reappraisal on these grounds alone.

The neglect by contemporary Kantian ethicists of Kant's first *Critique* has been particularly unfortunate. It forecloses a deeper understanding of Kant's own ethical views, and robs us of valuable resources for addressing contemporary issues in metaethics and applied moral philosophy. It is virtually impossible to understand Kant's conception of the categorical imperative in isolation from his account of reason in the first *Critique*'s Transcendental Dialectic; or his distinction between autonomy and heteronymy in isolation from his inchoate but suggestive formulation of the Two Standpoints Thesis in the solution to the Third Antinomy; or his elaboration of that thesis itself in Chapter III of the *Groundwork of the Metaphysic of Morals*[4] in isolation from the chapter on Noumena and Phenomena, the Refutation of Idealism, and the Fourth Paralogism in the A Edition of the *Critique*. Of course this is not to deny that these concepts can be put to excellent and fruitful use independently of ascertaining what Kant himself meant by them.

Moreover, the first *Critique* offers a developed conception of the self that provides a needed resource for defending Kantian ethics against anti-rationalist criticisms, such as that it is too abstract, alienating, altruistic, or detached from ordinary personal concerns to guide actual human behavior. The conception of the self to be found in the first *Critique* is, to be sure, a thoroughly rationalistic one that no antirationalist would accept. Its virtue, however, is to demonstrate convincingly that in ordinary personal concerns, as well as in the guidance of human behavior, the scope and influence of rationality is inescapable.

Corresponding to these two considerations, the purpose of this discussion is twofold. First, I want to shed some light on Kant's concept of personhood as rational agency, by situating it in the context of the first *Critique*'s conception of the self as defined by its rational dispositions. I hope to suggest that this concept of personhood cannot be simply grafted onto an essentially Humean conception of the self that is inherently inimical to it, as I believe Rawls, Gewirth, and others have tried to do.[5] Instead I will try to show how deeply embedded this concept of personhood is in Kant's conception of the self as rationally unified consciousness.

Second, I want to deploy this embedded concept of personhood as the basis for an analysis of the phenomenon of xenophobia. I focus on this phenomenon for two reasons. First, it is of particular concern for African-Americans. As unwelcome intruders in white America we are the objects of xenophobia on a daily basis. This pervasive fact of our experience conditions all of our social relations, and may itself engender a reciprocal form of xenophobia in self-defense. It is therefore doubly in our interests to understand this phenomenon and the defects in rationality it manifests. Second, Kant's conception of the self affords potent resources for understanding xenophobia as a special case of a more general cognitive phenomenon, namely the disposition to resist the intrusion of anomalous data of any kind into a conceptual scheme whose internal rational coherence is necessary for preserving a unified and rationally integrated self.

I begin by limning the conception of the self as rationally unified consciousness I want to defend on Kant's behalf. This conception differs from Kant's actual pronouncements in only one respect: I incorporate Strawson's suggestion that, among the candidates for innate concepts in Kant's Tables in the Metaphysical Deduction, only the subject-predicate relation can be understood as what Kant would call a transcendental concept or judgment-form. On this view, all other such concepts are empirical, including that of causality. I then formulate the issue of the relation between transcendental and empirical concepts or categories and its relevance to an analysis of xenophobia. Kant claims that anomalous data that fail to conform to the transcendental concepts of the understanding cannot be experienced by a unified self at all. Xenophobia is fear, not of strangers generally, but rather of a certain kind of stranger, namely those who do not conform to one's preconceptions about how persons ought to look or behave. It is therefore a paradigm case of resistance to the intrusion of anomalous data into an internally coherent conceptual scheme—a threat to the unity of the self defined by it. If a disposition to these preconceptions is innate, then xenophobia is a hard-wired, incorrigible reaction to a threat to the rational integrity of the self. If, on the other hand, a disposition to these preconceptions is the result of empirical conditioning, then xenophobia is corrigible in light of empirical data that may be realistically expected to compel the revision of those concepts.

In Section II I begin the exegetical part of this project by sifting through Kant's own claims about the relation between transcendental and empirical concepts, and conclude that empirical concepts, on Kant's view, instantiate transcendental ones.[6] In Section III I locate Kant's concept of personhood relative to the distinction between transcendental and empirical concepts by arguing that this concept has both transcendent and transcendental status for Kant. This implies that Kant's concept of personhood is innate, and not subject to empirical revision. However, the way in which this concept is instantiated or applied is not similarly fixed. On Kant's account, we identify others as persons on the basis of our own self-identification as persons; and Kant insists that the only self to which we have epistemic access is empirical. In Section IV I examine Kant's account of self-knowledge and argue that Kant's distinction between noumenal and empirical selves does not foreclose veridical identification of oneself as a person. I conclude that Kant's transcendent concept of personhood is instantiated by particular empirical exemplars of personhood, i.e., particular persons with particular personalities, among whom each of us necessarily identifies ourself and only contingently identifies others.

In Section V I then deploy Kant's concept of personhood and his distinction between transcendental and empirical concepts in the service of a detailed analysis of xenophobia. I argue that it is a self-protective reaction to violation of one's empirical conception of people, and involves a cognitive failure to apply the transcendent concept of personhood consistently across all relevant cases. I try to show that racism, sexism, homophobia, antisemitism, etc., are pseudorational responses to xenophobia that depend on the mechanisms of rationalization, dissociation, and denial; and on a deep personal investment in the resulting honorific stereotype of the valued group to which one belongs. Derogatory racial, gender, or ethnic stereotyping of others, on this view, is a reciprocally interdependent consequence of honorific stereotyping of oneself.

Finally, in Section VI I recur to the text, in order to settle the question of the cognitive status of xenophobia within Kant's theory. I offer two interpretations of Kant's requirement that all data of experience conform to categories constitutive of the rationally unified self. Interpretation (A) demands that all such data conform both to transcendental and to empirical concepts, whereas interpretation (B) requires that they conform only to the transcendental ones. If (A) is correct, then another who is anomalous with respect to one's empirical conception of people cannot be a person for one at all. So xenophobia is incorrigible. But if (B) is correct, then another might violate one's empirical conception of people but be nevertheless recognizable as instantiating one's transcendent concept of personhood. So it would be possible to recognize the other as a person even though she violated one's empirical presuppositions about what and who people are. In that case, even if a disposition to xenophobia were innate, particular manifestations of it would be the result of conditioning and therefore susceptible to empirical modification. I examine the textual evidence for each interpretation, and conclude that (B) is correct; and that Kant's conception of reason as theory-construction implies resources within the structure of the self for overcoming xenophobia—resources frequently overshadowed, however, by empirical conditioning.

I. KANTIAN RATIONALISM

In the first *Critique,* Kant tells us repeatedly that if a perception does not conform to the fundamental categories of thought that ensure the unity and coherence of the self, they cannot be part of our experience at all (A 112, 122, & B 132, 134).[7] Kant describes these fundamental categories as "*a priori* transcendental concepts of understanding," by which he means innate rules of cognitive organization that any coherent, conscious experience must presuppose. The Table of Transcendental Categories he offers in the Metaphysical Deduction is drawn largely from Aristotle, with considerable additional tinkering by Kant. They include substance, totality, reality, possibility, causality, and community, to name just a few. Some commentators have rightfully concluded that the most significant candidate for this elevated cognitive status is the subject-predicate relation in logic, from which Kant derives the relational category of substance and property in the Table of Categories (Kant regards this as the result of fleshing out the subject-predicate relation or "judgment form" with "transcendental content," i.e., the sensory data our experience presupposes rather than the sensations we perceive as a result of it (A 70/B 95–A 79/B 105)).[8] The idea, then, would be that organizing sensory data in terms of this relation is a necessary condition of experience. On this view, if we do not experience something in a way that enables us to make sense of it by identifying properties of it—for example, in propositions such as,

That car is dark red,

or

I am tired,

we cannot consciously experience that thing at all.

This thesis—call it the *Kantian rationalism thesis*—has the merit of plausibility over the archaic list of categories Kant originally furnished. It does not seem too controversial to suppose that any viable system of concepts should enable its user to identify states of affairs by their properties, since concepts just are of corresponding properties, and to ascribe a property to an object just is to subsume that object under the corresponding concept. So any system of concepts should enable its user to ascribe to objects those properties of which she has concepts. The Kantian rationalism thesis—henceforth the KRT—is so weak that it may even be defensible in the face of anthropological evidence that languages considerably remote from Indo-European ones evince a cognitive structuring to the user's experience that is so different from our own as to be almost unintelligible to us. It would be an argument in favor of the KRT if it could be shown that the subject-predicate relation held regardless of the other ways in which culturally specific conceptual organizations of experience differed among themselves.

More precisely formulated, then, the KRT says that if we do not experience something in such a way as to allow us to make sense of it in terms of a set of coherent concepts that structure our experience, *whatever those concepts are,* we cannot consciously experience that thing at all. On this thesis the innate capacity would consist in a disposition to structure experience conceptually as such, but not necessarily in accordance with any particular list of concepts,[9] provided that the particular, culturally specific set S of concepts $c_1, c_2, c_3 \ldots c_n$ that did so satisfied the following requirements:

(A) S observes the law of noncontradiction, i.e., the members of S are internally and mutually consistent in their application;
(B) Any particular c_i in S is either
  (1) an instantiation of some other c_j in S; or
  (2) instantiated by some other c_k in S; i.e., S is minimally coherent;
(C) for any cognitively available particular p, there is a c_j in S that p instantiates.

The suggestion would be that we can understand a particular state of affairs only if (A) the concepts by which we recognize it are neither internally nor mutually contradictory; (B) those concepts are minimally coherent with one another in that each particular identified by them satisfies the subject-predicate relationship with respect to at least one other of them; and (C) that particular itself instantiates at least one of them. I develop this suggestion at length elsewhere.[10] It says, roughly, that in order for something to register as a conscious experience at all for us, we have to be able to make sense of it in terms of some such concepts in the set; and that if we can't, it won't.

Suppose, for example, that we were to be confronted with some particular such that the concepts it instantiates satisfied (A) but violated (B), i.e. such that we could invoke a concept in identifying it consistently with the application of our other concepts; but that that concept itself bore no instantiation-relation to others in the set (i.e., aside from that of being a concept in the set). In this case, that which we invoked as a "concept" would in fact not be one at all, since the corresponding predicate would by definition denote only the single state of affairs it had been invoked to identify. Since there would be no further concepts in terms of which we might understand the meaning of that denoting term, it could not enter into any analytic truths. In short, this would be like cooking up a special noise to denote only one state of affairs on the single occasion of its occurrence. The enterprises of denotation and meaning themselves would fail.

Alternately, imagine what it would be like to be confronted by a particular such that its concept satisfied (B) but not (A), i.e., such that it enabled us to identify its properties in terms of concepts in the set, but that the application of those concepts themselves was internally or mutually inconsistent. In that event, it would be possible to ascribe to the thing the conjunction of some predicate F and some other one, G, that implied the negation of F.[11] Again the enterprise of identification itself would fail. If we were finally to fail to identify the thing or state of affairs in question as having a consistent set of properties, we would fail to identify it altogether. And then it could not be part of our conscious experience. If such cases characterized all of our encounters with the world, we would have no experiences of it at all and therefore no unified sense of self either.

These are the sorts of failures Kant has in mind when he avers, in the A Deduction, that

> without such unity, which has its rule *a priori,* and which subjects appearances to it, thoroughgoing, universal, and therefore necessary unity of consciousness would not be found in the manifold of perceptions. These would then not belong to any experience, therefore would be without object, and nothing but a blind play of representations, that is, less even than a dream. (A 112)

Kant is saying that if we do not organize cognitively the data of our senses according to consistent and coherent rules, we cannot be rationally unified subjects. "For otherwise," he adds in the B Deduction, "I would have as many-colored and diverse a self as I have representations of which I am conscious." (B 134) I would, that is, lack a sense of myself as the subject in whose consciousness those representations occur. For a Kantian rationalist, then, the cognitive organization of experience according to consistent and coherent concepts is a necessary condition of being a rationally unified subject.

The KRT as explicated claims that only the subject-predicate relation counts as what Kant would call a transcendental concept or judgment-form; all the rest are empirical. Empirical concepts may differ as to how deeply entrenched in our cognitive dispositions they are. But all empirical concepts, for Kant, apply to and are formed in response to particular empirical contexts, rather than being necessary preconditions of experience itself. However, Kant did not devote sufficient attention to explaining the relation between empirical and transcendental concepts. If empirical concepts are contingent rather than necessary determinants of experience, then presumably we might have a particular experience even though we lacked one particular empirical concept by which to make sense of it—i.e., in the case where we had some other, nonequivalent empirical concept that did the job equally well. And Kant is silent on the question of whether we might have a particular experience that conformed to the transcendental concepts but to none of our empirical concepts—for instance, of an empirical state of affairs for the evident properties of which we could find absolutely no fitting predicates at all. Is the formation of empirical concepts itself a necessary precondition of experience? Or is it as contingent on circumstance as those empirical concepts themselves are? Nor does Kant explain how susceptible to change our empirical concepts are, in light of their relation to transcendental ones on the one hand and to new or anomalous empirical data on the other.

These issues are central to the topic of this essay. Thomas Kuhn has documented the inherent impediments to paradigm shift in the natural sciences—their conservatism and constitutional insensitivity to the significance of new data, and their resistance to revising deeply entrenched theories in light of experimental anomaly.[12] Elsewhere I have argued that the resistance to integrating anomaly is a general feature of human intellection that attempts to satisfy a Kantian requirement of rational self-preservation.[13] I have also offered elsewhere a Kantian analysis of a certain brand of xenophobic resistance to anomaly that finds typical expression in racism, sexism, antisemitism, class elitism, and homophobia, among other types of discrimination.[14] The question at issue here is whether a Kantian conception of the self explains xenophobia as a necessary or a contingent attribute of the self; i.e., whether it is a hard-wired disposition to defend the self against attacks on its internal integrity that is impervious to modification, or whether a xenophobic fear of strangers as violating one's conceptual presuppositions about persons is contingent on such empirical conditions as upbringing, degree of exposure to diversity or integration, and peer-group reinforcement—and therefore revisable in light of new experience. Ultimately I think Kant's view implies the latter; I will try to show this in what follows.

II. TRANSCENDENTAL AND EMPIRICAL CONCEPTS

Kant says many things about the relation between transcendental and empirical concepts, most of which are inconclusive. He says that empirical concepts are based on transcendental ones (A 111), that they are grounded in transcendental ones (A 113), that they are subject to them (B 163), that they must agree with them (B 164), and that their source is in them (A 127). None of this is precise enough to shed light on the actual relation between them. A more specific but fallacious account of the relationship is suggested by Kant's assertion that empirical concepts are a consequence of transcendental ones (A 114). Regardless of whether by "consequence" Kant means "causal consequence" or "logical consequence," he clearly should not have said this: causality as itself a transcendental concept is not a relation that can be maintained to hold between transcendental and empirical concepts, and transcendental concepts cannot be supposed to imply empirical concepts (indeed, Kant as much as acknowledges this when he says later that empirical laws cannot derive their origin from transcendental concepts (A 128, B 165)). Nor is the extended account of the reproductive imagination in the A Deduction at A 119–24 and in the B Deduction at B 152 helpful in ascertaining exactly in what the relationship consists.

Surprisingly, Kant does admit the existence of "derivative pure *a priori* concepts." These are derived by combining the transcendental ones with one another or with "modes of pure sensibility," i.e., our innate disposition to structure our experience spatiotemporally. Whatever the character of this latter process of combination, it cannot be identical to or even very much like that involved in schematizing the categories in time, since this, Kant tells us, is what gives the transcendental concepts applicability to our sensory and spatiotemporal experience (A 140/B 179–A 142/B 181); it does not engender any derivative ones. Among these derivative necessary concepts are those of action, passion, and force, derived from the transcendental concept of causality; and the concept of presence and resistance, derived from that of community (A 82/B 108). The concepts of action and passion are of particular interest for understanding the role of human agency and inclination in Kant's moral philosophy, and it is useful to see them identified as necessary preconditions of experience so early on in the first *Critique*.[15] But Kant defers the project of enumerating all of these additional transcendental concepts to another occasion, and says nothing more about the nature of their process of derivation.

More helpful is Kant's assertion, in both the A and B Editions of the first *Critique,* that empirical concepts depend on the transcendental ones (A 114, B 164). This implies that transcendental concepts are a necessary but not sufficient condition of empirical ones, i.e., that transcendental ones make the empirical ones possible without ensuring any particular set of them. Earlier, in the Transcendental Logic, Kant had explained why transcendental concepts alone, i.e., in their corresponding logical forms of judgment, cannot furnish a sufficient condition of empirical truth. Although they do furnish criteria of logical truth,

> [t]hese criteria . . . concern only the form of truth, that is, of thought in general; and in so far they are quite correct, but not sufficient. For although our knowledge may be in complete

accordance with logical form, that is, may not contradict itself, it is still possible that it may be in contradiction with the object. (A 59/B 84)

Here Kant observes that the fact that a proposition may satisfy logical requirements does not by itself determine its content; indeed, it may happen that a system of propositions may satisfy these requirements, yet its content might be "contradicted," i.e., conclusively disconfirmed by the objective states of affairs it purports to denote (also see B 190, A 155–57).

The sufficient condition for the veracity of empirical concepts—i.e., that which ensures the consistent and coherent application of at least one specifiable *kind* of empirical concept rather than any other to a particular ("rabbit" or "gavagai" rather than "H_2O" to small furry entities with long ears, for instance)—is given by the source of their transcendental content. That transcendental content itself is what Kant calls the manifold, and he thinks that the process of synthesizing or unifying the manifold under concepts is what specifies their content:

Synthesis of the manifold (whether empirical or a priori) is what first produces a cognition, which certainly may be crude and confused at first and therefore in need of analysis. But synthesis alone is what actually collects the elements into a cognition, and unifies them into a particular content. (B 103/A 78)

The crucial missing link in these remarks is an answer to the question of whether a randomly chosen element of the manifold has attributes that lead us to collect it under one concept rather than another (i.e., whether natural kinds exist), or whether its attributes are conferred solely by the concepts that subsume it. Here Kant is silent on which account of transcendental content is correct, but later relies on the latter possibility to justify the need for a Schematism of the Pure Understanding (B 177/A 138). This latter possibility implies that any datum could be subsumed under any concept arbitrarily, and therefore that there is no systematic relation between our capacities of cognitive organization and the particular data we organize—hence the need for time as a schema that mediates between them. By contrast, the former implies that these data carry markers or clues to the concept that most appropriately subsumes them, and therefore that there is at least some minimal correspondence between the way we organize the world and the elements of the world that we organize. Kant furnishes no unambiguous evidence for this possibility (but see note 17, below).

And what about the source of this transcendental content? Its nature and ontological plausibility is a point of endless debate among Kant scholars. Here I will simply state (but not defend) the view that this source is what Kant describes, in a passage in the Schematism willfully mistranslated by Kemp Smith, as "the transcendental matter of all objects as things in themselves" (A 143/B 182[16]; also see A 20, A 28, A 30/B 46, B 60, B 75, B 125, B 145, A 168,

A 223, A 372, A 375, A 385, B 422a–423, A 581).[17] This is to suggest that first, in addition to our innate capacities for cognitive organization, a multiplicity of objects that are ontologically independent of us must provide us with the sensory data we organize, in order for empirical experience to occur; and second, if these objects provide such data, and our cognitive capacities are in good working order, systematically related empirical experience will occur.

This suggestion does not imply that the systematic relation we detect among empirical objects is identical to any relation that might obtain among ontologically independent objects that are by definition inaccessible to our empirical experience. Nor does it imply that the relation between these two sets of relations is one of causality as we now understand that term (although of course it might be). But it does imply that we are justified in thinking of the systematic coherence we discover in the empirical world we experience as at least a clue to the character of the coherence that may be presumed to actually exist among ontologically independent states of affairs as they are in fact. Indeed, in the ''Regulative Employment of the Ideas of Pure Reason'' Kant himself concedes this when, in arguing that the unity in nature we discover by exercising our rational capacities in inquiry and research is a necessary precondition of experience rather than a contingent outcome of it, he says,

> In fact it is hard to see how there can be a logical principle of the rational unity of rules, unless a transcendental principle is also presupposed, through which such a *systematic unity is* a priori *assumed to be necessarily attached to the objects themselves*. . . . The law of reason which requires us to seek this unity is a necessary law, since without it we would have no reason at all, and without this no coherent use of the understanding, and in the absence of this no *sufficient criterion of empirical truth. So in reference to this criterion we must necessarily presuppose the systematic unity of nature as objectively valid and necessary throughout*. (A 650/B 678–A 651/B 679; italics added)

Kant's point is that we are required, by the fact that reason and understanding must unify all of our experience under increasingly inclusive concepts in order for us to have experience at all, to conceive of all the possible objects of experience thus unified—i.e. the empirical world of nature *in toto*—as an ontologically independent system that is necessarily unified as well. Kant is not claiming that we detect that objective system in our necessarily limited experience of the natural world as it appears to us. He is not even claiming that we can infer any veridical characteristics of it from the areas of systematic structure we do empirically detect. He is claiming only that we must rationally conceive the totality of the natural world as an ontologically independent, systematically unified whole in order to experience any empirical part of it coherently; and the passages cited earlier demonstrate his own thinking as an example of this requirement.

The sufficient condition for the veracity of empirical concepts then—that which prevents conclusive disconfirmation (or "contradiction") of our explanatory theories by the objects we experience—is the natural world conceived as an ontologically independent phenomenon, unified under a maximally inclusive explanatory theory that can account for them, which we must presuppose in order to experience any of its natural objects at all. This assumption explains why, although an explanatory theory of the natural world might undergo revision in light of new empirical data, it can never be conclusively disconfirmed or "contradicted" by that data all at once. The more inclusive and sophisticated the theory becomes, the more anomalous data offer the challenge of revising and extending that theory into an even more powerful one that can integrate them, and the less susceptible the theory becomes to conclusive disproof by piecemeal anomalous evidence.[18] Only relatively primitive or provincial explanatory theories are vulnerable to the kind of attack Kant describes. I consider some in greater detail in Section V below, and argue elsewhere that the dogmatism with which such a theory is maintained is an index of its explanatory fragility.[19] The external natural world, then, conceived as an ontologically independent, systematically unified, and fully explicable whole, supplies the sufficient condition of empirical truth for Kant.

But now conjoin this suggestion to Kant's further claim that any conscious experience we have must conform to the transcendental concepts (B 162), and that empirical concepts are "special determinants" of transcendental ones (A 126, A 128). From this latter claim we can infer that an experience that conforms to empirical concepts thereby conforms in content to the transcendental ones that determine them. Now Kant does not say whether by the word "determine" he means "designate" or "ascertain" or "specify," nor does the German (*bestimmen*) enlighten us on this question.[20] I will assume that by "determine," when used in this context, Kant means "specify" since it is a broader term that can be used more or less synonymously with either "designate" or "ascertain" in most contexts. Kant is then saying, in the above-cited passages, that empirical concepts specify more precisely some of the same content that is structured by transcendental ones and initially generated by systematically related things in themselves.

Again this does not give us direct access to the nature of things in themselves, since the content of a more inclusive concept can be specified in a variety of nonequivalent ways by less inclusive ones. But the specification relation between transcendental and empirical concepts preserves relevant content from systematically interrelated things in themselves through transcendental and then empirical concepts that give it cognitive structure. And we can think of the specification relation as for present purposes equivalent to the instantiation relation described in Section I.B.1, such that

(A) c_i specifies c_j if and only if c_i instantiates c_j.

On this reading, empirical concepts instantiate transcendental ones, and the more inclusive properties corresponding to transcendental ones may be ascribed to the less inclusive properties corresponding to empirical ones—as, for example, the property of being a cause of change may be ascribed to a behavior, which in turn may be ascribed to an action. This reading accords with the KRT, according to which each (empirically contingent) concept within a subject's experience instantiates the (transcendentally necessary) subject-predicate relation or judgment-form relative to some others.

III. THE CONCEPT OF PERSONHOOD

The question of whether a Kantian conception of the self contains the resources for explaining and reforming xenophobia now can be reformulated more precisely as the question of whether an instantiation interpretation of the relation between concepts necessary for experience and those contingent to it can explain the phenomenon of xenophobia with respect to its degree of conceptual entrenchment and corresponding amenability to rational correction. Since xenophobia involves withholding recognition of personhood from those perceived as empirically different or anomalous, part of the answer to our question will turn on ascertaining the cognitive status of the concept of personhood in Kant's epistemology. To do this we first need to understand Kant's conception of the relation between transcendental and transcendent concepts.

Kant regards the ''transcendental judgment-forms'' as having two separate functions. The first, already discussed, is to structure cognitively the sensory data that unified experience presupposes. In that role Kant calls them ''transcendental concepts'' or ''categories.'' But these logical forms—which under the KRT reduce to the subject-predicate relation—have a second function as well. This is to reason, construct syllogisms and hypotheses, formulate theories, and make deductive inferences at increasingly abstract and inclusive conceptual levels from the unified experience thus structured. In this way these judgment-forms not only unify experience according to certain innate cognitive patterns, but unify the resulting multiplicity of unified experiences themselves under more abstract concepts and theories according to the same basic cognitive patterns:

> Understanding may be considered a faculty of the unity of appearances by means of rules, and similarly reason is the faculty of the unity of the rules of understanding under principles. Accordingly, reason never applies directly to experience or to any object, but to understanding, in order to give to its manifold cognitions a unity *a priori* through concepts, a unity which may be called the unity of reason, and which is of a very different kind from that which can be accomplished by the understanding (A 302/B 359). . . . In fact multiplicity of rules and unity of principles is a requirement of reason, in order to bring the understanding into thoroughgoing coherence with itself. . . . But such a principle . . . is merely a subjective law for the manage-

> ment of the resources of our understanding, in order to reduce their general use to the smallest possible number through comparison of its concepts. . . . (A 305/B 362–A 306/B 363)

In this second function, Kant refers to the transcendental judgment-forms as "*transcendent* concepts" or "ideas" of reason. Whereas the term "transcendental" refers to the necessary preconditions of experience, "transcendent" refers to that which exceeds or surpasses the limits of experience. Kant's notion is that abstract theories (whether moral, psychological, theological, or cosmological) that unify all the relevant data under a minimum of explanatory principles necessarily transcend in scope of application the contingent and piecemeal data that empirically confirm them. Thus the difference between transcendental concepts of the understanding and transcendent concepts or ideas of reason is ultimately a difference in degree of abstraction from experience rather than a difference in kind. (Compare Kant's account of judgment as knowledge by subsumption at A 68/B 93–A 70/B 95 with his account of knowledge from principles at A 300/B 357; also see A viii, A 302/B 359, A 311/B 368, A 329/B 386, A 409, A 643/B 671–A 644/B 672, A 651/B 679.)

As a transcendent concept (or idea), the concept of personhood gives coherence to our occasional, particular empirical experiences of these characteristics of human behavior by unifying them under this more abstract and inclusive notion that surpasses in scope of application any particular instance of human behavior that conforms to it. It thereby contributes to a standing expectation that other human beings will regularly behave as persons no matter how frequently this expectation is violated in fact.[21] As a transcendental concept, by contrast, it is what makes our particular empirical experiences of these same characteristics of human behavior possible. It is what enables us to recognize particular occurrences of consciousness, thought, rationality, and action for what they are. Whereas the transcendent concept of personhood supplies us with a higher-level *conception* of what being a person involves—a standing conception to which particular individuals may or may not conform on any given occasion, the transcendental concept of personhood enables us to recognize those occasions on which they do.

Kant clearly regards transcendent ideas of reason, like the transcendental categories of the understanding, as innate in the sense that reasoning beings are inevitably led to them by virtue of the categories of reasoning they use. But according to the KRT, only the subject-predicate relation, and so the substance-property transcendental category that corresponds to it, is a necessary condition of experience. From this it follows that only that transcendent idea of reason which is generated by the subject-predicate relation is similarly rationally inevitable, if any of them are.

Kant thinks the subject-predicate relation engenders the transcendent idea of a rationally unified, temporally continuous self as the content of the concept of personhood. His explanation in the Paralogisms of why he thinks this is not the most convincing argument available. What he could have said is just that the "I think" accompanies all our other concepts and therefore is instantiated in them, whereas it itself instantiates only the yet more inclusive substance-property concept. Being rationally inevitable, it is either just as innate conceptually as is that relation for Kant, or else is at least very deeply entrenched. This would be to suggest something like a hard-wired disposition to recognize others of our own (human) kind.

Because unified consciousness and thought presuppose cognitive structuring by rational categories, and because Kant believes reason can be motivationally effective, the concept of *personhood* also may be supposed to include, in addition to rationally coherent and persisting consciousness, the capacity for action. This departs from Kant's usage in the first *Critique* somewhat, where he uses that term in discussing only the former properties. But in the *Groundwork* his characterization of a person as a rational being (Ac. 428) makes explicit the first *Critique*'s connection between consciousness, rationality, and agency. Now there is no obstacle to conceiving of a being who has these properties but does not know that she does; indeed, Kant claims that this is precisely the human predicament, since genuine experiential knowledge of this topic is foreclosed to us. In order to prove the inevitability and so the transcendental necessity of this concept for human experience, Kant must show that we are disposed to identify ourselves as persons on the basis of evidence from which we cannot help but infer that we are.

Kant has plenty to say about each of the properties of personhood, and there is plenty of textual support for assigning the concept of personhood a transcendental as well as a transcendent status. For example, in the opening sections of the Transcendental Dialectic Kant treats the concept of virtue, which for him is part of the concept of a perfectly rational being (A 315/B 372, A 569/B 597) as a necessary practical idea of reason (A 317/B 374–A 319/B 376)—i.e., one that can motivate action. This implies a corresponding concept with transcendental status. This implication is strengthened by Kant's explicit assertion, in his discussion of the Platonic forms, that no human being coincides with the idea of what is most perfect in its kind, but nevertheless carries it—i.e., the idea of humanity—"in his soul as the archetype of his actions." (A 318/B 375) In the Ideal of Pure Reason Kant explicitly describes an "idea of perfect humanity" at A 568/B 596.

Similarly, Kant's treatment of the unity of the thinking subject as a transcendent concept or idea of reason that engenders the Paralogisms of Pure Reason implies transcendental status for the corresponding concept of the understanding, for example in the second paragraph at A 365. Indeed, he explicitly assigns that concept to the list of transcendental ones at A 341/B 399, and says of it,

> One quickly sees that this is the vehicle of absolutely all concepts, and therefore also of transcendental ones, and so is always conceived along with all of these, and therefore is itself equally transcendental.

A concept that is ''always conceived along with'' other concepts is instantiated by those other concepts. Therefore, empirical concepts instantiate more inclusive transcendent ones, and those, in turn, instantiate the most inclusive, highest-order transcendent concept of the thinking subject; and all of these instantiate the most inclusive transcendental concept of the substance-property or subject-predicate relation. This is just another way of suggesting—as Kant repeatedly does in the A and B Deductions—that the thinking self or ''I'' (as predicate) must be able to accompany (i.e., must be ascribable to) any experience (A 116–117a, A 123, B 131–36, B 140; note, however, that he never explicitly acknowledges that the ''I'' would have to denote a property, not a substance). All of these passages taken together provide especially compelling support for the KRT.

Moreover, in the A Paralogisms Kant denies that the concept of a unified thinking subject can come from any empirical source when he declares,

> Now I cannot have the slightest representation of a thinking being through any outer experience, but only through self-consciousness. So these sorts of objects are nothing more than the transference of this consciousness of mine to other things, which can be represented as thinking beings only in this way. (A 347/B 406)

He reiterates this at A 357, in the Second Paralogism. So he thinks that the concept of a unified thinking being is one I derive from the property of first-personal self-consciousness—a requisite, remember, for unified selfhood—and then ascribe to certain external empirical objects.

But which ones? How do I manage to ascertain which, among the array of available empirical objects, actually has that property, since I can find no empirical representation of it? Kant provides an answer to this question in the Solution to the Third Antinomy. There he first develops at length the thesis that the behavior of actual human beings is subject to empirical laws of causality in the natural world, such that our behavior from a third-personal, observational perspective is entirely predictable: ''[I]f we could exhaustively investigate all the appearances of the human power of choice,'' he tells us, ''there would not be found a single human action which we could not predict with certainty . . . if, that is to say, we are merely *observing*, and, as happens in anthropology, want to investigate physiologically the motive causes of someone's actions.'' (A 550/B 578)

But he also says that the situation is different from a first-personal perspective:

> Only a human being, who knows all of nature otherwise solely through the senses, also knows himself through pure apperception, and, indeed, in acts and inner determinations which he cannot class with impressions of the senses. . . . [W]hen we consider the same actions in relation to reason . . . in so far as reason is the cause *producing* them . . . we find a rule and order altogether different from the order of nature. (A 546/B 574; A 550/B 578)

That is, it is different from the rule and order of rationality, of reasoning and deliberating about actions and goals, of forming generalizations and making inferences, and of reaching conclusions about what is the case and what to do that move us to act accordingly. From the first-personal perspective, then, we are not just objects of empirical investigation, determined by causal forces, but thinking and reasoning persons, determining our own actions through rational intention and will.

Thus the rule and order of rationality ''shows, in its effects in appearance, a rule in accordance with which we may surmise rational motives and the kind of degrees of actions themselves, and judge subjective principles of the power of choice.'' (A 549/B 578) So Kant's solution to the problem of other minds, i.e., of how we can distinguish those third-personally observed objects who are similarly thinking subjects from those which are not, is to point out that although the behavior of all such objects satisfies the laws of causality, only that of some also may satisfy the laws of rationality. Only some external objects, that is, exhibit the capacity for rational *action*. The concept of a unified thinking being is, then, a transcendent and a transcendental concept we apply to those external empirical objects whose behavior gives evidence of being governed by the same laws of rationality we first-personally experience as governing our own.

IV. SELF-KNOWLEDGE

Now Kant does not think such ''acts'' of first-personal introspection give us knowledge of ourselves as we are in ourselves, i.e., as noumena, but only as we appear to introspection. Moreover, Kant warns us about the dangers of transcendental illusion inherent in the use of reason when he says,

> in our reason (considered subjectively as a human faculty of knowledge) there are basic rules and maxims of its use, which have all the look of objective principles, and through which it happens that the subjective necessity of a particular connection of our concepts is, to the advantage of the understanding, taken for an objective necessity in the determination of things in themselves. (A 297/B 353)

Kant is cautioning us against trusting our own, inescapable inference to the objective validity of our rational principles from their seeming necessity and universality. Our innate susceptibility to both of these conceptual traps raises the questions of whether our ascription of personhood to ourselves and others on the basis of our first-personal experience of the rule and order of rationality can have anything more than a contingent empirical foundation; and whether the concept of personhood itself can therefore claim any more validity than that.

Moreover, even if this concept should turn out to be necessary, it does not follow that we are necessarily justified in applying it to ourselves: if all we can know of ourselves is the way we appear to ourselves rather than the noumenal selves we are in actual fact, then the first-personal appearance of personhood may, for all we know, lack any basis in actual fact. Kant's distinction in Paragraph 25 of the B Deduction between what we can know—namely that of which we have empirical experience—and what we can consciously think or conceive—namely that about which the categories of thought enable us to reason, regardless of the extent to which it can be confirmed by experience—provides an answer to these questions.

Kant argues that it is the act of introspection (or—Kant's term—self-intuition (B 68–69, 153–56, 157–58a)) that enables one's self to appear to one at all. In the Transcendental Aesthetic Kant describes time as "the way in which the mind is affected through its own activity, namely by this situating (*setzen*) of its representation [in temporal relations], and so is affected by itself." This, he says, identifies time as an inner sense (B 68). Kant's idea here is that the mind's cognitive process of forming and organizing representations itself causes the mind to situate those representations in temporal succession; he elaborates on this idea at greater length in the Transcendental Deduction. A temporal succession of mental representations, however, is a property of the subject's interior consciousness, not of the external world; this is why Kant calls time an inner rather than an outer sense.

In the same passage, Kant goes on to say that the subject is itself the object of inner sense. What he means is that the temporal succession of mental representations that is a property of the subject's interior consciousness is identified by the subject as the subject's self when the subject turns its attention to it (cf. also B 140). This succession of mental representations is the appearance of the self that Hume found when he looked within and searched in vain for the enduring soul or substance that had been supposed to unify these representations. Kant calls it the empirical self, in contradistinction to (A) the underlying noumenal self that does the appearing; and (B) the transcendental subject that both undergoes those cognitive processes and also has such properties (we will suppose (A) and (B) to be materially equivalent for purposes of this discussion). The empirical self is the self as it appears to one when one looks for it. It is therefore the product rather than the presupposition of these cognitive processes (cf. also B

152–53, 155–56, 407). We can think of Kant's empirical self as equivalent to what I have elsewhere called one's *self-conception*.[22] Kant describes this as an appearance of the self because, he claims, the very act of looking for it is what causes it to appear:

> If the faculty of becoming self-conscious is to seek out (apprehend) what lies in the mind, it must affect the mind, and only in this way can it engender an intuition of itself . . . it then intuits itself, not as it would immediately and self-actively represent itself, but rather in accordance with the way in which it is internally affected, and so as it appears to itself, not as it is. (B 69)

However, Kant later warns us at least twice about investing too much credence in our empirical selves, or self-conceptions, as a source of self-knowledge. The first time is in the Solution to the Third Antinomy. There he maintains that "[t]he real morality of actions (merit and guilt), even that of our own conduct . . . remains entirely hidden from us. Our imputations can be referred only to the empirical character." (A 551/B 579a) This warning is echoed in Chapter II of the *Groundwork of the Metaphysic of Morals* in Kant's remarks on the perniciousness and ubiquity of the "dear self." There he cautions us that

> it often happens that in the keenest self-examination we find absolutely nothing except basic moral duty that could have been powerful enough to move us to this or that good action and so to greater sacrifice. But it cannot be ruled out with certainty that in fact some secret impulse of self-love, under the mere pretense of this idea, has been the actual, determining cause of the will. For this we gladly flatter ourselves, by falsely appropriating a nobler motivational basis. But in fact even the most strenuous probing of our hidden motives yields absolutely nothing, because when the issue is moral worth, it is not about the actions one sees, but rather about their internal principles one does not see. (Ac. 407; also see 419)

These caveats follow from Kant's previous remarks on the contingency and epistemic unreliability of the empirical self as a source of information about the transcendental subject to whom the empirical self appears. Here Kant is simply extending his remarks to cover the case of specifically moral self-knowledge as well. Thus the impossibility of knowing the noumenal self through acts of introspection would seem to foreclose reliance on first-personal consciousness, thought, rationality, and action as conclusive evidence of authentic personhood in both first- and third-personal cases.

Kant also distinguishes sharply between the active spontaneity of the act of introspection, and the empirical self that is caused by this act to appear. He thus rules out direct and unmediated knowledge of oneself as an active and spontaneous intellect. *A fortiori,* he rules out direct experience of oneself as initiating the processes of reasoning and cogitation that would conclusively identify one as a person (the terms "experience" and "knowledge" for Kant are usually synonymous). Indeed, Kant's description in the *Groundwork* of the imperfect human will as one which, on the one hand, "is determined by reason," but on the other, "is not necessarily obedient to it by nature" or "subjective condition" (Ac. 413), suggests that reasoning and intellection are processes we experience ourselves as passively and sometimes resistently undergoing rather than as actively initiating.

But Kant does acknowledge the possibility that a subject may nevertheless *represent* or conceive herself as an active, spontaneously reasoning and thinking subject (recall that this was the alternative he discarded in his account of self-intuition at B 69). The basis for this self-conception would not be the direct experience of active and spontaneous intellection. Instead it would be the apparently spontaneous, uncompelled character of the content of those mental "acts and inner determinations" themselves. As Kant puts it,

> I cannot determine my existence as a self-active being, but rather I represent to myself only the spontaneity of my thought, that is, of the determining, and my existence always remains sensibly determinable, that is as the existence of an appearance. But this spontaneity is why I call myself an intelligence. (B 158a)

Kant is, on the one hand, denying that I can ascertain my self-activity as a fact; but acknowledging, on the other, that I can conceive my thought as spontaneous in virtue of the autonomous character of my attempts cognitively to ascertain or specify things: it seems to me, that is, that my disposition to conceive and analyze are themselves self-initiated rather than externally caused or compelled (also cf. *Groundwork,* Ac. 448). Although I can ascertain my existence only through empirical means, and therefore as an appearance, it is because I try to ascertain or determine things cognitively at all that I identify myself as an intelligent being.

So although the subject cannot know herself as an active intelligence, she can still represent herself as one, on the evidence of the autonomous quality of her thought. And she can include this representation among those constitutive of her empirical self-conception. Thus a subject may at least reliably conceive herself as having the properties that identify her as a person, even if she cannot experience herself as having them.

But Kant's distinction between what can be known and what can be thought or conceived is not only useful in formulating our self-conception as persons. It is also useful in formulating the evidence on which that self-conception depends. "The use of reason," he tells us, "is not always directed to the determination of the object, therefore to knowledge, but also to the determination of the subject and of its volition. . . . " (B 166a). Following the suggestion in Section II that we translate *bestimmen* by the broad term "specify," Kant would then be saying that, in addition to ascertaining the nature of objects of knowledge, reason also can be used to shape the subject and its volition in certain specific ways. That is, reason can fix the form and specific content of the intentional object of the subject's will. It can fix the form of that intentional object in that it conceives the action that is its content as a valid conclusion of deductive and inductive reasoning. And reason can fix the content of that intentional object in that this reasoning process identifies a particular course of action as the rational one to pursue. This interpretation conforms to the instantiation interpretation of the relation between transcendental and empirical concepts offered in Section II. So although reason alone may not yield knowledge of the true nature of the self, it may yield a precise and recognizably rational formulation of the subject's particular deliberations, resolutions, and intentions. Although this would not count as self-knowledge in Kant's technical sense, it certainly would constitute evidence for one's self-conception as a reasoning subject.

Further support for this reading can be gleaned from Kant's characterization of reason in the Solution to the Third Antinomy as atemporal and unaffected by empirical states, but as itself nevertheless a determining influence on them (A 556/B 584). First, he describes the "appearances" of reason as "the ways in which it manifests itself in its effects." Presumably these effects are the particular, spatiotemporally specific instances of reasoning in accordance with the nonempirical canons of rationality. That Kant does not mean to identify the "effects" of pure reason with empirical action itself is clear from his assertion earlier in the same section that "the action, so far as it is to be ascribed to a way of thinking as its cause, does not thereby follow from it in accordance with empirical laws, that is, so that the conditions of pure reason precede it, but rather only so that their effects in the appearance of inner sense do." (A 551/B 579) If action is preceded by the effects of the conditions of pure reason in inner sense, it obviously cannot be identical with those effects. The only effects of pure reason in inner sense that can plausibly precede action are particular processes or occurrences of reasoning about what action to take. These empirical instances of valid reasoning specify the form and content of the intentional object of the will, as well as contribute to the motivational force of that will itself.

Second, at A 556/B 584 Kant also says of reason that it "is present in all human actions in all temporal circumstances and is always one and the same, but is not itself in time, nor falls somehow into a new state in which it was not before; it is determining, but not determinable in regard to this."[23] Here the idea is that the abstract canons of theoretical rationality themselves are not spatiotemporally local to any particular empirical action or situation, but are nevertheless locally instantiated by reasoning subjects who apply them to each such situation in such a way as to affect the action taken. The effect of reason on action cannot be merely to nudge it into existence causally as an occurrence. Instead it must affect action by specifying or fixing the form and intentional content of the action relative to universal and necessary rationality requirements that the subject applies to all actions.

Third, Kant maintains that "when we say that in spite of his whole previous course of life the liar could have refrained, this means only that the lie is directly under the power of reason, and reason in its causality is not subordinated to any conditions of appearance or the passage of time." This means that an agent who is assumed to have been capable of doing otherwise is supposed not to have been handicapped in doing otherwise by intervening causal variables that might have obstructed the effect of reason on her action. This does not conflict with Kant's earlier claim that reason manifests itself in empirical appearances, if we understand by this that the abstract canons of reason are instantiated in particular, empirical occurrences of reasoning. Rather, it merely denies that there are any other internal empirical processes—such as inclinations or emotions—that might interfere with the subject's ability to recognize what reason abstractly requires of a specific instance of reasoning, or obstruct the effect of that specific reasoning process on action.

Finally, Kant concludes this paragraph by asserting that "although difference of time can indeed make a big difference in the relations among appearances . . . it can make no difference to the action in relation to reason." By this Kant means that irrespective of when the action occurs, and when the particular reasoning process that ought to precede it occurs, the action itself is nevertheless subject to evaluation in terms of rational criteria. This is something that the agent can recognize in so far as there are no cognitive obstructions to the "direct power of reason" to fix the form and content of her particular reasoning process.

Taken together, these passages contribute to an explanation of why conscious subjects who think, reason, and act are inevitably led to identify themselves as *bona fide* reasoning and acting persons, even though they can have no knowledge of themselves as such. Centrally required for such identification is the subject's conception of reason as independent of and instantiated by particular empirical occurrences of reasoning that aspire to conform to it. This requirement is satisfied by the passages just considered. These provide evidence for adding the following to the conjunction of mental representations that constitute the empirical self:

(1) the representation of the form and intentional content of one's deliberations and intentions as fully specified by abstract canons of theoretical reason (from B 166a);
(2) the representation of particular empirical occurrences of reasoning as instantiations of these abstract canons of reason (from A 556/B 584);
(3) the representation of these abstract canons of rationality as thereby causally affecting subsequent action (from A 546/B 574, A 550/B 578, A 556/B 584); and

(4) the representation of (1)–(3) as evidence for one's self-conception as an active and spontaneous intellect (from B 158a).

Conjointly these identify any subject who finds them in introspection as a conscious subject, thinking, reasoning, and acting in accordance with the same rationality requirements that unify the self. Since those rationality requirements are innate, our capacity to identify these properties of personhood would be similarly innate, or at least very deeply entrenched. Under these circumstances, it would, indeed, be difficult to avoid including these properties in one's self-conception.

Notice the explanatory elegance and simplicity of Kant's account of personhood, under the assumption of the KRT: structuring our experience according to the subject-predicate relation gives it a basic consistency and coherence that extends to the particular set of contingent empirical concepts thus structured. Satisfying this structural requirement, in turn, is a necessary condition of a rationally unified self. A self that satisfies this rationality requirement thereby generates the cognitively inevitable concept of a reasoning and acting person, which it then applies, first to its own first-personal representations of unified rational agency; and second to those external empirical objects whose behavior exhibit similar adherence to rationality requirements. The concept of rational personhood thereby supplies simultaneously the principles of cognitive organization, self-identification, and recognition of other rational persons in Kant's system. To be a person is to be a self-consciously rational and unified self that manifests its rationality in action.[24]

Recalling the interpretation of the relation between transcendental and empirical concepts as one of instantiation, the proposal would then be that the transcendental concept of a unified rational person is instantiated by particular empirical exemplars of personhood, among whom each of us necessarily and first-personally counts herself, and inferentially and third-personally counts others. We each necessarily conceive of ourselves as persons, and then use this concept as a criterion for identifying others similarly.

V. XENOPHOBIA

In what follows I will use the terms *person* and *personality* to denote particular, empirical instantiations of personhood as analyzed above. These terms correspond closely to the nontechnical use of the terms. Thus when we refer to someone as a person, we ordinarily mean to denote at the very least a social being whom we presume—as Kant did—to have consciousness, thought, rationality, and agency. The term "person" used in this way also finds it way into jurisprudence, where we conceive of a person as a rational individual who can be held legally and morally accountable for her actions. Relative to these related usages, an individual who lacks to a significant degree the capacities to reason, plan for the future, detect causal and logical relations among events, or control action according to principles applied more or less consistently from one occasion to the next is ascribed diminished responsibility for her actions, and her social and legal status as a person is diminished accordingly.

Similarly, when we call someone a ''bad person,'' we communicate a cluster of evaluations that include, for example, assessing her conscious motives as corrupt or untrustworthy, her rationality as deployed for maleficent ends, and her actions as harmful. And when we say that someone has a ''good personality'' or a ''difficult personality,'' we mean that the person's consciousness, thought, rationality, and agency are manifested in pleasing or displeasing or bewildering ways that are particular to that individual. We do not ordinarily assess a being who lacks any of these components of personhood in terms of their personality at all. Persons, then, express their transcendent personhood in their empirical personalities.

With these stipulations in place, I now turn to an analysis of the concept of xenophobia based on the foregoing interpretation of Kant. Xenophobia is not simply an indiscriminate fear of strangers in general: it does not include, for example, fear of relatives or neighbors whom one happens not to have met. It is more specific than that. Xenophobia is a fear of individuals who look or behave differently than those one is accustomed to. It is a fear of what is experientially unfamiliar, of individuals who do not conform to one's empirical assumptions about what other people are like, how they behave or how they look. Ultimately it is a fear of individuals who violate one's empirical conception of persons and so one's self-conception. So xenophobia is an alarm reaction to a threat to the rational coherence of the self, a threat in the form of an anomalous other who transgresses one's preconceptions about people. It is a paradigm example of reacting self-protectively to anomalous data that violates one's internally consistent conceptual scheme.

Recall that on the KRT, if we cannot make sense of such data in terms of those familiar concepts, we cannot register it as an experience at all. I have argued elsewhere[25] that *pseudorationality* is an attempt to make sense of such data under duress, i.e., to preserve the internal rational coherence of the self, when we are baldly confronted by anomaly but are not yet prepared to revise or jettison our conceptual scheme accordingly. It is in the attempt to make sense of anomalous data in terms of empirically inadequate concepts that the mechanisms of pseudorationality—rationalization, dissociation, and denial—kick in to secure self-preservation. But they succeed in preserving only the appearance of rational coherence. In *rationalization,* we misapply a concept to a particular by distorting its scope, magnifying the properties of the thing that instantiates the concept, and minimizing those that fail to do so. So, for example, conceiving of a slave imported from Africa as three-fifths of a person results from magnifying the properties that appear to support this diminished concept of personhood—the slave's environmental and psychological disorientation, lack of mastery of a foreign language, lack of familiarity with local social customs, incompetence at unfamiliar tasks, etc.; and minimizing the properties that disconfirm it—her capacity to learn, to forge innovative modes of communication and expression, to adapt and flourish in an alien social environment, to survive enslavement and transcend violations of her person, etc. In *dissociation,* we identify something in terms of the negation of the concepts that articulate our theory: identifying Jews as subhuman, blacks as childlike, women as irrational, gays as perverts, or working-class people as animals, for example, conceives of them as lacking essential properties of personhood, and so are ways of defining these groups of individuals out of our empirical conceptions of people. In *denial,* we suppress recognition of the anomalous particular or property altogether, by ignoring it or suppressing it from awareness. For example, ignoring a woman's verbal contributions, or passing over a black person's intellectual achievements, or forgetting to make provisions at a Christmas celebration for someone who is a practicing Jew are all ways of eradicating the anomalous other from one's domain of awareness.

Thus xenophobia engenders various forms of discriminatory stereotyping—racism, sexism, antisemitism, homophobia, class elitism—through the pseudo-rational mechanisms of rationalization and dissociation, by reducing the complex singularity of the other to a set of oversimplified but manageable properties that invariably diminish our full conception of personhood. For the xenophobe, this results in a provincial self-conception and conception of the world, from which significant available data is excluded—data the inclusion of which would significantly alter the scope and content of the theory. And this provincial theory is sustained with the aid of denial, by enforcing those stereotypes through such tactics as exclusion, ostracism, scapegoating, tribalism, and segregation in housing, education, or employment.[26] My thesis is that xenophobia is the originating phenomenon to which each of these forms of discriminatory stereotyping is a response. The phenomenon of xenophobia is a special case of a perfectly general human intellective disposition to literal self-preservation, i.e., preservation of the internal rational coherence and integrity of the self against anomalous data that threaten it.

Nevertheless, to say this much is not to answer the question of how deeply entrenched xenophobia is in our cognitive scheme. Even if it is true that we are innately cognitively disposed to respond to any conceptual and experiential anomaly in this way, it does not follow that our necessarily limited empirical conception of people must be so limited and provincial as to invite it. A person could be so cosmopolitan and intimately familiar with the full range of human variety that only an "alien" would rattle her. On the other hand, her empirical conception of people might be so limited that any variation in race, nationality, gender, sexual preference, or class would be cause for panic. How easily one's empirical conception of people is violated is one index of the scope of one's xenophobia; how central and pervasive it is in one's personality is another. In what follows I will focus primarily on cases midway between such extremes: for example, of a white person who is thoughtful, well-rounded, and well-read about the problems of racism in the United States, but who nevertheless feels fearful at being alone in the house with a black television repairman. In all such cases, the range of individuals in fact identifiable as persons is larger than the range of individuals to whom one's empirical conception of people apply. In all such cases, I will argue, xenophobia can be understood in terms of certain corrigible cognitive errors, only the last of which constitutes full-blown xenophobia.

A. The Error of Confusing People With Personhood

Xenophobia is fueled by a perfectly general condition of subjective consciousness, namely the same first-/third-person asymmetry that, as we saw in Section III, led Kant to propose rational action as a basis for inferring another's personhood. Although I must identify myself as a person because of my necessary, enduring first-personal experience of rationally unified selfhood, my experience of you as a person, necessarily lacking that first-personal experience, can have no such necessity about it:

> Identity of person is . . . in my own consciousness unfailingly to be found. But when I view myself from the standpoint of another (as object of his outer intuition), this external observer considers me first and foremost in time. . . . So from the I, which accompanies all representations at all times in my consciousness, and indeed with full identity, whether he immediately concedes it, he will not yet conclude the objective continuity of my self. For because the time in which the observer situates me is not the same as that time to be found in my own, but rather in his sensibility, similarly the identity that is necessarily bound up with my consciousness, is not therefore bound up with his, i.e., with the outer intuition of my subject. (A 362–63)

Kant is saying that the temporal continuity I invariably find in my own consciousness is not matched by any corresponding temporal continuity I might be supposed to have as the object of someone else's consciousness. Since I am not always present to another as I am to myself, I may appear discontinuously to her consciousness in a way I cannot to my own. And similarly, another may appear discontinuously to my consciousness in a way I cannot to my own.

This is one example of how it can happen, on a Kantian conception of the self, that a necessary concept is instantiated by contingent ones: although personhood is a necessary concept of mine, whether or not any other empirical individual instantiates it is itself, from my point of view, a contingent matter of fact—as is the concept of that particular individual herself. Though you may exhibit rationality in your behavior, I may not know that, or fail to notice it, or fail to understand it. Nor can you be a necessary feature of my experience, since I might ignore or overlook you, or simply fail to have any contact with you. In any of these cases, you will fail to instantiate my concept of personhood in a way I never can. Because the pattern of your behavior is not a necessary and permanent, familiar concomitant of my subjectivity in the way my own unified consciousness and ratiocinative processes are, I may escape your personhood in a way that I cannot escape my own. For me the transcendent idea of personhood is also a transcendental concept that applies necessarily to me, but, from my perspective, only contingently and empirically to you.

Hence just as our empirical experience of the natural world is limited relative to the all-inclusive, transcendent idea of its independent unity, similarly our empirical experience of other persons is limited relative to our all-inclusive, transcendent idea of personhood. But there is an important disanalogy between them that turns on the problem of other minds and the first-/third-person asymmetry earlier described. For any empirical experience of the natural world we have, we must, according to Kant, be able to subsume it under the transcendent concept of a unified system of nature of which it is a part, even if we do not know what that system might be. By contrast, it is not necessarily the case that for any empirical experience of other people we have, we must be able to subsume them under the transcendent idea of personhood. This is because although they may, in fact, manifest their personhood in their personality, we may not be able fully to discern their personhood through its empirical manifestations, if those manifestations fall outside our empirical conception of what people are like.

Suppose, for example, that within my subculture, speech is used to seek confirmation and promote bonding, whereas in yours it is used to protect independence and win status[27]; and that our only interpersonal contact occurs when you come to fix my TV. I attempt to engage you in conversation about what is wrong with my TV, to which you react with a lengthy lecture. To you I appear dependent and mechanically incompetent, while to me you appear logorrheic and socially inappropriate. Each of us perceives the other as deficient in some characteristic of rationality: you perceive me as lacking in autonomy and basic mechanical skills, whereas I perceive you as lacking in verbal control and basic social skills. To the extent that this perceived deficit is not corrected by further contact and fuller information, each of us will perceive the other as less of a full-fledged person because of it. This is the kind of perception that contributes to one-dimensional stereotypes, for example of women as flighty and incompetent or of men as aggressive and barbaric, which poison the expectations and behavior of each toward the other accordingly.

Or take another example, in which the verbal convention in my subculture is to disclose pain and offer solace, whereas in yours it is to suppress pain and advert to impersonal topics; and that our only interpersonal contact occurs when I come to work as your housemaid. Again each of us perceives the other as deficient in some characteristic of rationality: you perceive me as dull and phlegmatic in my lack of responsiveness to the impersonal topics you raise for discussion, whereas I perceive you as almost schizophrenically dissociated from the painful realities that confront us. Again, unless this perceived deficit is corrected by further contact and fuller information, each of us will perceive the other as less of a person because of it, thereby contributing to one-dimensional stereotypes of, for example, blacks as stupid, or of whites as ignorant and out of touch with reality, that similarly poison both the expectations and the behavior of each toward the other.

In such cases there are multiple sources of empirical error. The first one is our respective failures to distinguish between the possession of rationality as an active capacity in general, and particular empirical uses or instantiations of it under a given set of circumstances and for a given set of ends. Because your particular behavior and ends strike me as irrational, I surmise that you must be irrational. Here the error consists in equating the particular set of empirical behaviors and ends with which I am familiar from my own and similar cases with unified rational agency in general. It is as though I assume that the only rational agents there are are the particular people I identify as such. Kant might put the point by saying that each of us has conflated her empirically limited conception of people with the transcendent concept of personhood.

B. The Error of Assuming Privileged Access to the Noumenal Self

But now suppose we each recognize at least the intentionality of the other's behavior, if not its rationality. Since each of us equates rational agency in general exclusively with the motives and actions of her own subculture in particular, each also believes that the motives and ends that guide the other's actions—and therefore the evidence of conformity to the rule and order of rationality—nevertheless remain inaccessible in a way we each believe our own motives and ends not to be inaccessible to ourselves. This third-personal opacity yields the distinction between the appearance and the reality of the self: you, it seems, are an appearance to me behind which is hidden the reality of your motives and intentions, whereas I am not similarly an appearance that hides my own from myself. The less familiar you are to me, the more hidden your motives and intentions will seem, and the less benevolent I will assume them to be.

Of course whom we happen to recognize as familiar determines whose motives are cause for suspicion and whose are not. There is no necessary connection between actual differences in physical or psychological properties between oneself and another, and the epistemic inscrutability we ascribe to someone we regard as anomalous. It is required only that the other seem anomalous relative to our familiar subculture, however cosmopolitan that may be, in order to generate doubts and questions about what it is that makes her tick. Stereotypes of women as enigmatic or of Asians as inscrutable or of blacks as evasive all express the underlying fear of the impenetrability of the other's motives. And someone who conceives of Jews as crafty, blacks as shiftless, or women as devious expresses particularly clearly the suspicion and fear of various third-personal others as mendacious manipulators that is consequent on falsely regarding them as more epistemically inaccessible to one than one is to oneself.[28]

Thus our mutual failure to identify the other as a person with the same status as oneself is compounded by skepticism based on the belief that each of us has the privileged access to her own personhood that demonstrates directly and first-personally what personhood really is. The inaccessibility and unfamiliarity of the other's conception of her own motives to our consciousness of her may seem conclusive justification for our reflexive fear and suspicion as to whether her motives can be trusted at all.

Now we have already seen in Section IV that Kant thinks the belief in privileged access is erroneous. From the first-personal relation I bear to my empirical self-conception which I lack to yours, it does not follow that my actual, noumenal motives are any more accessible to me than yours are. Therefore, regardless of how comfortable and familiar my own motives may seem to me, it does not follow that I can know that my own motives are innocuous whereas yours are not. In fact it is difficult to imagine how I might gain any understanding of the malevolent motives I reflexively ascribe to you at all, without having first experienced them in myself. Of course this is not to say that I cannot understand what it means to be the victim of maleficent *events* without having caused them myself. But it is to say that I must derive my understanding of the malevolent *intentionality* I ascribe to you from my own first-hand experience of it. Therefore your epistemic opacity to me furnishes no evidence for my reflexive ascription to you of malevolent or untrustworthy motives, although that ascription itself does furnish evidence for a similar ascription of them to myself. Thus Kant might put this second error by saying that we have been fooled by the first-/third-person asymmetry into treating the ever-present "dear self" as a source of genuine self-knowledge on the basis of which we make even faultier and more damaging assumptions about the other.

C. The Error of Failing Rationally to Conceive Other Minds

These two errors are interconnected with a third one, namely our respective failures to imagine each other's behavior as animated by the same elements of personhood that animate our own, i.e., consciousness, thought, and rationality. Our prior failure to recognize the other's behavior as manifesting evidence of these properties—a failure compounded by conceptual confusion and misascription of motives—then further undermines our ability to bridge the first-/third-person asymmetry by imagining the other to have them. Since, from each of our first-personal perspectives, familiar empirical evidence for the presence of these properties is lacking in the other, we have no basis on which to make the ascription, and so no basis for imagining what it must be like from the other's perspective. Our respective, limited empirical conceptions of people, which are the consequence of ignorance of others who are thereby viewed as different, delimit our capacity for empathy. This is part of what is involved in the phenomenon feminists refer to as objectification, and what sometimes leads men to describe some women as self-absorbed. Kant might put this point by saying that by failing to detect in the other's behavior the rule and order of rationality that guides it, we fail to surmise or imagine the other's motives and intentions.

This error, of failing to conceive the other as similarly animated by the psychological dispositions of personhood, is not without deleterious consequences for the xenophobe herself. Elsewhere I have described the self-centered and narrowly concrete view of the world that results from the failure to imagine empathically another's inner states, and its interpersonal consequences.[29] From the first-personal perspective, this error compounds the seeming depopulation of the social environment of persons and its repopulation by impenetrable and irrational aliens. This is to conceive one's social world as inhabited by enigmatic and unpredictable disruptions to its stability, to conjure chimeras of perpetual unease and anxiety into social existence. Relative to such a conception, segregation (assuming no relations of interdependence preclude it) is no more effective in banishing the threat than is leaving on the nightlight to banish ghosts, since both threats arise from the same source. Vigilance and a readiness to defend oneself against the hostile unknown may become such intimately familiar and constitutive habits of personality that even they may come to seem necessary requisites of personhood.

D. The Error of Equating Personality With Personhood

The three foregoing errors involve cognitive failures for which a well-intentioned individual could correct. For example, someone who regularly confuses people with personhood might simply take a moment to formulate a general principle of rational behavior that both applies to all the instances with which she is familiar from her particular community and has broader application as well; and remind herself, when confronted by anomalous behavior, to at least try to detect the operation of that principle within it. Similarly, it does not require excessive humility on the part of a person who falsely assumes privileged access to the noumenal self to remind herself that our beliefs about our own motives, feelings, and actions are exceedingly fallible and regularly disconfirmed; and that it is therefore even more presumptuous to suppose any authority about someone else's. Nor is it psychologically impossible to gather information about others' inner states—through research, appreciation of the arts, or direct questioning and careful listening, so as to cultivate one's imaginative and empathic capacities to envision other minds.

Thus it is possible for someone to exhibit these failures without being a xenophobe, just in case she has no personal investment in the defective empirical conception of people that results. A person has a *personal investment* in a conception or theory if (1) that theory is a source of personal satisfaction or security to her; (2) to revise or reject it would elicit in her feelings of dejection, deprivation, or anxiety; and (3) these feelings are to be explained by her identification with this theory. She *identifies with* this theory to the extent that she is disposed to identify it as personally meaningful or valuable to her.[30] A person could make the first three cognitive errors without taking any satisfaction in her provincial conception of people ("Is this really all there is?" she might think to herself about the inhabitants of her small town), without identifying with it (she might find them boring and feel ashamed to have to count herself among them), and without feeling the slightest reluctance to enlarge and revise it through travel or exploration or research.

What distinguishes a xenophobe is her personal investment in her provincial conception of people. Her sense of self-preservation requires her conception to be veridical, and is threatened when it is disconfirmed. She exults in the thought that only the people she knows and is familiar with (whites, blacks, WASPs, Jews, residents of Waco, Texas, members of the club, etc.) are persons in the full, honorific sense. This is the thought that motivates the imposition of pseudorational stereotypes, both on those who confirm them and those who do not.

To impose a *stereotype* on someone is to view her as embodying a limited set of properties falsely taken to be exclusive, definitive, and paradigmatic of a certain kind of individual. I will say that a stereotype

(a) equates one contingent and limited set of valued properties that may characterize persons under certain circumstances with the universal concept of personhood;
(b) restricts that set to exclude divergent properties of personhood from it;
(c) withholds from those who violate its restrictions the essential properties of personhood; and
(d) ascribes to them the essential, disvalued properties of deviance from it.

Thus a stereotype identifies as persons those and only those who manifest the valued properties in the set ((a) and (b))—call this set the *honorific stereotype*—and subsidiary ones consistent with it (such as minor personality quirks or mildly idiosyncratic personal tastes). And reciprocally, the honorific stereotype by implication identifies as deviant all those who manifest any properties regarded as inconsistent with it ((c) and (d))—call this second set of disvalued properties the *derogatory stereotype*. So, for example, an individual who bears all the valued properties of the honorific stereotype as required by (a) may be nevertheless disqualified for membership according to (b), by bearing additional disvalued ones as well—being related by blood or marriage to a Jew, for example; or having bisexual inclinations; or, in the case of a black person, an enthusiasm for classical scholarship. In virtue of violating (b), one may then fail to qualify as a full-fledged person at all (c), and therefore may be designated as deviant by the derogatory stereotype according to (d). The derogatory stereotype most broadly includes all the disvalued properties that fall outside the set defining the honorific stereotype (i.e., "us versus them"), or may sort those properties into more specific subsets according to the range of individuals available for sorting.

A stereotype generally is therefore distinguishable from an inductive generalization by its provincialism, its oversimplication, and its rigid imperviousness to the complicating details of singularity. Perhaps most importantly, a stereotype is distinguishable from an inductive generalization by its function. The function of an inductive generalization is to guide further research, and this requires epistemic alertness and sensitivity to the possibility of confirming or disconfirming evidence in order to make use of it. An inductive generalization is no less a generalization for that: it would not, for example, require working-class blacks living in the Deep South during the 1960s to dismantle the functionally accurate and protective generalization that white people are dangerous. What would make this an inductive generalization rather than a stereotype is that it would not preclude recognition of a white person who is safe if one should appear. By contrast, the function of a stereotype is to render further research unnecessary. If the generalization that white people are dangerous were a stereotype, adopting it would make it cognitively impossible to detect any white people who were not.

Thus Kant might describe the reciprocal imposition of stereotypes as the fallacy of equating a partial and conditional series of empirical appearances of persons with the absolute and unconditioned idea of personhood that conceptually unifies them. Whereas the first error—of confusing one's empirical conception of people with the transcendent concept of personhood—involves thinking that the only persons there are are the people one knows, this fourth error—of equating personality with personhood—involves thinking that the kind of persons one knows are all there can ever be. So unlike inductive generalizations, the taxonomic categories of a stereotype are closed sets that fundamentally require the binary operation of sorting individuals into those who fall within them and those who do not.[31]

As a consequence of her personal investment in an honorific stereotypical conception of persons, a xenophobe has a personal investment in an honorific stereotypical self-conception. This means that that self-conception is a source of personal satisfaction or security to her; that to revise or disconfirm it would elicit in her feelings of dejection, deprivation, or anxiety; and that these feelings are to be explained by her identification with this self-conception. In order to maintain her honorific self-conception, a xenophobe must perform the taxonomic binary sorting operation not only on particular groups of ethnic or gendered others, but on everyone, including herself. Since her self-conception as a person requires her and other *bona fide* persons to dress, talk, look, act, and think in certain highly specific and regimented ways in order to qualify for the honorific stereotype, everyone is subject to scrutiny in terms of it.

This is not only prejudicial to someone who violates these requirements and thereby earns the label of the derogatory stereotype. It is also prejudicial to someone who satisfies them, just in case there is more to her personality than the honorific stereotype encompasses and more than it permits. Avoidance of the negative social consequences of violating the honorific stereotype—ostracism, condemnation, punishment, or obliteration—necessitates stunting or flattening one's personality in order to conform to it (for example, by eschewing football or nightclubs and learning instead to enjoy scholarly lectures as a form of entertainment because one is given to understand that that is the sort of thing real academics typically do for fun); or bifurcating one's personality into that part which can survive social scrutiny and that "deviant" part which cannot (as, for example, certain government officials have done who deplore and condemn homosexuality publicly on the one hand while engaging in it privately on the other). One reason it is important not to equate personality with personhood is so that the former properties can flourish without fear that the latter title will be revoked.

Truncating one's personality in order to conform to an honorific stereotype in turn damages the xenophobe's self-esteem and also her capacity for self-knowledge. Someone who is deeply personally invested in the honorific stereotype but fails fully to conform to it (as everyone must, of course) views herself as inherently defective. She is naturally beset by feelings of failure, inferiority, shame, and worthlessness which poison her relations with others in familiar ways: competitiveness, dishonesty, defensiveness, envy, furtiveness, insecurity, hostility, and self-aggrandizement are just a few of the vices that figure prominently in her interpersonal interactions. But if these feelings and traits are equally antithetical to her honorific stereotype, then they, too, threaten her honorific stereotypical self-conception and so are susceptible to pseudorational denial, dissociation, or rationalization. For example, a xenophobe might be blindly unaware of how blatantly she advertises these feelings and traits in her behavior; or she might dissociate them as mere peccadilloes, unimportant eccentricities that detract nothing from the top-drawer person she essentially is. Or she might acknowledge them but rationalize them as natural expressions of a Nietzschean, *übermenschliche* ethic justified by her superior place in life. Such pseudorational habits of thought reinforce even more strongly her personal investment in the honorific stereotype that necessitated them, and in the xenophobic conception of others that complements it. This fuels a vicious downward spiral of self-hatred and hatred of anomalous others from which it is difficult for the xenophobe to escape. Thus the personal disadvantage of xenophobia is not just that the xenophobe devolves into an uninteresting and malevolent person. She damages herself for the sake of her honorific stereotype, and stunts her capacity for insight and personal growth as well.

A sign that a person's self-conception is formed by an honorific stereotype is that revelation of the deviant, disvalued properties provokes shame and denial, rather than a reformulation of that self-conception in such a way as to accommodate them. For example, a family that honorifically conceives itself as white Anglo-Saxon Protestant may deny that its most recent offspring in fact has woolly hair or a broad nose. Similarly, a sign that a person's conception of another is formed by a derogatory stereotype is that revelation of the other's nondeviant, valued properties provokes hostility and denial, rather than the corresponding revision of that conception of the other in such a way as to accommodate them. For example, a community of men that honorifically conceives itself in terms of its intellectual ability may dismiss each manifestation of a woman's comparable intellectual ability as a fluke.[32]

These two reactions are reciprocal expressions of the same dispositions in the first- and third-personal cases respectively. Shame involves the pain of feeling publicly exposed as defective, and denial is the psychological antidote to such exposure: for example, if the purportedly WASP offspring does not have negroid features, there is nothing for the family to feel ashamed of. So a person whose self-conception is defined by an honorific stereotype will feel shame at having disvalued properties that deviate from it, and will attempt to deny their existence to herself and to others. By contrast, hostility toward another's excellence is caused by shame at one's own defectiveness, and denial of the excellence is the social antidote to such shame: for example, if the woman is not as intelligent as the men are purported to be, then there is no cause for feeling shamed by her, and so none for hostility toward her. So a person whose self-conception is formed by an honorific stereotype will feel hostility toward a derogatorily stereotyped other who manifests valued properties that violate that derogatory stereotype, and will attempt to deny the existence of those valued properties in the other to herself and to others.

In the first-personal case, the objects of shame are disvalued properties that deviate from one's honorific stereotypical self-conception. In the third-personal case, the objects of hostility are valued properties that deviate from one's derogatory stereotypical conception of the other. But in both cases the point of the reactions is the same: to defend one's stereotypical self-conception against attack, both by first-personal deviations from it and by third-personal deviations from the reciprocal stereotypes this requires imposing on others. And in both cases, the reactions are motivated in the same way: the properties regarded as anomalous relative to the stereotype in question are experienced by the xenophobe as an assault on the rational coherence of her theory of the world—and so, according to Kant, on the rational coherence of her self.

Indeed, left untreated, all four of these cognitive errors—the conflation of the transcendent concept of personhood with one's provincial conception of people that another happens to violate; the ascription to the other of malevolent motives on the basis of an epistemically unreliable self-conception; the inability to imagine the other as animated by familiar or recognizably rational motives; and the equation of personality with personhood inherent in the imposition of reciprocal stereotypes—combine to form a conception of the other as an inscrutable and malevolent anomaly that threatens that theory of the world which unifies one's experience and structures one's expectations about oneself and other people. If this were an accurate representation of others who are different, it would be no wonder that xenophobes feared them.

VI. XENOPHILIA

Now recall once more Kant's original claim about the structure of the self (the KRT). He said that if a perception failed to conform to the categories of thought that unified and structured the self, it could not be experienced by that self at all. Also recall that we detected an ambiguity in Kant's claim: it was unclear whether a perception would have to conform to (A) both the transcendental and the empirical concepts that unified the self, or (B) only the transcendental ones, in order to be minimally an object of experience. Suppose (A) is correct, and perceptions must conform both to the transcendental and to the empirical concepts that structure the self and its experience. Then these sets of concepts are materially equivalent: something is a person if and only if it falls under one's empirical conception of people. Then someone must conform not only to my transcendental concept of personhood, but also to my empirically contingent and limited concept of what persons are like—i.e., of people—in order for me to recognize her as a person. Therefore, (A) implies that an anomalous other who violates my limited conception of people thereby violates my transcendental conception of personhood as well.

We have already seen in Section III that even if the concept of personhood is transcendental as well as transcendent according to Kant, this concept is at best an instantiation of the transcendental substance-property relational category.

Since my transcendental concept of personhood is not equivalent to the transcendental concept of a thing or substance in general, my failure to recognize the other's personhood does not imply a failure to recognize her as an object with properties altogether. I may recognize another who is anomalous with respect to my concept of personhood as consistent with my concept of objects in general. However, if the other must conform to my limited conception of people in order to conform to my concept of personhood but does not, then from my perspective, an object is all that she can ever be. In this case, xenophobia is a hard-wired cognitive disposition that is impervious to empirical modification.

But suppose instead that (B) furnishes the correct account of the relation between transcendental and empirical concepts, such that perceptions need conform only to the transcendental concepts and not necessarily to the empirical ones, in order to be part of one's coherent experience. (B) leaves open the possibility that a person might have an empirically limited conception of people yet fail to be a xenophobe, just in case she acknowledges as a matter of principle that there must be other ways to do things and other ways to live besides those with which she is familiar; and just in case she is able to put this principle into practice when confronted by some of them. This is the case described in Section V.D, of the individual who commits cognitive errors A–C, but has no personal investment in the defective empirical conception that results.

(B) also leaves open the possibility that one could be a xenophobe in the sense discussed in Section V.D, yet be corrigible in one's xenophobia. For (B) acknowledges the possibility that even though the xenophobe equates her limited conception of people with her transcendental concept of personhood, someone might conform to her transcendental concept of personhood without conforming to her empirical conception of people. That is, in this case it is cognitively possible to introduce into her range of conscious experience a new object the behavior of which satisfies the rule and order of rationality even though it fails to satisfy her honorific stereotype of personhood. And it is possible for her to recognize in this conceptually anomalous behavior the rule and order of rationality, and so the personhood of another who nevertheless violates that honorific stereotype.

Since recognition of the existence of such an anomaly constitutes a counterexample to her honorific stereotype of personhood, the xenophobe has two options according to (B). Either she may, through the mechanisms of pseudorationality, seek some strategy for explaining this anomaly away; or else she may revise her stereotypic and limited conception of people in order to accommodate it. Thus (B) suggests that it is in theory possible for the xenophobe to reformulate and reform that conception in light of new data that disconfirms it, and so to bring her reciprocal stereotypes closer to open-ended inductive generalizations.

Of course whether or not this occurs, and the extent to which it occurs, depends on the virulence of her xenophobia; and this, in turn, on the extent of her personal investment in her honorific, stereotypical self-conception. But if (B) is correct, and one can discern the personhood of someone who violates one's limited conception of people, then pseudorational dismissal of the stranger as a person is not a viable option. By hypothesis the properties that constitute her identity as a person cannot be denied. Attempts to dissociate them, i.e. to dismiss them as insignificant, alien or without value have unacceptable implications for one's own which similarly must be pseudorationalized out of the picture.[33] Moreover, attempts to rationalize them as flukes or mutations or illusions or exceptions to a rule undermine the universality of the rule itself. As in all such cases, pseudorationality does not, in fact, preserve the rational coherence of the self, but only the appearance of coherence in one's self-conception, by temporarily dismissing the anomaly that threatens it. In the event that a xenophobe is confronted with such a phenomenon, xenophobia conflicts with the requirements of literal self-preservation and finally must be sacrificed to it. So finally, the only way for the xenophobe to insure literal self-preservation against the intrusion of an anomalous person is to revise her reciprocal stereotypes of herself and others accordingly so as to integrate her.

There is evidence in the text of the first *Critique* that supports (B) as Kant's preferred alternative. These are in those introductory, explicative sections of the Dialectic in which Kant maintains that it is in the very nature of transcendent concepts of reason to have a breadth of scope that surpasses any set or series of empirical experiences we may have; indeed, to provide the simplest unifying principle for all of them and more. Thus, for example, he tells us that "the principle peculiar to reason in general, in its logical use, is: to find for the conditioned cognitions of the understanding the unconditioned whereby its unity is brought to completion." (A 307/B 364) By the "conditioned," Kant means those experiences and rules that depend on an inferential relation to other, more inclusive principles that explain them. And by the "unconditioned," Kant means those principles, concepts or ideas of reason that are not themselves dependent on any further ones but rather provide the explanation of all of them. What he is saying here is that rationality works interrogatively for us: given some datum of experience we understand, we reflexively seek to enlarge our understanding by searching for further data by which to explain it.

Kant then goes on to say in the same passage that this logical principle becomes a transcendent one through our assumption that if dependent explanatory rules and experiences are given, then the whole series of them, ordered in relations of subsumption of the sort that characterize a covering-law theory, must be given as well; and that this series is not itself dependent on any further explanatory principles.[34] Kant's point is that we assume that any limited explanation of experience we have is merely part of a series of such explanations that increase in generality and inclusiveness, up to a maximally inclusive explanation of all of them. Thus we regard each such partial experience of the world we have as one among many, all of which are unified by some higher-level theory. And later he says that

> [t]he transcendental concept of reason is none other than that of proceeding from a totality of conditions to a given conditioned. Now since only the unconditioned makes the totality of conditions possible, and conversely the totality of the conditions is itself always unconditioned; so a pure concept of reason in general can be explained through the concept of the unconditioned, so far as it contains a basis of the synthesis of the condition (A 322/B 379). . . . Concepts of pure reason . . . view all experiential knowledge as determined through an absolute totality of conditions. (A 327/B 384; also see A 311/B 368, B 383–85, A 409, A 509)

What he means is that we regard any particular phenomenon as embedded in a systematically unified series of such phenomena, such that if we can explain some partial series of that kind, then there is an entire series of which that partial series is a part that we can also explain; and such that that more inclusive explanation explains everything there is about the phenomenon to explain. So Kant is saying that built into the canons of rationality that structure our experience is an inherent disposition to seek out all the phenomena that demand an inclusive explanation, and to test its inclusiveness against the range of phenomena we find.

These remarks support (B) because they imply that the innate cognitive concepts that structure and unify our experience invariably, necessarily outstrip our empirical conceptions of it. Kant is saying that it is in the nature of our cognitive limitations—i.e., that we can only have knowledge of sense-based experience—that the explanatory scope of the innate concepts that structure and unify it necessarily exceeds that sensory basis itself. This means that we view any experience in implicit relation to other possible experiences of its kind, and finally in relation to some systematic explanation that makes sense of all of them. So no single experience, or series of experiences, can ultimately satisfy our appetite for conceptual completeness, because the scope of the higher-level concepts we invoke to explain them necessarily outstrips the limited number of those experiences themselves. There will always be a lack of fit between our innate rational capacity and the empirical theories it generates, because they will always appear limited in scope in a way our innate capacity for explanation itself does not. So no matter how much sensory data we accumulate in support of our empirical theories of ourselves or the world, we are so constructed intellectually as to be disposed to feel somewhat dissatisfied, inquisitive, restless about whether there might not be more to explain, and to search further for whatever our search turns up.[35]

But this means that we are disposed reflexively to regard anomalous data as more than mere threats to the integrity of our conceptions of the world and ourselves, for the disposition to inquire further and to seek a more inclusive explanation of experience remains, even when literal self-preservation has been achieved. We also are disposed to regard those data as irresistible cognitive challenges to the scope of our conceptions, and as provocations to reformulate them so as to increase their explanatory reach. Because, according to Kant, we are always seeking the final data needed to complete the series of experiences our conceptions are formulated conclusively to explain, it could even be said that we are disposed actively to welcome anomalies, as tests of the adequacy of the conceptions we have already formulated.

When applied specifically to the transcendent idea of personhood, this disposition to welcome anomaly as a means of extending our understanding amounts to a kind of xenophilia. That is, it amounts to a positive valuation of human difference as intrinsically interesting and therefore worthy of regard, and a disvaluation of conformity to one's honorific stereotypes as intrinsically uninteresting. It dismantles the assumption that there is any cause for self-congratulation or self-esteem in conforming to any stereotype at all, and represents anomalous others as opportunities for psychological growth rather than mere threats to psychological integrity. It implies an attitude of inquiry and curiosity rather than fear or suspicion, of receptivity rather than resistance toward others; and a belief that there is everything to be gained, and nothing to be protected, from exploration of another person's singularity.[36] We often see this belief expressed in the behavior of very young children, who touch, poke, prod, probe, and question one without inhibition, as though in knowledge of another there were nothing to fear. What they are lacking, it seems, is contingent empirical evidence to the contrary.

Wellesley College

NOTES

1 Work on this paper was supported by an NEH Summer Stipend and a Woodrow Wilson International Scholars' Fellowship. Portions are excerpted from Chapter 7 of a manuscript in progress, *Rationality and the Structure of the Self*. It has benefited from presentation to the Wellesley Philosophy Department Faculty Seminar and also from the comments of Anita Allen, Alison MacIntyre, John Pittman, and Kenneth Winkler.

2 Immanuel Kant, *Kritik der Reinen Vernunft,* herausg. Raymund Schmidt (Hamburg: Felix Meiner Verlag, 1976). All references to this work are parenthesized in the text. Translations from the German are my own. Connoisseurs will find my translations to be generally more literal than Kemp Smith's and (I think) more accurate in conveying not only the substance of Kant's claims but his manner of expression. Despite Kant's tendency to indulge in run-on sentences, he is by and large a plain speaker with a fondness for the vernacular, not the stilted, pretentious Prussian

Kemp Smith makes him out to be. But the major objection to Kemp Smith's translation is that he obscures important philosophical issues by overinterpreting Kant so as to resolve them before the monolingual English reader can become aware that there is anything to dispute. This is particularly evident in the debate about transcendental content (see below, Section II and notes 16 and 17).

3 P. F. Strawson, *The Bounds of Sense* (London: Methuen, 1968).

4 Immanual Kant, *Grundlegung zur Metaphysik der Sitten,* herausg. Karl Vorlander (Hamburg: Felix Meiner Verlag, 1965). All references to the Academy Edition are parenthesized in the text. Translations from the German are my own.

5 John Rawls, *A Theory of Justice* (Cambridge, Mass.: Harvard University Press, 1971), Chapters III and VII; Alan Gewirth, *Reason and Morality* (Chicago: University of Chicago Press, 1978), Chapter II; Thomas Nagel, *The Possibility of Altruism* (Oxford: Oxford University Press, 1975), Part Two. I discuss Rawls' recent transition away from a Humean model of rationality in ''Personal Continuity and Instrumental Rationality in Rawls' Theory of Justice,'' *Social Theory and Practice* 13, 1 (Spring 1987): 49–76, and Nagel's and Gewirth's reliance on a Humean model of motivation in Chapters II and III respectively of my *Rationality and the Structure of the Self.*

6 My exegetical remarks in this paper should not be mistaken for a defense of the extended overall interpretation of Kant they clearly presuppose. I defend this interpretation against the canonical views in *Kant's Metaethics* (in progress).

7 This thesis may be viewed as the resolution of a *Gedankenexperiment* Kant earlier conducts at A 89–91, in which he entertains the possibility of unsynthesized appearance. In any case, his ultimate commitment to this thesis is clear. See Robert Paul Wolff, *Kant's Theory of Mental Activity* (Cambridge, Mass.: Harvard University Press, 1968), for a discussion.

8 See, for example, Strawson, *The Bounds of Sense,* Chapter II.2. In hindsight Kant himself grudgingly admits that hypothetical and disjunctive syllogisms contain the same ''matter'' as the categorical judgment, but he refuses to budge on their essential difference in form and function. See Kant's *Logic,* trans. Robert Hartman and Wolfgang Schwarz (New York: Bobbs-Merrill, 1974), paragraphs 24–29, 60, note 2, especially pages 111 & 127.

9 This thesis is elaborated in the contemporary context by Gerald M. Edelman, *Neural Darwinism: The Theory of Neuronal Group Selection* (New York: Basic Books, 1987) and *The Remembered Present: A Biological Theory of Consciousness* (New York: Basic Books, 1989). See the review of Edelman and others by Oliver Sacks in ''Neurology and the Soul,'' *The New York Review of Books* 37, 18 (November 22, 1990): 44–50.

10 ''Rationality and the Structure of the Self,'' excerpted from *Rationality and the Structure of the Self* and delivered to the Association for the Philosophy of the Unconscious, American Philosophical Association Eastern Division Convention, Boston, Mass., 1986.

11 ''Rationality and the Structure of the Self.''

12 Thomas Kuhn, *The Structure of Scientific Revolutions* (Chicago: University of Chicago, 1971), Chapters VI–VIII.

13 A. M. S. Piper, ''Two Conceptions of the Self,'' *Philosophical Studies* 48, 2 (September 1985): 173–97, reprinted in *The Philosopher's Annual* 8 (1985): 222–46; also see A. M. S. Piper, ''Pseudorationality,'' in Amelie O. Rorty & Brian McLoughlin, eds., *Perspectives on Self-Deception* (Los Angeles: University of California Press, 1988), pp. 297–323.

14 ''Higher-Order Discrimination,'' in Amelie O. Rorty & Owen Flanagan, eds., *Identity, Character and Morality* (Cambridge, Mass.: Massachusetts Institute of Technology Press, 1990), pp. 285–309; reprinted in condensed form in the monograph series, *Studies on Ethics in Society* (Kalamazoo, Mich.: Western Michigan University, 1990).

15 Kant definitively identifies human desires and inclinations as empirical concepts at A 15/B 29. In the following sections I will offer an interpretation of the relation between transcendental and

empirical concepts as one of instantiation. This would treat the empirical concepts of desires and inclinations as instantiations of the transcendental concept of passion, and the empirical concept of intentional human behavior as an instantiation of the transcendental concept of action.

16 The German sentence runs as follows: «Da die Zeit nur die Form der Anschauung, mithin der Gegenstände, als Erscheinungen, ist, so ist das, was an diesen der Empfindung entspricht, die transzendentale Materie aller Gegenstände, als Dinge an sich (die Sachheit, Realität).»

17 Kant's statement here of course makes a great deal of trouble for his doctrine of transcendental idealism and therefore is not developed significantly in the first *Critique*. The Refutation of Idealism, for instance, provides no conclusive evidence either of his acceptance or rejection of such a view. However, there are other passages and problems in the first *Critique* and *Prolegomena* that furnish evidence of Kant's underlying commitment to it.

Specifically, the view that the sufficient condition for the correct application of empirical concepts is given by the transcendental matter of things in themselves answers a question regarding the status of what Kant entitles the "matter of appearance" that remains unanswered through both editions of the first *Critique*. In both editions, Kant clearly wants to say that the form of appearance is spatiotemporal intuition, which inheres innately in the transcendental subject and is empirically real. And in both editions he contrasts the form of appearance with its matter, which is "that in the appearance which corresponds to sensation" and is given a posteriori (A 20/B 34). But exactly where and to what the sensation is given, and what exactly is the nature of the correspondence, remains unclear. Kant defines sensation as "the effect of an object upon the faculty of representation, so far as we are affected by it" (A 19/B 34). Here he is clearly referring to the transcendental subject's faculty of representation. And since empirical objects are the consequence of that subject's cognitive activity, they cannot be supposed to exert causal influence on it. So by "an object" (*Gegenstand*), Kant must mean a nonempirical object, i.e., a thing in itself. So he is claiming that there is a nonempirical object that, by affecting the transcendental subject's faculty of representation, causes that subject to feel sensations.

Kant also denies that there is any "subjective representation, referring to something *outer*, which could be called objective *a priori*" (A 28/B 44). So, in particular, sensation (a subjective representation that, by corresponding to the matter of appearance, presumably refers to it) cannot be empirically real. Therefore, although sensation is the causal effect of an object on the transcendental subject, and although it refers to something outer, namely the matter of appearance, it is also a posteriori subjective representation that, unlike intuition, is not empirically real.

If sensation is a posteriori, one would expect to find it in the empirical world of appearance, and this is exactly where Kant locates it in the A Edition. There Kant's justification for assigning this status to sensation is that tastes, for example, belong to the "special constitution of sense in the subject that tastes it," and colors similarly are not properties of the objects we see, "but only modifications of the sense of sight, which is affected in a certain manner by light." By contrast with space, which is a necessary part of appearances, "[t]aste and colors are . . . connected with the appearances only as effects accidentally added by the particular constitution of the sense organs . . . grounded in sensation, and, indeed, in the case of taste, even upon feeling (pleasure and pain) as an effect of sensation" (A 28–29). So colors are effects of sensation, and taste is an effect of feeling, which in turn is an effect of sensation. And what is it that affects the sense organs, so as to give rise to the sensation that in turn causes one to perceive, say, colors? Kant tells us that it is light.

But light is itself an appearance, just as the sense organs are among the appearances of the empirical self and not part of the transcendental subject to whom the empirical self appears. So the secondary qualities of appearances such as color and taste must result from the effect of some of those appearances, such as light, on other appearances, such as the empirical self's sense organs. This explains how the empirical self comes to experience the secondary qualities of appearances: it experiences them as sensory effects of empirical appearances on its sense organs.

But the mere spatiotemporal *form* of an appearance cannot be supposed to have such causal efficacy. If anything about an appearance does, it must be its *matter*. So the matter of appearances cannot be supposed to be identical to the secondary qualities it may cause the subject to generate. So although these appearances have matter, they do not have secondary qualities except insofar as these are ascribed to them by a sensing empirical subject. Thus when Kant describes sensation as "corresponding" to the matter of appearance, he seems to be suggesting a three-place causal relation: the matter of appearance causes the empirical subject's sensation, which in turn causes the empirical subject to perceive the secondary qualities she ascribes to it.

Locating sensations in causal relations between the empirical self and the natural world of objects accords well with empirical psychology. The problem is that without explaining the connection between empirical sense organs and transcendental sensibility, this account obscures Kant's claim that sensations are the effect of a nonempirical object on the representational ability of the transcendental self. For since empirical objects are the product of transcendental cognitive activity, they cannot themselves engender the activity that produces them. And since things in themselves are supposed to be beyond our cognitive capacity to understand, Kant is not entitled to assert their effect on the subject, either.

What Kant should do is break his own rule of silence on what things in themselves can and cannot do, just this once. He should say that sense organs may be the way transcendental sensibility appears to the introspecting transcendental subject (see Section IV, below), just as empirical objects such as light may be the way things in themselves appear to that subject. That way the "*transcendental* matter of things in themselves" (A 143/B 182) could causally affect the subject's sensibility such that it then generated sensations, and so the secondary qualities of empirical objects. This would make sense of the sentence at A 143/B 182 that Kemp Smith mistranslates. It would stipulate a simpler, two-place causal relation between sensation and the transcendental matter that corresponds to it, namely that the latter causes the former.

Moreover, it would make sense of Kant's claim at A 20/B 34 about the matter of appearance corresponding to sensation. For if appearances could be the way things in themselves appear to the transcendental subject, and sensations occur in the transcendental subject, which itself appears as the empirical subject, then one way for both the matter of appearance and the transcendental matter of things in themselves to correspond to sensation would be if these two kinds of matter were, so to speak, materially equivalent. In this case, the causal relation of transcendental matter to the transcendental subject's sensations would appear as a causal relation between the matter of appearance and the empirical subject's sense organs.

Another benefit of this interpretation for the present discussion would be that it would supply detailed support for my suggestion, immediately following, that an instantiation relation between transcendental and empirical concepts preserves relevant content from systematically related things in themselves, through the transcendental and finally empirical concepts that structure that content. The material equivalence of transcendental and empirical matter would offer some evidence of what that content might be, and how increasingly specific conceptualizations of cognitively available particulars might preserve it.

This interpretation would only require Kant to revise the doctrine of transcendental idealism, not necessarily to abandon it. In particular, it would require him to revise his claim in the A Paralogisms, that

> in fact, when one regards outer appearances as representations, which are effected in us by their objects as existing things in themselves outside us, it is not possible to see how one can know their existence otherwise than through the inference from the effect to the cause, relative to which it must always remain doubtful whether the latter is in us or outside us. One can, indeed, concede that there may be something which is, in the transcendental sense, outside us and is the cause of our outer intuitions, *but this is not the object that we understand*

> *under the representations of matter and corporeal things; for these are merely appearances, i.e. mere types of representations, which are to be found only in us,* and whose reality is based on immediate consciousness, just as is the consciousness of my own thoughts. (A 372; italics added)

Consistent application of Kant's strictures about the unknowability of things in themselves would require Kant to replace the italicized passage, which makes a positive, substantive claim about what things in themselves cannot be, with one that admits our inability to *know whether or not* the "something which is in the transcendental sense outside us and is the cause of our outer intuitions" is "the object that we understand under the representations of matter and corporeal things." Kant is entitled to say that such an object is at least an appearance to be found in us. He is also entitled to say that, by hypothesis, we can know nothing about such an object beyond its appearance to us. But he is not entitled to deny that it might, in fact, accurately represent the nature of things in themselves as well.

This interpretation would, however, require Kant to jettison his allegiance to the traditional distinction between primary and secondary qualities. Since both would now be generated a priori by the subject's innate faculty of sensibility, and both would refer to something "outer"—respectively, the form and matter of appearance, the asymmetry between them would be far less striking. But Kant could still maintain that secondary qualities vary from person to person (i.e., to the extent that the transcendental subject's senses do) whereas primary ones do not; and so continue to insist that secondary qualities are not, unlike space and time, empirically real.

In the B Edition Kant moves closer to such a view. Here his argument for denying that sensations are empirically real is that "they belong merely to the subjective constitution of our *manner of sensibility,* for instance, of sight, hearing, touch, as in the case of the sensations of colors, sounds, and heat, which, since they are mere sensations . . . do not of themselves yield knowledge of any object" (A 28/B 44; italics added). On the next page Kant goes on to deny that colors and tastes can "be rightly regarded as properties of things, but only as changes in the subject, changes which may, indeed, be different for different people [and] with reference to color, can appear differently to every eye" (B 45; the passage in German runs, «jedem Auge in Ansehung der Farbe anders erscheinen kann.» Kemp Smith *again* willfully mistranslates this passage as "in respect of its color, can appear differently to every observer"). In this version of the argument Kant ascribes the five senses, and eyes in particular, to the subject's transcendental sensibility. Clearly this is a strategic error: Kant should not ascribe apparent properties of empirical objects, such as the sense organs human beings happen to have, to the transcendental subject to whom these properties empirically appear. But the interest of this *faux pas* is the evidence it provides of Kant's actual view. It clearly implies that he does think transcendental subjects have senses even if he shouldn't say so. And it supports the above suggestion that these senses can be understood as appearing empirically as sense organs to empirical observation or introspection.

What remains is to provide at least some textual evidence that the transcendental subject's sensations are caused by things in themselves. We have just seen that sensations cannot come from the empirical objects that are their consequences, as the A Edition suggests. Either they are self-generated by the subject or they come from something else. Now Kant insists that sensibility is a purely receptive capacity for "receiving representations through the way in which we are affected by objects" (A 19/B 33). Moreover, he later identifies and discusses that class of representations he thinks are actively generated by the mind's effect on itself (B 68–69; see Section IV, below). So we can infer that he doesn't think sensations can be actively self-generated. If they come from something else, this can only be from things in themselves. The above remarks, imploring Kant to speak up about the behavior of things in themselves, offers a possible account of this behavior that would square nicely, not only with A 143/B 182, but with A 19/B 34 as well.

Now for Kant actually to state this in the *Critique* would constitute a commitment to causal realism that conflicted with his strictures that we can know nothing of things in themselves, and in particular cannot assert the applicability of the categories to them. So Kant refrains from any such claim in the first *Critique*. Luckily for us, by the time he writes the *Prolegomena* he is ready to tip his hand. There Kant states quite clearly, in contrasting his own view with that of the idealist:

> I, on the contrary, say that things as objects of our senses existing outside us are given, but we know nothing of what they may be in themselves, knowing only their appearances, *that is, the representations which they cause in us by affecting our senses. Consequently I grant by all means that there are bodies without us, that is, things which, though quite unknown to us as to what they are in themselves, we yet know by the representations which their influence on our sensibility procures us*. (Immanuel Kant, *Prolegomena to Any Future Metaphysic*, tr. Lewis White Beck (New York: Bobbs-Merrill, 1950), Ac. 288, italics added)

Surely Kant's considered commitment to causal realism, i.e., to things in themselves as causal sources of the appearances they effect in us by impinging on our senses, a commitment achieved with intellectual and temporal distance from the many ambiguities and confusions of the first *Critique*, could not be any clearer than this.

18 Scientific paradigm shifts needn't invalidate Kant's insight, since a "gavagai" doesn't stop being a "gavagai" when we discover that it is "really" a perturbation in the electromagnetic field. I discuss the requirement of inclusiveness at greater length in " 'Seeing Things,' " *Southern Journal of Philosophy* 21, Suppl. Vol. (1990): 29–60.

19 Piper, "Pseudorationality."

20 The use of *bestimmen* can also mean to decree or ordain someone to do something; but it cannot mean merely to cause something. *Bestimmen* always carries the connotation of shaping some idea or event by cognitive means. Therefore it does rule out "cause" as a synonym for "determine." Kant's usual words for causality are *Kausalität* or *Ursache*. So *Selbstbestimmung* would refer to the cognitive activity of resolving to be or act in a certain way, not to that of merely causing oneself to do so. The tendency to think of Kant's concept of self-determination on analogy with that of causal determination should be resisted at all costs.

21 I develop this claim at greater length in "The Meaning of 'Ought' and the Loss of Innocence," invited address delivered to the American Philosophical Association Eastern Division Meeting, Atlanta, Geor., December 1989. Abstracted in the *Proceedings of the American Philosophical Association* 63, 2 (October 1989): 53–54.

22 Piper, "Two Conceptions," and "Pseudorationality."

23 Lest I be charged with the same fault I charge Kemp Smith, I note the ambiguity of the German: «Sie, die Vernunft, ist allen Handlungen des Menschen in allen Zeitumständen gegenwärtig und einerlei, selbst aber ist sie nicht in der Zeit, *und gerät etwa in einen neuen Zustand*, darin sie vorher nicht war; etc.» (italics added). A literal translation of this passage would make the meaning incoherent, so I infer that Kant was expressing himself ungrammatically.

24 Now in the *Groundwork*, Kant claims that "the human being and in general every rational being *exists* as end in himself, *not merely as means* for arbitrary use by this or that will, but rather must be viewed as *at the same time an end* in all of his actions, whether directed to himself or to other rational beings. . . . [R]ational beings are called *persons* because their nature distinguishes them as ends in themselves, i.e. as something that must not be used merely as means, and thus so far restricts all power of choice (and is an object of respect)" (Ac. 428). Besides an immediately

preceding paragraph that introduces these concepts with definitions of them, there is little in the *Groundwork* of an explicit nature to have prepared the reader for these remarks on personhood as an end in itself, so it may seem that Kant has simply pulled these intuitively appealing ideas out of a hat. Moreover, Kant does not explain in the *Groundwork* why it is that personhood or rational nature deserves to be regarded as an end in itself, or even what he thinks an end in itself is.

The explanations of Kant's claims lie, rather, in the first *Critique*. There Kant characterizes an end as a species of idea (A 318/B 375). As we have seen, an *idea* is for Kant a technical term that denotes a final outcome of the rational disposition to generalize inclusively from lower-level to higher-level concepts, principles, and theories. He also describes the peculiar sphere of reason as an order of ends which is at the same time an order of nature, and human beings as the only creatures in nature who can contain the final end of this order in themselves and also exempt themselves from it through morality (B 425). So the sphere of rationality is one in which all of our experience is systematically organized and unified according to inclusive theoretical concepts in the manner already discussed. Human beings both contain the final end of this natural order within themselves and also can transcend it through moral conduct. In the Canon of Pure Reason, Kant tells us what this final end is: it is the idea of a natural world made moral, in which the free power of choice of rational beings "has, under moral laws, thoroughgoing systematic unity as such, as much with itself as with the freedom of every other." (A 808/B 836) In this moral world, the supreme good is happiness as directly apportioned to moral worth by a Supreme Reason that rules according to moral law, and we are rationally compelled to envision this world as the outcome of our efforts to achieve moral worthiness to be happy (A 809/B 837–A 811/B 839, A 813/B 841–A 816/B 844). The ultimate end, Kant tells us, is the entire vocation of man, and this is treated by moral philosophy (A 840/B 868). So Kant says in the *Groundwork* that personhood is an end in itself because a person has the capacity rationally to represent to herself, as a final end of her moral conduct, a divinely just moral order in which she participates as an equal member. This is the same vision that lies behind Kant's obscure remarks about membership and lordship in the kingdom of ends (Ac. 433–34).

25 Piper, "Two Conceptions" & "Pseudorationality."

26 Piper, "Higher-Order Discrimination."

27 This is the main thesis of Professor Deborah Tannen's fascinating *You Just Don't Understand: Women and Men in Conversation* (New York: William Morrow and Co., Inc., 1990), a popularization of her research in linguistics on gender differences in language use.

28 I chart the systematic use of such disvaluative properties in "Higher-Order Discrimination."

29 "Impartiality, Compassion and Modal Imagination," *Ethics* 101, 4: Symposium on Impartiality (July 1991), 726–57.

30 The concept of personal investment is discussed in my "Moral Theory and Moral Alienation" *The Journal of Philosophy,* LXXXIV, 2 (February 1987): 102–18. Also see Notes 13 & 14.

31 I am indebted to Rüdiger Bittner for pressing this question in discussion of my "Higher-Order Discrimination," although I was unable to address it properly in that context.

32 See Note 14 for a fuller discussion.

33 A case study of this phenomenon might be the postmodernist attitude of mourning over the loss of value and meaning in contemporary creative and intellectual products of "western civilization" at just that historical moment when the longstanding contributions to it by women and people of color are gaining recognition.

34 I argue that Kant's moral theory is a descriptive, explanatory theory that fits the deductive-nomological model in "The Meaning of 'Ought' and the Loss of Innocence."

35 This idea of theoretical rationality and theory-building as an innate disposition is given some support by Robin Horton's crosscultural work. See his "African Traditional Thought and West-

ern Science,'' in *Rationality,* ed. Bryan Wilson (Evanston, Ill.: Harper and Row, 1970), 131–71. As I understand Horton's conclusions, the main difference between western scientific theories and the cosmologies of traditional societies is that the latter lack the concept of modality, i.e., recognition of the conceptual possibility that the favored and deeply entrenched explanation may not be the right one or the best one. They therefore lack the attitude of epistemic uncertainty that leads in the west to the joint problems of scepticism and solipsism. To this extent the stance of intellectual dissatisfaction I am attributing to Kant's epistemology may be culturally specific.

36 Thus xenophilia in the sense I am defining it should be distinguished from a superficially similar, but in fact deeply perverse form of xenophobia, in which the xenophobe reinforces her honorific, stereotypical self-conception by treating the other as an exotic object of research, whom (like a rare species of insect) it is permissible to examine and dissect from a superior vantage-point of inviolate disingenuousness. By contrast, the xenophile acknowledges the disruption and threat to the integrity of the self caused by the other's difference, and seeks understanding of the other as a way of understanding and transcending the limitations of her own self-conception.

en a person has suffered a grave misfortune the type of moral will serve to help that person to recover must be sensitive to the s in which the misfortune is likely to affect her or his life. This ust the physical damage that has been wrought to the person's body, in which the person will be haunted by painful memories, the ings of emotional and social vulnerability, and so on. For as I have dily damage can, itself, be negligible. It is not in the damage done hat the horror of armed robbery necessarily lies—since there might t in the damage done to the victim's sense of self. Again, while rape be physically violent, it need not be, as the idea gaining acceptance ce rape reveals.[3]

sure, there are many misfortunes, at the hands of other, which any can experience, and so which are independent of social categories. k of these as generalized misfortunes. Anyone can be robbed, or be a car accident caused by an intoxicated driver, or be hit by a stray ne can lose a loved one owing to a flagrant disregard for human misfortunes do not know the boundaries of social categories. And can be difficulties, perhaps insuperable ones in some instances, individuate (events that are) misfortunes, when people have expe-ralized misfortunes of the same type, then they have considerable ne another's suffering. The experience of losing a leg as a teenager alitatively different from that of losing a leg as an adult of 50, but two experiences are far closer qualitatively than is either to the losing a parent as a teenager or as an adult of 50. And between two h of whom lose a leg, it perhaps matters if one is an athlete and one

trasted with generalized misfortunes are misfortunes that are quite ished social categories—misfortunes owing to oppressive, if not egative attitudes about the members of well-defined diminished ries. As it happens, the diminished social category may be coex-a natural category, as may be the case with gender.[5] I shall use the 'hostile misfortunes'' to refer to these misfortunes, where ''hostile'' capture both that the misfortune is owing to agency and that the respect to the relevant set of acts, is owing to morally objectionable rding the diminished social category. I shall often refer to a person egory as a category person.

ne in a diminished social category experiences all, and to the same stile misfortunes specific to that category, but being in a diminished ry makes it exceedingly likely that one's life will be tinged with hostile misfortunes specific to that diminished social category.

MORAL DEFERENCE*

LAURENCE THOMAS

> Why is this peach-tree said to be better than that other; but because it produces more or better fruit?. . . In morals, too, is not *the tree known by the fruit?*
>
> David Hume, *Enquiry Concerning the Principles of Morals* (V, IIn1)

In ''What Is It Like To Be a Bat?,'' Thomas Nagel tells us that we hardly come to know what it is like to be a bat by hanging upside down with our eyes closed.[1] That experience simply tells us what it is like to be a human behaving or attempting to behave like a bat. If bats were intelligent creatures possessing a natural language, which we could translate, surely we would have to take their word for what it is like to be a bat. If, in batese, bats—including the most intelligent and articulate ones—generally maintained that ''Hanging upside down is extraordinarily like experiencing death through colors,'' we human beings would probably not know how to get a handle on what was being claimed, since the notion of experiencing death already strains the imagination. Just so, we would be in no position to dismiss their claim as so much nonsense because we cannot get a handle on it—because, after all, we humans experience no such thing when we engage in bat-like behavior. On this matter, bats would be owed deference.

Some people are owed deference—moral deference, that is. Moral deference is meant to stand in opposition to the idea that there is a vantage point from which any and every person can rationally grasp whatever morally significant experiences a person might have. A fundamentally important part of living morally is being able to respond in the morally appropriate way to those who have been wronged. And this ability we cannot have in the absence of a measure of moral deference. David Hume's position on the human sentiments gives us insight regarding the matter. Or so I claim in Section III. The full account of moral deference is offered in Section IV, the final section. I maintain that the attitude of moral deference is, as it were, a prelude to bearing witness to another's pain, with that person's authorization—the person's blessings, if you will.

On my view, moral deference is the bridge between individuals with different emotional category configurations owing to the injustices of society. I do not claim that moral deference will serve as a bridge between intelligent creatures who differ radically in their biological constitution from one another, though moral deference may nonetheless be owed. Moral deference, as I conceive of it, is not about whether individuals are innocent with respect to those who have been treated unjustly; rather, it is simply about the appropriate moral attitude to take when it comes to understanding the ways in which another has been a victim of social injustice. A person's innocence or lack thereof is irrelevant.

SOCIAL CATEGORIES

If one encounters a Holocaust survivor, it would be moral hubris of the worst sort—unless one is also such a survivor—to assume that by way of rational imaginative role-taking, à la Kohlberg,[2] one could even begin to grasp the depth of that person's experiences—the hurts, pains, and anxieties of that individual's life. There is not enough good will in the world to make it possible for persons (who are not Holocaust survivors) to put themselves imaginatively in the mind of a Holocaust survivor, to do so simply as an act of ratiocination.

The slaveowners who lived among slaves and, in fact, ruled the very lives of slaves knew a great deal about slaves. In many cases, slaveowners knew more about the intimate lives of slaves than a person has the right to know about another's intimate life (unless such information is freely and voluntarily offered in a noncoercive context). Yet, for all that white slaveowners knew about black slaves, the owners did not know what it was like to be a slave. Naturally, there were slave uprisings; but no slaveowner knew what it was like to be a slave on account of being a victim of such uprisings.

If a woman has been raped, it is clear that the last thing in the world that a heterosexual man should say is, "I can imagine how you feel." A great many men can barely imagine or grasp the fear of rape that, to varying degrees, permeates the lives of women, let alone the profoundly violent act of rape itself. Few actions could be more insensitive to victims of rape than a man's supposition that via a feat of imagination he can get a grip on the pain that a victim of rape has experienced.

I am, of course, aware that heterosexual men can be raped. But given the assumption of heterosexuality, male victims of rape, unlike female victims of rape, do not in general have the awkwardness of seeking to be personally fulfilled romantically by forming a relationship with a person who belongs to the

very same social category as does the person
case, do males have to contend with social a
explicit—that make them the target of sex
significance of their consent as an appropri
Lesbians do not escape this latter injustice;
Given the assumption of heterosexuality, wh
recover from the mental anguish of having b
a man does not involve being able to have se
complete recovery is not a matter of his b
conjuring up the pain of rape. By contrast,
generally seen along precisely these lines.
man involves nothing like the phenomenal
woman.

Why is it that we cannot simply imaginati
Holocaust survivor or, in the case of a man
answer is painfully obvious: even if we ha
son's experiences, we would nonetheless no
Nor would we have the painful memory o
ences. So a description, no matter how fu
counts to capture the subjective element o
namely, the memories—is far from trivial,
experiences shape our lives is through the
selves upon our lives. In fact, there are tim
rience upon our lives would be virtually nu
lives are affected by the memories of it.

Suppose that one has been robbed at gunp
to much at all, say $20 or $30. Suppose o
mental abuse, since two police officers cam
event may alter the way in which one lives f
realize how lucky one was. It is just that o
might have happened but for a fluke of luck-
cripples one emotionally. Rehearsing an ex
ingly reveal just how lucky one was. A w
having sex with her male partner, which ha
only to find that she can no longer continu
been assailed by the painful memories of b

No amount of imagination in the world c
subjective imprimatur of the experiences
individual's subjective imprimatur makes a
things together.

There can be appropriate and inappropr

another. W
response th
adverse wa
includes not
but the wa
person's fee
noted, the b
to the body
be none—b
can certainl
of acquaint

Now, to
human bein
We may thi
the victim o
bullet. Any
rights. Thes
though ther
with how to
rienced gen
insight into
is perhaps
no doubt th
experience
teenagers b
is not.[4]

To be co
tied to dim
prevailing,
social categ
tensive with
euphemism
is intended
agency, wit
attitudes reg
in such a ca

Not every
extent, the h
social categ
some of th

Moreover, if one is not in that diminished social category, the likelihood of one's experiencing any of the hostile misfortunes will be virtually nil. I regard gender, ethnicity, and race as obviously involving diminished social categories of this kind, though there need not be hostile misfortunes specific to every ethnic and racial group. Although people of the same diminished social category do not all endure the same hostile experiences, the relevant experiential psychological distances between their lives will be less than such distances between their lives and the lives of those who do not belong to any diminished social category or to a very different one. Interestingly, there can be subgroups within a diminished social category, and hostile misfortunes tied to those subgroups. For instance, there are very light-complexioned blacks (some of whom are phenotypically indistinguishable from whites) and there are darker-complexioned blacks; and each subgroup has its own hostile misfortunes, in addition to those associated simply with being black. Finally, it is possible for the hostile misfortunes of two different diminished social categories to parallel one another to a considerable degree. Such may be the case with the hostile misfortunes of African-American and Hispanic-American peoples. Individuals from these groups do not experience exactly the same hostile misfortunes. But there appears to be considerable overlap. The hostile misfortunes of a diminished social category group need not be fixed. Hence, there could be less overlap between two groups at one time than at another time.

As with generalized misfortunes, though, I shall assume that when two people of the same diminished social category experience the same type of hostile misfortune, then they have considerable insight into one another's experiencing of that misfortune. Of course, the problem of individuating types of events does not disappear here. Numerous refinements are possible. However, I shall leave such matters aside. Furthermore, there is the very thorny issue of when the hostile misfortunes of two diminished social category groups are similar enough to one another that each group has some insight into the moral pains of the other. There is certainly no reason to rule this out of court on conceptual grounds; on the other hand, one of the worst mistakes that can be made is for one diminished social category group to assume, without having attended to the matter, that its suffering gives it insight into the suffering of another diminished social category group. But this issue, too, I shall leave aside.

Now, the knowledge that someone belongs to a diminished social category group does not, in and of itself, give one insight into the subjective imprimatur of that individual's experiences of and memories stemming from the hostile misfortunes tied to the category to which the person belongs. If so, then a very pressing question is: how is it possible to be morally responsive in the appropriate way to those belonging to a diminished social category if one does not belong to that category? Here is where moral deference enters into the picture, though first more needs to be said about being a member of a diminished social category.

BEING SOCIALLY CONSTITUTED

David Hume observed that "Human nature cannot by any means subsist, without the association of individuals . . . ."[6] His point can be rendered in a contemporary vein as follows: we are constituted through others, by which I mean that the way in which we conceive of ourselves is, at least in part, owing to how others conceive of us, and necessarily so. The way in which we think of ourselves is inextricably tied to the way in which others think of us. In a fully just world, all would be constituted through others so as to be full and equal members of society. That is, each member would be constituted so as to see her or himself in this way. By contrast, in an oppressive society, the victims of oppression—diminished social category persons, I mean—are constituted, in both masterfully subtle ways and in ever so explicit ways, so as not to see themselves as full and equal members of society. I shall refer to this as downward social constitution. Each group of diminished social category persons in society experiences different forms of downward social constitution, although I have allowed that there may be overlap. Painfully, social groups that are themselves victims of downward social constitution may engage in downward social constitution of one another. Victims of sexism can be antisemitic; victims of racism can be sexist. And so on for each diminished social category group. Even worse, perhaps, there can be downward social constitution by members within a group. In an oppressive society, downward social constitution is an ongoing and pervasive phenomenon, which is not to deny that there can be pockets of relief to varying degrees. Needless to say, a society with diminished social categories will have one or more privileged social categories, the members of which are favored and have full access to the goods of society.

One of the most important ways in which downward social constitution occurs pertains to expectations. It is just assumed, often without awareness of what is being done, that this or that category person cannot measure up in an important way. The reality that we do not expect much of a person on account of her category can be communicated in a thousand and one ways. One may listen inattentively, or interrupt ever so frequently, or not directly respond to what the person actually says, or not respond with the seriousness that is appropriate to the persons concerned. Most significantly, owing to meager expectations, one may fail to give the benefit of the doubt to the diminished social category person. We often do not realize that we are participating in the downward constitution of others because communicating favorable and negative expectations with regard to others is a natural part of life. Further, behavior that contributes to the downward constitution of another may manifest itself in other contexts that have nothing to do with downward constitution. After all, one can listen inattentively simply because one is preoccupied. Or, one can fail to respond directly because one misunderstood what the person said. Accordingly, negative expectations toward a member of a diminished social category need not feel any different from negative expectations toward any other member of society, nor need the behavior bear a special mark. Except for the blatant bigot or sexist, participating in the downward social constitution of another rarely has any special phenomenological feel to it.

Thus, it is interesting that for most people the evidence that they do not engage in downwardly constituting behavior is that they do not have the appropriate feelings. It is true that if one has and sustains the appropriate feelings, then one is an X-ist (racist, sexist, and so forth), or one has acted in an X-ist way if such feelings fuel one's behavior; on the other hand, it is manifestly false that if one lacks such feelings, then X-ism is not a part of one's life.

I have said that in an oppressive society downward social constitution is an ongoing and pervasive phenomenon despite pockets of relief. Such constitution may show up in advertisement, in the casting of characters for a film (play or television program), in the assumptions about the interests (as well as professional aims and hobbies) that a person has or what such a person should be satisfied with. The list goes on. Further, an expression of downward constitution may manifest itself at almost any time in almost any context. An expression of downward constitution may come from those who are so eager to put up an appearance of caring that they deceive themselves in believing that they actually care. Such an expression may even come from those who in fact care.[7]

To be a member of a diminished social category group is invariably to have to contend with what I shall call the problem of social category ambiguity. Often enough the question will be: was that remark or piece of behavior a manifestation of downward social constitution or something else or both? It may not have been, but the very nature of the context and one's social reality as a diminished social category person does not allow one to rule out that possibility with the desired confidence. On the one hand, one does not want to accuse someone falsely; on the other, one may not want to put up with an affront owing to being a member of a diminished social category. Yet, there may be no way to inquire about the matter without giving the appearance of doing the former. Finally, there is the painful reality that one may not be able to share one's feelings about one's social category status with those who do not belong to that category, without giving the impression of being overly concerned with such matters—even with those who regard themselves as friends. It is a reality that sometimes requires a kind of profound disassociation from one's own experiences, at least momentarily.

Together, these things all speak to a profound sense of vulnerability that comes with being a member of a diminished social category. Part of that vulnerability is owing not just to being a subject of downward social constitution, but to the memories of such experiences. Invariably, the diminished social category person will be haunted by some of these memories to varying degrees. Then there is the fact that a memory (sometimes painful, sometimes not) of an experience of downward social constitution can be triggered by any number of things, including the witnessing of another's experience of downward social constitution, or another such experience of one's own. There is a sense in which one can be assailed by the memories of past undesirable experiences. A diminished social category person is vulnerable in this way. People who are downwardly constituted socially are victims of a social claim about them—not just any old claim but the claim that they lack the wherewithal to measure up in an important social dimension. In this regard, diminished social category persons are vulnerable on several counts. First, there is the vulnerability owing to being weary of always feeling the need to prove that this social claim is a lie—if not to themselves then to others. Second, there is the vulnerability owing to the reality that there is almost nothing that diminished social category persons can do which will decisively establish the falsity of the social claim. Third, there is the vulnerability owing to the weariness of it all that stems from the feeling that one must speak up because no one else will, although one is concerned that continually speaking up will diminish one's effectiveness. Obviously, diminished social category persons cope with these vulnerabilities in a variety of different ways and with varying degrees of success. But successfully coping with a vulnerability is hardly tantamount to not being vulnerable, any more than not showing anger is tantamount to not being angry.

The remarks in the preceding two paragraphs are meant to bring out the sense of *otherness* that inescapably comes with being a person belonging to a diminished social category, the sense of what it means to be socially constituted as such a person. This sense of otherness is not something that a person who does not belong to one's particular diminished social category can grasp simply by an act of ratiocination. In particular, it is not something to which people belonging to privileged social categories can grasp. People who belong to a privileged social category can, of course, experience insults and affronts to their person, even at the hands of those belonging to a diminished social category. Indeed, privileged social category persons can experience these things precisely because they belong to a privileged social category. But, clearly, just as a person does not know what it is like to be a bat by hanging upside down with closed eyes, a person does not know what it is like to be a member of a diminished social category merely on account of having been affronted and insulted by diminished social category persons for being a privileged social category person. For the hallmark of a diminished social category person is that of being a person whose life has been downwardly constituted socially, with all that this implies in terms of vulnerability as noted above. A privileged social category person who has experienced affronts at the hands of diminished social category persons has no more had a downwardly constituted life on that account, with all that this implies in terms of vulnerability, than has a seventy-year-old person led a life marred by sickness for having had to spend three weeks at twenty in the hospital for exposure to meningitis and again at fifty for exposure to hepatitis.

EMOTIONAL CONFIGURATION

Hume seems to have held that if our natural capacity for sympathy and benevolence were sufficiently cultivated, we would have adequate insight into the weal and woe of others.[8] I disagree, although I think that his heart was in the right place. In a world without hostile misfortunes and diminished social category groups, and so without privileged social category groups, I think that Hume's position would, indeed, be correct or very nearly that. I hesitate only because it might be that even in a perfectly just world some differences might be impassable despite unqualified good will on all accounts. Hume's point holds given two assumptions: (a) the emotional capacities of people are essentially the same; (b) the configuration of these emotional capacities through society is essentially the same, the primary difference with respect to the latter being in their development. Thus, for Hume, Nero is simply one whose capacity for benevolence and sympathy virtually went uncultivated. By contrast, Hume thought it obvious that anyone who had benefited from some cultivation of these sentiments could not help but see that Nero's actions were criminal.[9]

Such social phenomena as downward social constitution and diminished social categories would not have occurred to Hume. Specifically, and more pointedly, it would not have occurred to him that a person's emotions could be configured along a dimension other than the extent of their cultivation, the case of gender aside.[10] So, given Hume's moral psychology, anyone whose capacity for sympathy and benevolence was properly cultivated was in a position to understand sufficiently the moral experiences of all others. I am suggesting that Hume's moral psychology must be adjusted to take into account the reality that the emotional makeup of persons can be configured along dimensions other than cultivation. There is what I shall call emotional category configuration.

In a sexist society, a politically correct male who abhors violence against females, and understands ever so well why a victim of rape would rather be comforted by a female rather than a male nonetheless does not have the emotional configuration of a female. This is because the kind of fears that he experiences when he walks alone at night do not have as their source a concern about sexual violence; whereas they do for a woman whether or not she has been raped.[11] In a sexist society, at any rate, the emotional category configuration of women and men are different. This follows from women and men being socially constituted differently.

Likewise, a white can be attacked by blacks, and that attack can be brutal and absolutely inexcusable. As a result, the person may be emotionally crippled in terms of his fear of interacting with blacks. This is painfully sad. All the same, this suffering experience does not parallel the suffering of blacks. His fear of blacks may very well be a reminder of the random brutality of some blacks and of the moral squalor in which some wallow. The experience may seal his conviction that blacks lack the wherewithal to live morally decent lives.

But for all of that, the experience will not be a reminder that he is a second-class citizen. It will not make him vulnerable to that pain. He will not have the pain of being scarred by those who in fact have power over so very much of his life. By and large, the white will not really have to concern himself with having to trust blacks who have power over him, as with a little effort and creativity the white can avoid situations of this kind; whereas for the black, having to trust whites who have power over him is a real possibility. So, whereas some physical distance from blacks, coupled with time, might serve to heal the wounds of the white, this healing route is not a genuine possibility for a black. This is yet another dimension along which the black will live with his pain in a quite different manner than the white. Certainly no innocent white should be a victim of black anger and hostility; certainly no innocent black should be either. The moral wrong may be equal in either case. My point is that because the black and the white have different emotional category configurations, each will experience their respective pain in a radically different manner. While economic differences could be factored in here, I did not develop the point with such differences in mind. The force of the point is not diminished in the least if both the white and the black are quite upper middle-class people enjoying equal salaries.

A fortiori, we have a difference in emotional category configuration here rather than a difference in the cultivation of the emotions if we suppose that the black and the white went to the very same kind of schools, read many of the same books, and have overlapping interests and musical tastes. We can imagine that they have similar personalities, and have had similar maturation experiences and wrestled with many of the same issues. Nonetheless, it is most likely they will be socially constituted in different ways. In the case of the black, strangers might be surprised that he was not born poor, or wonder where he learned to speak so well. The police at the university where he has just joined the faculty might regard him with suspicion. Or, at the checkout desk at the university library, the staff person might ask him for a piece of photo-identification to confirm that he is actually the owner of the university library card (which does not have a photograph on it) that he presented. These experiences will not be a part of the white person's life.

The cumulative effect of these experiences contributes to the significant difference in the emotional category configuration of which I have been speaking. Time and time again, a well-off black must steel himself against such experiences in settings of equality, while a white need not. Ironically, some of the experiences of downward social constitution—some of the insults—that a black will encounter, the person could only encounter if she were well-off, since a black in the throes of poverty would be too far removed from such social situations in the first place.[12] A black American in the throes of poverty is not apt to experience racism in a Middle Eastern or European hotel by a white American.

Nothing that I have experienced in my entire life had prepared me for the shock of being taken as a would-be purse snatcher in a Middle Eastern hotel by a white American who saw me enter the hotel lobby from the guest rooms. The person leapt for her pocketbook on the counter as if she had springs on her feet, although people had been sitting in the lobby all along. Worse still, she and I had been sitting in the lobby opposite one another only two days earlier. As I play back the experience in my mind, it seems so incredibly surrealistic to me that I continually find myself stunned. Even granting racism, and that she had been robbed by a black man while she was in Harlem, just how reasonable under the circumstances could it have been for her to suppose that *I* was a poor black out to steal her purse? After all, it takes more than cab fare to get from New York, New York, to any place in the Middle East.[13] I have been called a "nigger" to my face three times in my life. One of them was in Harvard Yard between Widner and Emerson. If I were to walk around with a fear that whites might call me "nigger," I would surely be taken as mad by most of my friends and acquaintances. Or, I would be seen as having enormous and unjustified hostility against whites.

Hume's moral psychology cannot account for the emotional vulnerability that comes with the above experience. This is because it would not have occurred to him that a person would be treated as anything other than a full citizen of the world on a par with all others—at least among other equally cultivated individuals—*if* the individual displayed the refinements of education and culture. It would not have occurred to him that persons displaying such refinements could be the object of hostile misfortunes. For on his view, the display of these things should suffice to elicit admiration.[14]

THE IDEA OF MORAL DEFERENCE

Moral deference is owed to persons of good will when they speak in an informed way regarding experiences specific to their diminished social category from the standpoint of an emotional category configuration to which others do not have access. The idea behind moral deference is not that a diminished social category person can never be wrong about the character of his own experiences. Surely he can, since anyone can. Nor is it that silence is the only appropriate response to what another says when one lacks that individual's emotional category configuration. Rather, the idea is that there should be a presumption in favor of the person's account of her experiences. This presumption is warranted because the individual is speaking from a vantage point to which someone not belonging to her diminished social category group does not have access. It is possible to play a major role in helping a person to get clearer about the character of an experience delivered from the vantage point of an emotional category configuration. But helping someone get clearer is qualitatively different from being dismissive. Indeed, how a person feels about a matter can be of the utmost importance even if the individual's feelings are inappropriate, since inappropriate feelings can shed considerable light on the very appearances of things in themselves.

While I do not think that moral deference is owed only to persons of good will who are members of diminished social categories, my account begins with such persons. The assumption here is that in characterizing their feelings and experiences as diminished social category persons, those of good will do not tell an account that is mired and fueled by feelings of rancor and bitterness. This is not to suggest that persons of good will never experience tremendous anger and rage on account of experiences of downward social constitution. They sometimes do, and rightly so. Occasionally experiencing anger and rage, though, is by no means the same thing as becoming consumed by these feelings. A complete account of moral deference would have to be extended to include those who, understandably or not, have come to be full of bitterness and rancor owing to the ways in which they have been downwardly constituted socially. It becomes especially important to extend the account in this direction if one considers that oppression, itself, can render its victims so full of rancor and bitterness that the manifestation of these sentiments can blind us to their underlying cause, namely oppression itself.

Moral deference is meant to reflect the insight that it is wrong to discount the feelings and experiences of persons in diminished social category groups simply because their articulation of matters does not resonate with one's imaginative take on their experiences. Moral deference acknowledges a vast difference between the ideal moral world and the present one. In the ideal moral world there would be only one category of emotional configuration, namely the human one—or at most two, allowing for differences in the sexes. So, given adequate cultivation of emotions and feelings, everyone would be able to get an imaginative take on the experiences of others. Interestingly, this way of understanding the role of emotions in the ideal world might point to a reason for making them irrelevant entirely; for if rightly cultivated emotions would result in everyone's making the same moral judgments on the basis of them, then the emotions do not make for a morally relevant difference between people, at least not among those with rightly cultivated emotions. On this view, the emotions can only make a morally relevant difference if they are seen as a constitutive feature of what it means to be a person, and so of moral personhood. But, alas, philosophers often seem anxious to deny that the emotions have any moral relevance, in and of themselves, at the foundational conception of moral personhood.[15]

In a far from ideal moral world, such as the one we live in, which privileges some social categories and diminishes others, it stands to reason that there will be emotional boundaries between people, owing to what I have called emotional category configuration. This is one of the bitter fruits of immorality. Recall Hume's question: "In morals, too, is not the tree known by its fruits?" The idea of moral deference is true to the moral reality that the mark of an immoral society is the erection of emotional walls between persons. It is true to the reality that social immorality cannot be eliminated in the absence of a firm grasp of how it has affected its victims. It is not enough to be confident that social immorality harms. One must also be sensitive to the way in which it harms. Thus, the idea of moral deference speaks to an attitude that a morally decent person should have in an immoral society.

We can best get at what moral deference involves, and its importance, by thinking of what it means to bear witness to another's moral pain with that person's authorization. To bear witness to the moral pain of another, say, Leslie, with Leslie's authorization, is to have won her confidence that one can speak informedly and with conviction on her behalf to another about the moral pain she has endured. It is to have won her confidence that one will tell her story with her voice, and not with one's own voice. Hence, it is to have won her trust that one will render salient what was salient for her in the way that it was salient for her; that one will represent her struggle to cope in the ways that she has been in getting on with her life; that one will convey desperation where desperation was felt, and hurt where hurt was felt. And so on.

To bear witness to Leslie's pain is not to tell Leslie's story of pain as a means to explicating how her pain has affected one's own life. Accordingly, to be authorized by Leslie to bear witness to her pain is to have won her confidence that telling her story of pain will not take a back seat to telling one's own story of pain as caused by her story. Not that it will always be impossible for people to make reasonable inferences about how one has been affected. It stands to reason that how one has been affected will surely be obvious in some cases. Rather, whatever inferences reasonable people might be able to draw, the point of bearing witness to the moral pain of another will not be so that others can see how one has been affected by the other person's pain. Thus, to be authorized to bear witness for another is to have won her confidence that one will tell her story with a certain motivational structure.

Now, it may be tempting to think that bearing witness to the moral pain of others requires something amounting to a complete diminution of the self, to becoming a mere mouthpiece for another. But this is to think of bearing witness to the moral pain of others as something that happens to one—a state that one falls into or whatever. Perhaps there are such cases of bearing witness. I do not write with them in mind, however. Instead, as I conceive of the idea, bearing witness to the moral pain of another is very much an act of agency and, as such, it can be an extremely courageous thing to do. During the time of slavery, whites who endeavored to bear witness to the moral pain of blacks were sometimes called "nigger lovers." In Nazi Germany, some who endeavored to bear witness to the moral pain of the Jews were killed. Nowadays, those who endeavor to bear witness to the moral pain of lesbians and homosexuals are often branded as such themselves. Far from being an activity only for the faint of heart, bearing witness to the moral pain of others can require extraordinary courage and resoluteness of will.

Well, needless to say, there can be no bearing witness, as I have explicated it, to the moral pain of another without having heard his story and heard it well. One will have had to have heard the glosses on the story and the nuances to the story. One will have had to have been sensitive to the emotions that manifested themselves as the story was told, and to the vast array of nonverbal behavior with which the story was told. One will have to have heard his story well enough to have insight into how his life has been emotionally configured by his experiences. One rightly authorizes a person to bear witness to his moral pain only if these things are true.

To have such insight into another's moral pain will not be tantamount to having that person's fears or being haunted by his memories, but it will entail having a sense of the kinds of things and circumstances that will trigger his fears and memories. It will not entail being vulnerable when he is downwardly constituted on account of his diminished social category, but it will entail a sense of the kinds of social circumstances that will give rise to such vulnerability. Moreover, it will entail being appropriately moved on account of these things. To have such insight is to be in as good a position as one can be to understand while yet lacking a complete grasp of another's moral pain.

Moral deference, then, is the act of listening that is preliminary to bearing witness to another's moral pain, but without bearing witness to it. I do not see the step from moral deference to bearing witness as an easy one. A person may lack the fortitude or courage to bear witness, however well he might listen. Moral deference is not about bearing witness. It is about listening, in the ways characterized above, until one has insight into the character of the other's moral pain, and so how he has been emotionally configured by it. In any case, moral deference may be appropriate on occasions when bearing witness is not. You may not want me to bear witness to your moral pain; yet, you may be deeply gratified that I have listened well enough that I could in the ever so unlikely event that you should want me to.

Moral deference, too, is not an activity for the faint of heart. For it is a matter of rendering oneself open to another's concern, and to letting another's pain reconstitute one so much that one comes to have a new set of sensibilities—a new set of moral lenses if you will. Moral deference is rather like the moral equivalent of being nearsighted, putting on a pair of glasses for the first time, and discovering just how much out there one had been missing. Of course, one had always seen trucks, cars, people, and so forth. But there were designs on cars and trucks, and sayings on shirts, and facial expressions that people displayed, and minute movements that people made, and slight variances in colors—none of which one could see at a distance. With moral deference one acquires sensibility to the way in which a self-respecting oppressed person lives in the world. Hence, to engage in moral deference is to allow oneself to become affected in a direct interpersonal way by the injustices of this world. While not the only way in which to do this, it is a very important way in which to do this. Thus, it is a fundamentally important mode of moral learning. It is a mode of moral learning which those who have been oppressed are owed in the name of eliminating the very state of their oppression. In the absence of such learning, oppression cannot but continue to be a part of the fabric of the moral life. Indeed, the absence of such learning, the studied refusal to engage in such learning, is one of the very ways in which oppression manifests itself. Worse, such studied refusal to learn adds insult to injury.

Significantly, moral deference involves earning the trust of another—in particular, the trust of one who has been oppressed. And earning the trust of another, especially someone who is weary of trusting anyone from a different social category (diminished or privileged), is an act of great moral responsibility—something not to be taken lightly in the least. It would be morally egregious in the very worst of ways to earn such a person's trust, and then abuse it or merely withdraw from the person. If the struggle for equality is ever to be won we must be strong enough to be vulnerable. That is, we must be strong enough to prove ourselves worthy of the trust of those whom we have oppressed. This is well-nigh impossible in the absence of moral deference given to those whom we have oppressed. Moral deference is by no means a weakness. It is quite a matter of courage, instead.

In an important essay entitled "The Need for More than Justice," Annette Baier explains the significance of departing from John Rawls's claim that justice is the first virtue of social justice.[15] One thing that is needed is the appropriate moral posture toward those who have been oppressed. Without it, we often blithely trample upon those whom we mean to help. The notion of moral deference is meant to give expression to one aspect of what that posture calls for. It is impossible to responsively help those who have been hurt if one does not understand the nature of their pain. And while it may be true that we can know what is right and wrong behavior for others without consulting them, it is simply false that, in the absence of similar experiences, we can know how others are affected by wrongdoing without consulting them.

Let me repeat a point made at the outset: the idea of moral deference helps us to understand the inadequacy of the response that one has not contributed to another's oppression. To the extent that it is true, the response does not entail that one understands another's downward social constitution. Moral innocence does not entail understanding. Neither, for that matter, does good will. Nor does either entail that one has earned the trust of one who has been downwardly constituted by society. It goes without saying that the innocence of others should never be discounted; neither should it be trumpeted for what it is not, namely understanding and the earned trust of others.

A final comment: the account of moral deference offered suggests why both those who have been downwardly constituted by society and those who have not been should think differently of one another. If, as I have argued, those who have not been should be willing to earn the trust of the downwardly constituted, then the downwardly constituted must not insist that, as a matter of principle, this is impossible. Understandably, it may be difficult to earn the trust of those who have been downwardly constituted by society. And it may, in fact, not be possible for some outside of the social category in question actually to do so. But what has to be false is that, as a matter of principle, it is impossible for anyone outside of that social category to do so.

Apart from the context of the loves of friendship and romance, there is no greater affirmation that we can want from another than that which comes in earning her or his trust. If we should be willing to accept moral affirmation from others, then surely we are more likely to treat them justly. Moral deference embodies this idea.

Syracuse University

NOTES

* This paper owes its inspiration to my 1991 Winter Quarter class on the Gilligan-Kohlberg debate (which I taught while visiting at the University of Chicago); Alison M. Jaggar's, "Love and Knowledge: Emotion in Feminist Epistemology," in eds. Alison M. Jaggar and Susan R. Bordo, *Gender/Body/Knowledge: Feminist Reconstructions of Being and Knowing* (New Bruns-

wick: Rutgers University Press, 1989); and Seyla Benhabib's "The Generalized and the Concrete Other: The Kohlberg-Gilligan Controversy and Moral Theory," in eds. Eva Feder Kittay and Diana T. Meyers, *Women and Moral Theory* (Rowman and Littlefield, 1978). I see moral deference as a way of responding to the moral significance of the concreteness of others. I received instructive comments from Norma Field, John Pittman, and Julian Wuerth. At various times, conversations with Linda Alcoff, Alan J. Richard, Michael Stocker (always a present help), and Thomas Nagel (over the penultimate draft) were very helpful. A special debt of gratitude is owed to writer Jamie Kalven whose life reveals the richness that moral deference can yield.

Some recent works on the subject of racism have been most illuminating: David Theo Goldberg, "Racism and Rationality: The Need for a New Critique," *Philosophy of the Social Sciences,* Vol. 20 (1990); Adrian M. S. Piper's paper "Higher-Order Discrimination," in Owen Flanagan and Amelie Oksenberg Rorty, *Identity, Character, and Morality: Essays in Moral Psychology* (Cambridge: Massachusetts Institute of Technology Press, 1990); Elizabeth V. Spelman, *Inessential Women: Problems of Exclusion in Feminist Thought* (Beacon Press, 1988). My essay has very nearly turned out to be something of a companion piece to Michael Stocker's wonderful essay "How Emotions Reveal Value" (unpublished).

1 In *Mortal Questions* (Cambridge University Press, 1979).

2 *The Philosophy of Moral Development* (New York: Harper & Row, 1981). See especially the essay entitled "From Is to Ought: How to Commit the Naturalistic Fallacy and Get Away with It."

3 See, for instance, "Tougher Laws Mean More Cases are Called Rape," *The New York Times,* 27 May 1991: p. 9.

4 For a very important discussion of events, and their individuation, see Judith Jarvis Thomson, *Acts and Other Events* (Cornell University Press, 1977).

5 That gender is both a biological and a social category is developed at length in my essay "Sexism and Racism: Some Conceptual Differences," *Ethics* (1980).

6 *Enquiries Concerning the Principles of Morals* (Section IV, para. 165).

7 For an absolutely masterful discussion of these matters, see Adrian Piper, "Higher-Order Discrimination."

8 *Enquiries Concerning the Principles of Morals:* V, pt. II, pars. 183, 189; IX, pt. I, par. 220.

9 *Principles of Morals,* Appen. 1, 241.

10 For an important discussion of Hume regarding gender, see Annette Baier, *A Progress of Sentiments* (Cambridge: Harvard University Press, 1991), pp. 273–75. Hume thought that women who desired to become wives and to bear children should be held to stricter standards of chastity than men. Cf. David Hume, *Enquiries Concerning the Principles of Morals,* Section V, Section VIII, par. 215 and, especially, Section VI, part I, par. 195.

11 Perhaps male child victims of male rape can approximate such fears in their own lives. Still the adult life of such males will be qualitatively different from the adult life of females, owing to great differences in the way in which society portrays women and men as sex objects. See the discussion in Section I above. This, of course, hardly diminishes the pain of having been a male victim of child rape.

12 Bernard Boxill, in a very powerful essay, "Dignity, Slavery, and the 13th Amendment," has demonstrated the deep and profound way in which slavery was insulting. His essay appears in Michael J. Meyer and William A. Parent (eds.), *Human Dignity, the Bill of Rights and Constitutional Values* (Cornell University Press, 1992).

13 I was so enraged by the experience that it was clear to me that I had better channel my rage lest I do something that I would regret. Fortunately, I had a micro-cassette recorder with me. I walked the streets of Tel Aviv and taped the essay "Next Life, I'll Be White," *The New York Times/*

Op-Ed page (13 August 1990), an expanded version of which appeared in *Ebony Magazine* (December, 1990). It is, among other things, profoundly insulting when the obvious is discounted at one's own expense.

14 *Enquiries Concerning the Principles of Morals:* V, pt. II–180; VIII.

15 Cf. my ''Rationality and Affectivity: The Metaphysics of the Moral Self,'' *Social Philosophy and Policy* 5 (1988): 154–72.

16 *Morality and Feminist Theory, Canadian Journal of Philosophy,* Supp. Vol. 13 (1987). Rawls's first sentence is ''Justice is the first virtue of social institutions as truth is of systems of thought,'' *A Theory of Justice* (Cambridge: Harvard University Press, 1971), p. 3.

As I was typing the final draft of this essay, Martha Minow's book, *Making All the Difference: Inclusion, Exclusion, and American Law* (Ithica: Cornell University Press), was brought to my attention. But I did read the Afterword in which she writes: ''Claiming that we are impartial is insufficient if we do not consider changing how we think. Impartiality is the guise that partiality takes to seal bias against exposure'' (p. 376). This essay points to a way in which that change must go.

RACE, CLASS, AND THE SOCIAL CONSTRUCTION OF SELF-RESPECT

MICHELE M. MOODY-ADAMS

INTRODUCTION

In the mid-1950s, when Kenneth Clark first investigated the influence of racial prejudice on children, discrimination appeared to pose a serious threat to the self-conception of many Black American children.[1] Clark's famous "doll study" of racial preferences in children tested black and white children in several age groups to determine which of two dolls—black or white—they preferred. A majority of Black children in every age group studied expressed a preference for the white doll and rejected the black doll. Of course, not every child who grew up during this period would have displayed such a response, but the self-conceptions of those who did seemed to have been distorted by the complex consequences of discrimination. Many social theorists hoped that social reforms of the 1960s might help remedy the problem. Yet when the study was recently repeated, the results were surprisingly similar to Clark's original findings: a majority of the Black children studied expressed the same kind of racial preferences as those of similar children in the 1950s.[2]

Anecdotal accounts suggest that the increasing economic isolation of some Black children in American cities may compound the effects of discrimination. A public teacher in a major American city recently reported a disturbing conversation with a ten-year-old Black child who was asked to explain his disruptive classroom behavior. When this student was cautioned that he was preventing his classmates (all of whom were Black) from learning, he replied that it didn't matter, since they were "nothing." Reminded that he was disrupting his own education, he answered that he, too, was "nothing," and added "my mother told me I ain't nothing."[3]

This article describes and defends a new way of understanding the notion of self-respect, as a contribution to philosophical psychology and as an attempt to understand why the relevant social reforms seem to have failed the child in my example—and others like him. The first section defines and describes the two distinct components of self-respect and discusses the influence of social conditions on each component. I also distinguish self-respect from self-esteem and discuss the complicated relation between the two phenomena. The second section shows how socially developed expectations about persons and their capacities help shape self-conceptions and ultimately influence the ability to have and affirm self-respect and self-esteem. I show, further, how socially developed expectations—especially those bound up with class and race—sometimes undermine the capacity to develop a *robust* sense of self-respect. Finally, the third section discusses the most important social bases of self-respect. Social reforms may be a necessary component of any effort to ensure the socially widespread emergence of robust self-respect. Yet we can restore the social bases of self-respect only if we also seek to revise destructive expectations about persons and their characteristics—including many self-regarding expectations—that have supported unreformed social practices.

WHAT IS SELF-RESPECT?

Self-respect, or due respect for one's own worth, has two fundamental components. The first, more fundamental, component involves the conviction that one best affirms one's own value by using one's abilities and talents to contribute to one's survival. One who fails to act on this conviction fails to affirm self-respect, while one who lacks the conviction fails to have self-respect. Yet the conviction and the readiness, together, are just the minimum content of self-respect; a *robust* sense of self-respect is far more than simply a concern to use one's talents in the interest of self-preservation. Further, even the minimum content of self-respect is itself more than simply a concern for one's survival. A person might care about her own survival and yet be unwilling to try to contribute to it: such a person places some value on her own existence but lacks the attitude properly called self-respect. A person has self-respect only when the value she places on her own survival is sufficient to make her willing to contribute to it.

What constitutes contributing to one's survival will always be relative to the specific circumstances of an individual life. For instance, what might be a significant affirmation of the minimum content of self-respect for a hostage bound and gagged in a dark cell would be relatively insignificant for a person not confined in this way.[4] But virtually no human beings who are capable of consciousness and reflection are incapable of having and actively affirming the minimum content of self-respect. A mentally handicapped person who seeks employment, a young child who wants to be allowed to choose what to wear to school, even a person wishing to end some addictive behavior by first acknowledging a need for the assistance of others—all of these people affirm their possession of the minimum content of self-respect. Finally, most people have a tenacious and regularly observable tendency to seek, and to try to protect, the minimum content of self-respect. As I suggest below, even people who have suffered severe economic and social deprivation typically bear out this observation.

The second component of self-respect is a willingness to do whatever is within one's power to enhance or develop one's abilities and talents. A person who must travel long distances to work, for instance, might need to learn to drive if she cannot take public transport to work. The willingness to develop one's talents initially emerges because, usually, one can best exercise one's abilities when these abilities have been adequately developed.

The relation between the two aspects of self-respect is typically unproblematic—it is generally easy to reconcile concerns that might be generated by the two aspects of self-respect. However, certain circumstances may complicate the relation between the two components of self-respect, making it difficult to reconcile their demands. The first complication arises because human beings have the capacity to place intrinsic value on the development and exercise of some kinds of abilities—such as artistic abilities and moral capacities. Concerns generated by the development and exercise of such abilities may even take priority over concerns associated with the minimum content of self-respect. When this happens, self-forgetfulness and even self-sacrifice can be transformed into manifestations of self-respect.[5] A great writer who works to exhaustion to complete her book, or a lifeguard who risks his life to save a child from drowning, both illustrate this kind of transformation.

But a second, very different kind of complication arises when a person is consistently thwarted in her efforts to develop or exercise her talents and abilities. Such a person may begin to mistrust her abilities; severe frustration and disappointment can make the exercise of one's abilities and talents seem antithetical to self-preservation. One may even come to believe that one's misfortune and unhappiness actually result from the exercise of one's talents and abilities—even when, as a matter of fact, one is not responsible for the unhappiness suffered. Thus children who suffer extreme abuse, for example, can come to hate the exercise of their distinctive talents and abilities—with dire consequences for their sense of self-respect.

Of course the relation between the two components of self-respect can be more harmonious: indeed, a robust sense of self-respect must comfortably combine the two components (to some degree) over a lifetime. Moreover, a robust sense of self-respect is a central ingredient of a satisfying life. To see why, we must understand, first, that the two components of self-respect are often mutually reinforcing. The satisfaction that often accompanies the development of one's distinctive talents and abilities typically increases one's enjoyment of life. This increase may in turn strengthen one's conviction of the importance to one's self-respect of using and developing those abilities. Second, a robust sense of self-respect typically generates a wish to formulate and pursue an effective life plan rather than to seek self-preservation merely by means of ad hoc reactions to circumstances. One is likely to lead a better life in virtue of having and acting upon such a wish than if one never developed, or acted upon, such a wish. Thus John Rawls is right to view self-respect as a good that any rational person will want, whatever else she might want.[6] Finally, a robust sense of self-respect generally makes one better able, and more willing, to engage in the social cooperation that makes possible the rational pursuit of life plans. Since it is in general rational to want to encourage such cooperation, it is also rational to want every member of one's society to be given the fullest possible chance to develop a robust sense of self-respect.[7]

I distinguish self-respect from self-esteem. My account thus departs substantially from Rawls's claims about the content of self-respect. Rawls contends that "a person's sense of his own value" is equivalent to that person's "secure conviction that his conception of his good, his plan of life, is worth carrying out" (TJ 440). Rawls also claims that "self-respect implies a confidence in one's ability, so far as it is within one's power, to fulfill one's intentions" (TJ 440). Like other critics of this claim, I think that what Rawls describes here is not self-respect but the phenomenon of self-esteem.[8] Moreover, the distinction between self-esteem and self-respect is crucial. How else can we understand that a person might lose confidence in the worth of some particular life plan without at the same time questioning her value as a person?[9] People can sometimes refine, revise, or relinquish a life plan (or some portion of it) should circumstances require them to do so. This is because self-respect is both more fundamental, and less fragile, than self-esteem.

But while self-esteem—confidence in one's life plan—is distinct from self-respect—a due sense of one's own worth—severe diminutions in self-esteem may nonetheless have devastating effects on self-respect. Such effects are most likely when a loss of confidence in one's plans causes a further loss of confidence in one's abilities to attend to one's own preservation. For instance, a person might attribute some drastic failure of his plans to his own mistakes (correctly or incorrectly) rather than to bad fortune or human malevolence. Should such a belief diminish his confidence in his abilities—and, especially if the failure is extreme enough—his self-respect will be severely diminished. In a very different sort of case, a person's response to misfortune (rather than to her own mistakes) might diminish her self-esteem so severely as eventually to diminish her confidence in her abilities and talents. Repeated or extreme bad fortune forges a particularly close link between the fragility of self-esteem and the fragility of self-respect. To be sure, we can neither insulate people from all imaginable misfortune nor prevent them from making mistakes. Yet we can support a socially sanctioned scheme of education that teaches people how to avoid those mistakes most likely to undermine self-respect. We can also try to remedy at least some accidents of fortune that pose the gravest danger to self-esteem and hence to self-respect. But once we have sought the appropriate remedies, we must leave people free to make mistakes. A robust sense of self-respect develops only if one is allowed to learn the extent and the limits of one's own powers; here, experience is the best teacher.

While some circumstances threaten self-respect indirectly through self-esteem, a variety of circumstances can pose a *direct* threat to self-respect. Every society gradually develops a set of mechanisms—social, political, and economic institutions and practices—through which its members typically learn to seek constructive affirmations of self-respect. Yet one's access to mechanisms for the constructive affirmation of self-respect can be artificially limited. For instance, societies with a tradition of discrimination (de jure or de facto) against some groups of people may effectively exclude those people from the typical mechanisms for affirming self-respect. The mere fact of discrimination alone (however arbitrary or unjust its basis) is unlikely to pose a direct threat to the self-respect of its victims. Self-respect is rarely so fragile. But when a scheme of discrimination is rooted in a complex network of degrading and dehumanizing fictions about its victims it can become truly dangerous to self-respect. The more entrenched this network of fictions, the more likely discrimination is to pose a threat to the self-respect of those subjected to it.

Such a scheme demands of those whose choices it restricts that they learn to reconcile two conflicting messages: (1) that self-respect is affirmed and experienced through participation in a particular set of social practices, but (2) that one is nonetheless effectively excluded from these practices. Some who are affected by such a scheme may also fail to discover alternative constructive means to affirm their worth, and they may not recognize the destructive cultural fictions as fictions. For such people, social exclusion is almost certain to weaken self-respect. Moreover, the responses of those who are continually excluded may have powerfully damaging consequences for themselves and their societies. Of course, we cannot ensure that all those who are able to participate in constructive social practices will actually choose to do so; it would be wrong to try if we are to protect the personal liberty that is central to self-respect. Yet we can identify those lingering effects of discrimination that continue to prevent people from choosing to accept or reject the relevant mechanisms. Though these effects are more complex than is often acknowledged, they can be remedied once we understand them.

THE SOCIAL CONSTRUCTION OF SELF-RESPECT

I have so far assumed that the ability to have and affirm a robust sense of self-respect is greatly influenced by social circumstances. Important facts about the contexts in which people initially develop self-conceptions support this assumption. First, the vocabulary in which one learns to give expression to one's self-conception, and even the concepts that initially shape that self-conception, are products of the linguistic conventions of a given community. These conventions embody that community's normative expectations about emotion, thought, and action, and as these expectations change or become more complex so, too, will the self-conceptions of the members of that community. For instance, changes in the way American society views women's choices about work and marriage have changed the way women view themselves and have produced a variety of new and complex expectations about women and their sense of self-worth. Second, a society's normative expectations about emotion, thought, and action have an especially powerful influence on the development of self-respect. Every society gradually develops intricate patterns of normative expectations about what talents and abilities one ought to use in the service of self-preservation—even about what really constitutes survival or self-preservation. A complex society will produce intricate and overlapping patterns of such expectations. Further, self-contained communities within complex societies sometimes produce their own self-contained expectations about selves and self-respect. The self-conceptions of those in such communities will overlap very little with the self-conceptions of those outside such groups. Consider, for instance, the self-contained expectations that shape life in America's Old Order Amish communities.[10]

Socially developed patterns of expectations about self-preservation, and about the acceptable means to that end, constitute what I call the *social construction of self-respect*. The social construction of self-respect is so important because it sets down the parameters within which we initially learn to evaluate our own worth. In twentieth-century America, for example, a powerful set of normative expectations encourages Americans to link their worth as persons to the kind of work they do. As we might expect, people who conform to such expectations find that their self-respect tends to rise and fall with the character of their employment prospects. But complex societies produce overlapping patterns of expectations governing self-worth. Thus some Americans are more influenced by expectations linking self-worth with material possessions than with honest and productive work. In this regard, the Wall Street stockbroker whose bumper sticker announces that "Whoever dies with the most toys wins" bears important similarities to the urban high-school student preoccupied with getting the latest running shoes or a bigger piece of gold jewelry. Finally, the overlapping patterns of expectations that gradually evolve in complex societies—especially in their coarser adaptations—may conflict with each other. Contemporary American society provides striking examples of the very common conflict between the pursuit of honest work and the pursuit of material possessions. The stockbroker who turns to insider trading in pursuit of his "toys"—and the urban high-school student who sells drugs in pursuit of his—reveal the complexity of the social construction of self-respect in America.

One's ability to conform to any pattern of expectations about appropriate ways to affirm self-respect will be affected by one's social, political, and economic circumstances. A variety of circumstances can be relevant—including geographical location, religion, or native language, as well as class and race. The relevance of any particular circumstance is a function of each society's history and traditions. In a society with a long history of relative ethnic and racial homogeneity, for instance, one's class position may be the most important such circumstance. But in many societies, including American society, there are two such circumstances: class position and membership in a particular racial, ethnic, or religious group. Moreover, in such a society the influence of class position is usually registered most directly on the phenomenon of self-esteem—affecting one's confidence in the worth and attainability of one's life plans. In contrast, the influence of race designations (like that of ethnic or religious group membership) is typically registered most directly on self-respect.

The influence of class is due partly to the typically close connection between life plans and economic resources, but its influence also depends upon each person's understanding of how this connection affects her own life. Awareness of one's class position tends to have the most immediate effects on self-esteem, particularly on one's confidence in one's ability actually to carry out one's life plans. This awareness often determines a young person's sense of what *sort* of life plan she ought to pursue. Indeed, a young person's conviction of severe economic limitations on her life plans may even diminish her confidence in the worth of her most valued plans. Such a loss of confidence, as Rawls has suggested, can have devastating consequences—including apathy and cynicism about the worth of pursuing any constructive projects (TJ 440). Finally, the effects of class on self-esteem and motivation may be compounded by geographical isolation or by membership in a historically disfavored racial group—as the lives of some people in America's Appalachian region, and of some in America's urban underclass, reveal.[11]

Though the loss of self-esteem need not diminish self-respect, those who believe themselves confined in an unfavorable class position may find that circumstances directly affecting self-esteem ultimately pose a threat to their self-respect. The experience of one who believes himself economically confined may even be *phenomenologically* like the experience of legally enforced discrimination: it may be felt as exclusion from accepted social mechanisms for affirming self-respect. To be sure, families can sometimes mitigate the potentially destructive effects of economic limitations. Thus many political philosophers—especially in the liberal tradition—view the family as a private buffer against an array of potential assaults on self-esteem and self-respect.[12] But even in societies where laws protect the internal operations of the family as private, the family is a social and economic institution that registers the effects of social and economic isolation. The strain of membership in economically marginal positions may take a severe toll on the structure and well-being of the family itself. When social and economic marginality persist for several generations of one family, the family may even be the principal vehicle for conveying the belief that social isolation is a permanent fact of experience. As in my example of the child whose mother believes that he is "nothing," the economic isolation of a family may reinforce the tendency for diminutions in self-esteem to be transformed into challenges to self-respect.

The direct influence of racial designations—of "race"—on self-conceptions is registered in different and somewhat more complex ways. Not surprisingly, these designations can have especially damaging effects if a society has ever given explicit legal protection (and implicit social support) to racial discrimination. In such a society, merely outlawing discrimination will be unlikely to immediately undo its effects. For in a country not subject to authoritarian rule, legal rules persist for several generations only if there is relatively widespread acceptance of those rules. In order to understand obedience to law as something more than mere observable regularities in behavior, we must acknowledge the existence of what H. L. A. Hart has called an "internal perspective" on the rules of a legal system.[13] According to Hart, an adequate account of a legal system must recognize the existence of a perspective from which agents subject to legal rules take demands for conformity to the rules, and criticisms of breaches of the rules, to be justified. But if we accept Hart's view, as I think we should, we shall have to relinquish the notion that changing discriminatory laws might automatically eliminate discrimination—or its lingering structural consequences.

Yet accepting the plausibility of this view commits us to two important conclusions about discrimination in America. First, we must acknowledge the existence of a complex internal perspective on the legally supported exclusion of Black people from the social mechanisms for affirming self-respect. A complex set of beliefs and attitudes, transmitted from one generation to another for at least three hundred years, helped shore up the institution of American slavery, and the legally protected discrimination of subsequent periods. Second, it is simply implausible that this internal perspective on the exclusion of Black Americans might have magically ceased to exist with the bitterly contested end of legally-sanctioned discrimination in America.[14] In the "Letter from Birmingham Jail," Martin Luther King vividly described some of the ways in which legally enforced segregation "distorts the soul and degrades human personality" for both the segregator and those subjected to segregation.[15] I contend that many of the relevant distortions will still be transmitted from one generation to another, as part of the social construction of self-respect, long after the "official" end of segregation.

Thus I claim that, in America, the social construction of self-respect continues to bear the complex and often unacknowledged stamp of racial discrimination. What does it mean to claim this? First, in subtle—and sometimes blatant—ways, any group that has been legally excluded from American mechanisms for affirming self-respect will remain a disfavored group for some time. The "conceptual space" that a society historically marks out for a disfavored group places very definite boundaries on what those not in that group will think of them. Changing laws will not automatically alter these boundaries, and many people will unreflectively continue to accept the conceptual boundaries that have been imposed upon the disfavored group. In such a context, even some who actively try not to be "racists" may nonetheless perpetuate the very distortions used to justify discrimination. One of the most dangerous—and least questioned—distortions is the notion that the disfavored group has some psychological and behavioral "essence" that is allegedly genetically transmitted and inescapably possessed by all members of the group.[16] Moreover, beliefs about the alleged essence of some group need not be primarily negative in order to have destructive consequences. For the notion is destructive principally in the way it blinds those who believe in it to the obvious diversity to be found within each group. The Asian American student who neither likes nor excels at mathematics, and the Black American student who prefers physics to basketball alike suffer from the notion of racial essence. Nor is this notion any less destructive when it is unreflectively accepted by the disfavored group themselves as a self-conception. It is particularly destructive when they unreflectively accept a notion of their own "essence" that remains entangled in distortions bound up with the tradition of discrimination. Indeed, to accept such a notion, as I show below, is to participate in one's own victimization.

But the social construction of self-respect typically sustains discriminatory attitudes in yet a second way. For the social transmission of norms of self-respect continues to encourage many people to believe that they must measure their worth primarily by *comparison* with those in the disfavored group. In particular, some social norms governing self-respect lead many persons to believe that preserving their sense of self-respect depends upon being able to prove that they are "superior" to members of some disfavored group. The more precarious the class position of such people, the more they will learn to fear any changes in the "inferior" status of the disfavored group as challenges to the alleged certainties that shore up their sense of self-respect. This phenomenon obviously informs much recent racial discord in the urban centers of America. The more complex the hierarchies of class and ethnicity in a community—and the greater the sense of economic uncertainty there—the more complicated these fears and the resultant conflicts become.

Yet the distorting lessons of discrimination and exclusion are not always manifested in violent conflict: they continually deform and distort the most ordinary social interactions. Consider a college mathematics professor who unreflectively continues to accept unfounded preconceptions about the intellectual capacities of Black students. How might such a professor respond to a Black student's expression of confusion on some point in her class lecture? Coming from a white student, such a confusion would probably be viewed as a simple error, or even as a request for help. But this professor is likely to interpret the Black student's comment as though it were evidence of basic intellectual weakness. If the Black student has expressed confusion on previous occasions, his comments may then become evidence that Black students in general can't "keep up," or even won't try—that they are, in short, "inferior." Similar conduct from a white student would not be taken to support any analogous generalization about all white students. It would simply be a sign that this individual student can't, or even won't, keep up with the class. Moreover, the professor's preconceptions imply that the Black student who has in fact excelled is somehow suspect. Because this professor expects Black students to be weak at mathematics, she will regard a Black student's mathematical success as somehow a "fluke"—she may even question the student's honesty. Crucial social interactions can thus be shaped—one might say deformed—by discriminatory attitudes that commit those who hold them to profoundly *irrational* judgments about the abilities of those in some disfavored group.

Such distortions have consequences that transcend any single social interaction. To understand these consequences, we must take note of two important phenomena identified by social scientists. Robert Merton has described the phenomenon of the "self-fulfilling prophecy" whereby expectations of certain behavior in others often tend to evoke that very behavior.[17] For instance, a Black student might cease to put effort into a class taught by a professor who expects him to be inferior; the student may well presume (correctly) that his effort won't be taken seriously. Of course, he would then do poorly or even fail, thereby seeming to bear out the professor's prediction of failure. But this phenomenon calls attention to a second, described by Gordon Allport as the "reciprocal conduct of human beings in interaction."[18] Allport notes that in social interactions our expectations of others, and the behavior they then tend to display, will constantly reinforce each other in a complex reciprocal fashion. To be sure, sometimes the effects of this reciprocal process are benign or even beneficial. But when the process begins either with racial exclusion, or with open expression of hatred based on ethnic or religious group membership, dangerous consequences may follow. The experience of hatred and exclusion will sometimes produce extreme anger and bitterness in its victims. Further, those who—for various reasons—come to believe that there is nothing to be gained by restraining their anger may openly display such feelings. But of course, behavioral manifestations of these feelings may then be taken by those not in the disfavored group to "confirm" the culture's reasons for hate and exclusion. Racial and ethnic hatred and exclusion thus initiate processes that distort and deform social interactions by generating mistrust and suspicion, and sometimes violent conflict.

I have so far discussed attitudes that devalue the *abilities* of those in the disfavored group. Yet in many contexts discrimination embodies an effort to devalue, degrade, or discount the worth of persons themselves—not just their talents and abilities. Consider the following example. A dispatcher in an urban police station who has been taught to believe that Black people are not fully human will very likely treat Black victims of crime with less seriousness than victims who are not Black. For instance, he may view a Black person's call for emergency police assistance as relatively unimportant, with potentially disastrous consequences for those who seek that assistance. He may even attempt to rationalize the low priority he gives to emergency calls from Black callers: he might claim that statistics about violence in the caller's neighborhood support his belief that Black people "don't really care" about violence or that giving the call greater priority "won't do any good." The prevalence of such rationalizations, in turn, will have destructive reciprocal effects. People who expect to be viewed with less seriousness when they are victims of crime will learn to mistrust the institutions that view them in this way, and their mistrust can have devastating effects.

Yet the distorting effects of discrimination do not simply shape the attitudes of "outsiders" toward the disfavored group or vice-versa. Discrimination may also have a profound influence on the self-conceptions, and the sense of self-respect, of some within the disfavored group. Of course, even in the face of the cruellest racism, many people are able to affirm a robust sense of their own worth—and of any group with which they identify—in a variety of satisfying ways. Understanding their success, as I suggest below, yields invaluable lessons about the social bases of self-respect. Yet, like King and Clark, I contend that segregation can distort the self-conception of the segregated as well as of the segregator. The analysis of self-respect introduced in the first section allows me to show *how* some of these distortions take place. The principal distortions of self-respect take two forms: (1) the mutually reinforcing relation between the two components of self-respect may be undermined, or (2) the minimum content of self-respect may itself be distorted. Ironically, the most important distortions reveal just how valiantly people will fight to retain a minimum degree of self-respect, even in the face of challenges to their sense of self-worth.

The first kind of distortion occurs when one's wish to preserve oneself is somehow pried apart from the willingness to develop one's abilities and talents. This separation most often takes place when a person experiences severe disappointment and frustration in the exercise of her abilities. Surprisingly, this process begins as a perfectly ordinary tendency to risk-aversion: in particular, it starts as an aversion to the psychological discomfort of severe disappointment. People with weak voices, for instance, seldom like to sing in public. But what starts as fairly ordinary risk-aversion can develop into extreme self-mistrust, and it may then take on a markedly self-destructive character. Familiar, but distressing, examples of this self-destructive process are common in settings where social and economic isolation compounds the lingering effects of discrimination.

The two components of self-respect are strikingly separated in the tendency of some Black school-aged children in poor urban areas to gradually lower their expectations of themselves, until they effectively relinquish any ambitions of academic success. Hence, the high drop-out rate in these areas. Of course, some students who drop out may have lowered expectations not of themselves but of the society that they believe excludes them. They may simply lose confidence that it is prudent for them to continue in school. Still others may drop out principally because they mistrust the facilities available to them. But caring and hardworking teachers—many of whom are also Black—conclude that many Black students who drop out have learned to mistrust *themselves* because they have gradually internalized prejudicial assumptions that they cannot succeed. Such students provide distressing evidence of the pervasiveness of the self-fulfilling prophecy: the student who believes that he shouldn't even try certainly will not succeed. Moreover, such a student is liable to mistrust students who excel (or simply try to excel), branding them with the label of what he mistrusts most: they are "trying to be white." Students who make such comments are reluctant to identify successful students as "really Black" because they have come to identify being Black with failure. They have thus internalized the very preconceptions that historically have been used to exclude Black Americans from constructive affirmations of self-respect.

But accepting a view of oneself as intrinsically bound for failure can wreak havoc even on the *minimum content* of self-respect. The student who claims to believe that he is "nothing" provides unfortunate evidence of this second kind of distortion of self-respect. Now it is unlikely that this student consistently believes that he really is "nothing." Rather, his efforts to understand his experience lead him to suffer moments of extreme self-doubt and self-mistrust. Yet few children who experience this degree of self-mistrust could emerge with the minimum content of their sense of self-respect untouched. As I suggested earlier, we are unlikely to find any person totally lacking in self-respect. But one can certainly become unable to distinguish self-destructive behavior from behavior that actually promotes one's well-being. Such a confusion between self-destructive and self-preserving behavior is manifested in the disruptive and ultimately self-destructive classroom behavior of the young boy in my example. His behavior prevents him from learning how to read well or how to manipulate the mathematical concepts he requires to survive economically.

As he develops into a young man, he will become increasingly aware of a set of expectations about selves and self-respect that govern much of his daily life. Some of these expectations will differ very little from those in the larger society: a Wall Street stockbroker and an inner city youth alike may be tempted to measure self-worth by means of their possessions. A second group of expectations will differ radically from those of the larger social group—insofar as they embody a rejection of some of the discriminatory attitudes toward Black Americans. But often, a third category of expectations unintentionally incorporates the exclusion and marginalization that most people in his community would, on reflection, obviously prefer to reject. Familiar patterns of behavior manifest the relevant structure of expectations: membership in youth gangs that promise as great a risk of death as they do protection and camaraderie, drug abuse, and various kinds of violent crime. These patterns of behavior are rooted in dangerous and destructive expectations concerning selves and self-respect.

But the appeal to a Black American teenager of membership in an urban street gang provides an important lesson. For as Rawls once argued, one's sense of one's worth is often bound up with one's sense that one is valued by others; ties of membership in associations and communities typically encourage and support one's sense of self-respect (TJ 440–42). The distressing irony of the urban street gang is that instead of providing a real remedy for the social isolation and exclusion of its members—as a college fraternity, for instance, might—it actually *intensifies* that isolation. Like the young Black student who identifies "Black" with "failure," an older gang member comes to identify "Black" with "marginal." But in viewing his membership in a gang as an affirmation of self-respect, the gang member reveals just how completely he has internalized society's effort to marginalize him. For he has come to see himself precisely as he is seen by those who wish to exclude him: as essentially a threatening "outlaw," a permanent possibility of danger. Moreover, he will sometimes act on that self-conception in a self-destructive fashion and will often wreak havoc on his community in the process. The gang member's self-conception provides a powerful example of the way in which—even in an effort at self-assertion—one can accept a vision of oneself that remains too entangled in a tradition of discrimination and exclusion to be a constructive category for self-reflection.

THE SOCIAL BASES OF SELF-RESPECT

But how might a young child who claims to think that he is "nothing" learn to seek more constructive categories for self-reflection and self-understanding? An important part of the answer requires reflection on the experience of Black Americans who have been able to disentangle their self-conceptions from a conceptual scheme that threatens to confine them to marginality and failure. Such people have relied upon two principal vehicles to disentangle their sense of self-worth from the legacy of discrimination. First, their experience has typically included membership in various communities and associations that *constructively* affirm their worth as persons. For many, of course, the most important such community has been the family. But associative ties outside of a family may supplement the family's influence—or sometimes even remedy the effects of a damaged family.[19] Second, the sense of self-worth of many Black Americans has been sustained by a sense of history and social traditions. Of course, one consequence of American slavery is that many Black Americans have no detailed or particular knowledge of the national (as opposed to continental and geographical) origins of their families. Moreover, discriminatory policies bound up with slavery—and its long aftermath—have often made it difficult, it not impossible, for Black Americans to have access to written history. But the kind of oral history that is seldom preserved in formal educational institutions (for any group) was often an important and constructive alternative. Black Americans who, for many years, managed to develop constructive means for affirming self-respect—often in spite of great hardship—were once a prominent presence in Black communities. Their successes and their failures were an important source of knowledge of how one might preserve one's self-respect—not just in response to exclusion and discrimination but in spite of it. The greater mobility of some Black Americans thus unwittingly deprives other Black people of access to those parts of their history that they may need most.[20] Further, as successful Black residents leave Black communities, many of the communal associations that provided constructive ties of membership leave with them or die off altogether. To be cut off from membership in associations that constructively affirm one's value and to be cut off from an appreciation of how others have found constructive categories for self-reflection and choice in spite of hardship is to be cut off from the two most important social bases of self-respect. Finding ways to develop the social bases of self-respect in communities set apart by class and race will surely require the participation of Black people who have learned to resist internalizing assumptions about marginality and failure. Even small-scale social programs that vividly display the concern of "sucessful" Black Americans might help provide models of constructive affirmations of self-respect—even if only as an incentive to seek altogether new models.[21]

But no social order can command the respect of people whom it continually fails to respect and for whom (as a consequence) both self-mistrust and widespread mistrust of social institutions come to seem a rational adaptation to circumstances. The possibility of social cooperation thus also imposes an *obligation* on those not in the disfavored group to relinquish the discriminatory attitudes that persist. As I have shown, this requires far more self-scrutiny—and, ultimately, a more serious revision of self-conceptions—than is acknowledged in most discussions of social reform. The police dispatcher who encourages mistrust of the police, and the professor who encourages mistrust of her students' abilities, both endanger the complex social cooperation that underwrites the pursuit of rational life plans for everyone. Still further, restoring the social bases of self-respect will require social policies that recognize the important fact that no human being is ever *simply* a victim. Even a victim retains the fundamental human need to exercise and develop his own abilities and talents in the effort to help remedy his suffering. One develops the self-trust that is fundamental to a robust sense of self-respect only by means of experiences that also require that one take responsibility for the consequences of one's choices—to an extent compatible with one's knowledge and experience. Some social ''reforms'' of recent years have treated the recipients of assistance simply as victims, thus encouraging the reformers, and those people whom they sought to aid, to ignore important facts about the nature of self-respect.[22]

Finally, as William Julius Wilson has suggested, efforts to encourage a robust sense of self-respect can succeed only alongside efforts to remedy the structural causes of economic and social isolation that seriously endanger self-respect (TD 1987). I have argued that some of the people who most need the benefits of economic reform have become deeply mistrustful of social institutions and—even worse—sometimes, of themselves. Their lack of trust may well hinder their capacity to take advantage of opportunities that might arise with structural changes in the economy. Finding the remedy for this mistrust will require a concerted effort to reshape the social construction of self-respect—not just for the disadvantaged but for any group whose sense of self-worth seems to ''require'' them to accept the isolation of the truly disadvantaged (of any race or ethnic group) as an unrevisable fact of experience.

Indiana University

NOTES

* An earlier version of this paper was read at a conference at Brown University. Helpful comments on that version were provided by Howard McGary, Lucius Outlaw, and Laurence Thomas.

1 Kennth B. Clark, *Prejudice and Your Child* (Boston: Beacon Press, 1963).

2 Daniel Goleman, ''Black Child's Self-View Is Still Low, Study Finds,'' *New York Times,* Aug. 31, 1987, p. A 13.

3 I am indebted to Shirley Moody for this example.

4 A hostage might vigorously attempt to protect her sanity, or her memory of the past, or even simply to keep track of the passage of time—thus exercising, relatively speaking, a significant degree of control over the conditions of her own survival.
5 On some understandings of the self—say, on which one's identity is partly constituted by one's membership in a group—a willingness to sacrifice one's physical body might be required to reveal one's self-respect. See Karl Duncker, "Ethical Relativity? (An Enquiry Into the Psychology of Ethics)," *Mind*, vol. 48: 39–57, for a discussion of the moral consequences of this view of the self.
6 John Rawls, *A Theory of Justice* (Cambridge, Mass.: Harvard University Press, 1971), p. 440 (hereafter abbreviated TJ).
7 Many important human ends and purposes can be fulfilled only in a context of social cooperation. Thus I reject the libertarian notion that social cooperation is somehow incidental to self-preservation.
8 See Bernard Boxill, *Blacks and Social Justice* (Totowa, N.J.: Rowman and Allenheld, 1984), p. 189.
9 Rawls's analysis thus encourages ambiguity: he sometimes treats "self-respect" and "self-esteem" as equivalent expressions (TJ 440–42).
10 For an intriguing discussion of an Old Order Amish community, see Donald Kraybill, *The Riddle of Amish Culture* (Baltimore: Johns Hopkins University Press, 1989).
11 See David Looff, *Appalachia's Children* (Lexington: University Press of Kentucky, 1971); Douglas Glasgow, *The Black Underclass: Poverty, Unemployment and Entrapment of Ghetto Youth* (New York: Vintage Books, 1980); and William Julius Wilson, *The Truly Disadvantaged: The Inner City, The Underclass and Public Policy* (Chicago: University of Chicago Press, 1987) (hereafter abbreviated TD).
12 See James Fishkin, *Justice, Equal Opportunity and the Family* (New Haven, Conn.: Yale University Press, 1983), for discussion of some problematic consequences of this view for liberal theorists.
13 H. L. A. Hart, *The Concept of Law* (Oxford: Oxford University Press, 1961).
14 Even the Austinian or Benthamite legal positivist must explain the persistence of legally protected segregation in America. This theorist may appeal to the notion of entrenched "habits of obedience"—but *entrenched* habits, as we all know, do not magically disappear.
15 Martin Luther King, "Letter from Birmingham Jail," in King, *Why We Can't Wait* (New York: Mentor Books, 1964), p. 82.
16 This and other difficulties with the genetic notion of race are discussed in several of the essays in Ashley Montagu, ed., *The Concept of Race* (New York: The Free Press, 1964).
17 Robert Merton, "The Self-Fulfilling Prophecy," *The Antioch Review*, vol. 8: 193–210.
18 Gordon Allport, *The Nature of Prejudice* (Reading, Mass.: Addison-Wesley, 1954).
19 As a matter of historical fact, Black churches and their associated organizations (choirs, youth groups, and so forth) have often been a powerful force in the lives of many Black Americans. Though an organization need not be rooted in shared religious beliefs in order to successfully underwrite self-respect, the experience of the Old Order Amish provides interesting reflection. When a community is largely self-contained (whether as a result of unchosen external forces, or—as in the case of the Amish—as a result of choice), shared religious beliefs often provide a more coherent and more constructive self-conception than any other phenomenon.
20 Critics of W. J. Wilson's stance in *The Truly Disadvantaged* would do well to consider this fact.
21 Douglas Glasgow (1980) urged similar participation by Black Americans.
22 I discuss the topic of responsibility and victims of economic and social deprivation in M. M. Moody-Adams, "On the Old Saw That Character Is Destiny," in O. Flanagan and A. O. Rorty, ed., *Identity, Character and Morality: Essays in Moral Psychology* (Cambridge, Mass.: Massachusetts Institute of Technology Press, 1990).

THE ROLE MODEL ARGUMENT AND FACULTY DIVERSITY

ANITA L. ALLEN

INTRODUCTION

Proponents of faculty diversity in higher education sometimes advance the "role model" argument.[1] The argument is a familiar player in confrontations over race, gender, and the allocation of employment opportunities. In these contexts, the role model argument asserts that colleges and universities ought to hire females of all races and male members of minority groups to insure that undergraduate, graduate, and professional school students will have appropriate role models among their teachers.[2] The role model argument is popular because the belief that young people need role models is pervasive. In words so familiar that they bear the stigma of cliché, many say that if students are to realize their full potential as responsible adults, they need others in their lives whom they can emulate and by whom they will be motivated to do their best work.

Academic philosophers have seldom shown signs of taking the popular role model argument seriously. To be sure, philosophers who wrote about the moral foundations of civil rights policy in the 1970s and 80s invariably mentioned the argument.[3] But they mentioned it in passing as an argument—though not the most powerful or interesting argument—for a permissive, liberal stance toward policies they labelled "affirmative action," "preferential treatment," "reverse discrimination," or "quotas." Even philosophers like Bernard Boxill, who defended liberal, race-conscious policies for minority and female inclusion, gave the role model argument cursory treatment.[4] Everyone seemed content to regard the role model argument as ancillary to more powerful and interesting arguments for distributive and reparative justice. By the 1990s an apparent consensus had been reached in philosophical circles: the role model argument may reflect legitimate utilitarian concerns, but it does not deserve to be taken seriously as an independent argument for recruiting traditionally excluded minorities and white women.[5]

The persistent popularity of the role model argument in rationales for diversity and affirmative action have made it increasingly important to rethink the consensus. Accordingly, I will examine the power and limitations of the role model argument here. My focus will be the case for black female law teachers as role models for black female law students. The high standing of lawyers in American society justifies close attention to issues within *legal* education. I focus on *black women* in legal education for three reasons. First, black women are one of several groups in higher education still described as excluded or underrepresented. Second, according to one study, black and other minority women who manage to enter law teaching are "at the bottom" of their profession, "hindered by their sex rather than aided by it" when it comes to tenured teaching positions at the nation's law schools.[6] Third, recent events at Harvard University called the nation's attention to black women law teachers and to a particularly strong version of the role model argument made on behalf of black women law students. The events at Harvard prompted a number of minority scholars to assess the logic and politics of the role model argument.[7]

In the spring of 1990, protests by Harvard Law School students demanding faculty diversity culminated in a "sit-in" demonstration outside the office of Dean Robert Clark. Professor Derrick Bell, Harvard's first and most senior black law professor, stated publicly that he would take an unpaid leave of absence until the law school tenured a black woman. Two years later, Harvard had tenured no black woman, students again demonstrated at the Dean's office, and Bell made plans to be away from the law school for a third year.

Bell's actions were praised in some quarters, criticized in others. Critics charged that Bell's demand for a woman of color on the faculty was unreasonable, in view of the limited pool of qualified minority candidates. Bell replied that the pool of qualified black women candidates appears prohibitively small only because Harvard is determined to perpetuate narrow, self-serving criteria of qualification. Bell's critics also stressed that Harvard's law faculty of about seventy already included six black men, three of whom were tenured, and five tenured white women. To this, Bell responded that the presence of white women and black men on the teaching staff did not answer the full demand for diversity: black women law students, he said, need black women law teachers.

One man's sacrifice in the name of black female role models for black female students drew the attention of the national media. In the wake of publicity, one organization approvingly named Bell "Feminist of the Year." Belittling Bell's efforts in an editorial praising Harvard for offering tenure to four white men, a journalist quipped that "[o]nly in the curious world of university campuses could anyone argue that professors should be judged by their skin color, gender or sexual practices instead of their merit as teachers."[8] Some members of the general public took umbrage at the idea that a school might be pressured by politics to favor a black woman over outstanding white teachers. For them, Bell's demand symbolized the demise of excellence and the excesses of preferential affirmative action policies. Yet, as affirmative action entered its third decade, black women remain largely absent in most fields as higher education teachers. The population of black women tenured as professors of philosophy, mathematics, economics, and the natural sciences is exceedingly small.

From the point of view of Professor Bell and the law students of all races who have risked arrest in the name of faculty diversity, being and providing role models is a distinct moral imperative for faculty and administrators in American higher education. More precisely, being and providing *same-kind* role models is often a moral imperative: black men for black men, black women for black women. Some who oppose the political tactics employed by Bell and the Harvard law students nevertheless share their perspective on the importance of same-kind role models. Indeed, as elaborated below, I share the perspective that minority students need same-kind faculty role models. The demand for same-kind role models is not illegitimate in principle.

The stance that institutions and appropriate individuals ought to provide same-kind role models does not, however, translate into unqualified endorsement of the role model argument for faculty appointments. On the contrary, one might believe, as I will argue here, that when it is used as the centerpiece of the case for minority faculty appointments, the role model argument is profoundly problematic. Obscuring both the varied talents of minority teachers and the varied tasks their institutions expect them to perform, "centerpiece" uses of the role model argument impede fairness and honesty in the faculty appointments process.

AGAINST THE ROLE MODEL ARGUMENT

Who is a Role Model?

I maintain that, despite the very real value to students of faculty role models, we should abandon the minority role model argument heard today in the context of faculty appointments. However, before turning to the case for outright abandonment, I want to make the case for a weaker claim—that greater care should be taken in the phrasing of the role model argument.

The role model argument tolerates an intolerable degree of ambiguity about what it means to be a "role model." Judith Thomson, George Sher, and other philosophers who have attempted to assess the role model argument for race-based and gender-based preferences, have not grappled with the ambiguity of the concept.[9] Thomson's admirable defense of the role model argument was undercut by ambiguity about precisely what she understood a role model to be.

Not everyone means the same thing when they refer to themselves or others as "role models." For example, one academic dean may describe excellent classroom teachers who rarely counsel students outside of class as role models.

Another dean may reserve the term for teachers who also counsel students outside of class about career and personal concerns. Different individuals may define ''role model'' differently; but also, the same individual may define it differently in different settings. A university provost may on one occasion employ ''role model'' as a term applicable to all faculty members and administrators, yet on another occasion employ it as a term of special approbation for outstanding faculty and administrators.

The ambiguity of the expression ''role model'' is not so fundamental that moral claims about the importance of role models cannot be sustained. However, it is incumbent upon those who rely upon the term to get beyond the initial ambiguity of ''role model.'' It is helpful to being by distinguishing the three most common senses in which educators currently employ the term. When we say that a teacher is a ''role model,'' we generally mean that that individual serves as one or more of these:

(1) an *ethical template* for the exercise of adult responsibilities;
(2) a *symbol* of special achievement;
(3) a *nurturer* providing special educational services.

Philosophers must hope in vain to alter by fiat the ordinary language practices of the general public. However, it would greatly clarify academic debates about the value of role models and the role model argument were the academic community always to specify whether the role models at issue in a given instance are supposed to be templates, symbols, or nurturers.

All teachers are ethical templates, but only some significantly function as symbols and nurturers. When teachers teach, they model the role of teacher. They are ethical templates, men and women whose conduct sets standards for the exercise of responsibilities. Like other teachers, law school teachers are role models in the ethical template sense. The manner in which faculty members exercise their responsibilities as teachers sets standards for how those responsibilities ought to be exercised. How law school teachers speak and behave will suggest something to their students about how law school teachers ought to speak and behave. Because most law professors are also members of the bar or bench, the conduct of law professors also carries general messages about the exercise of responsibility in adult roles other than teaching, especially the roles of attorney and judge.

As ethical templates, teachers can set high standards or low. An alcoholic teacher who routinely teaches classes in a state of intoxication would set an arguably low standard. Even if the content of an inebriated teacher's lectures were otherwise adequate, one could still argue that the lecturer was a poor role model. An arguably praiseworthy role model who set a high standard may not be viewed as such by students. When visiting professor Patricia Williams taught a commercial law course at a prestigious law school several years ago, students quickly devalued her modeling of the commercial law professor role.[10] As a black female professor attempting to advance original scholarly perspectives, Williams represented a new kind of template. Many students admired her teaching and some said they admired her clothes; but a number wanted a traditional professor's perspective and complained about Williams' teaching to the Dean.

All teachers are ethical templates, but only some are symbols of special achievement. The "symbol" is the kind of role model philosophers most commonly acknowledge. As explained by Thomson and Sher, "role models" are individuals who inspire others to believe that they, too, may be capable of high accomplishment.[11] Kent Greenawalt had this same understanding in mind when he described the utilitarian, "role models for those in the minority community" argument for racial preferences:

> If blacks and other members of minority groups are to strive to become doctors and lawyers, it is important that they see members of their own groups in those roles. Otherwise they are likely to accept their consignment to less prestigious, less demanding roles in society. Thus an important aspect of improving the motivations and education of black youths is to help put blacks into positions where blacks are not often now found so that they can serve as effective role models.[12]

Like members of racial minority groups and white women, white men can also be symbols of special achievement. A criminally delinquent white juvenile who reformed himself and became a respected professional could serve as a role model for others of his same background.

If an individual is to serve as a symbol of special achievement for a group, group members must recognize the individual as belonging to their group. A recognizability requirement thus constrains would-be role models. With this in mind, some have occasionally argued that institutions seeking to hire blacks as role models should hire blacks who "look black" rather than blacks who "look white." But such a requirement does not follow from the recognizability imperative. Physical appearance is only one basis for racial recognition. Outward appearance has never been the only basis of racial identification, not under American race law and not under prevailing American custom. For African Americans, Native Americans, and Hispanic Americans who look—or look to some—like Caucasians, recognition by strangers as members of minority groups may require deliberate verbal disclosure.

Disclosure is essential for the identification of members of a number of minority groups. The faculty diversity movement at Harvard included a demand for openly gay and lesbian law teachers. One cannot be a gay or lesbian role model if no one knows one is gay or lesbian. Serving as a symbol of gay achievement depends upon first disclosing that one is gay. The situation is somewhat analogous for blacks, Native Americans, and Hispanics who "look white." The mere fact that a person is not visually recognizable to strangers as a member of a racial minority group does not mean that such a person will not eventually disclose their racial affiliation and become an effective symbol of special minority achievement. A light-skinned person with African ancestors and a black cultural self-understanding can be as effective as a dark-skinned person with African ancestors and a black cultural self-understanding. Throughout American history black communities have embraced high-achieving blacks of whatever hue as symbols of special achievement for the race, where a black racial heritage was discernable either through appearance, family history, or credible self-disclosures. Indeed, a number of historically important black political leaders have been men of mixed race ancestry who "looked white," but opted against "passing."[13]

Teachers who directly engage students through mentoring, tutoring, counselling, and special cultural or scholarly events are role models in a final sense. They are nurturers. Educators sometimes assume nurturing roles as personal, supererogatory commitments to students they believe would not be adequately served by mere templates and symbols.

The role of template, symbol, and nurturer are typically conflated in the role model argument for including minorities in higher education. Yet, being a minority group member is neither a necessary nor a sufficient condition for being a "role model" for minority students in every sense identified. For example, a black woman's mere presence in an institution can help to reshape conceptions of who can be a law teacher. Her style and perspectives can perhaps reshape conceptions of what it is appropriate for law teachers to do and say.

But only some black women teachers are role models in the sense of "symbols" of special achievement and "nurturers" of students' special needs. Blacks nominally hired as symbols may turn out to be nurturers. In this vein, Robert K. Fullinwider once hinted that implicit in the rationale for placing blacks in "visible and desirable positions" is the possibility that individual blacks will provide "better services to the black community."[14]

However, some black women "symbols" do not give a "nurturer"'s priority to the advancement of the interests of black students and wider black communities. These women would understandably resent students and colleagues who assume on the basis of their race and gender that they are willing to add nurturing to a long list of tasks that include teaching, writing for publication, and committee assignments. In arguments for academic role models for black women, a high degree of clarity requires specification of the tasks one expects the role model to perform. Not every black woman will be willing or able to perform every task.

The Cost to Integrity and Well-Being

We can continue to speak ambiguously about role models and breed misunderstanding. Or, we can begin to speak less ambiguously, as I suggest, about templates, symbols, and nurturers. But the ambiguity of the expression "role model" is only a small part of what makes the role model argument problematic. Even after conceptual clarity is achieved about what "role model" denotes, premising minority recruitment centrally on the capacity to serve as role models proves too costly.

One cost is that reliance upon the role model argument helps to sustain the widespread prejudice that African Americans, Hispanics, and members of certain other minority groups are intellectually inferior to whites. Faculties typically use the role model argument for minority appointments in situations in which they would rarely think to cite role modeling capacities as a reason for hiring whites. They hire white men on the expectation that they will excel as teachers, scholars, or administrators. They hire minorities, notwithstanding a presumption of lesser talent, on the expectation that they will serve as minority role models. The role model argument therefore functions as an excuse for employing someone regarded as lacking full merit.

Believing that they are better than prejudiced colleagues assume they are, and knowing that they will in fact serve as templates, symbols, or nurturers, some minority job candidates may be content to secure academic employment on grounds that imply inferiority. This is why conservative efforts to shame minorities out of accepting affirmative action appointments have largely failed. Minorities understand how valuable they are to their institutions, even if conservative opponents to minority recruitment do not. Yet to escape the degradation of fair process that role model-based recruitment represents, higher education has two choices consistent with integrity. It can limit minority recruitment to individuals who satisfy the traditional, narrow conceptions of merit purportedly applied to white men. Or, it can premise recruitment on revised, broader conceptions of merit proposed by progressives who aggressively contest tradition.

A second cost of the role model argument relates to the first. It perpetuates institutional bad faith. The role model argument mires those who rely upon it in self-deception. The role model argument dishonestly understates the actual contributions of minority faculty. Like nonminority colleagues, minority faculty must prepare and teach courses, supervise student projects, write for publication, and serve on committees. The role model argument obscures these typical responsibilities. Blacks retain posts as pilots, not because they are role models, but are skilled at keeping their aircraft aloft. By analogy, black college and university professors ultimately receive tenure, not because they are symbols and nurturers, but because they provide essential services. Colleges and universities should not be permitted to pretend that the only valuable service performed by minority faculty is role modelling.

The role model argument has a third cost. Reliance on the role model argument can easily result in the search for someone's stereotype of the best or the most "positive" minority. Those charged with making judgments about who is and is not a positive minority role model can easily run amok. Blacks and other minorities who look, sound, or think like upper middle class whites may be overvalued by decision makers who are not at ease with cultural diversity. Those with the power to appoint faculty may interpret traits of ethnic differences as indicia of lesser competence.

But by the same token, minorities with "white" attributes may be undervalued by decisionmakers who see no point to hiring minorities who are not discernably ethnic in appearance, speech, or perspective. At Harvard Law School, Professor Bell and the student diversity activists expressed a preference for minority faculty with culturally distinct perspectives, significant ties to the minority community, and an express willingness to nurture.

The knowledge that they are hired as minority role models in an atmosphere penetrated by stereotypes of race and gender can impose undue psychological burdens on affected faculty. The burden in question is the burden of measuring up to an unreasonable number of externally imposed standards as a condition for community approval. It can make a black woman feel that she must be perfectly black, not just black; perfectly female, not just female. Even an enthusiastic role model can tire of the extraordinary service she is expected to give her school. She can grow weary under the weight of having to wear her racial commitment and feminism always on her sleeve.

A final cost of the role model argument is that it can signal to white male faculty that they do not have role-modeling obligations toward minority students. The possibility that white faculty may regard minority students as unreachable and thus, to an extent, unteachable, is an alarming one. Even today, white males are the predominant group in most departments in most institutions in the United States. It is from white men that black women, for example, are required to learn most of what they need to know. Race-related faculty indifference is a commonly heard student complaint. Appointing a quota of same-kind role models in response to such complaints may strike some whites as all they need to do to address the special needs of minority students. Minority students can greatly benefit from same-kind minority role models. But it does not follow that black role models on campus leave white faculty with less than equal educational obligations towards minority and nonminority students.

Affirmative Action

I support many of the goals and practices of affirmative action in faculty appointments, especially the practice of relying upon broad criteria of merit that encompass a range of talents and methods. Yet one could easily mistake my criticism of the role model argument for a criticism of affirmative action in faculty appointments. This is because, in the political realm, the role model argument is closely associated with the case for affirmative action. The role model argument ties the case for affirmative action in student admissions to the case for affirmative action in faculty appointments in the following way. Once historically white institutions begin to admit minority group members in large numbers, they create a need for minority teachers to teach, inspire, and mentor. The role model argument acknowledges the needs of affirmative action students for affirmative action to supply appropriate faculty.

However, the logical relationship between the affirmative action and role model argument is less snug than first appearances might suggest. In theory, a staunch opponent of affirmative action could advocate hiring minority role models to improve the educational experiences of "wrongly" admitted, "unqualified" affirmative action students. To put it starkly, even a racist or sexist could advance the role model argument.

The soundness of the role model argument does not entail or presuppose the soundness of all of the liberal egalitarian arguments for affirmative action found in the philosophical literature.[15] In fact, because what I am calling the role model argument defends minority faculty recruitment on utilitarian grounds referring to student and institutional need, rather than on grounds referring to compensatory justice, reparative justice or moral desert, the role model argument is neutral as among affirmative action's possible forward- and backward-looking rationales. Possibly some of the best reasons for providing minority students with same-kind teachers relate narrowly to educational necessity rather than broadly to the moral necessity of redressing slavery or addressing current economic injustices in the wider society.

In light of the foregoing, the logical linkage between the role model argument and the case for affirmative action is attenuated. Nevertheless, some for whom the end of increasing the number of minority faculty is paramount may object on practical grounds to my call for the abandonment of the role model argument. "Sure, the role model argument has the drawbacks you identify; but it works to get minorities onto faculties; it therefore has strategic value for minority inclusion and empowerment."

This strategic defense of the role model argument is ultimately unpersuasive. To counteract myths of minority inferiority, while avoiding stereotyping and institutional self-deception, minority appointments must be made on grounds that yield to or aggressively contest traditional notions of merit. It is tempting to view the presence of institutionally designated minority role models as necessarily a step toward satisfying the need for better representation and resources for minority communities. But it is unrealistic to suppose that an isolated black woman law teacher or Latina mathematician represents meaningful gains in minority power. Minority professors are sometimes disaffected by their labors and marginalized by their colleagues. The presence of minority faculty does not guarantee that minorities share power in the simplistic cause-and-effect fashion suggested by defenders of strategic approval of the role model argument.

THE NEED FOR SAME-KIND ROLE MODELS

The claim Professor Bell made for a black female law professor for black female students at Harvard Law School struck many as untenable. I would conjecture that most in higher education greet the claims made for same-kind role models with frank skepticism. Would law students of any race or status be better off if schools provided more same-kind faculty role models? There appears to be evidence to the contrary. Blacks who attend historically black colleges, where black faculty role models abound, receive lower scores on average on the law school admissions test than blacks who attend historically white schools.[16]

Some critics dismiss the claim for same-kind role models as just so much political rhetoric. Black "role models," they argue, have political, not educational importance. Mere politics should not, the argument continues *reductio ad absurdum,* lead schools to invest in endless searches for black females, handicapped lesbians, and every other minority group that might claim special needs.

To get beyond this skepticism, some insight is needed into the experiences of persons from traditionally excluded minority groups, such as black women. Until recently, little was known about the experiences of black women in legal education. The number of black women law teachers and students was small and their misfortunes were their closely guarded secrets.

First as a student and professor in the field of philosophy, and later as a student and professor in the field of law, I have had numerous experiences that point toward the need for faculty diversity and same-kind role models. My experiences, sketched below in illustrative examples, suggest why so many minority group members and their supporters strongly believe in the need for minority templates, symbols, and nurturers. As the dates of each of my examples suggest, there may be as much old-fashioned prejudice and insensitivity to contend with in the 1990s as there was in the infancy of the civil rights and women's movements, over two decades ago.

Perhaps the most important rationale for same-kind role models is this. White men, who predominate in higher education, have frequently failed to communicate confidence in the possibility of minority achievement. Snap judgments made on the basis of skin color alone are not uncommon; nor are begrudging affirmative action appointments. Black women have been made to feel inferior and out of place in higher education:

(1) In 1971, a white male classics professor to a black female student: ''Why don't you forget about college and become an airline stewardess?''
(2) In 1976, a white male undergraduate to his black female teaching fellow in philosophy on the first day of class: ''What gives you the right to teach this class?''
(3) In 1978, the white chairman of a philosophy department to a black female candidate for an assistant professorship: ''You don't have the kind of power we are looking for, but I am personally committed to affirmative action.''

Increasing the number of minority faculty could increase the chances that minority group members will find peers and role models in the ivory tower capable of believing sincerely in their competence. Moreover, a flourishing minority community within an institution could reduce the tendency to stereotype nontraditional students and faculty members as third-rate intellects.

White male professors have often defined agendas that ignore the intellectual needs of minority students. This can happen when ''traditional'' faculty take narrowly western perspectives or exclude from their courses issues affecting minority communities. It can also happen, however, when ''progressive'' faculty view their classrooms as opportunities to convert conservative students into radicals:

(4) In 1982, a white male law professor to a black female law student: ''I'm not aiming this class at people like you, I'm aiming it at the conservative white males headed for Wall Street.''

In law schools, one problematic side effect of white professors ignoring the intellectual needs of minority students is that students come to believe that whites teach an established ''white'' version of the law, and blacks teach a different ''black'' version:

(5) In 1987, a black male law student to a black female professor: ''I'm not taking any courses from blacks; I want to learn the same thing the white boys are learning.''

In a different vein, white professors' racial slights can seriously undercut professional relationships based on mutual respect:

(6) In 1981, a distinguished white male philosophy professor to a black female, now a professional colleague: ''You look like the maid my family once had.''
(7) In 1990, a white colleague to a black female colleague with curly hair tied back with a bandanna: ''You look like Buckwheat.''

Sexual harassment, including unique, race-related forms of sexual harassment can also undercut professional relationships:

(8) In 1977, a white male professor to a black female former student who dropped him as an advisor after an uninvited kiss: "I thought you were my student; I was surprised to learn you'd completed your dissertation under someone else."
(9) In 1990, a white male college professor to black female law professor at a conference panel on discriminatory harassment on campus: "You shouldn't mind being called a jungle bunny; bunnies are cute and so are you."

Painful, demoralizing experiences such as these lead black women to develop personal skills, social perspectives, and concerns to which their students are beneficially exposed throughout the course of formal education. It can teach a black female student a great deal to have access to black women teachers who have negotiated the gauntlet of racism and sexism that she, too, must negotiate.

It is important for minorities training to be professionals to know how to maintain composure and self-respect in situations like these:

(10) In 1983, a white female undergraduate in a class on the subject of affirmative action taught by a black female: "There are no intelligent black people in Oklahoma."
(11) In 1983, a partner at a prestigious law firm to a black woman law student working as his summer intern: "Write a memo explaining why legislation requiring private eating clubs to admit minorities and women would be unconstitutional."
(12) In 1990, a white female law student to an Hispanic student in the presence of a black woman law professor: "Forget about trying to improve this school's loan forgiveness program for public interest lawyers. If you ever have any problems paying back your student loans you can always contact me, a person of privilege and increasing privilege for help."

Those who disparage the demands for same-kind role models must try to understand the kinds of life experiences that prompt them. Behind the demands for same-kind black female faculty role models for black female students lies a fundamental sense of abandonment. As undergraduate, graduate, and professional school students, black women often feel that their institutions have abandoned them to racism, prejudice, and indifferent or hostile teachers.

This feeling of abandonment increases the alienation and hostility of minority students. It may correlate with underachievement among black women who attend even the best predominately white schools; and it may help to explain the high rate of minority undergraduate attrition. Quite possibly, good black female students would do even better if "same kind" role models were available to serve as examples (ethical templates), motivators (symbols of special achievements), and attention givers (nurturers).

Although white males, black males, and other categories of teachers could serve black women in these ways, the fact of the matter is they do not, they have not, and, to some extent, they cannot in the current social and political climate. The demand for same-kind role models heard today underscores the diversity of student needs that results from the diversity of Americans' social experiences.

CONCLUSION

My thesis has the flavor of a paradox. I argue for role models, but against the role model argument. But it is no paradox to say that we should praise faculty role models who take seriously their power and responsibilities as templates, symbols, and nurturers—but condemn uses of the role model argument that treat minorities like inferiors. Nor is it a contradiction to say that we should praise the minority and white female faculty who are willing to accept jobs others believe they are not qualified to hold, but condemn those who offer jobs to minorities and white women whose professional equality they are not prepared to admit.

After twenty years in higher education as a student and teacher, I have come to accept as true empirical claims commonly made by friends of the argument for same-kind role models: minority students have special role modeling needs that minority faculty are uniquely placed to service. The same decades of experience point toward the need for an egalitarian and empowered vision of minority teachers, scholars, and administrators. The "role model" argument for minority appointments simply obstructs such a vision.

Higher education has taken on the education of students from all segments of the community. In doing so, it has assumed an obligation to provide role models for students who need them. To meet this obligation, colleges and universities will have to diversify their faculties to include men and women of varied backgrounds. The goal of faculty diversification is distorted when the search for minority candidates—and not others—is understood principally as a search for role models rather than as a search for talent in its many and diverse forms. Faculties will have to diversify their talent, but diversification is not enough to satisfy the need for role models. Schools will have to encourage their faculties to be more responsive and respectful than ever before.

Georgetown University

NOTES

1 Portions of this paper are adapted from a longer essay. *See* Anita L. Allen, "On Being a Role Model," 6 *Berkeley Women's Law Journal* 22 (1990–91).

2 Bernard Boxill has suggested that even if affirmative action "sins against a present equality of opportunity, [it may be acceptable because it] promotes a future equality of opportunity by providing blacks with their own successful 'role models.' " *See* Bernard Boxill, *Blacks and Social Justice* (Totowa, N.J.: Rowman and Allenheld, 1984), p. 171.

3 See Robert Fullinwider, *The Reverse Discrimination Controversy: A Moral and Legal Analysis* (Totowa, N.J.: Rowman and Littlefield, 1980); eds. M. Cohen, T. Nagel, T. Scanlon, *Equality and Preferential Treatment* (Princeton, N.J.: Princeton University Press, 1977); Kent Greenawalt, *Discrimination and Reverse Discrimination* (New York: Alfred Knopf, 1983); Boxill, *Blacks and Social Justice,* pp. 147–172.

4 See Boxill, *Blacks and Social Justice,* p. 171.

5 See Gertrude Ezorsky, *Racism and Justice: The Case for Affirmative Action* (Ithaca, N.Y.: Cornell University Press, 1991). Ezorsky does not name the need for role models as an argument for affirmative action. Ibid. at pp. 73–94.

6 "Minority Women at the Bottom of Law Faculty," *New York Times,* April 3, 1992.

7 See, for example, Linda Greene, "Tokens, Role Models, and Pedagogical Politics: Lamentations of an African American Female Law Professor," 6 *Berkeley Women's Law Journal* 81 (1990–91). Professor Greene's essay was part of a symposium issue of the *Berkeley Women's Law Journal* entitled "Black Women Law Professors: Building a Community at the Intersection of Race and Gender," consisting of 15 essays by black women law teachers.

8 L. Gordon Crovitz, "Harvard Law School Finds Its Counterrevolutionary," *Wall Street Journal,* March 25, 1992.

9 I refer to essays by Thomson and Sher reprinted in Cohen, Nagel, & Scanlon, eds., *Equality and Preferential Treatment.*

10 Cf. Patricia Williams, *The Alchemy of Race and Rights* (Cambridge, Mass.: Harvard University Press, 1991), p. 95.

11 According to Thomson,

> [W]hat is wanted is *role models.* The proportion of black and women faculty members in the larger universities (particularly as one moves up the ladder in rank) is very much smaller than the proportion of them amongst recipients of Ph.D. degrees from those very same institutions. Blacks and women students suffer a constricting of ambition because of this. They need to see a member of their own race or sex who are [sic] accepted, successful, professional. They need concrete evidence that those of their race *can* become accepted, successful, professional. (Emphasis in original)

Thomson, "Preferential Hiring," in Cohen, Nagel, & Scanlon, *Equality and Preferential Treatment,* p. 22.
Sher considered the argument that:

> [P]ast discrimination in hiring has led to a scarcity of female "role models" of suitably high achievement. This lack, together with a culture that inculcates the idea that women should not or cannot do the jobs that . . . men do, has in turn made women psychologically less able to do these jobs. . . . [T]here is surely the same dearth of role models . . . for blacks as for women.

Sher, ''Justifying Reverse Discrimination in Employment,'' in Cohen, Nagel, and Scanlon, eds., *Equality and Preferential Treatment,* p. 58.

12 Greenawalt, *Discrimination and Reverse Discrimination,* p. 64.

13 Their stories are told in F. James Davis, *Who Is Black? One Nation's Definition* (State College: Pennsylvania State University Press, 1991).

14 Fullinwider, *The Reverse Discrimination Controversy,* p. 18.

15 For a recent survey of the arguments generally, see Ezorsky, *Racism and Justice.*

16 Of course, the racial composition of their faculties is not the only respect in which white and black colleges differ.

ALIENATION AND THE AFRICAN-AMERICAN EXPERIENCE

HOWARD MCGARY

The term "alienation" evokes a variety of responses. For liberals, to be alienated signals a denial of certain basic rights, e.g., the right to equality of opportunity or the right to autonomy.[1] On the other hand, progressive thinkers believe that alienation involves estrangement from one's work, self, or others because of capitalism.[2] However, recent discussions of alienation have cast doubt on whether either of these theories totally capture the phenomenon. Drawing on the experiences of people of color, some theorists maintain that to be alienated is to be estranged in ways that cannot be accounted for by liberal and Marxist theories of alienation.[3]

The concept of alienation is often associated with Marx's conception of human beings in capitalist societies. However, non-Marxists have also used the term alienation to explain the experiences of human beings in relationship to their society, each other, their work, and themselves. But liberal theories of alienation have been criticized by Marxists for two reasons. First they see liberal theories of alienation as describing a psychological condition that is said to result from a denial of basic individual rights rather than the result of a systematic failure. Second, liberals have an account of human nature that is ahistorical, one that fails to consider the changes in human nature that result from changes in social conditions.

For the Marxist, alienation is not simply a theory of how people feel or think about themselves when their rights are violated, but an historical theory of how human beings act and how they are treated by others in capitalist society. The Marxist theory of alienation is an explanatory social theory that places human beings at the center of the critique of socioeconomic relations. Marx's human being is not a stagnant given, but a product of an explanatory social theory. For Marx, alienation is something that all human beings experience in capitalist societies; it is not something that certain individuals undergo because they are neurotic or the victims of some unjust law or social practice.

It is clear that African-Americans have not always been recognized and treated as American citizens or as human beings by the dominant white society. Both of these forms of denial have had serious negative consequences and numerous scholars have discussed what these denials have meant to African-Americans and to the rest of society. However, it does not directly follow from the fact of these denials that African-Americans are alienated because of these things. In this paper, I shall attempt to understand this new challenge to the liberal and Marxist theories of "alienation" and its impact, if any, on the masses of African-Americans.

THE NEW ACCOUNT OF ALIENATION

According to the new account of alienation that is drawn from the experiences of people of color, alienation exists when the self is deeply divided because the hostility of the dominant groups in the society forces the self to see itself as loathsome, defective, or insignificant, and lacking the possibility of ever seeing itself in more positive terms. This type of alienation is not just estrangement from one's work or a possible plan of life, but an estrangement from ever becoming a self that is not defined in the hostile terms of the dominant group.

The root idea here is not just that certain groups are forced to survive in an atmosphere in which they are not respected because of their group membership, but rather that they are required to do so in a society that is openly hostile to their very being. The hostility, according to this new account of alienation, causes the victims to become hostile toward themselves. Those who are said to be alienated in this way are thought to be incapable of shaping our common conception of reality and thus they play little, if any, role in their self-construction. The self is imposed upon them by social forces, and what is even more disturbing, no individual self can change the social forces that impose upon members of certain groups their negative and hostile self-conceptions.

Is this new account of alienation just another way of saying that people of color have had their humanity called into question? We might begin to explore this question by examining the claim that having one's humanity recognized and respected means having a say about things that matter in one's life, and having such a say means that one is unalienated. To be more specific, having opinions about things and the ability and freedom to express one's opinions is the mark of the unalienated person. This response is helpful, but it does not fully capture what recent writers have meant by alienation. It assumes that the alienated self is secure, but constrained by external forces that prevent the person from becoming fully actualized: from having one's voice recognized and respected in the moral or political process.

The above account of what it means to recognize and respect a person's humanity fails to fully appreciate that human selves result, at least in part, from social construction. How we define who we are, our interests, and our relationship with others, involves a dynamic process of social interaction. To assume that what recent writers have meant by alienation is the failure by some to be able to express and have their opinions heard misses the mark. This view of things assumes that (1) people are clear about their interests, but have not been allowed to express them and (2) those who have power and privilege will be able to understand and fairly assess claims made by those who lack power and privilege if they were only allowed to express their opinions. Even if (1) and (2) are true, we still have not captured what recent writers have meant by alienation. This account focuses incorrectly on what the self is prevented from doing by forces external to it. However, the new account of alienation primarily concentrates on the fragility and insecurity of the self caused by the way people who are victims view and define themselves. According to this view, even if the external constraints were removed, the self would still be estranged because it has been constructed out of images that are hostile to it.

One might think that this new account of alienation is not saying anything new because Americans (including African-Americans) have always believed that people should be free to decide what kind of persons they want to be provided that in doing so they don't violate the rights of others. At least in principle, Americans have endorsed this idea. If this is so, what is new in these recent accounts of alienation? Perhaps we can gain some insight into this question by taking a closer look at the African-American experience.

African-Americans have had a paradoxical existence in the United States. On the one hand, they have rightfully responded negatively to the second-class status that they are forced to endure. On the other hand, they believe that America should have and has the potential to live up to the ideas so eloquently expressed in the Bill of Rights and in Martin Luther King, Jr.'s "I Have a Dream" speech.[4] It is clear that there was a time when African-Americans were prevented from participating in the electoral process and from having a say in the shaping of basic institutions. Many would argue that there are still barriers that prevent African-Americans from participating in meaningful ways in these areas. If this is so, does this mean that most (many) African-Americans are alienated from themselves and the dominant society?

African-American leaders from the moderate to the militant have emphasized the importance of African-Americans' making their own decisions about what is in their interests.[5] The right to self-determination has been seen as a crucial weapon in the battle against the evils of racial discrimination. These thinkers have also recognized that one must have an adequate understanding of one's predicament if one is to devise an effective strategy for overcoming the material and psychological consequences of racial injustice. Insight into the African-

American experience has come from a variety of sources. Some of these insights have been offered by social and political theorists, others have been advanced in literature and the arts.

Ralph Ellison, in his brilliant novel, *The Invisible Man,* describes what he takes to be a consuming evil of racial discrimination.[6] According to Ellison, African-Americans are not visible to the white world. They are caricatures and stereotypes, but not real human beings with complex and varied lives. In very graphic terms, Ellison reveals what it is like to be black in a world where black skin signifies what is base and superficial. Ellison skillfully describes how blacks are perceived by white society, but he also tells us a great deal about how blacks perceive themselves. It is clear that African-Americans have struggled to construct an image of themselves different from the ones perpetrated by a racist society, but this is not an easy thing to do. W. E. B. DuBois spoke to the struggle and the dilemma that confronts African-Americans when he identified what he called "the problem of double-consciousness" in *The Souls of Black Folk*:

> It is a peculiar sensation, this double-consciousness, this sense of always looking at one's self through the eyes of others, of measuring one's soul by the tape of a world that looks on in amused contempt and pity. One ever feels his twoness—an American, a Negro; two warring ideals in one dark body, whose dogged strength alone keeps it from being torn asunder.[7]

DuBois is pointing to what he takes to be the mistaken belief held by many blacks and whites, namely that a person cannot be both black and an American. According to DuBois, for far too many people this was a contradiction in terms. DuBois strongly disagreed and spent a great deal of his energy arguing against this conclusion. But why this false view was held by so many people can be traced to an inadequate conception of what it means to be "black" and what it meant to be "American." According to DuBois, race and class exploitation contributed greatly to these false conceptions. For DuBois, it was no surprise that African-Americans had such a difficult time identifying their true interests.

THE LIBERAL RESPONSE

Liberal political theorists rarely discuss alienation. This is in large part because alienation is seen as something that comes from within. For them alienation often is the result of injustice, but even so, it is something that can be overcome if only the individual would stand up for her rights. Liberals may realize that this might come at some serious personal cost to the individual, but they believe that the individual can and should bear these costs if they are to remain autonomous unalienated beings. For example, liberals often sympathize with white, highly educated, wealthy women who live alienated lives, but they believe that it is within the power of these women to end their estrangement or alienation even though it may be extremely difficult for them to do so. The critics of the liberal account of women's oppression have argued that liberals fail to see that capitalism and the negative stereotyping of women causes even educated and economically secure women to be at the mercy of sexist practices and traditions.

The critics of liberalism have also argued that liberalism places too much emphasis upon individuality and thus the theory fails to recognize how our conceptions of who we are and what we see as valuable are tied to our social relations. They insist that we are not alone in shaping who we are and in defining our possibilities. Society, according to these critics, plays a more extensive role than liberals are willing to admit.

Although liberals have recognized the alienation that people experience in modern society, their individual-rights framework has not readily lent itself to an in-depth analysis of this phenomenon. I disagree, however, with the critics of liberalism when they contend that the individual-rights framework is inadequate to describe the nature of alienation. I shall attempt to show that liberals can describe the nature of alienation in capitalist society even though the theory is inadequate when it comes to addressing what the liberals must admit to be a violation of important rights.

Liberal theorists might characterize this new form of alienation in terms of a denial of the rights to such things as autonomy and self-determination and claim that these denials rob persons of their freedom. Alienation on their account is just another way of saying that people are unfree and further that they don't appreciate that this is so. But if the liberal response is to be helpful, we need to know more precisely in what sense alienation is a denial of important rights, e.g., the right to be free.

In what sense is the alienated person unfree? Can a person be alienated even if she has basic constitutional rights, material success, and a job that calls upon her abilities and talents in interesting ways? Some theorists think so. If alienation is a lack of freedom as the liberal theory suggests, in what sense are the people who have constitutional rights and material well-being unfree? The liberal theorist Joel Feinberg has discussed the lack of freedom in terms of constraints.[8] If we define alienation as constraint, then alienated persons are unfairly constrained in the ways that they can conceive of themselves in a culture that defines them in stereotypical terms. But what are these constraints? To borrow Feinberg's terminology, are these constraints external or internal? According to Feinberg, "external constraints are those that come from outside a person's body-cum-mind, and all other constraints, whether sore muscles, headaches, or refractory 'lower' desires, are internal to him."[9]

If we employ the language of constraints to understand alienation as a kind of unfreedom, should we view this unfreedom in terms of external or internal constraints or both? On a liberal reading of DuBois's and Ellison's characterizations of the African-American experience, this experience is characterized by a denial of opportunities because of a morally irrelevant characteristic, a person's race. It is plausible to interpret them in this way because this is clearly one of the consequences of a system of racial discrimination. However, I believe that they had much more in mind. The focus on the denial of opportunities is the standard liberal way of understanding the consequences of racial injustice. This is why you find liberal writers like Feinberg discussing freedom in terms of the absence of constraints and John Rawls concentrating on designing social institutions such that offices and positions are open to all under conditions of self-respect.[10] The focus by liberals has been primarily on what goes on outside of the body-cum-mind.

This is not to say that they completely ignore such psychological harms as self-doubt and a lack of self-respect that can result from injustice. In fact, Feinberg notes that things like sickness can create internal constraints which serve to limit a person's freedom.[11] Rawls, as well, appreciates the impact that injustice can have on a person's psyche. Thus he spends some time expounding on the connection between justice and a healthy self-concept.[12] He argues that in a just society social institutions should not be designed in ways that prevent people from having the social bases for self-respect. So both Feinberg and Rawls recognize that such things as freedom and justice go beyond removing inappropriate external constraints. But nonetheless, I don't think that Feinberg and Rawls can fully capture the insight offered by DuBois and Ellison because their emphasis on the external constraints causes them to underestimate the internal ways that people can be prevented from experiencing freedom.

Since Isaiah Berlin's distinction between positive and negative freedom, liberals have recognized that such things as ignorance and poverty can limit a person's freedom.[13] Recognition of the limitations caused by internal constraints has led some liberals to argue that a society cannot be just if it does not address internal constraints on people's freedom. Such liberals would be open to the idea that an examination of the African-American experience would reveal the obvious and subtle ways that a lack of education and material well-being can lead to a sense of estrangement, a lack of self-respect. They would argue that this is true even when formal equality of opportunity can be said to exist. On their view, the real problem is not the lack of laws that guarantee equality under the law, but finding ways to make real these guarantees. For them it is not so much how African-Americans are viewed by the rest of society, but rather that they should be treated in ways that make it possible for them to act and choose as free persons. According to this view, things are just even if people are hated by the rest of the community, provided that they are guaranteed equal protection under the law and steps are taken to ensure real equality of opportunity. These liberals insist that there is a large area of human affairs that should escape government scrutiny. In these areas, people should be able to pursue their own conceptions of the good provided that they don't cause direct harm to others. I should add that these liberals also believe that those who fail to provide such necessities as food and education to those who are in need of them cause direct harm by failing to do so.

However, some communitarian critics of liberalism have argued that this way of understanding the requirements of justice underestimates the importance of how we form a healthy self-concept in a community.[14] They emphasize the importance of being seen and treated as a full member of society as opposed to a person who must be tolerated. They question the wisdom and usefulness of attempting to find impartial norms that will guarantee each person the right to pursue his own unique conception of the good constrained by an account of the right defined by impartial reasoning. This concern has led some communitarians to reject the search for impartial ideals of justice in favor of a method of forging a consensus about justice through a process of democratically working across differences through open dialogue. According to this view, we will not be able to put aside our partialities, but we can confront them through discourse.

Communitarians would contend that African-Americans or any minority group that has been despised and subjugated will feel estranged from the dominant society if they are merely tolerated and not accepted and valued for their contributions. They believe that the liberalism of Feinberg, Rawls, and Nozick can at best produce toleration, but not acceptance. But this view, of course, assumes that we can identify some common goods (ends) to serve as the foundation for our theory of justice. This is something that liberals who give priority to the right over the good deny.

The communitarians, whether they realize it or not, have pointed to a persistent problem for African-Americans—the problem of recognition. How do African-Americans become visible in a society that refuses to see them other than through stereotypical images? One need only turn to the history of black social and political thought to see that African-Americans have wrestled with the question of what the appropriate means are for obtaining recognition and respect for a people who were enslaved and then treated as second-class citizens. Some argued that emigration was the only answer, while others maintained that less radical forms of separation from white society would do. Others contended that blacks could obtain recognition only if they assimilated or fully integrated into white society.[15] Neither of these approaches so far have been fully tested, so it is hard to say whether either approach can adequately address the problem of the lack of recognition for blacks in a white racist society.

The new alienation theorists believe that liberals cannot adequately describe or eliminate the kind of estrangement experienced by African-Americans and other oppressed racial groups. Is this so? Yes and no. I shall argue that liberals can describe the experience of estrangement using the vocabulary of rights and opportunities, but I don't think that they can eliminate this experience and stay faithful to their liberal methodology.

Typically when we think of a person being denied rights or opportunities we think of rather specific individuals and specific actions which serve as the causes of these denials. For example, we might think of a specific employer refusing to hire a person because he or she is black. The black person in this case is denied job-related rights and opportunities by a specific person. But even if we changed our example to involve groups rather than individuals, the new alienation theorists would maintain the experience of estrangement that they describe goes beyond such a description. According to their account, African-Americans who have their rights respected and don't suffer from material scarcity still are estranged in a way that their white counterparts are not.

Are these theorists correct or do prosperous and highly regarded middle-class and wealthy African-Americans serve as counterexamples to the above claim? Don't such persons enjoy their rights and opportunities? If not, what rights and opportunities are they being denied? I believe that rights and opportunities are being denied, but it is more difficult to see what they are in such cases. I think that liberals can contend that middle-class and wealthy African-Americans are still alienated because they are denied their right to equal concern and respect in a white racist society. Even though they may be able to vote, to live in the neighborhood of their choice, and to send their children to good schools, they are still perceived as less worthy because of their race. The dominant attitude in their society is that they are less worthy than whites. The pervasive attitude is not benign. It acts as an affront to the self-concept of African-Americans and it causes them to expend energy that they could expend in more constructive ways. The philosopher Laurence Thomas graphically described this experience in a letter to the *New York Times*.[16] For example, African-Americans are too aware of the harm caused by being perceived by the typical white as thieves no matter what their economic and social standing might be. African-Americans, because of the dominant negative attitudes against them as a group, are denied equal concern and respect.

It is difficult to see that this attitude of disrespect is a denial of rights because we most often associate political rights with actions and not with attitudes. In fact, it sounds awkward to say that I have a right that you not have a certain attitude towards me. This statement seems to strike at the very heart of liberalism. However in reality it does not. Liberals can and do say that human beings should be accorded such things as dignity and respect, and they believe that this entails taking a certain attitude or having dispositions towards others as well as acting or refraining from acting in particular ways. So, it is not that they cannot account for the particular estrangement that blacks experience because of the attitude of disrespect generated by the dominant society, but that they don't seem to have the theoretical wherewithal to resolve the problem.

Since liberals assign great weight to individual liberty, they are reluctant to interfere with actions that cause indirect harm. So even though they recognize that living in a society that has an attitude of disrespect towards African-Americans can constitute a harm, and a harm caused by others, they are reluctant to interfere with people's private lives in order to eliminate these harms.

How can liberals change white attitudes in a way that is consistent with their theory? They could mount an educational program to combat false or racist beliefs. Liberals have tried this, but given their strong commitment to things like freedom of thought and expression, and the fact that power and privilege is attached to seeing nonwhites as less worthy, educational programs have only had modest success in changing white attitudes. Critics of such educational programs argue that these programs can never succeed until racism is seen as unprofitable.

Let us assume that the critics are correct. Can liberals make racism unprofitable and respect individual liberty, one of the cornerstones of their theory? There are two basic approaches available to liberals: they can place sanctions on all harmful racist attitudes or they can provide people with incentives to change their racist attitudes. But in a democracy, the will of the majority is to prevail. If the attitude of disrespect towards African-Americans is as pervasive as the new alienation theorists suggest, then it is doubtful there will be the general will to seriously take either of the approaches. I don't think that liberals can eliminate harmful racist attitudes without adopting means that would be judged by the white majority as unjustified coercion. However, they can adequately describe the alienation that African-Americans experience even if they cannot eliminate it.

THE MARXIST ACCOUNT

The Marxist explanation of the African-American condition assumes that the problems experienced by this group can be traced to their class position. Capitalism is seen as the cause of such things as black alienation. For the Marxist, a class analysis of American society and its problems provides both a necessary and sufficient understanding of these things. According to the Marxist, alienation be it black or white is grounded in the labor process. Alienated labor, in all of its forms, is based in private property and the division of labor. On this account, if we eliminate a system of private property and the division of labor, we will eliminate those things that make alienated relations possible.

The Marxist does recognize that political and ideological relations can and do exist in capitalist societies, and that these relations do appear to have the autonomy and power to shape our thinking and cause certain behaviors. But, for the Marxist, these relations only appear to be fundamental when in reality they are not. They can always be reduced or explained by reference to a particular mode of production. Racism is ideological; an idea that dominates across class lines. However class divisions explain racial antagonisms, it is not the other way around.[17] But Marxists don't stop here. They also contend that in order to eliminate racism, we must eliminate class divisions where class is defined in terms of one's relationship to the means of production.

Classical Marxists would oppose the new account of alienation advanced by recent theorists. The classical Marxists would insist that all forms of alienation, no matter how debilitating or destructive, can be explained in terms of the mode of production in which people are required to satisfy their needs. For them, it is not a matter of changing the way blacks and whites think about each other or the way blacks think of themselves because ideas don't change our material reality, relationships with others, or our self-conceptions. Our material conditions (mode of production) shape our ideas and our behavior.

On this account, African-Americans are estranged from themselves because of their laboring activity or lack of it. They view themselves in hostile terms because they are defined by a mode of production that stultifies their truly human capacities and reduces them to human tools to be used by those who have power and influence. This all sounds good, but many black theorists (liberal and progressive) have been skeptical of this account of the causes and remedy for black alienation and oppression. They argue that the conditions of black workers and white workers are different and that this difference is not merely a difference in terms of things like income and social and political status or class position. The difference cuts much deeper. In a white racist society, blacks (workers and capitalists) are caused to have a hostile attitude towards their very being that is not found in whites. The new alienation theorists contend that the classical Marxist explanation of African-American alienation is too limiting. It fails to recognize that alienation occurs in relationships apart from the labor process. W. E. B. DuBois, although a dedicated Marxist, claimed that the major problem of the twentieth century was race and not class. Some theorists have contended that Marxists are too quick in dismissing the significance of race consciousness.[18] I think the facts support their conclusion. In the next section, I will focus directly on this issue of African-American alienation.

AFRICAN-AMERICANS AND ALIENATION

I believe that the atmosphere of hostility created against African-Americans by our white racist society does amount to a serious assault on the material and psychological well-being of its African-American victims. I also believe that this assault can, and in some cases does, lead to the types of alienation discussed above. However, I disagree with those who conclude that most or all African-Americans suffer from a debilitating form of alienation that causes them to be estranged and divided in the ways described in the new account of alienation. I also reject the implication that most or all African-Americans are powerless, as individuals, to change their condition. The implication is that group action as opposed to individual effort is required to combat this form of alienation. There is also the implication that revolution and not reform is required in order to eliminate this form of alienation.

I don't wish to be misunderstood here. It is not my contention that capitalism is superior to socialism, but only that it is possible for African-Americans to combat or overcome this form of alienation described by recent writers without overthrowing capitalism.

Are African-Americans, as a group, alienated or estranged from themselves? I don't think so. Clearly there are some African-Americans who have experienced such alienation, but I don't think this characterizes the group as a whole. African-Americans do suffer because of a lack of recognition in American society, but a lack of recognition does not always lead to alienation. Even though African-Americans have experienced hostility, racial discrimination, and poverty, they still have been able to construct and draw upon institutions like the family, church, and community to foster and maintain a healthy sense of self in spite of the obstacles that they have faced.

Although African-Americans have been the victims of a vicious assault on their humanity and self-respect, they have been able to form their own supportive communities in the midst of a hostile environment. During the long period of slavery in this country, African-Americans were clearly in an extremely hostile environment. If there ever was a time a group could be said to be the victims of the assault caused by white racism, slavery was such a time. Slaves were denied the most basic rights because they were defined and treated as chattel. Some scholars, like Stanley Elkins, have argued that slavery did cause African-Americans as a group to become less than healthy human beings.[19] On the other hand, there is a group of scholars who argue that slaves and their descendants were able to maintain healthy self-concepts through acts of resistance and communal nourishment.[20] I tend to side with this latter group of scholars.

What is crucial for the truth of their position is the belief that supportive communities can form within a larger hostile environment that can serve to blunt the assault of a hostile racist social order. This, of course, is not to say that these communities provide their members with all that is necessary for them to flourish under conditions of justice, but only that they provide enough support to create the space necessary for them to avoid the deeply divided and estranged selves described in some recent work on alienation.

The history and literature of African-Americans is rich with examples of how communities have formed to provide the social and moral basis for African-Americans to have self-respect even though they were in the midst of a society that devalued their worth. Once again, I think it bears repeating. I don't deny that a hostile racist society creates the kind of assault that can lead to alienation, but only claim that this assault can be and has been softened by supportive African-American communities.

The sociologist Orlando Patterson disagrees. Patterson has argued that African-Americans are alienated because slavery cut them off from their African culture and heritage and denied them real participation in American culture and heritage. He characterizes this phenomenon as "natal alienation."[21] African-Americans, on Patterson's account, feel estranged because they don't believe that they belong. They are not Africans, but they also are not Americans. One might argue that the present move from "black American" to "African-American" is an attempt to address the phenomenon of natal alienation. According to Patterson, the past provides us with crucial insight into the present psyches of African-Americans. On his view, the fact of slavery helps to explain the present condition and behavior of African-Americans, including the present underclass phenomenon.[22]

I disagree with Patterson's conclusions. He falls prey to the same shortcoming that plagues the liberal and the Marxist accounts of the African-American experience. They all fail to appreciate the role of ethnic communities in the lives of individuals and groups. Although DuBois never played down the horrors and harms of racism, he refused to see the masses of black people as a people who were estranged or alienated from themselves. In fact, in his *Dusk of Dawn,* DuBois describes how black people have been able to draw strength from each other as members of a community with shared traditions, values, and impulses.[23] Being anchored in a community allows people to address and not just cope with things like oppression and racism.

The work of the historian John Blassingame can also be used to call into question Patterson's natal alienation thesis and it also provides some support for the importance of community in the lives of African-Americans. Blassingame argued that even during the period of slavery, there was still a slave community that served to provide a sense of self-worth and social cohesiveness for slaves. In my own examination of slave narratives, first-hand accounts by slaves and former slaves of their slave experiences, I found that all slaves did not suffer from a form of moral and social death.[24] By moral and social death, I mean the inability to choose and act as autonomous moral and social agents. Of course this is not to deny that slavery was a brutal and dehumanizing institution, but rather that slaves developed supportive institutions and defense mechanisms that allowed them to remain moral and social agents.

But what about the presence of today's so-called black underclass? Does this group (which has been defined as a group that is not only poor, poorly educated, and victimized by crime, but also as a group suffering from a breakdown of family and moral values) squarely raise the issue of black alienation or estrangement? Some people think so. They argue that Patterson's natal alienation thesis is extremely informative when it comes to understanding this class. Others reject the natal alienation thesis, but remain sympathetic to the idea that where there once was a black community or institutions that served to prevent the erosion of black pride and values, these structures no longer exist to the degree necessary to ward off the harms of racism and oppression.

In *The Truly Disadvantaged,* William J. Wilson argues that large urban African-American communities are lacking in the material and human resources to deal with the problems brought on by structural changes and the flight of the middle class.[25] According to Wilson, these communities, unlike communities in the past, lack the wherewithal to overcome problems that are present to an extent in all other poor communities. If Wilson is correct, the resources may not exist in present day African-American communities to ward off the assault of a hostile racist society. I am not totally convinced by Wilson's argument, but I think his work and the work of the supporters of the new account of alienation make it clear that there needs to be further work which compares African-American communities before the development of the so-called "black underclass" with urban African-American communities today.

At this juncture, I wish to distinguish my claim that supportive African-American communities have helped to combat the effects of a racist society from the claims of black neoconservatives like Shelby Steele. In *The Content of Our Characters,*[26] Steele argues that African-Americans must confront and prosper in spite of racism. Steele's recommendations have a strong individualist tone. He argues, like Booker T. Washington, that racism does exist but that African-Americans who are prudent must recognize that if they are to progress, they must prosper in spite of it. In fact, Steele even makes a stronger claim. He argues that African-Americans have become accustomed to a "victims status" and use racism as an excuse for failing to succeed even when opportunities do exist.

I reject Steele's conclusions. First, I don't think that individual blacks acting alone can overcome racism. Individual blacks who succeed in this country do so because of the struggles and sacrifices of others, and these others always extend beyond family members and friends. Next, I reject Steele's claim that the lack of progress by disadvantaged African-Americans is due in any significant way to their perception of themselves as helpless victims. Such a claim depends upon a failure to appreciate the serious obstacles that African-Americans encounter because of their race. Even if it is true that African-American advancement is contingent on African-Americans helping themselves, it does not follow that African-Americans should be criticized for failing to adopt dehumanizing means because they are necessary for their economic advancement.

African-Americans should not be viewed as inferior to other groups, but they should also not be seen as superior. Racial injustice negatively impacts the motivational levels of all people. African-Americans are not an exception. Steele makes it seem as if poor and uneducated African-Americans lack the appropriate values to succeed. He contends that the opportunities exist, but that too many African-Americans fail to take advantage of them because they cannot break out of the victim mentality. I reject this line of reasoning. As I have argued elsewhere,[27] this way of thinking erroneously assumes that most disadvantages result from a lack of motivation. In reality, it would take exceptional motivational levels to overcome the injustices that African-Americans experience. Because some African-Americans can rise to these levels, it would be unreasonable to think that all could. Steele underestimates the work that must be done to provide real opportunities to members of the so-called black underclass who struggle with racism on a daily basis.

I would like to forestall any misunderstandings about my emphasis on the role that supportive communities play in the lives of oppressed groups. I am not maintaining that African-Americans don't experience alienation because they are able to draw strength from supportive communities. My point is that supportive communities can, in some cases, minimize the damaging effects caused by a racist society. Nor is it my intention to deny that African-Americans and other groups must constantly struggle to maintain a healthy sense of self in a hostile society that causes them to experience self-doubt and a range of other negative states.

Rutgers University

NOTES

1 Liberal thinkers tend to argue that alienation results when human beings can no longer see themselves as being in control of or comfortable in their social environment, and they contend that this discomfort occurs when crucial rights are violated, e.g., the right to autonomy. In an interesting twist on the liberal position, Bruce A. Ackerman argues in *Social Justice and the Liberal State* (New Haven, Conn.: Yale University Press, 1980), esp. pp. 346–47, that the right to mutual dialogue is necessary to protect the autonomy of individuals in a community.

2 See, e.g., John Elster (ed.), *Karl Marx: A Reader* (Cambridge: Cambridge University Press, 1986), Chapter II; Bertell Ollman, *Alienation* (Cambridge: Cambridge University Press, 1976),

Part III; Robert C. Tucker (ed.), *The Marx-Engels Reader* (New York: W. W. Norton & Co., 1978) pp. 73–75, 77–78, 252–56, 292–93.

3 See Frantz Fanon, *Black Skin/White Masks* (New York: Grove Press, 1967), Chapter 1; June Jordan, "Report from the Bahamas," *On Call* (Boston: South End Press, 1985), pp. 39–50.

4 The famous speech delivered by Martin L. King, Jr. at the March on Washington, D.C., August, 1963.

5 See Howard Brotz (ed.), *Negro Social and Political Thought 1850–1920* (New York: Basic Books, 1966).

6 Ralph Ellison, *The Invisible Man* (New York: New American Library, 1953).

7 W. E. B. DuBois, *The Souls of Black Folk* (New York: New American Library, 1969), p. 45.

8 Joel Feinberg, *Social Philosophy* (Englewood Cliffs, N.J.: Prentice-Hall, Inc., 1973), Chapter 1.

9 Feinberg, *Social Philosophy,* p. 13.

10 John Rawls, *A Theory of Justice* (Cambridge, Mass.: Harvard University Press, 1971), Section 67.

11 Feinberg, *Social Philosophy,* p. 13.

12 Rawls, *Theory of Justice,* pp. 440–46.

13 Isaiah Berlin, *Two Concepts of Liberty* (Oxford: Clarendon Press, 1961).

14 See, Alasdair MacIntyre, *After Virtue* (Notre Dame, Ind.: University of Notre Dame Press, 1981), Chapter 17; Michael Sandel, *Liberalism and the Limits of Justice* (Cambridge: Cambridge University Press, 1982), pp. 59–65, 173–75.

15 Howard McGary, Jr., "Racial Integration and Racial Separatism: Conceptual Clarifications," in Leonard Harris (ed.), *Philosophy Born of Struggle* (Dubuque, Iowa: Kendall/Hunt Publishing Co., 1983), pp. 199–211.

16 Laurence Thomas, in *The New York Times,* August 13, 1990.

17 See Bernard Boxill, "The Race-Class Question," in Harris, *Philosophy Born of Struggle,* pp. 107–16.

18 See, e.g., Howard McGary, Jr., "The Nature of Race and Class Exploitation," in A. Zegeye, L. Harris, & J. Maxted (eds.), *Exploitation and Exclusion* (London: Hans Zell Publishers, 1991), pp. 14–27; and Richard Schmitt, "A New Hypothesis About the Relations of Class, Race and Gender: Capitalism as a Dependent System," *Social Theory and Practice,* Vol. 14, No. 3 (1988), pp. 345–65.

19 Stanley Elkins, *Slavery: A Problem in American Institutional and Intellectual Life* (Chicago: University of Chicago Press, 1976).

20 John Blassingame, *The Slave Community: Plantation Life in the Antebellum South* (New York: Oxford University Press, 1972), esp. pp. 200–16.

21 Orlando Patterson, *Slavery and Social Death* (Cambridge, Mass.: Harvard University Press, 1982).

22 Orlando Patterson, "Towards a Future that Has No Past: Reflections on the Fate of Blacks in America," *The Public Interest,* Vol. 27, 1972.

23 W. E. B. DuBois, *Dusk of Dawn* (New Brunswick, N.J.: Transaction Books, 1987), esp. Ch. 7.

24 See Howard McGary & Bill E. Lawson, *Between Slavery and Freedom: Philosophy and American Slavery* (Bloomington: Indiana University Press, 1992).

25 William J. Wilson, *The Truly Disadvantaged* (Chicago: University of Chicago Press, 1987).

26 Shelby Steele, *The Content of Our Characters: A New Vision of Race in America* (New York: Saint Martin's Press, 1990), especially Chapters 3 and 4.

27 Howard McGary, "The Black Underclass and the Question of Values," in William Lawson (ed.), *The Underclass Question* (Philadelphia: Temple University Press, 1992), pp. 57–70.